Interventions with
Children
& Youth
in Canada

Maureen Cech

With a Forward by the Honourable Landon Pearson, O.C.

SECOND EDITION

OXFORD
UNIVERSITY PRESS

OXFORD
UNIVERSITY PRESS

Oxford University Press is a department of the University of Oxford.
It furthers the University's objective of excellence in research, scholarship,
and education by publishing worldwide. Oxford is a registered trade mark of
Oxford University Press in the UK and in certain other countries.

Published in Canada by
Oxford University Press
8 Sampson Mews, Suite 204,
Don Mills, Ontario M3C 0H5 Canada
www.oupcanada.com

Library and Archives Canada Cataloguing in Publication

Cech, Maureen, 1951-, author Interventions with children and youth in Canada / Maureen
Cech. -- Second edition.

Includes bibliographical references and index.
ISBN 978-0-19-900890-2 (pbk.)

1. Social work with children--Canada--Textbooks. 2. Social
work with youth--Canada--Textbooks. 3. Problem children--
Canada--Textbooks. 4. Problem youth--Canada--Textbooks.
I. Title.

HV745.A6C42 2015   362.70971   C2015-900351-2

Cover image: RunPhoto/Getty Images. Chapter 2 opening epigraph from SPIN A SOFT BLACK SONG: POEMS
FOR CHILDREN © 1971 by Nikki Giovanni. Reprinted by permission of Farrar, Straus, and Giroux, LLC. All Rights
Reserved. Chapter 11 opening epigraph from COUNTING STARS Written by Ryan Tedder © 2014 Sony/ATV Tunes
LLC & Midnite Miracle Music. All rights administered by Sony/ATV Music publishing LLC., 424 Church Street,
Nashville, TN 37219. All rights reserved. Used by permission.

Oxford University Press is committed to our environment. This book is printed on Forest Stewardship Council® certified
paper and comes from responsible sources.

Printed and bound in Canada

1 2 3 4 — 18 17 16 15

Contents

Figures and Tables

Figures

Tables

Foreword

By the Honourable Landon Pearson, O.C.

We were all children once and as we grow older and take on adult roles we continue to be surrounded by children. Consciously or unconsciously we interact with them all the time. Whether or not we intervene in their lives is quite a different question. But, if we do, then this is the book to guide us.

In his book *The Ecology of Human Development*, the distinguished American psychologist Urie Bronfenbrenner posits three systemic categories to describe the complicated overlapping environments we should be aware of when we think about working with children and young people. The first is the global macrosystem that we and our ancestors have constructed through our individual and collective actions over many centuries. As a system it is constantly changing, of course, and some parts of it are more beneficial to children than others. But every choice we now make about what to believe, who to vote for, what to buy or sell or how many children we will have (supposing, in that case, that we have any choice at all) will have an impact on both today's and tomorrow's children. Whether we like it or not, we are all connected, all members, as the Charter of the United Nations reminds us, of "the human family."

We rarely think about the macrosystem when we are with children, for it is in the mesosystem—that intermediate space between the world out there and the family—that most of us act when we are working professionally with them. Only when we comprehend how a mesosystem is structured, how inequalities of power and money can shape a school or a neighbourhood and how prejudice and discrimination can shape attitudes to children and youth, can we be more constructive in these settings.

Surrounded by and at the heart of the other two systems is the child's microsystem where he or she lives together with parents, caregivers, or guardians—the family into which he or she is born and, usually, grows up. While many of the children and young people with whom professionals interact are no longer in their family homes, the long reach and the power of this system has to be acknowledged if an intervention is to be successful.

The approach of this book is not just a structural one, however; it is also strengths-based. And this, to my mind, is what makes it so valuable. A strengths-based approach is bound to incorporate a child rights perspective; the two are so complementary. Since the end of the Second World War, the United Nations has developed a powerful body of instruments, international treaties, and conventions designed to protect, promote, and fulfill the rights of every human being, including children. The UN Convention on the Rights of the Child is among them and has been adopted by virtually every country in the world, even if all of them, including our own, fail to implement it fully. Nevertheless, it is out there in a child's macrosystem, affirming that he or she has the same inherent and unalienable rights as every other human being augmented by some special ones that recognize his or her vulnerability and developmental requirements. Among the most important of these rights is the right to be heard. In my experience, the child who is not heard is unlikely to listen no matter how sensible our advice may be!

The strengths- and rights-based approach, so well delineated in *Interventions with Children and Youth in Canada,* is practically guaranteed, I am convinced, to transform "problem" children into children with problems that he or she will find it possible to resolve with professional help and support. I envy the students who will have the privilege of learning from this textbook. They will make a difference.

Preface

There was an old woman who lived in a shoe;
She had so many children, she didn't know what to do.
She gave them some broth without any bread;
She spanked them all soundly, and sent them to bed.

—(Anonymous)

The old woman in the shoe spanked them all soundly and sent them to bed. The next morning the children awoke, played, misbehaved, and the routine was repeated. She again spanked them all soundly and put them to bed. Like the old woman in the shoe who has no bread, we repeat traditional interventions: spanking, restraints, incarceration, foster care. They work for a while, at least until the next day, when there still is no bread.

Wisdom resides in traditional folk tales and stories for children. I teach through the medium of children's stories and have sprinkled some of my favourite passages throughout this book to entice the reader into further exploration of children's literature. A wealth of information on children's behaviour, language, and life experience is revealed within the pages of these books. Some children's stories provide the wisdom that is lacking in adult reports. Truths are revealed by the old woman in the shoe— the futility of punishment rather than such structural interventions as fixing the shoe, supplying the bread, and providing adequate education for both parent and child.

This book interweaves the wisdom of children's stories with current Canadian medical, psychological, sociological, and educational information. No single science provides the requisite background for working with children. This tapestry of ideas, plus a few of my own, challenges us to work with children, rather than on them, and engage with children as persons with rights. Like all new ways of working, this requires adjustment on the reader's part and even further change on the part of the practitioner.

This necessary shift in practice is grounded in tradition, however, through our Canadian respect for the child as a member of the community and our respect for Mother Earth. The structural approach that positions a child in the centre of a structure reflects the Medicine Wheel of interconnectedness in which the child is the hub of the wheel. This Medicine Wheel reminds us how our lives connect to the land, to one another, and to the values that we share. Unlike the biomedical model, this wheel does not crush the child under a label or medicate the child to run faster and faster around the wheel. The structural and strengths-based approach is a response to the child as a person, a citizen of Canada today (not a future citizen) with rights and responsibilities.

In recognizing the child as a person and as a citizen we move from the privileged position of experts with universal wisdom who label misbehaving children as individuals who have gone "wrong" in a society based on what is "right." We move also from the privileged sector of adulthood with its generalized air of universal wisdom that convinces many in society that children need tough love and punishment. Rather than assessing, labelling, and punishing children, we assess and label the structural determinants of children's behaviour, growth, and development. Perhaps society is not always "right," particularly when it reflects multiple layers of oppression in which children try to live productive lives. We assess and label these structural determinants and advocate for change. That is our role in the intervention. We don't change behaviour—that is the child's role.

But, back to the bread. The old woman in the shoe did the best she could within her shoe, but she always came back to that empty cupboard. There was no bread. She knew it and the children did, too. What to do? Traditional interventions (spanking) work in the short term. But the long term begs for a full cupboard and a bigger shoe, the structural and strengths-based approach taken in this book.

This is not a do-it-yourself book or instructional manual for parents as stressed as the old woman in the shoe who didn't know what to do; nor is it a cookbook full of intervention recipes that can be pulled out and followed to make children better. There are already many such books available for sale and resale because they offer panaceas, those short-term repair jobs on children, always on the assumption that the children need repairs, rather than the shoe. This book suggests another way of working with the child as a person with rights and a child of Mother Earth.

Organization

There are 12 chapters in this book, each one presenting a theoretical basis for the next. Within each chapter are additional kinds of information: Points to Consider with thought-provoking questions; Notes from the Field, with case studies and scenarios; and Group Exercises that offer group experiences related to the chapter topic. Each chapter ends with a summary, review questions, and discussion questions. The review questions prompt the reader's understanding and recall of the material within that chapter, and provide a review of the key points. The discussion questions invite the reader to further explore the topic, either internally as part of self-reflection and personal development, or externally as a part of applications in work practice in the community.

Chapter 1 is the foundation for the ensuing chapters. It describes the structural and strengths-based approach of the book, mainly by contrasting this approach with more traditional approaches to children. Three key structural determinants for children in Canada are examined: poverty, the *DSM-V*, and the Convention on the Rights of the Child. Each one of these structural determinants affects the daily life of children, particularly at moments of high risk when children may need adult intervention and support. This support is provided by workers who are categorized by mandates and roles. Interventions are divided, fracturing the child in the process.

Chapter 2 examines our changing social construction of the child. In pioneering Canada, the child was seen as valuable; in a more industrialized and urbanized twentieth century, the child was seen as vulnerable. Today, the child is seen as social capital. On the margins are children who are developmentally delayed, children with different abilities, children who live in poverty, First Nations and Inuit children, and children of new Canadians. Their marginalized location, always subject to adult control, determines the services available to them, as well as the structural determinants impacting their daily lives. Their location is determined also by their age, and these shifting age limits create problems, placing responsibilities in some areas, and removing freedoms in others, depending on where children live in Canada. These age and social limits frame the social construction of the child.

How social location and structural determinants affect children's development is explored in Chapter 3. Children have specific developmental needs that may or may not be met. As children grow and develop they form a more stable picture of their own gender and sexual orientation, and this picture may or may not meet adult approval. Their needs in these critical learning periods call for both a caregiver and a structural response.

The importance of this response is the focus of Chapter 4. When this response is synchronous and nurturing, the child usually thrives. When this response is neglectful and dismissive, the child may be injured to the core and may suffer cognitive, emotional, and physical delays. These attachment injuries happen in foster care, adoption, intercountry adoption, and deculturation, resulting in behaviours that are often misunderstood. Understanding these injuries lays the foundation for developing a healthy working relationship with the child.

What that relationship looks like is explained in Chapter 5. The relationship theories of Carl Rogers infuse this chapter because they demand an equality that is vital to affirming the child's personhood. The Rogerian relationship based upon congruence, respect, and empathy equalizes the power construct between child and worker so that both are engaged in exploring behaviours, documenting plans, and managing change. This relationship does not happen in isolation but is framed by a structure that is empowering, as exemplified in community capacity building in which the child is a participant and a problem solver rather than a problem.

Understanding the child and ourselves in a mindful way leads to praxis in which we reflect upon this knowledge, theory, and previous action before we respond. Chapter 6 introduces praxis as well as guidelines for the first meeting with the child. The worker listens to the child's culture while the child informs, engaging with the child through genograms, sociograms, or lifelines. In this meeting the worker tries to understand the child's meaning of the presenting problem from multiple perspectives within the family and community.

Listening to the child is not as simple as leaning forward and paying attention. Listening is a learned skill that demands authenticity, affirmation, and presence, all of which culminate in the AHA! Moment described in Chapter 7. Listening prompts telling, which then demands more attentive listening as the child combines memories, emotions, and reactions into a life narrative. This weaving, or autobiographical reasoning, happens naturally as the child tries to make sense of the world and the people within it. When the child's story becomes problem-saturated and the child turns to the worker for help, the worker can support the child to externalize then contextualize these problems so that they become part of a more hopeful, re-authored life narrative.

Most often the telling of these stories is through play as children try to make sense of their world and the world of the adults with whom they interact. They choose specific materials to express their emotions, memories, abuse, neglect, and long hidden trauma, and the worker listens and observes through the lens of psychoanalysis, family relations, object relations, or cognitive-behavioural theory. In Chapter 8, the meanings beneath and within the play are webbed and mapped until they become clearer.

Outside of the playroom, working relationships with children and youth can happen online through e-counselling. Workers listen online and respond both synchronously and asynchronously; in the latter case, the child can take time to savour the worker's response before replying and pushing the send button. Chapter 9 offers a menu of digital interventions that complement and sometimes substitute for face-to-face meetings. Digital technology allows continuous connectivity and instant linking to social supports. It also raises new questions about the privacy, boundaries, and confidentiality described in Chapter 5.

Because of the social constructions around childhood and children, workers are conditioned to believe that certain behaviours are negative, while others are positive. Workers are also conditioned to use behavioural controls and restraints rather than supports, to react rather than respond. In Chapter 10, we look at the role and meaning of behaviour, even in crisis situations as workers keep the child safe while respecting the child's pivotal role in behavioural change.

These crisis situations alert us to situations of high risk in which the child may be injured or worse. In Chapter 11, we find out about these situations through listening and observing closely the play of children, and by responding appropriately to disclosures of risk through this play. Our response may be crucial to the child's safety. Our response is framed by law and by "best practice," as well as by our own respect for the personhood of the child. Traditional interventions such as apprehension and placement of children do not always work, as the "no-home" placements of some children indicate. Structural interventions that focus on moving and changing structural supports rather than moving and changing children are often more successful.

We conclude by examining an increasingly popular intervention with children—group work. In Chapter 12, we compare groups and gangs, and examine why children voluntarily join neighbourhood gangs but are often assigned to groups. The dynamics, leadership, communication styles, and membership are factors that determine how effective this intervention is for children. Gangs and groups once again affirm the interconnectedness of the Medicine Wheel. The child is a person and a social being. The child wants that interconnectedness with peers, with the community, and with the family. How to make that connection affirming and hopeful is the challenge for workers who are asked to facilitate groups for children.

The Children

"Children and youth" is the current Canadian phrase describing a full range of persons up to the age of 24. However, the contradictory meanings, boundaries, and dimensions of the word "youth" are described in Chapter 2. These contradictions, and the central role of the Convention on the Rights of the Child, have led this author to favour the word "children," and to often use that word alone. This category is clear and defined by the Convention as including persons up to the age of 18.

This category of children includes those whom the Youth Criminal Justice Act (YCJA) calls "youth," the 12- to 17-year-olds who fall under this legislation. This category of children excludes the 18- to 24-year-olds who also are called "youth" by Youth in Care Canada. This category also excludes the 18- to 26-year-olds who are called "youth" by the Royal Canadian Mounted Police (RCMP) when referring to youth gangs.

The word "children" reminds us that the 15-year-old living on the street is a child with a right to shelter, and that the 14-year-old expelled from school is also a child with a right to education. The Convention defines these rights, and it is our responsibility as adults to ensure that Canadian children are accorded these rights in their daily life. Naming persons up to the age of 18 "children" is a first step to acting on this responsibility.

Acknowledgements

The list of references at the end of this book indicates many researchers and practitioners who have led the way. Thanks to them, and to my students who took the time and trouble to alert me to updates. Reviewers added their expertise; in particular I would like to thank Ken Barter of Memorial University, Phil Jones of the University of Lethbridge, Christine Slavik of the University of the Fraser Valley, and Frances Owen of Brock University for their helpful suggestions. I am indebted to Leah-Ann Lymer and Joanne Muzak of Oxford University Press who used the strengths-based approach to coach me through the revisions, catching those ripples that could have easily washed away my meaning. The careful attention of all of these reviewers, plus Carl's constant support, made the fine-tuning of this book pure pleasure.

Maureen Cech
October 2014

1 The Structural and Strengths-Based Approach

We have to be more than just observers of children's suffering; we have to be partners in their struggles.

—The Honourable Landon Pearson, O.C.

The line at the checkout is long. People wait, looking at their carts and the food they want to buy, glancing at their watches as the dinner hour approaches. At the front of the line, a woman's bank card is rejected, causing a further delay. At the back, one of the latecomers abandons his cart with a growl and heads for the exit. A child begins to cry—first quietly, then louder—while the parent tries unsuccessfully to get her to sit still in the shopping cart.

When a child misbehaves in public, all eyes focus on two people. The first is the child. The second is the parent. The customers look at the child, then the parent, and wonder why that child doesn't stop crying and why that parent doesn't get his or her child to "behave." These two questions also form the dominant discourse of countless books on children's behaviour that offer behaviour modification advice to parents, workers, and teachers. This reaction to children's behaviour is repeated in the classroom, the emergency ward, the courtroom, the community centre program, and the **child welfare** meeting room. Professionals and members of the public look at the child, then at the parent to decipher the origin of the child's behaviour. Rarely do they use a wide-angle lens to focus on the structure of the overall environment and to refocus on the strengths within the child, the parent, and the family.

This myopic viewpoint is changing as rapidly as the culture of childhood. **Evidence-based practice** is challenging conventional wisdom about child development and behaviour and widening the lens to include the environmental structure. It is now evident that the answers to both where behaviour originates and how to change it lie within a structure that includes social assistance, education, health, child welfare, and youth justice. Canadian writer Paul Tough (2012) cautions that the child's character, genetics, and cognitive ability are not the only factors to consider in behavioural change. Structural change is what makes the difference in children's lives. "We can argue about whether those interventions should be provided by the government or non-profit organizations or religious institutions or a combination of the three. But what we can't argue anymore is that there's nothing we can do" (Tough, 2012: 196).

In this chapter, we examine what it means to take a structural and strengths-based approach to understanding and modifying behaviour, and how workers can use this approach with children. We give particular attention to three **structural determinants** of behaviour, the most important of these being poverty. The second structural determinant of behaviour—the *Diagnostic and Statistical Manual of Mental Disorders (DSM-V)*—appears to be an innocuous assessment and categorization tool for children's disorders, but, in fact, it is a structural determinant that categorizes children only by their deficits, rather than by their strengths. The third determinant we will focus on is the United Nations Convention on the Rights of the Child (UNCRC). Few children know about or understand this international legislation, a lack of knowledge that in itself, as we will see, is the result of deliberate socio-political action by adults. Brian Howe and Katherine Covell (2007: 241) call children's rights outlined in the UNCRC "Canada's best-kept secret."

The structural and strengths-based approach to behaviour has been applied to adults and to families, but workers rarely apply this approach to children. This omission is intentional and reflects a pervasive **childism** that positions children as inferior and incapable persons who are unable to understand structural determinants. In this chapter, we will see how this childism can harm children and how the structural and strengths-based approach can benefit them. This approach also may influence our own behaviour in such community contexts as the grocery store lineup. Rather than focusing only on the child or the parent (or even on both individuals), the structural and strengths-based approach widens our focus to include determinants such as accessibility to food, nutritional norms, and patterns of consumerism, all of which impact children's behaviour. When these determinants change, so does the child's behaviour. Knowing how these determinants can change allows us to refocus on the child's strengths and readiness for change and empowers us to facilitate change so that the child stops crying, the parent relaxes, and the lineup slowly moves forward.

Objectives

By the end of this chapter, you will:

- Understand the structural and strengths-based approach to children's behaviour.
- Identify the key structural determinants of health in children's lives.
- Demonstrate how to take the structural and strengths-based approach to a child's behaviour.

What Do We Mean by "Structure"?

The child is located within a **social structure** that determines the legal framework for the child's rights, the social assistance for the child's family, and the **child protection** system that moves the child into **foster care**. The structure determines whether or not the child will be born in a hospital, and whether or not the child will receive requisite care after birth. And it continues to affect every aspect of the child's life—from education, to health, to socialization, to recreation—even though the child cannot necessarily identify or name each particular structural determinant. The child is inside the structure and, like a fish in a bowl, rarely sees the constricting glass even when colliding with it. It is unlikely that the very young child can identify **homophobia**, for example, even as the child's parents are experiencing this structural determinant during a preschool interview with the child's teacher.

The **structural approach** focuses on how this complex social structure affects every aspect of the child's life and how the child can, in turn, affect this structure. The **strengths-based approach** assumes that the child has the strength and capability to both understand and affect this structure. In combination, the structural and strengths-based approach locates problems within the structure rather than within the child who is assumed to be capable of solving problems; as a result, problems are solved by changing the structure rather than the child. This structural and strengths-based approach widens the consideration of behavioural **interventions** beyond the child, family, and worker and into the social structure itself.

Urie Bronfenbrenner's (1979) ecological model is fundamental to this approach. His ecological model centres on the child's being continuously impacted by several systems or structures, each interacting with the other. The smallest one is the **microsystem** in which the child interacts with caregivers, parents, or guardians. The most obvious microsystem is the home in which the child lives. The daily life of the newborn is experienced very much at the microsystem level. The microsystem nests within a **mesosystem** that includes all of the settings in which the child lives and plays: the school and daycare, community centres and drop-in clinics, arenas and skating rinks. The largest structure is the **macrosystem**. At the macrosystem level are the structural determinants that affect the child, determinants that Bronfenbrenner (1979: 13) described as "forces emanating from more remote regions in the larger physical and social milieu."

Bronfenbrenner's ecological model positions the child at the centre of these nesting, interrelated systems; however, the child is the focus of investigation and diagnosis. The problems are located within the child or the child's family. The structural and strengths-based approach also positions the child centrally, but the focus of investigation and diagnosis is the structure. The emphasis is on the child's strengths within this structure or macrosystem that impacts the child's life context and behaviour. This change in emphasis is illustrated in Figure 1.1.

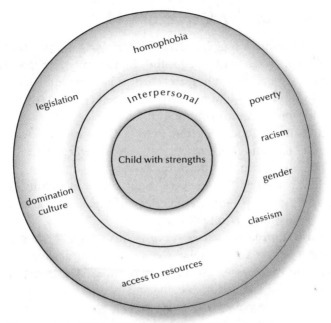

Figure 1.1 The Structural and Strengths-Based Approach

Anne-Marie Ambert (2007: 23) describes the macrosystem in Canada as one in which the nurturance of children, and children themselves, are devalued and disempowered. The Public Health Agency of Canada's description of population health demonstrates Ambert's description. Eight of the eleven **determinants of health** are structural ones over which children have little or no control and even less input: income and social status, social support networks, education and literacy, employment and working conditions, social and physical environments, health services, gender, and culture.

Similar determinants of health for children are used in the National Longitudinal Survey of Children and Youth (NLSCY), and in Human Resources and Skills Development Canada's (HRSDC's) document *A Canada Fit for Children* (2004). The latter describes children as "powerful agents of social and cultural change" and goes on to state, "We in Canada recognize the importance of participation of children to their own healthy development, as well as to the development of the communities in which they live and to society at large" (HRSDC, 2004: 54). This federal **affirmation** of children as "powerful agents" recognizes that children can decide to change and have the ability to change, an affirmation that is strengths-based and fully in line with the intent of the United Nations Convention on the Rights of the Child (UNCRC). However, this affirmation is not accompanied by the necessary structural supports for this participation.

The eight structural determinants identified in the population health approach remain problematic in the lives of children. A child living in poverty simply does not have regular, consistent access to nutritious food, adequate clothing, standard housing, or recreational facilities. The child may *want* to become healthy through exercise and eating well, but without the prerequisite structural changes, the child's achievement of health is unlikely. More often, the child still is considered to be both the problem and the nexus of the solution: if only the child ate properly and exercised more, the obesity problem would be solved. According to this approach, rather than Canadian society being refitted to support the child, it is up to the child to fit into *"A Canada Fit for Children."*

 Group Exercise   **1.1**

Structural Determinants

This group exercise demonstrates how the structural and strengths-based approach changes the dynamic of any intervention. The work of each small group is captured on posters affixed to the wall so that other groups can add their ideas to the poster when they come to it.

The exercise begins with a review of the structural approach by the group leader. Each small group is then given a poster board on which a child's challenge is printed; for example, obesity, low birth weight, eating disorders, inability to read, or homelessness. The small group then identifies the structural determinants that create or maintain this challenge and prints these determinants on its poster board.

When the groups have completed their poster boards, the leader signals each group to move to the poster board of the group nearby. Each group adds ideas to this poster board and then moves on, until all of the small groups have had a chance to add their ideas to all of the poster boards. Then, the full lists of structural determinants are read aloud and discussed as a whole by the larger group. The leader assigns a final task: to identify or to recommend structural supports that would counter the structural determinants so that these challenges for children can be met and overcome.

Poverty

Poverty has been identified as the most significant structural determinant or **risk factor** in a child's life (Hill et al., 2013). The Government of Canada's report *The Well-Being of Canada's Young Children* (2011: 41) repeats the message of the four previous reports that higher family income is associated with better child well-being.[1] This does not mean that parents living in poverty are necessarily inadequate parents, or that children raised in poverty have no chance of reaching their potential or their optimal developmental level. What it does mean is that poverty is the greatest structural determinant affecting a child's present and future life. Poverty makes childhood harder—much harder. Because of the connection between poverty and negative outcomes for children, Willms (2002: 8) suggests that describing children to be **"at risk"** is almost the same as describing children who are living in poverty.

Poverty is measured in many different ways; the internationally accepted standard of measurement is the **low income measure after tax (LIM)**. Statistics Canada still uses low income cut-off (LICO) but does not endorse LICO as either a measure or a definition of poverty. According to LIM, the number of children living in poverty in Canada has remained consistent since 1980, varying from 14 per cent to 17 per cent, with the number of children living in poverty in First Nations communities being about 40 per cent (Macdonald and Wilson, 2013: 9). Poverty is measured annually by Campaign 2000,[2] but these measurements do little to help children who live in either persistent or transitory poverty.

Persistent poverty is a chronic condition in which families struggle throughout their entire lives, or even through successive generations, to make ends meet. Poverty becomes a lifestyle; as certain kinds of doors remain closed, it feels to the impoverished that there is no way out of such grinding and deep deprivation. Persistent poverty in the family is said to be the most difficult and damaging kind of poverty for children (Covell and Howe, 2001: 43). These children report going straight outside to the school-yard at lunchtime because they do not have a lunch at school; skipping school on field trip days because they do not have the money to participate; and feeling embarrassed about living in a shelter or about having a parent who is unemployed. Because they lack adequate nutrition, they do not have the stamina to participate actively in sport and, consequently, do not develop psychomotor skills to optimal levels. They often do not have adequate shelter or may have to move frequently and so miss out on school as well as necessary peer relationships, neighbourhood social opportunities, and peer play. These inadequacies are **co-relational**; that is, one inadequacy reinforces another.

Still taken from the Canadian Tire Jumpstart Charity television advertisement and reproduced with permission.

Photo 1.1 This boy is looking for work to pay for his hockey equipment.

Persistent poverty can cause children to suffer from exhaustion because of excessive household chores, including caring for siblings, meal preparation, cleaning, and laundry. Persistent poverty can also mean a lack of any or all of the following:

- adequate nutritious food;
- adequate shelter, which often results in frequent moves as the family seeks affordable housing; may entail the misery or dangers of inadequate heat, light, cooling, safe water, etc.;
- adequate clothing;
- recreational outlets and equipment for participating in sport;
- access to technology in the home;
- reading materials in the home, including newspapers, books, and magazines;
- adequate school supplies;
- dental care, eye care, medication, and special health services;
- transportation to school, medical appointments, and recreation; and
- access to music, art, drama, dance, or other cultural activities; instruction in music, art, drama, or dance; materials for creative and constructive projects.

Short-term or **transitory poverty** is also called income instability (Hill et al., 2013). Transitory poverty arises when unanticipated events impact the family income; for example, the sole income earner in the family may die or require expensive medication for a sudden illness; a child may become ill and need specialized home care; a parent may become redundant in the workplace; or parents may separate or divorce. All of these unexpected events can force the family to drop below LIM and live in transitory poverty. The Canadian Council on Social Development (2013) reports that food bank users increased by 31 per cent between 2008 and 2012. Most of these food bank users were persons living in transitory poverty, squeezed between rising prices and lower (or no) wages.

Children of food bank users are often seen as inadequate and lazy—as little "criminals-in-waiting."[3] However, the reality of their lives tells another story. They often work harder than their wealthier counterparts: some care for their younger siblings, while others care for family members with developmental disabilities, mental health issues, chronic or terminal illness, or addictions. They live on or beyond the edge of what most think of as "customary" in Canadian life. They are not allowed to work legally to buy their food, clothing, and shelter; nor are they allowed to apply for social assistance until they are 16 years of age.[4] Poverty is *done to* them. This power-lessness to change their own condition adds to their feelings of alienation, shame, hopelessness, and depression as they absorb the cultural message that their poverty is somehow a personal failing. Paul Tough (2012: 20) reports on the effects of poverty on children's school success and concludes, "It wasn't poverty itself that was compromising the executive-function abilities of the poor kids. It was the stress that went along with it."

Point to Consider   1.1

Quebec's Structural and Strengths-Based Approach

In 1959, the fertility rate in Quebec was 4.0 children per woman; this fell to 1.47 by 1998 (Baker, 2005: 17), leaving Quebec with one of the lowest birth rates in the world. Then the structural and strengths-based approach was applied as part of the provincial government's poverty reduction plan. This plan included financial support for low-income families with children under the Parental Wage Assistance (PWA) program; accessible, quality child care (at a cost of $5 per day); and the Quebec Family Allowance. Structural supports were accompanied by a strengths-based approach to children, who were positioned as assets to the province (Baril, Lefebvre, and Merrigan, 2000). By 2002, the birth rate began to rise, and this shift continued. In 2007, 84,200 babies were born in Quebec, a startling figure that reflects the baby boom that began in 2002. The example of Quebec demonstrates that, with adequate structural and strengths-based support, adults can and will plan responsibly to become parents.

Diagnostic and Statistical Manual of Mental Disorders (DSM-V)

The *Diagnostic and Statistical Manual of Mental Disorders* was compiled by an expert panel of doctors drawn from several branches of the traditional medical community. The fifth edition (*DSM-V*) was published by the American Psychiatric Association in 2013. This reference text of disorders is designed to be used by mental health specialists and health care providers with extensive clinical training. Non-clinicians may consult the *DSM-V* to obtain information only, and not to make diagnoses. However, a diagnosis based on the *DSM-V* is the basis for securing specialized services for a child or financial reimbursement for the child's medication. As a result, frontline workers in education, child care, and social services use this manual as their standard reference tool. In this way, the *DSM-V* is a powerful structural determinant in shaping, funding, and delivering services for children.

Mental disorders have been added to and subtracted from the *DSM* since its first edition in 1952. In 1974, for example, homosexuality was withdrawn as a mental disorder. Prior to that date all homosexual persons were deemed to have a mental disorder, and were excluded from certain occupations as a result (Greenberg, 2013). This erroneous labelling is only one example of the subjective nature of this influential manual, which draws symptoms of mental disorders from both scientific studies and conventional wisdom. As Canadian therapist Stephen Madigan (2011: 31) writes concerning the dangerous power of diagnostic labels, "The power to advise or label someone is often a source of unquestioned authority and privilege by both professionals and those who seek our help."

Another example of such labelling is the category of attention deficit hyperactivity disorder (ADHD), which was added to the revised third edition of the *DSM* in 1987 (*DSM-III-R*). This category was split into three subtypes of ADHD in the *DSM-IV* with symptoms that included inattention, distractibility, impulsivity, and hyperactivity. These are also "symptoms" of many children who are forced to sit at desks inside a stuffy classroom on a sunny June day. ADHD includes many more symptoms and is a serious condition, but on the basis of the *DSM-IV* symptoms, many children were subsequently misdiagnosed and pathologized. The label of ADHD connotes a sickness or deficit, and these children became known by the deficit above all else. Their label followed them for years and curtailed any possibility of change. Charles Whitfield (2006: 96) asks, "How helpful is it to label children with new disorders such as ADHD when, instead, the child's behaviour may be a normal reaction to an abnormal environment? The child's dysfunctional educational system, teachers, parents and exposure to toxic media may be a major part of the problem."

Once a child has been assessed on the basis of the *DSM-V*, this costly assessment tends not to be repeated. As a result, a child may carry the *DSM-V* label long after the identified and assessed behavioural symptoms have faded. Because, for example, Colin feels distracted and fails to manipulate objects effectively in a testing sequence on the testing day, he may be labelled as "delayed" and may carry this label for years. The boy hears the label repeated by the worker, foster parent, and other professionals and paraprofessionals, and may ask for details. The worker's response reinforces Colin's identification with the label, and causes him to behave in ways that are consistent with and that reinforce the original label. Colin is no longer Colin: he is a very delayed boy. As Colin reinforces the validity of the original label, the behavioural descriptors increase, and the assessors (adults) feel validated in their original diagnosis. Michael Ungar (2006: 295) observes, "Interventions by professionals and the diagnostic assessments to which high-risk youth are subjected cause more harm than good when these labels become yet another barrier to a child's healthy constructions of self."

David Rosenhan's (1973) research study in the mental health field illustrates the enormous power of labels. Rosenhan began by asking hospital staff volunteers from 12 different US hospitals to admit themselves to several local psychiatric hospitals, reporting to the admissions clerk that they had been "hearing voices." All but one of these eight volunteer participants, or pseudo-patients, were admitted to hospital under the label "schizophrenic" rather than under their own behavioural descriptors ("hearing voices"). Once admitted to the hospitals, the participants behaved normally, read their books, and engaged in routines. All of them exhibited no signs of schizophrenia or abnormal behaviour. Despite this consistently normal behaviour, all of the participants continued to be diagnosed as "schizophrenic" by staff nurses and doctors. They had difficulty getting out of hospital, and one of the participants was released only after 52 days of hospitalization. As so often happens with children, the biomedical label caused others to view the research participants in a different way. The person became equated with the label (schizophrenia) even though not one of these persons was actually schizophrenic.

Assessments of children in foster care in Ontario follow the biomedical, deficits-based approach of the *DSM-V*. Both the Ontario Looking After Children (OnLAC) assessment project and the Child and Adolescent Functional Assessment Scale (CAFAS) use *DSM* categories to measure functional impairment in children who exhibit behavioural, emotional, psychological, psychiatric, or addictive difficulties. The Assessment and Action Record (AAR), a monitoring instrument used within OnLAC, consists of a clinical checklist of multiple-choice questions for the child's foster parents and the child's worker. The child is positioned in the checklist as an object of concern with deficits rather than as a subject with strengths.

Certain sections of these assessments are completed by foster parents and workers who may or may not know the child well and who may or may not have had adequate training in assessment administration. These caregivers are expected to comment about and on behalf of the child, even when the child is available and able to speak, and the test results reflect their third-party comments. This structure of third-party assessment implicitly suggests that children are "not competent articulators of their own experiences" (James and Jenks, 1996: 329). Because of this biomedical test design, children in care are very often incorrectly assessed, and they carry their diagnostic labels for years.

United Nations Convention on the Rights of the Child

When Canadian adults discuss the law or their legal rights, they refer most often to the Canadian Charter of Rights and Freedoms. Canadian children might cite their own charter (the United Nations Convention on the Rights of the Child) if they knew about its legal power over their lives. The UNCRC is rarely displayed in daycares, schools, child welfare agencies, community centres, health care centres, or family resource centres, and is seldom posted on any of the government websites for parents, children, and families; in fact, three-quarters of Canadian children do not even know that the UNCRC exists (Canadian Coalition for the Rights of Children, 2012: 22). This failure to display and popularize the UNCRC is deliberate. Denying Canadians knowledge of children's rights also denies citizenship status for children. Children in Canada may be citizens according to the law; however, they are typically counted as future citizens who live outside the current body of citizens.

A decade after the Convention was adopted by the United Nations, Elections Canada and UNICEF organized an activity designed to inform Canadian school children about the UNCRC by asking them to vote for their favourite Convention article. Even this token activity was resisted. One school board trustee in Abbotsford, British Columbia, warned, "It undermines the integrity of the family and involves children in a political undertaking. There is a gradual erosion of parental authority and this is one more step in that direction" (Howe and Covell, 2005: 3). His reaction to the Convention continues to be both common and widespread, resulting in a lack of information about children's rights that negatively impacts all Canadian children. The outcome of the Elections Canada vote by three-quarters of a million Canadian children in

UN Convention
on the Rights of the Child
In Child Friendly Language

"Rights" are things every child should have or be able to do. All children have the same rights. These rights are listed in the UN Convention on the Rights of the Child. Almost every country has agreed to these rights. All the rights are connected to each other, and all are equally important. Sometimes, we have to think about rights in terms of what is the best for children in a situation, and what is critical to life and protection from harm. As you grow, you have more responsibility to make choices and exercise your rights.

Article 1
Everyone under 18 has these rights.

Article 2
All children have these rights, no matter who they are, where they live, what their parents do, what language they speak, what their religion is, whether they are a boy or girl, what their culture is, whether they have a disability, whether they are rich or poor. No child should be treated unfairly on any basis.

Article 3
All adults should do what is best for you. When adults make decisions, they should think about how their decisions will affect children.

Article 4
The government has a responsibility to make sure your rights are protected. They must help your family to protect your rights and create an environment where you can grow and reach your potential.

Article 5
Your family has the responsibility to help you learn to exercise your rights, and to ensure that your rights are protected.

Article 6
You have the right to be alive.

Article 7
You have the right to a name, and this should be officially recognized by the government. You have the right to a nationality (to belong to a country).

Article 8
You have the right to an identity – an official record of who you are. No one should take this away from you.

Article 9
You have the right to live with your parent(s), unless it is bad for you. You have the right to live with a family who cares for you.

Article 10
If you live in a different country than your parents do, you have the right to be together in the same place.

Article 11
You have the right to be protected from kidnapping.

Article 12
You have the right to give your opinion, and for adults to listen and take it seriously.

Article 13
You have the right to find out things and share what you think with others, by talking, drawing, writing or in any other way unless it harms or offends other people.

Article 14
You have the right to choose your own religion and beliefs. Your parents should help you decide what is right and wrong, and what is best for you.

Article 15
You have the right to choose your own friends, and join or set up groups, as long as it isn't harmful to others.

Article 16
You have the right to privacy.

Article 17
You have the right to get information that is important to your well-being, from radio, newspaper, books, computers and other sources. Adults should make sure that the information you are getting is not harmful, and help you find and understand the information you need.

Article 18
You have the right to be raised by your parent(s) if possible.

Article 19
You have the right to be protected from being hurt and mistreated, in body or mind.

Article 20
You have the right to special care and help if you cannot live with your parents.

Article 21
You have the right to care and protection if you are adopted or in foster care.

Article 22
You have the right to special protection and help if you are a refugee (if you have been forced to leave your home and live in another country), as well as all the rights in this Convention.

Article 23
You have the right to special education and care if you have a disability as well as all the rights in this Convention, so that you can live a full life.

Article 24
You have the right to the best health care possible, safe water to drink, nutritious food, a clean and safe environment, and information to help you stay well.

Article 25
If you live in care or in other situations away from home, you have the right to have these living arrangements looked at regularly to see if they are the most appropriate.

Article 26
You have the right to help from the government if you are poor or in need.

Article 27
You have the right to food, clothing, a safe place to live and to have your basic needs met. You should not be disadvantaged so that you can't do many of the things other kids can do.

Article 28
You have the right to a good quality education. You should be encouraged to go to school to the highest level you can.

Article 29
Your education should help you use and develop your talents and abilities. It should also help you learn to live peacefully, protect the environment and respect other people.

Article 30
You have the right to practice your own culture, language and religion - or any you choose. Minority and indigenous groups need special protection of this right.

Article 31
You have the right to play and rest.

Article 32
You have the right to protection from work that harms you, and is bad for your health and education. If you work, you have the right to be safe and paid fairly.

Article 33
You have the right to protection from harmful drugs and from the drug trade.

Article 34
You have the right to be free from sexual abuse. (Article 35No one is allowed to kidnap or sell you.

Article 36
You have the right to protection from any kind of exploitation (being taken advantage of).

Article 37
No one is allowed to punish you in a cruel or harmful way.

Article 38
You have the right to protection and freedom from war. Children under 15 cannot be forced to go into the army or take part in war.

Article 39
You have the right to help if you've been hurt, neglected or badly treated.

Article 40
You have the right to legal help and fair treatment in the justice system that respects your rights.

Article 41
If the laws of your country provide better protection of your rights than the articles in this Convention, those laws should apply.

Article 42
You have the right to know your rights! Adults should know about these rights and help you learn about them, too.

Articles 43 to 54
These articles explain how governments and international organizations like UNICEF will work to ensure children are protected with their rights.

QUEEN ALEXANDRA FOUNDATION FOR CHILDREN

Canadian Heritage   Patrimoine canadien

UNICEF Canada

Photo 1.2 This UNCRC poster is designed for display in schools, daycares, and youth shelters. Retrieved from: www.unicef.org/rightsite/files/uncrcchilldfriendlylanguage.pdf

1,900 schools was telling. Canadian children voted Article 9, the right "to live with a family that cares for you," as the "number one" right. Pretty radical stuff!

The final report of the Standing Senate Committee on Human Rights, *Children: The Silenced Citizens* (2007), documents this overt acceptance and covert denial of the UNCRC within various Canadian structural systems. The following is a brief summary of the findings of that report, as well as an update on the acceptance and denial of the UNCRC in Canada, and the implications for children of this socio-political message.

In 1989, 192 member countries of the United Nations supported and signed the Convention on the Rights of the Child. The signatories were required to implement through legislation the 54 articles of the Convention, and to co-operate with annual United Nations inspections of their legislative compliance. These inspections by United Nations officials were designed to be the basis for annual reports on the state of children in the world; in other words, the UNCRC would provide a baseline for each signatory to measure individual national standards.

The UNCRC officially elevates children to the status of rights-bearing persons with rights in three broad categories: provision of education, health care, and welfare; protection from violence, abuse, **neglect**, and exploitation; and participation in civic affairs.

All of these rights are seen to be equal and universal; in other words, one child is equal to another, regardless of where the child lives in the world or who the child is. This rights-based approach challenges childism, a pervasive bias that positions children as objects of charity who need to be protected and regulated by adults who claim to work in the **best interests of the child**. While some charities do contribute to the **empowerment** process for children, most simply reinforce adult power and the **commodification** of children. These charities distribute children like commodities to the families and agencies who want them.

Although the Convention is an international, legally binding treaty signed by the Canadian federal government, many of its 54 articles continue to be either contradicted or unsupported by laws in Canada. Judges may refer to the Convention in legal cases involving children, but they cannot call upon it as a legislative power as they do with the Charter of Rights and Freedoms. An important precedent was set in 2010 when the Supreme Court of the Yukon recognized the UNCRC and ruled that, under Article 3, children do have the right to be heard in custody cases. This legal precedent only applies in the Yukon, however, and not in other provinces and territories. Other articles of the Convention pose particular challenges in Canadian law.

- Articles 3 and 12 defend children's rights to participate in affairs that directly concern them in their own daycares, schools, recreation facilities, or hospitals. However, in Canada this participation is limited to fundraising, entertainment, and focus **groups**, and does not include decision making. As child and youth care expert Karas Gharabaghi (2012: 11) explains "Youth engagement typically entails a thinly guised attempt to give legitimacy to adult-designed and operated initiatives by having some carefully selected young people endorse what is being offered."

- Articles 16 and 17 defend children's right to privacy and their own personal information. This right is contravened in Canada when children in schools are searched without a warrant, their bags and their lockers are searched, and their personal diaries, letters, blogs, phone records, and emails are read by caregivers, workers, or parents. In most provinces and all territories children do not have the right to their own birth information if they are adoptees or if they were conceived through sperm donations.

- Article 18 defends children's rights to quality accessible and affordable care while their caregivers are working. This right is contravened in Canada by the lack of national child care. Child care is supported for a limited group of children under the age of six through a monthly payment (Universal Child Care Benefit) to the child's primary caregivers who may or may not be working.

- Articles 19, 28, 37, and 38 defend children's right not to be hurt or abused. This right is contravened by Section 43 of the Criminal Code of Canada, which allows children to be hurt as part of discipline.

- Article 24 defends children's right to be protected from environmental toxins. This right is contravened when Canadian children are exposed to pesticides, mercury, nicotine, and other toxins in the air, water, and food they consume, and when their housing, playing fields, and schools are built on toxic soil. The elementary school in Attawapiskat First Nation in Northern Ontario, for example, was built on a toxic waste dump and was closed in 2000 only after the children in the school protested the toxic conditions (Wilson, 2011).

- Article 34 defends children's right to be protected from sexual exploitation. This right is contravened by the lack of a national registry of child sexual abuse offenders and the failure to enforce maximum penalties for adults engaging in sexual activities with children.

- Article 37 defends children's right to be incarcerated with other children instead of with adults. This right is contravened when children are incarcerated with adults and not offered rehabilitative services because of the lack of youth detention facilities in northern and remote Canadian communities.

The list of UNCRC contraventions is long, with **marginalized** groups suffering the most. Because federal transfer payments have increased by only 2 per cent since 1996 and have not adjusted for population growth, Aboriginal children living on reserve often do not have access to local community health services, and some do not even have clean drinking water in their homes (Macdonald and Wilson, 2013: 6). They are allocated $2,000 to $3,000 less school funding per child per year than other Canadian children (Canadian Coalition for the Rights of Children, 2011), and they make up almost half of the population in alternative (foster) care in Canada.[5]

The impact of reduced funding is directly felt by Aboriginal children living on-reserve. One such child was Jordan River Anderson from Norway House Cree Nation. As the First Nations Child and Family Caring Society of Canada website explains, Jordan was born with complex medical needs that required supports that his family and community could not afford, and the province would not provide because Jordan was **Aboriginal**. Jordan was kept in hospital for two years while provincial and federal governments argued over his health care costs. While they continued to argue, Jordan died alone in hospital when he was only five years old. Jordan's case became the impetus for the framing of "Jordan's Principle," a child-first document that upholds a child's right to health care as a citizen of Canada. Jordan's Principle was unanimously supported in Parliament in December 2007, but like the UNCRC, this principle has never been enacted in legislation that would protect the health care rights of all Aboriginal children in Canada.[6]

Despite the guarantees of universality in the UNCRC, there is less funding for the education, child welfare, and health services for Aboriginal children today than there is for these same services for non-Aboriginal children. In 2008, the Canadian Human Rights Tribunal began consideration of this discrimination, and their consideration continues. Discrimination against Aboriginal children ultimately affects all Canadian children. A fifteen-year-old respondent to a 2011 UNCRC survey explained, "I do not hear the term 'children's rights' very much, and I think that some people may not think of it very seriously. I think that it is important, not only for the well-being of children, but hopefully, if children care about their rights, when they grow up they will be more proactive about human rights of all sorts" (Canadian Coalition for the Rights of Children, 2012: 27).

Structural Assets

Three structural determinants (poverty, the *DSM-V*, and the UNCRC) have been described in this chapter. Each of these determinants impacts the child's overall health or wellness. Poverty affects both short- and long-term outcomes for children. The *DSM-V* is being used in a way that unfairly assesses, labels, and, in some cases, overmedicates children. The Convention (UNCRC) makes promises it cannot keep because corresponding legislation has not been enacted in Canada to provide enforcement of all of its articles.

Fortunately, Canadians also enjoy structural assets or health-enhancing resources that improve the child's overall outcomes. When an active, engaged, and competent child interacts with these structural assets, a positive outcome is likely. A child who has support from an adequate income, knowledge, **advocacy** skills related to basic Convention rights, and specific health supports to match specific needs, is more likely to reach full potential. Peter Benson (2006) and Peter Scales, Arturo Sesma, and Brent Bolstrom (2004) describe 40 developmental assets, 20 of which are external to the child and under significant control by communities. The scientific foundation for these 40 assets in 8 categories is described in more detail in Peter Scales and Nancy Leffert's *Developmental Assets: A Synthesis of the Scientific Research on Adolescent Development* (2004). Central to these researchers' description is the belief that the child both affects and is affected by the structural assets listed in Table 1.1.

Table 1.1 Structural Assets

Asset	Examples
Support	Family support, positive family communication, other adult relationships, caring neighbourhood, caring school climate, and parental involvement in schooling
Empowerment	Community valuing of children, view of children as resources, children's provision of service to others, and safety
Boundaries and expectations	Family boundaries, school boundaries, neighbourhood boundaries, adult role models, positive peer influence, and high expectations for children
Commitment to learning	Creative activities, children's programs, religious community, and time at home

This range of structural assets provides a framework for civic planning in a country that respects and values its youthful citizens and plans for their active participation and engagement. Support, empowerment, **boundaries**, and a commitment to learning: these assets seem simple enough to provide for a child. However, the child does not always feel safe and supported in a community that is sexist and violent; where expectations for the child are low because of the child's ethnicity, race, or ability; and where there is little or no commitment to meeting the child's learning needs. This kind of community fails because it offers neither positive adult **role models** nor positive peer influences, both essential parts of boundaries and expectations, structural assets described by Scales and Leffert (2004).

 Point to Consider   1.2

Children's Rights Programs

Provincial education programs that include the Convention have demonstrated cross-curricular educational benefits. In Nova Scotia, the health and social studies curriculum for kindergarten to Grade 6 includes information on the Convention that has resulted in a wider understanding of citizenship responsibilities in these young children (Levine, 2000). In Saskatoon, at Princess Alexandria School, the Convention is the basis for a rights-based discipline policy. Schissel (2006: 150–3) describes an environment in which "negative" behaviours are countered with options for the student so that the individual child has positive possibilities for personal growth and change: "At a general level, the students are treated with the respect that adults, at least formally, are granted by society." Because of the rights-based conduct policy, expulsion and suspension are not used; instead, the focus is on providing support to keep children in school for as long as it takes them to learn the elementary school curriculum. Children, thus, are acknowledged as having the right to an education.

The Workers

Just as children are categorized, so are their workers. Children's workers are categorized not by the *DSM-V* but by their roles, each of which has qualifications and boundaries that are defined by the particular ministry, department, or agency that funds or oversees the work. Table 1.2 presents these role categories.

Table 1.2 The Workers

Job Title	Role	Minimum Training Level: C (certificate), D (diploma), U (university degree)
Educational assistant	Support the child's assessed cognitive, socio-emotional, and physical needs	D: Developmental Services Work D: Early Childhood Education D: Child and Youth Work
Family support worker	Assess parental capacity; link families to social, health, and legal services; facilitate parent education	D: Social Services Work U: Bachelor of Social Work
Youth outreach worker	Counsel youth on the streets, in shelters, youth centres, and drop-ins; link youth to services	D: Child and Youth Work D: Social Services Work
Respite worker	Provide care for children of parents in shelters, homes, and treatment programs	D: Early Childhood Education D: Child and Youth Work
Child care provider Daycare worker	Provide care and education for children and respite for parents	D: Early Childhood Education
Residential care worker Direct care staff Frontline worker	Counsel youth; individual program planning; behaviour modification and management; group home management; group work; provide daily care for children and youth	D: Developmental Services Work D: Child and Youth Work D: Social Services Work U: Behavioural Science Technology
Special needs worker	Provide daily care (feeding, bathing, lifting and transferring, leisure activities) for children with special needs	D: Developmental Services Work U: Behavioural Science Technology
Foster care worker	Train and support foster parents; oversee care of foster children	D: Social Services Work U: Bachelor of Social Work
Child protection worker	Respond to disclosures and reports of abuse and neglect; risk assessment; investigate alleged abuse and neglect	U: Bachelor of Social Work

Job Title	Role	Minimum Training Level: C (certificate), D (diploma), U (university degree)
Service worker for young single parents	Counsel parents; facilitate parent education; link parents to services	D: Social Services Work U: Bachelor of Social Work
Foster parent	Provide daily care for children and youth in the foster home	Agency training
Welfare worker	Assess eligibility of youth for social assistance or training subsidies	D: Social Services Work U: Bachelor of Social Work
Addictions counsellor	Support and counsel children and youth with addictions	C: Addictions Counselling
Clinical social worker (hospital setting)	Support and counsel children with chronic or terminal illness, eating disorders, mental health issues, addictions, trauma, or other medical issues	U: Masters of Social Work
Child life specialist	Assess needs of child and family when child is hospitalized; provide play-based interventions for child and family	U: Masters of Social Work
Crisis counsellor Trauma counsellor	Counsel children and youth in crisis situations	D: Child and Youth Work D: Social Services Work U: Ph.D. (psychology)
Play therapist	Support children to uncover and deal with emotional trauma	U: Bachelor of Social Work or BA (Psychology) + Play therapy certificate C: Play therapy

This categorization works well for the management of staff and services, but this categorization does not serve the child well. As stated in the Preface to this book, no single science provides the requisite background for working with children. A worker trained in early childhood education may understand how to observe play but will not understand how to handle disclosures of abuse. Similarly, a child protection worker does not have the training to set up play spaces and observe play. The roles of these workers overlap and mix, negatively impacting children and youth whose lives do not fit into neat categories of separate service provision. In addition, most of these frontline workers are called direct service providers, a title that suggests that they provide the direct services. This is misleading as the direct services are typically provided through referrals to another layer of workers: public health nurses, family doctors, school principals, dentists, psychologists, and other professionals.

Because no single worker is responsible for the whole child there is little consistency in services or messaging. A boy with diagnosed bipolar disorder who lives in a group home, for example, may have to tell and re-tell his story to five workers: foster care worker, child protection worker, residential care worker, mental health worker, and educational assistant. This does not include the doctor and psychologist whom he sees at regular intervals and the teacher he sees in his classroom every day. The number of workers and their differing schedules, vacations, and leave times only exacerbate his stress and insecure attachment. The mental health worker may not understand the group home culture and may suggest programs that do not fit that model of care. The educational assistant may suggest parental involvement when the boy has not seen his parents for years. The same educational assistant may assess the boy's behaviour as too disruptive for extracurricular activities. The result may be many referrals but no actual services in place because of program exclusions and waiting lists. "Many young people spend their teenage years moving from one service to another, failing at all of them, and being told that their specific circumstances just don't fit the helping systems available. Imagine the message: 'You're not good enough to be helped.'" (Gharabaghi, 2012: 7).

The pervading childism among frontline workers also impacts service. Childism suggests that children are vulnerable and unable to understand the structural determinants impacting their lives. Child and youth workers Elicia Loiselle, Sandrina de Finney, Nishad Khanna, and Rebecca Corcoran (2012: 186) know the frustration that youth in care feel when they are "helped" rather than empowered and involved in service planning: "Such conceptualizations assume that young people are not already aware of and engaged with issues that have shaped generations of their families, and that effective "care" and "helping" should involve apolitical, uncritical, color-blind "relational practices" that are disconnected from what is going on in their lives and communities." Childism prompts workers to apportion resources to children rather than engage them in egalitarian relationships or advocacy work. Workers are often disempowered themselves and struggling with structural determinants such as homophobia and punitive labour practices, so disempowering children feels natural. Their fallback position is the agency protocol, government guidelines, and departmental requirements. Consider the following situations. Although the names are fictitious, these are real situations involving Canadian children.

- Randy has pervasive developmental disorder and hates it when people sing. Last summer his foster parents sent him to camp. When the children sang around the campfire Randy screamed at everyone to stop and pushed one of the counsellors who was playing guitar. The camp director sent Randy home. The following summer his foster parents enrolled Randy at a different camp. They hoped that he had outgrown his aversion to singing and they wanted him to enjoy the camping experience. At the first campfire Randy screamed at everyone to stop singing and threw a campfire log at the other campers. One camper was gouged above her eye and knocked unconscious. When her parents found out about Randy's behaviour at both camps they decided to sue Randy's foster parents and the camp director.

- Erin, an educational assistant, encouraged Mildred's classmates to include her in their games and push her in her wheelchair. During a game of capture the flag an enthusiastic classmate pushed Mildred and overturned her wheelchair, causing numerous abrasions on Mildred's face. Her parents were horrified and are suing both Erin and the school.
- Candy lives in a group home run by the local youth services bureau. She developed a serious lung infection as a result of mould in her bedroom. After she was admitted to hospital a municipal health inspector condemned the group home, citing numerous health violations and the unsanitary condition of the premises. Candy's brother intends to sue the bureau and the residential care worker for failing to keep Candy safe.
- Stephanie started going to a youth drop-in with her friends and became involved with many of the fundraising activities there. One of the youth outreach workers advised Stephanie that the birth control medication she was taking could have dangerous long-term side effects. As a result, Stephanie stopped the medication and became pregnant three months later. When she told her parents about the worker's advice her parents decided to sue the worker for damages.

In all of these workplaces the workers were unprotected and unsupported. They were responsible for getting (and paying for) their own legal representation. This lack of protection and support left them feeling vulnerable and disempowered, not a safe place from which to do frontline work. Bernard Schissel (2011: 11) reminds us, "Many of those in charge of children and youth in society earn insufficient wages given the importance of their work and . . . often work in the context of scarce resources and without much political support, and often aggressive political opposition."

Workers who are supported and protected feel empowered to take the structural and strengths-based approach. They can in turn empower children to make decisions and to advocate for structural change. Robbie Gilligan (2006: 21) tells the story of his friend, Debra Fearn, who grew up in foster care and later went on to become a university professor. Debra reflects on a teacher who was empowered to engage her in a structural and strengths-based intervention in the educational system:

> She saw a spark in me and for the next seven years ensured that the spark became a flame that did not extinguish itself. She believed in me, and gave me courage and a belief in myself that could have easily been lost along the way. When I failed Maths and French . . . , she ensured that I received extra tuition after school, and she gave me the belief that I would be successful the second time around. . . . What makes her stand out in my mind is that she cared for me and she liked me.

Note from the Field   1.1

Emergency Foster Placement

Some workers believe that only adults understand structural determinants. When they work with children who are impacted by structural determinants these workers attempt to amuse and distract the children rather than engage them in structural change. Consider the following two dialogues. Both child protection workers have just apprehended a three-year-old boy from his home and are driving him to an emergency foster home. This drive can involve navigating unfamiliar roads and highways, hearing the child scream and cry, and mentally preparing the **case note** of the **apprehension** and placement, plus the supporting documentation for the risk assessment. One worker distracts the child, while the other supports the child's voice and (limited) power within this system.

Dialogue 1 begins with positive messages intended to distract the crying child during the drive to the emergency foster home. This dialogue positions the foster home as better and more fun than the child's own home. The worker promises the boy, "You will have a great time."

W: We'll be there soon and you'll have lots of fun with the other kids.
C: Do they have a dog?
W: No, but they have two cats and a great big swimming pool too!
C: I want to go home.
W: I know. But we're almost there and you will have a great time.

Dialogue 2 also begins with reassurances, and then the worker validates the child's grief and his concern for his mommy. The worker's attentive listening reassures the child that questions are encouraged and that the child's feelings and concerns are heard. The only promise that is made—giving the boy's picture to his mother—is one that the worker is able to fulfill. In this second dialogue, the boy is charged with making a picture (message) for his mom. In doing this, he moves from the powerless position of being carried away in a stranger's car to playing an important role in his move to the foster home.

W: We'll be there soon.
C: Do they have a dog?
W: No, no dog as cute as Rusty (child's dog). Your grandma has promised to take care of Rusty while you're gone.
C: I want to go home. I want Rusty.
W: Rusty wants you too. But Rusty needs some extra things now that grandma can give him. He needs walks and some food and a cozy bed at night. Mommy and I are going to get together tomorrow to try to get

> all those things that you and Rusty both need. Those things are hard to get here in Winnipeg even when you try really hard to get them.
>
> C : I could help mommy.
>
> W: Yes, you can. Maybe you can make mommy a drawing of the bed that you want for Rusty, and I can take your drawing to mommy tomorrow. That would help.
>
> C : Would it?
>
> W: Yes. It would give mommy a better idea of what bed Rusty needs.
>
> C : What else can I do?
>
> W: Right now you and I can talk and make a plan.
>
> C : I'm hungry.
>
> W: You must be! We can make a snack together when we get to your foster home. You can show me what you like to eat and we can eat it together while you make your drawing for mommy.
>
> C : Okay.

This intervention may seem too simple: "she cared for me and she liked me." But decades later, and more than 20 workers and 12 foster homes later, Debra remembers that one teacher who believed in her strength and capabilities and gave her the specific attention that she needed at the time. Her teacher did not pity Debra or give her referral forms. Her teacher made those structural adjustments (e.g., arranging for tutoring, re-scheduling exams) to enable her success. Debra's experience is replicated in the foster homes of Ontario youth. Their academic success increases when their foster parents feel empowered to advocate on their behalf, changing the system rather than assessing, changing, or blaming the children in their homes. Gilligan (2006), Masten (2006), Cheung, Lwin, and Jenkins (2012), Tough (2012), and others continue to provide research examples of children and youth who are positively impacted by this structural and strengths-based approach.

The Workers' Mandate

There is no federal Ministry of the Child, and federal oversight of children's services is limited to recommendations and reports, both without the strength of federal legislation. Those who work with children in Canada have different mandates in each agency, province, and territory, and this structural determinant affects all of the workers' interventions with children and youth.

The lack of a national mandate affects Canadian children directly as they move on and off reserve, from province to territory, and even from city to city. There have been calls for equal treatment of all Canadian children for over a century, but the response has been limited to reports. Health, education, child care, child welfare, labour, recreational opportunities, alternative care, adoption, family preservation and supports, and the list continues: all of these interventions with children are funded and administered differently for Aboriginal and non-Aboriginal children, in each province and territory, and in some cases (child care, schools, recreational opportunities) in each municipality.

Child labour laws, for example, vary from coast to coast, resulting in irregular school attendance and child injuries and deaths. In most provinces, the minimum age to work is 14, but in British Columbia and Alberta 12-year-olds may work a certain number of hours each day. In Quebec, there are no age restrictions and no limit on hours worked, and some children work long hours in the fields during harvest season. These children handle machinery and loads well beyond their capabilities and, as a result, they make up a disproportionate percentage of workplace accident victims in that province (Arsenault, 2008).

Federal oversight does apply to "delinquent" children. This has been a consistent federal mandate from the Juvenile Delinquents Act (1908–84), to the Young Offenders Act (1984–2003), and now the Youth Criminal Justice Act (last amended on April 1, 2014). The Youth Criminal Justice Act (YCJA) applies to children between the ages of 12 and 17, removing them from the UNCRC child category and re-categorizing them as "young offenders." The focus of the YCJA is on non-punitive measures and restorative justice, and its implementation has resulted in 15 per cent more children being held in remand (pre-trial detention) and 30 per cent fewer children appearing in court from 2002/3 to 2009/10. Figure 1.2 (Youth Court Cases in Canada, 2002/3–2009/10) illustrates these declining numbers of youth in court. Canada's overall youth incarceration rate, which includes both custody and detention, has been almost halved under the YCJA, from thirteen youths per 10,000 in 2002/3 to seven youths per 10,000 in 2008/9.

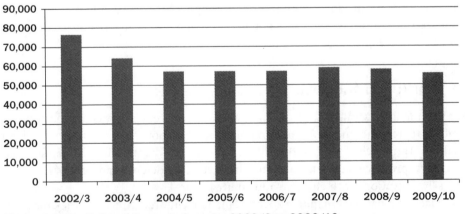

Figure 1.2 Youth Court Cases in Canada, 2002/3 to 2009/10

Source: Statistics Canada, Youth Court Survey, 2002/3 to 2009/10, Canadian Centre for Justice Statistics, 2013. Reproduced and distributed on an "as is" basis with the permission of Statistics Canada.

The federal government also has a mandate to regulate **child support** payments, provide certain child benefits such as the Universal Child Care Benefit (UCCB), transfer funds for certain children's services, and provide direct funding for child care programs that serve First Nations communities, military families, immigrants, and refugees. The federal government also issues periodic reports on children's issues. These include *Children Come First* (2002), *A Canada Fit for Children* (2004), *Every Image, Every Child* (2007), *Child Care in Canada: The Federal Role* (2007), *National Children's Agenda* (2007), and *Population Health* (2011). Each report deals with one aspect of children's service, summarizes federal initiatives, and provides recommendations. In addition, there are many non-governmental national organizations, associations, councils, partnerships, leagues, and foundations working hard on behalf of all Canadian children. These national groups issue periodic reports and warnings but are dependent upon membership and donations for the continuation of their research and advocacy work. These groups provide estimates of children who are in foster care or who are adopted, children completing high school or dropping out of school, and children living in poverty. There is no systematic federal counting of these children, which seems to suggest that children in Canada do not count.

Because of this lack of federal oversight there are also no national standards for education, child protection, child care, health care, or alternative care. Don Giesbrecht, president of the Canadian Child Care Federation, commented on the fact that 80 per cent of Canadian children are in unlicensed and unregulated child care: "In this country we have national standards for light bulbs but not for children" (CBC News, 2013). In Bolton, Ontario, in 1986 four children died in a fire in their unlicensed daycare. Their untrained caregiver was too drunk to get them out to safety. The coroner's recommendations were never implemented and certainly were not in place in 2012 in Ottawa, Ontario, when two-year-old Jérémie Audette drowned in a backyard pool that was being used by 31 other children in their unlicensed daycare. One of his caregivers was fined $2,000, and the other $750. Neither caregiver spent a day in jail. Andre Marin's report on this legislative failure was simply titled, *Careless about Child Care* (2014). The lack of a national mandate for children is a structural detriment that, in some cases, proves to be deadly.

Structural and Strengths-Based Interventions

Structural and strengths-based interventions do what the Honourable Landon Pearson suggests in the epigraph to this chapter: they make the worker a partner with the child and change the "me" to "we." Rather than assessing the deficits of the child and imposing remedies or medication on the child ("me"), the structural and strengths-based worker and the child ("we") collaborate to identify and assess both the structural determinants and the child's strengths or assets. The worker acknowledges the role that adults play in disempowering the child and works to correct this power imbalance. The worker also remembers that, when pointing out structural determinants, the other three fingers of the hand point backwards: the worker and the child together are responsible for advocating for structural change. Dennis Saleebey (2002: 13–14) summarizes this type of intervention beautifully:

> Every individual group, family, and community has its strengths; trauma and abuse, illness and struggle may be injurious but they may also be sources of challenge and opportunity; assume that you do not know the upper limits of the capacity to grow and change and take individual, group, and community aspirations seriously; we best serve clients by collaborating with them; every environment is full of resources; and caring, care taking, and context count.

These interventions assume that children have the ontogenetic capacity to understand the impact of structural determinants and to work towards modifying their impact in order to manage and change their behaviour. This assumption is empowering. Instead of, "Look out, you're going to fall," with its corresponding assumption of failure, the worker offers affirmation and encouragement: "One more step to climb!" The child's opinions and preferences are recognized and heard, rather than dismissed and disregarded in favour of "adult wisdom." The child plans and chooses solutions and takes responsibility for making these chosen solutions or new behaviours work. This process of empowerment affirms the child's capabilities and sense of control and requires the child to assume ownership of both the problem and the solution—the sense of responsibility articulated in the UNCRC. In effect, the worker says to the child, "You are in charge of this. You decide where you want to go with this." The choice of intervention or resources is in the hands of the one who is most familiar with the impact of structural determinants in daily life: the child.

Structural and strengths-based interventions empower the child to make decisions and to move forward. When the child demonstrates a need to engage in physical play rather than sit at a desk for hours, the worker advocates for the child's acceptance into alternate, more physically satisfying programs. When the child talks about teasing by classmates, the worker listens and helps the child to reframe the teasing and devise new responses to it. The worker also addresses the structure and engages the school and classroom teacher in anti-bullying strategies. This does not diminish or excuse the child's responsibility for having hit others. On the contrary, this increases the child's responsibility to advocate for change and to make that change happen. Three case examples demonstrate these interventions.

Consider Tammy, a biracial seven-year-old with language delays who lives in a white neighbourhood and attends the local school. The deficits-based biomedical approach is to pathologize Tammy's language skills (screen for language deficits or delays) and assign a label or diagnosis. Perhaps the *DSM-V* is used, or a speech pathologist administers a written or oral language test. Then Tammy is given medication, speech/language intervention, or extra tuition, while her parents are reprimanded, coached, or given instructions on improving their communication with Tammy. They may be told to sign off on her homework, hire a tutor, or read stories to her every night before bedtime. Tammy and her family, or Tammy alone, is fitted into an existing program. Because of the scarcity of health care resources, both the clinical assessment and the intervention may not take place until months or years after the initial identification of the language delay.

On the other hand, the educational assistant may take the structural and strengths-based approach as shown in Table 1.3. The educational assistant identifies the cause of Tammy's behaviour (delayed language) within the larger structure rather than within Tammy. The worker pinpoints poverty, racism, assessment models, and the education system as specific structural barriers to Tammy's success. The worker also identifies and acknowledges Tammy's strengths: her enthusiasm, health, intellectual ability, willingness to learn, strong interpersonal relationships within her family, cultural and racial pride, **resiliency**, and an engaged and concerned family. With the parents' collaboration, the educational assistant arranges for child care within the home and a school subsidy that allows Tammy to take a break from her caregiving responsibilities and join an after-school social group. The family, Tammy, and the educational assistant make a plan to engage the school in an anti-racism program that includes racial pride activities as part of the curriculum. Tammy is central to this program and gets that chance to speak out and communicate with her peer group, and so her expressive language and her advocacy skill develop.

Consider six-year-old Tyler, described by his teacher as hyperactive because he gets up from his table too often and fights with the other boys. The teacher recommends that Tyler be prescribed the stimulant medication Ritalin. The family support worker does not dispute the teacher's diagnosis or his single mother's frustration with Tyler's behaviour, or in any way excuse Tyler's aggressive behaviour. However, before intervening or medicating the child, the worker conducts a structural and strengths-based assessment as shown in Table 1.4.

Table 1.3 Tammy

Structural Determinants	Impact on Tammy	Tammy's Strengths/Assets
Poverty	· Caregiving responsibilities that preclude socializing after school · No home computer · Two working parents · Few resources	· Maturity and ability to provide care for siblings · Strong extended family · Healthy attachment to family
Racism	· Bullying at school and in her (white) neighbourhood	· Cultural and racial pride within a biracial family
DSM-V/Biomedical model	· Stigma of being labelled "delayed"	· Resiliency · Family support for education
Education system	· Stigmatization of an educational assistant · No free after-school programs	· Cognitive ability · Receptive language skills · Enthusiasm for learning

Table 1.4 Tyler

Structural Determinants	Impact on Tyler	Tyler's Strengths/Assets
Education system	· 2 hours outdoor play per day · 6 hours indoor sitting per day	· Psychomotor skills
Gender roles	· Action and battle role play · Little interest in art, dance, music, reading	· Plays well with boys · Role plays warriors, battles · Strong, healthy
DSM-V/Biomedical model	· Potential for being labelled "ADHD" and being prescribed psychotropic drugs	· Respect for teacher
Childism	· Accepts authority · Obeys teacher and parent · Feels powerless in school	· Understands rules and consequences

Tyler signals to the family support worker his readiness to change—a readiness prompted by his mother's anxiety plus lunch hours spent in the principal's office rather than outside with his friends. The worker listens to Tyler's signal and responds with an affirmation that Tyler is capable of taking ownership over his behaviour. Tyler's identified strengths in psychomotor skills and understanding prompt corresponding structural and strengths-based interventions. The grade one curriculum requires Tyler's compliance and attention to classroom activities. The worker and the mother together offer Tyler a chance to join a sports team before school and after school. This provides an outlet for Tyler's energy and strength and a chance to learn team skills from the older boys. Because these demanding games with older boys are exciting for him, Tyler now has a reason to attend to his teacher during class. The older boys in turn reinforce Tyler's growing understanding of co-operation and teamwork, rather than bullying and winning.

The impact of gender roles on Tyler is counterbalanced by the team coach who is both male and nurturing. The worker supplements this positive male role model by pointing out examples of other caring males. Tyler and the worker dialogue around issues of aggression and expressing feelings through words rather than fights. By working together they are able to postpone his medication. Ritalin may be necessary for Tyler in the future but, at the moment, Tyler is able to take control of his own behaviour through this modification of structural determinants. These interventions acknowledge Tyler's strengths in communication, psychomotor skills, and socialization, and take advantage of the pre-existing structural supports for change. Tyler controls each of these interventions and takes responsibility for the change. The structure adapts to support this change. The child, even at six years of age, can control the timing and the amount of change, and can continue learning in school without medication and its accompanying label.

Point to Consider   1.3

A Community Faces Poverty

In 2005, the Municipal Council in Hamilton, Ontario, acknowledged that 20 per cent of the city's population—roughly 100,000 people—were living in households subsisting below the poverty line. Instead of taking the "charity" approach and setting up new food banks and clothing distribution posts, the Council asked for solutions from the people in the poorest neighbourhoods. The goal was to make Hamilton the best place to raise a child. The people in the poorest neighbourhoods developed community action plans that identified specific projects they felt would result in better outcomes for children. Their expertise was acknowledged and valued and formed the core of the Hamilton Roundtable for Poverty Reduction. Some of their community initiatives were

- Tastebuds, a student nutrition collaborative project involving community volunteers and children in 100 schools;
- Kids Unlimited, a program of mentoring and of joint corporate-children projects; and
- Best Start, an early childhood education program involving parents and educators in the community.

These three projects, among others, were undertaken by people in the poorest neighbourhoods, together with people from outside these neighbourhoods. This shared goal and shared power resulted in new relationships and community collaboration within other areas of mutual interest. In a community focused on poverty as a structural determinant of child health (Chamberlain and Weaver, 2008), the poverty rate was lowered significantly.

The third case example is that of Tibo, a 15-year-old young offender who engages in self-harm as well as abusive behaviour towards others. Tibo has used self-harm successfully as a way to cope with the absence of a consistent caregiver during his entire childhood. He has seen adults come and go at his place and has suffered neglect as well as physical and sexual **abuse** within his home. At the same time, he has been the primary caregiver of his two younger brothers. Because he is a resident of a northern community with no youth detention facilities, he has been incarcerated with adult men, most of whom abuse both drugs and alcohol.

Tibo expresses to his youth outreach worker that he does not want his brothers to visit him, nor does he want them to end up in juvenile detention with him. The worker affirms Tibo's maturity, street smarts, and skill in caregiving, and his resilience in managing the trauma of attachment injuries and childhood sexual abuse. The worker empowers Tibo to reframe his current situation within structural terms in order to understand how structural determinants have impacted his behaviour. In this way, Tibo can begin to forgive himself for leaving his younger brothers outside while he is inside. Incarceration can engage Tibo in a treatment program, counselling, and a chance to work through some of the abuse he has suffered. In time, Tibo may want to advocate for change. He may want to express his anger by identifying and charging his childhood abusers. He may want to proactively communicate with previous teachers who failed to report the abuse. Active decision making is empowering and can replace helplessness with hopefulness. A structural and strengths-based approach to Tibo is described in Table 1.5.

What we know about successful interventions is that they are structural and strengths-based and planned to match the needs of the individual child. These interventions are based on a belief that the child is competent, has the personal resources to change, and will change when structural supports are adequate. The worker respects both the strengths of the child and the child's capacity for change and identifies to the child the structural supports needed to support the child's decision to change.

Table 1.5 Tibo

Structural Determinants	Impact on Tibo	Tibo's Strengths/Assets
Legislation (YCJA)	· Incarcerated for 12 months with adult offenders	· Physical strength and size · Resiliency · Street smarts
Gender roles	· Assumes male role as tough, violent, and callous	· Close relationship with his younger brothers, and desire to protect them
Biomedical model	· Seven years on Ritalin	· Willingness to consider a substance abuse program
Lack of affordable and accessible child care	· Cared for two younger siblings throughout elementary school, and survived a succession of inept and abusive caregivers during his early childhood	· Actively self-medicates to dull the pain from childhood abuse and attachment injuries · Secure attachment to his younger brothers · Capable and caring
Childism	· Disclosed childhood sexual abuse through his aggressive behaviour in elementary school, but his disclosures were never reported	· Distrust of adults and authority figures · Resiliency

Summary

The structural and strengths-based approach to working with children differs significantly from the traditional biomedical or deficits-based approach which usually begins with the identification of a behaviour problem within the child. The child is constructed as a problem and is assessed, and the usual intervention is a requirement for the child to change. The structural and strengths-based approach, on the other hand, locates the problem within the structure. The child is assumed to be competent and able to problem solve with an adult in order to make structural changes. In advocating for and making structural changes, the child is empowered to continue problem solving.

This chapter introduces three particular structural determinants that directly impact the lives of children in Canada and elsewhere. Poverty is an overriding factor, causing children to miss out on structural supports and opportunities and, in some cases, even the basic necessities of life. The second structural determinant is the *Diagnostic and Statistical Manual of Mental Disorders*, fifth edition (*DSM-V*), which offers a stark contrast to the structural and strengths-based approach in its diagnosing and labelling of children's behaviours as the result of disorders. Finally, the Convention on the Rights of the Child (UNCRC) frames all of the basic rights of children, but the lack of legislative application in Canada of this important document illustrates why children's legal rights are so often neglected. In subsequent chapters, we will see the structural and strengths-based approach in action as we learn to listen to children and to understand their behaviours. Keep in mind these three structural determinants as they circumscribe all of our work with children.

Review Questions

1. How would you use the structural and strengths-based approach with a toddler who continually runs away from a caregiver?
2. What is the major difference between Bronfenbrenner's ecological approach and the structural approach to working with children and youth?
3. Why is poverty the most important structural determinant for children in Canada? Use the eight determinants of population health as your guide in providing examples.
4. How is the *DSM-V* used, and what are the inherent drawbacks of this diagnostic tool?
5. Explain any three articles of the UNCRC that are contravened in Canada today.
6. Name ten different roles played by workers with children and youth and explain why education and training is so important in each of these roles.
7. Explain how the lack of a federal mandate for children's services impacts both children and their workers in Canada. Give examples.

8. What does changing "me" to "we" mean?
9. Why might some workers prefer to use the traditional, deficits-based approach?
10. In the examples of Tammy, Tyler, and Tibo, how did strengths become assets that were used to overcome structural impediments?

Discussion Questions

1. "Empowerment" is a term often used in the helping professions because one of the goals of caring for others is to support them in ways that move them into independence and self-actualization. How can you create an empowering relationship with children? Is this something you might want to do? How might the goal of empowerment affect your work with children?
2. Do you think that children have too many rights in Canada today? Which articles of the Convention on the Rights of the Child do you not support and why?
3. When working with children like Tammy, Tibo, and Tyler, described in this chapter, how would you engage the family and teachers in the structural and strengths-based approach?

2 The Social Construction of the Child

daddy says the world is
a drum tight and hard
and i told him
i'm gonna beat out my own rhythm

—Nikki Giovanni, "The Drum"

Google the word "child" and you will find screens of definitions and descriptions. Definitions of "child" vary according to the **social location** of the definer, usually an adult, who decides the age limits, descriptors, and behaviours that combine to form the **social construction** of a "child." In one social location, the definer may construct the child to be property of the family and may see children as persons under the age of 10. In another, the child may be viewed as a citizen of the world with universally acknowledged rights. In Canada, the social construction of "child" continues to evolve as our understanding of the definition, boundaries, and dimensions of childhood changes.

The social location of the definer reflects the socio-political constructs of the time. In a period of pioneering and settlement, a child is a valuable property who can work in the fields, cook, and clean. In more affluent times, a child is a cherished accessory to be cosseted, trained, and valued for "refined" accomplishments. In this chapter, we will trace the social construction of the child through a century and a half of Canadian life. This history is not a comprehensive account of childhood and children, which is the subject of many books listed in the references (Janovicek and Parr, 2003; Kail and Zolner, 2005; Stearns, 2006). Instead, this brief review explores the social construction of children in each period to uncover socio-political underpinnings, boundaries, and dimensions.

During the first 50 years of this period (1850–1900), the Canadian child was positioned as a valuable commodity. Families were large, infant mortality rates were high, and every hand in the family was needed for survival. In the next half-century or so (1900–1950s), the child was positioned as vulnerable and needing moral correction, training, and education. From the 1960s onwards, the child was positioned as **social capital**—a valuable collective investment shared between family and state. Throughout this 150-year period, of course, some children grew up on the margins because of their language, culture, race, ability, or life situation. They were marginalized, subjected to a societal bias that excluded them from the benefits of inclusion in the thriving central culture. These children felt the broad brush strokes of the socio-political constructs of the time, but they felt these strokes in much different (and often cruel) ways.

Current government funding, reports, and projects may suggest that children have better lives today than they did in the 1850s. In many ways they do. Infant mortality rates are much lower. A premature infant of three pounds is likely to live today, and the average Canadian child is likely to have at least two meals a day. The ignorance of the past—the beatings, the servitude—appears to have been replaced by enlightened and nurturing parenting in a child-focused Canada. However, many Canadian children would disagree that their reality is promising, and their rates of poverty, illness, and suicide attest to this. As Janet Ruane and Karen Cerulo (2004: 31) note, "While we idealize childhood, the reality for Canadian children is anything but ideal. Indeed, despite the pro-child stance, many children find childhood too difficult to endure." Let's look at the various constructions and experiences of childhoods now, in each of the three periods, to understand the validity of this comment.

Objectives

By the end of this chapter, you will:

- Understand how the concept of "child" has been socially constructed and how this affects the relationship between children and adults.
- Identify the variety of age limits that define a person as a child and the legislation that sets these limits.
- Deconstruct your current perceptions of the concept of "child" as they affect your interventions with children.

Social Construction

"Construction" is a building process, planned and deliberate. Accordingly, social construction is less planned, but formed nevertheless by deliberate acts that build meanings or affirm culturally shared assumptions. This construction process is gradual and covert, with most people unaware of the process in which they participate. They are aware only of the end product: the socially constructed value they have assumed, adopted, or reinforced.

The recognition that childhood is a socially constructed concept indicates that the identity of "child" does not exist objectively but is both time- and culture-bound. Children and childhood are perceived differently by different people at different times. Our exploration of the concept of childhood in Canada begins by examining the basic culturally shared assumptions underlying this constructed entity at various times in our society's history. The first assumption is boundaries: who belongs in the category of "child" and who is excluded.

Boundaries begin with the **categorization of persons,** a socio-political act that enables state management and control of individuals. Constructing the category of "senior citizens," for example, allows the state to manage persons of a specified age as a group and to control aspects of their behaviour ("we will help you in these ways but not those") through the provision of tax benefits, allowances, and special subsidies. Similarly, slotting individuals of a specified age into the category of "child" allows the state to manage and control them as a group. Categorization according to age is called **generationing**. This age division places children in a social location that is very different to the location occupied by adults.

Each generation is then subdivided into more than one category. The category of "infants" is a subcategory of "children." Infants can range in age from birth to six weeks or to six months, depending on the definer's understanding of the age limits of infancy. Then, at the upper end of childhood, there is, as of the 1950s, the constructed category of "youth," "adolescents," or "teenagers." The construction of this category is significant because of both the size of the age group (comprising seven years from ages 13 to 19) and the negative attributes frequently associated with this subcategory of children. These negative attributes have a spillover effect on all children, impacting their treatment by adults and by society at large.

The research work of G. Stanley Hall, Anna Freud, and other early twentieth-century thinkers supports the creation of the category of "teenager" to refer to persons at the upper limit of the childhood stage. This category was originally termed "adolescence" by Hall and was defined both by age boundaries (the "teen" years—ages 13 to 19) and by characteristic behaviours, and the behaviours soon became more important than the age. Over time, a self-fulfilling prophecy emerged: the category increasingly came to represent a set of circumscribed behaviours instead of an age range, as individuals were socialized to absorb the behaviours and the norms of the category in which they had been positioned. Thus, children who behave in a certain way came to be categorized as adolescents, youth, or teenagers, regardless of their age. This category still does not exist in many cultures and countries in which puberty rites signal a passage from childhood directly to adulthood. Children in such contexts never become categorized as adolescents, youth, or teenagers. They remain children until, through puberty rites, they become adults.

The categorization process sets age and behaviour boundaries. The next step in social construction is **characterization**. Who are these children and what purpose do they serve? The process of characterization serves a particular socio-political interest

Group Exercise   2.1

Generationing

This group exercise demonstrates how behaviours define generations rather than vice versa. It also demonstrates the cultural context of this process.

The exercise begins with an explanation of generationing. The leader then explains that a statement of behaviour will be read, after which the group members will vote on the generation associated with that behaviour. The group will choose from three generations: child, teenager/adolescent, or adult. The group members may use audience response cards (clickers); game cards marked "child," "teen," "adult"; or a simple show of hands. The show of hands method does have a contagion effect, however, in that some group members may raise their hands simply because those nearest to them have done the same.

When the group understands how to vote, the leader then reads aloud each of the following statements, pausing after each one to count and record the votes.

- Crystal can barely draw a stick figure.
- Mohammed hangs around restaurants a lot looking for his friends.
- Russell likes to log online after midnight.
- Samantha is moody and depressed and sometimes sleeps all day.
- Wei-ling scores coke when he can, and sometimes deals to his friends.

By the time that this last statement is read, the voting will be confused and sporadic, with some group members choosing not to vote. At this point, the leader will ask the non-voting members to explain why they have chosen not to vote. Their answers will lead to a group discussion on behaviours and generationing, and why behaviours do not always reflect the generation with which they are associated.

at a particular time. In harsh and lean times, problem children may be characterized as expendable. They represent another mouth to feed, so if they cannot work or contribute to the family, their survival is compromised. The premature infant, the child who fails to thrive, or the child with a disability gets less attention and less sustenance than the child who can contribute to the family pot. In times of affluence, on the other hand, children are better appreciated and cherished. The child in both cases has the same personal qualities, but the social construction of the child characterizes the child in tough times as inessential (another mouth to feed) or in easier times as essential (warm, cuddly, and part of the family).

The meaning, social significance, and experience of childhood also vary among generations and among cultures and belief systems. A mother's childhood may have been quite different from the childhood that her own child experiences; for example, a street child in Ecuador (in this instance, the mom) will have experienced a very different childhood from that of her child raised in Canada in an affluent neighbourhood. Children and families are shaped by the culture in which they are situated and, at the same time, they reproduce that culture through the way they operate and behave in their daily lives.

The social construction of the concept of childhood is controlled and sustained by adults who position themselves as socially, politically, and economically superior to children. Adults decide which persons are to be categorized as children, and how these persons are to be described. After all, children do not vote or pay taxes or hold positions of political power. They are dependent on the actions of parents, guardians, or the state acting in the place of a legal guardian, and usually they are described as vulnerable, dependent, and helpless. This description also validates the **dependency** positioning of children as recipients of adult care even after they are well beyond their early infant years.

Adult power is reinforced when a child is described as irresponsible—or even as playful or fanciful. When a child is asked to tell a story or to offer an opinion, adults often automatically filter the content or dismiss it completely in their official reports. When a child testifies in court, this testimony is questioned solely on the basis that the person offering it is a child. As Allison James and Chris Jenks (1996: 329) comment, "Children's words may continue to be viewed with suspicion or indifference by an adult, as in cases of child sexual abuse where age, rather than experience, may still often be deemed the more important indicator of a child's ability to tell, or even to know, the truth."

Perhaps the most damaging descriptor applied to children, and the one that permeates most of the early childhood literature, is "developing." Children are socially constructed as incomplete persons or "human becomings" (Garrett, 2003: 26) who will be complete persons only when they have achieved adulthood. This perceived quality of incompletion is considered a deficit, a negative. In fact, many of the adjectives used to describe childhood and children—"innocent," "ignorant," "incompetent," "vulnerable"—have negative connotations. Innocence suggests naïveté; ignorance, a lack of knowledge; incompetence, a lack of ability; and vulnerability, powerlessness. These adjectives simultaneously position adults as the rescuers and protectors, the authorities and guides of the incapable, helpless, and vulnerable (children). The "science" of child development taught in colleges and universities exemplifies this childism in claiming that healthy **development** results in a child becoming a responsible adult. Unhealthy development, on the other hand, may result in a child remaining a child, which is presented as a decidedly inferior position.

In this state of incompletion and learned helplessness, children may be deprived of their rights (see Chapter 1) and of opportunities to take responsibility for their own actions. They may be offered choices about clothing and food—whether to wear the blue or green shirt or to eat one sandwich or two—but they are prevented from contributing to major decisions about their education, health, family structure, or home location. Children are positioned as needing competent and knowledgeable adults to speak for them, to protect them, and to make decisions "in their best interests." These knowledgeable adults typically are a child's parents or the state acting in the role of the parents (**in loco parentis**). Adults decide what children should do at given times: what they should eat, how they should play, with whom they must live. Adults hold this power or responsibility because they are older and perhaps wiser and also because they have been socially constructed as competent.

The French philosopher Michel Foucault (1977: 140–8) describes the ways in which adults control children through routine. **Routine,** the regularity and rhythm in a child's activities and tasks, is a structure that helps the child feel more organized and confident. Routine inculcates regularity in eating and sleeping habits, play and work. However, the routines that are imposed on children are often dictated by adults to suit their own social needs. Early toilet training means fewer diapers; regular naps and early bed times mean more free time for adults. This adult-imposed routine benefits adults but does not teach the child to listen to or trust natural bodily rhythms. Inevitably, adult-imposed routines can undermine the child's self-confidence and sense of personal responsibility.

Foucault describes how this happens in the child's classroom. School is presented to children as a learning experience when, in Foucault's terms, it simply teaches children to obey, accept, and conform to a series of disciplines that reinforce adult power and control. The child learns at an early age to behave according to rules established by adults in school, no matter what the rules are or how meaningless and trite they may be. The child may be asked to face the front, put up a hand, and sit up straight; the one who conforms is the one who will be called on and given the teacher's approbation. The classroom message to all of the children is this: what is to be learned (e.g., the math lesson) is less important than obedience and submission to adult power. As Jenks (2005: 81) notes, "The whole premise of adult interaction with the child, even often in pleasure, is control and instruction. All conditions combine and conspire to that end."

When children do not conform to adults' rules and routines and act

Photo 2.1 Asking for permission to speak in school.

as persons, they challenge the prevailing social construction of childhood. These children are punished and excluded from the category of children. Children who run away from home, for example, are called "street youth" even at 11 or 12 years of age. Children who injure other family members are called "delinquents" or "young offenders"; others are labelled "brats," "deviants," "monsters," and "not children at all." Such was the case with 12-year-old Jasmine Richardson; in 2006, in Medicine Hat, Alberta, Jasmine helped her 23-year-old boyfriend to murder her parents, Marc and Debra, and her brother Jacob. Tried under the Youth Criminal Justice Act as a youth instead of as a child, she was convicted, and much was made of her relationship with her boyfriend and her sexual activities, both of which put her outside the fairytale version of childhood. The press described Jasmine as "depraved" and "a monster" but never as "a child" or "a little girl" despite her young age and diminutive size.

Similar descriptions were applied to the 14-year-old shooter at W.R. Myers High School in Taber, Alberta, in 1999; the 17-year-old shooter in the hallway of C.W. Jefferys Collegiate Institute in Toronto in 2007; and the 17-year-old shooter at Central Technical School in Toronto in 2010. In West St Paul, Manitoba in 2009, a 15-year-old who stabbed his friend to death was excused for this crime because he had been on Prozac for three months. In the same year, a 14-year-old brutally sexually assaulted a girl who was a year younger. Two years later, this boy stabbed another boy to death at Portage Place Mall in Winnipeg. All of these children were described as "teen murderers" with the usual characterizations of adolescence applied to them.

Katharine Kelly and Mark Totten (2002) argue that children who commit such assaults are categorized as "youth" and tried under the Youth Criminal Justice Act because they do not fit our social construction of children. They are powerful persons who can act independently without the direction and control of adults, and their acts are planned and deliberate; in short, they are human beings rather than "human becomings." Bernard Schissel (2006: 13) goes further in describing Canada today as a child-hating country. When children act independently as persons, he notes, they are moved to another category (youth), or simply described as monsters and aberrations. Omar Khadr knows this. Omar was accused of killing an American soldier and planting mines to target US convoys in Afghanistan. His actions as a child soldier

Photo 2.2 Omar Khadr at age 14.

© Mike Cassese/Reuters/Corbis

Group Exercise   2.2

Meeting the Child

The brief visual and auditory experience of this large-group exercise demonstrates how the position of children as vulnerable and helpless is socially constructed.

The exercise begins with one volunteer who sits in front of the group and takes on the persona of the child. The group members are asked to print on a sticky note the first word that comes to their minds when they think of a child. The group members then affix their notes to the volunteer while saying their words. This part of the exercise should be done quickly to deter group members from searching for politically correct phrases or words. Some words, such as "innocent," "young," "helpless," "vulnerable," and "cute" will be repeated. When all the words are said, the volunteer should be covered with sticky notes.

The group leader then asks the volunteer how it feels to be described in this way. The volunteer may remark on how demeaning this exercise feels and how the repetition of particular labels is hurtful. The leader then thanks the volunteer, perhaps patting his or her head or hair. The volunteer may spontaneously react to this; if not, the leader asks the volunteer how it feels to be touched this way by a stranger. This leads to a discussion of why children's personal space often is invaded by adults. The discussion can be enlarged to include social construction; the repetition of words (labels) is part of this social construction as people begin to associate these words with children. The group members may want to repeat this exercise to deconstruct the labels. This time, the participants may choose to use only strengths-based words to describe a child. The exercise is repeated, with the volunteer being asked to compare experiences of being labelled "helpless" versus being labelled "strong." During the deconstruction, the group leader does not touch the volunteer or invade the volunteer's personal space. Instead, the volunteer is respected as a person with the right to space and dignity.

---

led him to lose his Convention rights even though he was only 15 years old. Instead, he was incarcerated for ten years in a brutal adult prison at Guantanamo Bay, Cuba, deprived of family and of any children his own age, and left outside of Canadian society until May 2013, when he was moved to a maximum-security prison in Edmonton, Alberta.

The social construction of childhood positions children as passive victims of abuse or as wide-eyed innocents who dream of being adopted. Gerry Fewster (2002: 18) argues, "By definition, childhood is a diminished state—interesting only as a preparation for adulthood but not to be taken seriously." However, the reality is that children are not property to be protected or pitied. They are persons with a full range of emotions who can act independently—including ways that are not expected and sanctioned by society.

Children are not lesser, incomplete entities that are in the process of developing into the "better" and complete state of adulthood; they are growing persons who have voices, intellects, and opinions that need to be heard.

The Marginalized Child

Histories of Canadian childhood (e.g., Janovicek and Parr, 2003) contrast the stories of mainstream children with those of children marginalized by the socio-political constructs of race, ability, socio-economic status, language, class, culture, and ethnicity. These childhoods have been, and continue to be, very different from the mainstream. Marginalized children have confronted bias and stereotyping from infancy and often are perceived stereotypically as representatives of a group rather than as unique individuals or children. Their stories have only begun to be heard, but they help us to understand the difference that marginalization makes in the social construction, and the lived experience, of childhood.

In the late nineteenth century and through much of the twentieth century, while most mainstream Canadian children were dealing with discipline and work at an early age, their First Nations peers in northern and western Canada often were worse off. Changes to the Indian Act in 1920 made it punishable by law for Indian parents to withhold their children from attending residential schools, and these schools were often far away from the parents' home. Children as young as five years of age were forcibly taken away from their families (Rogers, deGagné, and Dewar, 2012: 37). One residential school survivor, Madeleine Dion Stout, recollects beings separated from her parents: "I beg my mother and father not to leave me. I cry until my nose bleeds. Then and there colours fade. There is nothing left to say; hearts break and moments die" (Rogers, deGagné, and Dewar, 2012: 47).

Some workers at the residential schools replaced the children's names with numbers or new English names, cut their hair, and replaced their clothing with uniforms (Sinclair, Hart, and Bruyere, 2009).Through these imposed changes in name, hair, clothing, language, and religion, these children underwent **deculturation,** the process of having one's culture systematically devalued and stripped away (see Chapter 4). Some children died in the process, often by suicide; others escaped, only to be rounded up again and punished (Schissel and Wotherspoon, 2003; Davis, 2009). Every one of the remaining survivors carries memories of this dehumanizing experience. Fred Kelly recalls, "Immediately upon entry into the school, the staff began to beat the devil out of us. Such was my experience. We were humiliated out of our culture and spirituality. We were told that these ways were of the devil" (Rogers, deGagné, and Dewar, 2012: 64). Despite this well-known history and the modern understanding of it, however, more First Nations children are in state (residential) care today than at the height of the residential schools era (Sinha et al., 2011).

Even more severely marginalized were the children of First Nations mothers and white trader fathers, as they were made to feel that they belonged to neither culture. Girls often were indulged by their white trader fathers; but boys tended to be shunned by them and described as "wild as an Indian." The mothers, whether married to the trader fathers or not, occupied a tenuous and usually inferior social position, their loyalties divided between their partners and their children, each of a separate culture. The children, too, held divided loyalties, and had difficulty fully identifying with either of the cultures that infused them. As Juliet Pollard (2003: 65) remarks, "Métis offspring of the traders challenged the dominant culture and often consciously chose to reject white society in favour of perpetuating a [distinct] cultural identity which they retain to this day." This cultural identity, however, still causes them to be denied some of the government services available to First Nations children, and to be equally excluded from programs for mainstream children.

As Canadian immigration expanded to include people from all parts of the world, children of particular non-European backgrounds also were ostracized and marginalized. In British Columbia, Chinese Canadian families provided labour, taxes, and service, but their children were shunned in the school system (Janovicek and Parr, 2003). Despite their being second-generation Canadians, they were called "Orientals" and categorized as inferior. Timothy Stanley (2003: 126) notes, "In British Columbia, white supremacy was often expressed in the notion that BC was, and should be, a white man's country." These beliefs were put into action in 1922, when the Victoria School Board forcibly removed Chinese Canadian children from their classes and marched them to Chinese-only schools.

If race, ethnicity, and language were barriers for children in late nineteenth- and early twentieth-century Canada, so was socio-economic status. The children of **lone mothers** and of the poor were marginalized by mainstream society and socially constructed as morally tainted or sinful. In a society dominated by conservative, intolerant mores, a child born to a lone mother was labelled a "bastard"— a product of sin (sex outside of marriage) who was undeserving of title rights or of inheritance rights. The survival and upbringing of these children was determined by mainstream society. Such social reformers as Helen Gregory MacGill and Emily Murphy (of the Famous Five[1]) linked illegitimate babies to mentally unfit mothers and advocated for the forcible sterilization of these women.

Then, there were the children marginalized on the basis of ability. Until the 1980s, most children with developmental disabilities were either institutionalized or home-schooled instead of being integrated into the mainstream educational system, under the assumption that their disability was contagious. Frances Owen and her co-authors (2008: 165) describe this institutionalization of children: "They were subjected to medical experimentation, substandard living conditions, and, involuntarily, sterilization. They were also over-medicated and victimized through abuse, neglect, or cruel and unusual punishment." Similarly, children with visual, ambulatory, hearing, or learning needs were encouraged to attend special schools and institutions, usually located in rural areas far away from their homes. In fact, these situations still exist today: "The rights of children . . . with . . . disabilities to live in their family homes, to have access to education or educational support systems, and in some cases to life-saving medical treatment remain issues of controversy" (Owen et al., 2008: 163).

Children marginalized on the basis of race, ethnicity, culture, class, or ability nevertheless are aware of the experiences of children in mainstream society. They watch and

Point to Consider 2.1

Auton v. British Columbia

Connor Auton, a British Columbia toddler, was diagnosed with autism in 2000. His parents were surprised to find out that their son's applied behavioural analysis (ABA) and intensive behavioural intervention (IBI) therapies, while recognized as valid and reliable health care for autism, were not funded by the government. So they, along with several other parents, brought a class action suit against the government of British Columbia. Their suit was impacted by many layers of often conflicting legislation, including the Canada Health Act, the Constitutional Act, the Medical and Health Care Services Regulation (BC), the Interpretation Act (BC), and the Medicare Protection Act (BC).

The British Columbia Supreme Court agreed that early intensive intervention using ABA/IBI therapy was essential to Connor's health and well-being, and cited the Convention on the Rights of the Child in their decision. Articles 23 and 28 of the Convention specify children's right to health care and educational services that provide appropriate supports for children with special needs. However, this ruling was overturned by the Supreme Court of Canada because the intensive daily therapies needed by children with autism were not considered "core service" provided by "health care practitioners." Despite the negative impact of the ruling on Connor and other children with autism, it did affirm that children are persons with the same health care rights as adults. However, they do not have the same right to work as adults because provincial labour laws preclude them from paid work, and so they are unable to pay for their own therapy, eye care, and dental work. This once again disempowers children and positions them as dependent and vulnerable.

wonder at the inequality of their treatment. They may try to fit in with the mainstream by hiding their ethnicity, language, or disability. They may protest—only to be punished in an adult detention facility. They may seethe with silent anger throughout their childhood years. Each of these potential reactions is unique to each child and each child's social location. That such behaviour is a reaction to marginalization needs to be acknowledged and understood before we begin to work with these children on the margins.

The Economically Valuable Child (1850–1900s)

In nineteenth-century Canada, when childbirth was difficult and infant mortality rates were high (one out of five children died before the age of one), very young children were socially constructed as dispensable (Knapp, 1998: 318). This construction enabled mothers to accept the continual loss of their babies. Those children who did survive their first five precarious years were considered economically valuable and were put to work in the family and sometimes in the community. Work, rather than school, was regarded as the best education for children at the time. In 1850, the Superintendent of Education, Egerton Ryerson noted that there were "nearly one hundred thousand children of school age in Upper Canada not attending any school" (qtd in Davey, 2003: 108). His estimate located the majority of children in Upper Canada in the workforce rather than the classroom.

Childhood was viewed both as a time of innocence and as a time of waywardness, and children were thought to be vulnerable to corruption, "simultaneously innocent and evil; in danger but also dangerous" (Chunn, 2003: 192). Work, it was thought, could cure a multitude of sins, from laziness to delinquency to sexual promiscuity. Children required moral and physical structure and care, which were provided by hard work and by the traditional family, with father as breadwinner and mother as homemaker. The parents, especially the father, had property rights over their children.

Those without a family, or those whose parents were unavailable, were expected to get their moral order and guidance solely from work. Under Britain's Poor Law, 80,000 poor British children—some orphans, others separated from their parents— were transported to Canada between 1880 and 1930. These were the British "Home Children" who were placed with Canadian families as farm labourers and domestic servants, forced to toil without pay because it was thought that this work would be an education for them and redeem them from the sin of their poverty. Poor Canadian children were expected to work, too, and work they did, enduring long hours of toil

Isaac Erb, Library and Archives Canada. PA-041785

Photo 2.3 British "Home Children" on their way to Canada.

while their pay was handed directly to their owner-parents. In 1890, 21.5 per cent of the miners in Nova Scotia were boys under the age of 18, some as young as 8 years, and all were involved in back-breaking and isolating labour in the mines. Farmhands in the West were no better off, working from before dawn milking the cows until after dusk, bedding these same animals. Seeding, harvesting, logging, washing, and building: all were children's jobs on the farm (Janovicek and Parr, 2003).

In the cities, poor children were put to work early and routinely, and their wages were expected to help support the family. It was taken for granted that the child's wages would belong to the parents, just as the child did. There were not many factory jobs for children, but girls found jobs in domestic service, and boys found jobs as messengers and newspaper sellers (Janovicek and Parr, 2003). Maureen Baker (2007: 76) explains, "As soon as working-class children were old enough, they were expected to contribute to the family economy in some way, first helping around the house and garden and later contributing their labour or wages to support the household. . . . In other words, childhood . . . was not much different from adult life in nineteenth-century low-income families."

Children who could not work were just another mouth to feed. Those who were seen as "retarded" or disabled, and those who were unable to engage in conventional forms of work, were put to work in freak shows, orphanages, and houses of prostitution. Every child was required to have an economic value, and those who did not were allowed to quietly slip away or starve (Owen et al., 2008: 166).

The Vulnerable Child (1900–1950s)

These attitudes towards children remained prevalent into the twentieth century. However, significant socio-political changes at the end of the 1800s affected the economic value of children and shifted the social construction. Canada became a country in 1867, and, between 1898 and 1914, the Canadian economy boomed as never before. Many Canadian families moved from farms to cities where there were jobs that paid well in the steel and iron industry, manufacturing, banking, and other services. In 1881, the numbers of people employed in agricultural and non-agricultural pursuits were almost equal but, thirty years later, the people employed in agriculture were half those of their non-agricultural counterparts (Statistics Canada, 2009b).

This economic and geographic shift had two effects on the social construction of children. The first was that the harsh treatment of children was more visible. Strangers now saw the cruelties inflicted on children that previously were kept within the circle of the family, and some Canadians began to question the appalling conditions in which some children lived. The second effect was that children were less economically valuable in the more urbanized economy in which jobs required skills beyond simple lifting and carrying. Compulsory schooling removed some of these children from the streets, and parents were urged to register their children in school so that they could learn the skills required in the urban workplace. Children were now seen as vulnerable to the perils of inactivity and potential mischief on the city streets, and long hours in the classroom coupled with rigid physical discipline could save children from both immorality and future unemployment.

New education legislation, lower infant mortality rates, and an early emotional investment in children convinced parents to send their children to school. Peter Stearns (2006: 56) notes, "With fewer children overall and with each young child far less likely to die, emotional investment in the individual child rose." Lucy Maud Montgomery's famous Anne books illustrate this social shift. Anne Shirley was a plucky Canadian heroine made popular in *Anne of Green Gables* (1908). In a sequel to this novel, *Anne's House of Dreams*, Anne relinquishes her dreams of being a writer and leaves her post of principal at Summerside High School for the higher dream of being a mother with her "prince," Gilbert Blythe, beside her. Her motherhood is the high point of her life in an era in which motherhood was constructed as more fulfilling than any career, and the child was positioned as vulnerable and at risk of going astray without this maternal care and guidance.

Late nineteenth- and early twentieth-century psychologists and psychiatrists such as G. Stanley Hall, William Healy, John Watson, and Sigmund Freud warned that maternal neglect could cause terrible damage to the child. By the 1940s, Dr Benjamin Spock and others were encouraging mothers to become more involved in their children's lives so as to better guide and educate their children. Dr Spock's message of maternal involvement in their children's lives was echoed in Dr Ernest Couture's *The Canadian Mother and Child*, first published by the Canadian Ministry of Pensions and National Health in 1940 and reprinted nine times up to 1991. The message was clear: there were no bad children, only bad mothers.

This construction of the mother's role and the child's vulnerability was given credence by attachment theorists such as John Bowlby and Konrad Lorenz (see Chapter 4), whose research indicated that early **bonding** or **attachment** with the mother was the basis for a child's health and emotional wellness. A child with a healthy attachment had a chance to succeed; a child who missed out on such bonding was said to suffer an **attachment injury** and to be less likely to succeed. The child was thus positioned as vulnerable and needing the secure attachment to a nurturing mother, either a birth mother or an adoptive one.

Socio-political events reinforced attachment theory and the message conveyed by *The Canadian Mother and Child*. Soldiers returning from the Second World War took the jobs women had held during the war, and this was seen as only right, considering the soldiers' sacrifices overseas. Daycares that had flourished during the war years were closed, and new government family allowances offered a further financial incentive (albeit small) for mothers to stay home and do the child rearing. Attachment theorists, politicians, and economists were united on this front: children belonged at home in the nurturing arms of their mothers.

The Child as Social Capital (1960 to the Present)

In the first half of the twentieth century, traditional Christian morality dominated family life and government, and politicians used this morality to justify their laws, their tax increases, and their treatment of the poor. This shared and widely understood morality was the glue that kept the construction of the vulnerable child together. The postwar child of the 1950s was still seen as morally vulnerable and liable to fall into evil ways, immorality, and poor habits without the nurturance and guidance of a mother. In the 1960s, this glue began to lose its strength, and this social construction came unstuck. The 1960s were characterized by prosperity, social revolution, political protest, and experimentation with drugs and sex. This decade also saw the huge numbers of postwar babies (the baby boom) becoming teenagers who questioned parental authority, sexual rules, and the **authoritarian** parenting of the past. Their mothers began to question their own stay-at-home status, too, and many of these mothers entered the workforce. With their new jobs they gained financial independence and access to those increasingly popular consumer goods of the burgeoning market economy. Bonnie Fox (2001: 163) notes that 90 per cent of Canadian women aged 25 to 29 had children in 1961. This percentage dropped to 70 per cent by 1971, then to 60 per cent by 1991 as more and more women chose careers rather than children.

In 1965, US President Lyndon Johnson announced the launch of Head Start, a government program that promised education, health, nutrition, and parent involvement services to low-income children and their families. Mother care alone began to lose its lustre as the Head Start model began to be developed in Canada, along with more nursery schools, preschools, and daycares. The cost of these programs was carried largely by the state, but groups such as Children's Television Workshop also contributed. In 1969, they launched *Sesame Street*. Like Head Start, this popular television show was soon seen to be the medium for early literacy and numeracy skill development. Children were constructed as belonging equally to the family and the state, and they were viewed as social capital—workers in training for a flourishing workforce in which success was possible for anyone. Steen Esbensen's 1985 report to the Task Force on Child Care, *Good Day Care Makes a Difference*, summarized the research supporting the value of daycare over mother care.

In 1966, the government of British Columbia introduced maternity leave, and five years later the federal government followed suit. The Canada Labour Code was amended to allow postpartum women to claim up to 15 weeks of unemployment insurance money provided they had at least 20 weeks of insurable earnings. In 1984, this benefit was extended to include adoptive mothers. In 1990, the phrase "maternity leave" was dropped in favour of a "parental leave" of 25 weeks for all parents, both adoptive and birth. Birth mothers were given an additional 15 weeks of maternity leave on top of parental leave. In 2001, the universal parental leave portion was increased to 35 weeks.

The 1990s continued this cultural shift from mother care to daycare, and the continued provision of limited government funding supported this change. The National Children's Agenda (1992), a joint federal-provincial-territorial initiative aimed at improving the well-being of children, prompted the Brighter Futures Program (1992), the Aboriginal Head Start Program (1995), and the Centres of Excellence for Child Well-Being (2000) all across Canada. This support was predicated on full workforce participation by mothers. Lone mothers were not exempted from this expectation, and there was little or no value attributed to their in-home caregiving. As Caroline Beauvais and Jane Jenson (2001: 5) note, "Caring for children as a lone mother is no longer accepted as a substitute for labour force participation." Programs such as Ontario Works (implemented in April 1996) required lone parents either to work or to attend training in order to receive social assistance.

Governments referred to this kind of support for childcare and early childhood education as "investment." Providing daycares, Head Start programs, and parental leaves was not constructed as a moral action; it was constructed as a wise *economic* decision concerning a commodity (the child) that could have an enormous payback (the grown child's value to the government as a taxpayer) if that commodity were properly groomed for the workforce.

Government "investments" ranged from early childhood education programs to integrated service provision to income transfers. The language of investment and of children as social capital permeated every project. For example, one Ontario provincial government report stated, "Investment by all sectors of society in the early years is as important as our investment in education to ensure Ontario has a highly competent and well-educated population, all necessary for a strong economy and a thriving democracy" (McCain and Mustard, 1999: 2). In 2006, when the Canadian federal government introduced the Universal Child Care Benefit of $100 per month for each child up to and including five years of age, the benefit was described as an investment. Children were positioned as workers of the future, and investing in them made financial sense. James Heckman and Dimitry Masterov (2007) and other economists also defined children as social capital that could be shaped to become an effective workforce in the future.

This construction formed the premise for the governmental shift from supporting parents at home to supporting children in the wider society. Schools provided breakfast and sex education, and big-box daycares such as Kids and Company and ABC Learning Centre filled the national childcare gap. The family, the state, and business became partners in the guidance and nurturance of children. When Sandra Griffin, past president of the Canadian Child Care Federation, wrote the 2007 report *Why the Investment in Children? Costs and Benefits of Investing in Children* nobody questioned her use of language. By 2007, the words "children" and "investment" were inextricably linked and this report was welcomed as sound economic advice from an early childhood educator working in partnership with the state. If taxpayers questioned the linkage, politicians reminded them, "It takes a village to raise a child."

In the 1980s, educational systems across Canada were gradually reoriented from the experiential and discovery learning of the 1960s to the business model of outcomes-based learning. Each skill learned in the classroom was tied to a measurable outcome. This model was designed to prepare children for their entry into the workforce. Those who could not make the grade were identified through early testing, which could qualify them for additional educational supports (see Chapter 1). Early diagnosis and special needs assessments were part of a plan to identify those children who were least likely to contribute as social capital. Though this analysis may seem like an oversimplification, the evidence is overwhelming: the development of centres, support, funding, and classes for children with special needs continues to move these children further away from the integration and inclusion model of the 1980s. These children may be housed in regular classrooms but their educational assistant works solely with them and not with the other children in the classrooms. Controversy continues to follow this separation of those seen to be less able to meet measurable learning outcomes or, as an economist might say, "deficit social capital." However, it is clear that the emphasis remains on the child as social capital, an investment with dividends.

To further prepare children for their participation in a capitalist, free-market economy, they were groomed simultaneously as consumers. As children received more, they craved more, and their craving was given structural support with lists of "essential" sports equipment and school supplies and buying seasons such as "Back to School Days." Children became "six pocketers," receiving cash from the pockets of a minimum of six adults: mom, dad, two grandmas, and two grandpas. Canada's "tweeners" (10- to 14-year-olds) had a spending power of over $2.9 billion a year in 2010, and the teens (15- to 19-year-olds) spent 90 per cent of their average annual income on entertainment (Lamb et al., 2012: 167). Sandra Smidt (2013: 9) describes the beauty products aimed at girls so that they can look like their mothers, and the games aimed at boys so that they can play with their dads: "Younger and younger children were encouraged to dress glamorously or casually but in the fashion of the day; to acquire jewellery and use facial products; to consider their nails and have more than one pair of shoes; to explore fantasy worlds through electronic toys."

Children of all ages were seen to have a huge influence over family purchases. Advertisements targeted children for sales and encouraged children to teach their parents what to buy. Dubbed "**kidfluence**," children's influence on family purchases was estimated to be enormous. Rather than contributing to family income as in earlier days, the contemporary Canadian child drains that income.

The Boundaries of Childhood

The concept of children has changed as much as the age boundaries of that childhood. In the nineteenth century, 10-year-olds were considered fully capable of being employed as adults for 12-hour workdays outside the home. Today, such participation in the workforce is not expected of a 10-year-old child, although some child actors and fruit harvesters still work for lengthy periods of time, and labour laws vary across Canada (see Chapter 1).

The constructed age limits that define childhood are not based on biology. On the one hand, they are culturally determined, reflecting the culture of society and the family. On the other hand, they are co-relational, as one age limit for an activity (working, smoking, or driving) affects the age limit for a related activity. Being a child allows a person to engage in certain acts and not others. Being a youth rather than a child has similar co-relational effects.

A "child" is defined variously as a person under the age of 6; a prepubescent child, or under the age of 13; or a not-yet-adult, under the age of 16. Under provincial adoption law in most provinces of Canada, an adopted person (regardless of age) forever remains a "child" of a parent without the rights to birth information if the birth mother forbids disclosure. These different upper age limits, from 6 to 60, affect the child's access to legal rights, social services, and birth information and affect the boundaries of the worker–child relationship. When an adult discloses abuse to the worker, the worker listens and counsels. When a child does the same, the worker is bound by law to break confidentiality.

Adults decide on the age parameters of the category of child, and these decisions are said to be based on **best practice**. However, it often seems as though this categorization meets adult needs rather than those of the children. Whether childhood is constructed as ending at age 12, 14, 16, or 18 depends on which construct benefits the adults most. For example, when the labour market is full and unemployment rates rise (as was the case in Ontario in 2006 and New Brunswick in 1999), mandatory schooling is extended from age 16 to 18, thereby keeping children out of the job market. When the need for seasonal farm help is high, even 14-year-olds can skip school to work in the fields with their parents' permission.

Childhood may begin in utero, as some health professionals suggest; or it may begin after birth. Age limits at either end of childhood are an outcome of deliberate socio-political and economic decisions that have profound effects on the children within and outside these age limits. Where childhood begins and ends is very important to the issue of the child's social location and experience. Table 2.1 provides an overview of various constructions of the 12-year-old in current Canadian legislation.

Table 2.1 Constructions of the 12-Year-Old in Canadian Legislation

Criminal Code of Canada, Section 43	May be spanked by a parent or an adult in a position of authority in order to be disciplined or corrected.
Youth Criminal Justice Act	Included in a category called "youth" with persons up to the age of 17, and can be incarcerated.
Canada Health Act	Can obtain a therapeutic abortion without parental consent.
Child Welfare Acts (provincial and territorial)	Can be removed from the family if seen to be at risk of abuse and/or neglect, but cannot press assault charges against the alleged abuser.
Social Assistance (provincial and territorial)	Cannot receive social assistance until age 16 unless the child is a parent.
Bill C-2 (Legal age of consent to sexual activity)	Cannot engage in sexual activity with persons 17 years of age or older.[2]

Lower Age Limits

Canadian law does not recognize a child as a person until that child is born. From the time of ossification, or bone formation (approximately eight weeks after conception) until birth, the developing prenatal organism is called a fetus rather than a person or a child. The fetal period is marked by continuing, rapid growth of the specialized systems that emerge during the embryonic phase. A one-inch embryo at 8 weeks, the fetus develops to have sex organs by 12 weeks, hair by 16 weeks, eyes by 24 weeks, and so on.

Under the law, decisions during the first nine months of fetal growth are solely the prerogative of the woman carrying the fetus. She decides whether or not to participate in prenatal care. She decides how much alcohol and drugs the fetus will consume, whether or not the fetus will be deprived of oxygen in the blood, what stress and risks the fetus will have to manage, and what food the fetus will have. She chooses to use vitamin supplements or not. She chooses to increase or decrease the risks of disability in her fetus. She can also decide whether to remove the fetus through abortion at any stage of fetal growth. She makes all of these decisions for the fetus until birth, when the child becomes a legal person (Chamberlain, 1995).

For the early months during the nine-month gestation period, the woman may be unaware that she is pregnant. If she is aware, she may not be planning to carry the fetus through to birth, or she may not be planning to care for the child after the birth. During her pregnancy, she may be drinking, doing drugs, eating little, and may be under severe physical and emotional stress; she may be alone and without support. In August 1996, this was the situation for a Winnipeg mother of three when she came to the attention of Winnipeg Child and Family Services. Two of the woman's three previous children had been born permanently disabled and were permanent wards of the Crown. Superior Court Judge Perry Schulman ordered her held in residential treatment for her glue and solvent sniffing. However, the court's *parens patriae* jurisdiction (the power to act as a child's parent in order to intervene with an abusive or neglectful parent) was successfully contested on appeal as such intervention would contravene the woman's rights under the Canadian Charter of Rights and Freedoms. As a result, the woman was not detained, and she continued her addictions. Her child was born prematurely and was developmentally delayed. In the same year, Brenda Drummond of Ottawa chose to shoot herself in the abdomen, causing brain damage to the fetus she was carrying. Her son was also born developmentally delayed. Both of these cases demonstrate that the only right recognized by the courts is that of the already born person (the mother).

Cultural beliefs and medical practice contradict this legal position. The fetus is more photographed and scanned now than ever before in history. Mothers are advised to avoid drugs and alcohol, take folic acid and multivitamins, increase calcium intake, listen to classical music, avoid stress, and get regular exercise while carrying the fetus. The woman carrying the fetus is told that her pregnancy term comprises the first nine months of childhood, and that these nine months are critical to the child's development of organs, cognitive and physical skills, and a healthy attachment. The study of fetal learning has become a science, and prenatal stimulation is considered to be a way to enhance the future intelligence of the child.[3]

The contradiction between the social constructions of fetus as active learner and fetus as passive tissue affects the social and legal perceptions of what constitutes the first year of the child's life. Does the year end at 12 months after birth or does it include the 9-month fetal stage and end at 3 months after birth? How this first year is defined may determine whether the mother can be held accountable for prenatal stimulation or the lack of it. The accepted definition also determines the point at which the child becomes a person under Canadian law and therefore has legal rights.

Although the Convention on the Rights of the Child recognizes the child as a person in the first year of life, Canadian law does not. If a child is killed in the first 24 hours of life, the legal term for the act is post-natal abortion or **neonaticide**. If the child is older than a day but younger than a year, the act is called

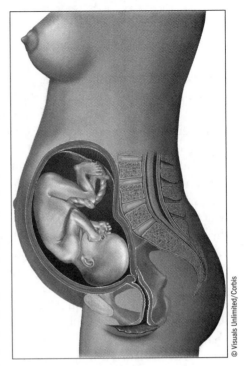

Photo 2.4 Six-month-old fetus.

infanticide. Neonaticide is typically punished with a conditional sentence or probation. Infanticide carries a maximum five-year punishment. The act of killing a person, however, is called murder and carries the much more severe maximum punishment of life imprisonment. Children in their first year of life are deemed expendable, despite current cultural beliefs, medical practice, and the Convention on the Rights of the Child. The notion that these children are expendable was challenged by the courts in 2005 when Katrina Effert of Edmonton, Alberta, was twice found guilty of murder for strangling her newborn son (Rodney) and throwing his body into a neighbour's yard. This was the first time in Canadian history that neonaticide was deemed to be murder (Nesca and Dalby, 2011). Effert was given a suspended sentence for the murder of her son and released.

Upper Age Limits

Just as the argument over the beginning of childhood has continued over the years, so the debate over the upper limit of childhood persists. While some frontline workers, legislators, counsellors, and judges hold that childhood ends at puberty, others—primarily parents and educators—tend to believe that childhood ends when public schooling does. Even child welfare professionals do not agree on the upper age limits of childhood as Table 2.2 indicates.

Table 2.2 Age Limits for Children in Child Welfare

Province or Territory	Ministry	Legislation	Age Limit
British Columbia	Child Protection Division, Ministry of Children and Family Development	Child, Family and Community Service Act	Under 19
Alberta	Child and Family Services Authorities, Ministry of Children and Youth Services	Child, Youth and Family Enhancement Act	Under 18
Saskatchewan	Ministry of Social Services	Child and Family Services Act	Under 16
Manitoba	Child and Family Services Division, Ministry of Family Services and Consumer Affairs	Child and Family Services Act	Under 18
Ontario	Children's Aid Societies, Ministry of Children and Youth Services	Child and Family Services Act	Under 16
Quebec	Ministry of Health and Social Services	Youth Protection Act	Under 18
New Brunswick	Dept of Social Development	Family Services Act	Under 16
Nova Scotia	Children Youth and Families Division, Dept of Community Services	Children and Family Services Act	Under 16
Prince Edward Island	Child and Family Services Division, Ministry of Social Services and Seniors	Child Protection Act	Under 16
Newfoundland and Labrador	Dept of Child, Youth and Family Services	Children and Youth Care and Protection Act	Under 16
Northwest Territories	Dept of Health and Social Services	Child and Family Services Act	Under 16
Yukon	Family and Children's Services, Dept of Health and Social Services	Child and Family Services Act	Under 18
Nunavut	Dept of Health and Social Services	Child and Family Services Act	Under 16

Source: This material is derived partly from the still unpublished document, "Lexicon of Child Welfare" (CWLC, 2013); Table 1-1 of the *Child Incidence Study of Reported Child Abuse and Neglect* (Public Health Agency of Canada, 2010); and from an Internet search of individual ministries and departments in each province and territory. Continual administrative changes in child welfare makes it essential to use several reference sources.

These upper age limits are important as they define both legal rights and access to services for the child. The upper age limit in the UNCRC is 18, but this upper age limit does not always apply in Canada where the **age of majority**, or the threshold of adulthood as legally determined, is considered to be 18 or 19. In Alberta, Saskatchewan, Manitoba, Ontario, Quebec, and Prince Edward Island, the age is 18; in British Columbia, Nova Scotia, Newfoundland and Labrador, New Brunswick, the Northwest Territories, Yukon, and Nunavut, it is 19. Canadian federal law requires parents (or the state in the role of the parents) to provide for their children until they are 19 years of age. This leaves parents in Canada responsible for their child's debts until that child is 19 even though the child may have left home at 16 (Cottrell, 2003: 4). Even within a particular province or territory, a child's legal status is complex. Table 2.3 sets out the contradictions in the legal status of a 16-year-old in Ontario.

A further complication is the Youth Criminal Justice Act (YCJA), federal legislation that removes children aged 12 and older from the category of "children." Section 61 of the YCJA permits each province and territory to set an age at which young persons between ages 14 and 16 can be sentenced as adults for specific crimes. As a result, a 14-year-old Canadian is tried under the YCJA in one province, but faces an adult hearing and adult sentencing in another. This age discrimination is specifically forbidden by the UNCRC.

Some legal experts contend that children should be held accountable for their crimes, even when they are younger than 12 years of age. Relatives of persons who have

Table 2.3 Legal Rights of a 16-Year-Old in Ontario

Area of daily life	Has the right to . . .	Does not have the right to . . .
Health	Smoke cigarettes in public places	Buy a package of cigarettes until age 19
Education	Attend school or be home-schooled with Ministry permission	Leave school until age 18
Social	Marry with parental consent; leave home without parents' consent	Marry without parental consent; work during school hours; enter foster care; receive support from a children's aid society; live in a homeless shelter in most municipalities
Finance	Apply for social assistance as a single parent or under special circumstances, and receive social assistance through a trustee	Work full-time
Civil rights	Apply for information under the Freedom of Information Act	Get birth information as an adoptee; vote

been murdered by young children in Canada and elsewhere usually support this call for culpability. In contrast, others argue that the constructed stage of childhood should be extended, and that children should be given child welfare protection beyond age 18. This controversy is enlightened by the voices of children and youth under child welfare protection who lose their financial and educational supports when they turn 18 even though most Canadian children enjoy their parents' support and their home until they are well beyond the age of 21.[4]

Summary

This chapter positions the child in Canada in a historical context. Social constructions of the child have evolved over the last hundred and fifty years, up to the current construction of the child as social capital. Although most children are viewed this way today, children who are new to Canada (immigrants and refugees), children with different abilities, children who live in reserves and rural areas, and children who live in poverty, all are treated as deficits; they are marginalized and largely forgotten in the language of investment.

Also discussed in this chapter are the age limits of childhood—specifically how variations in legally specified age limits affect the child's access to certain activities, placements, rights, and resources. Now that we are familiar with the ways in which the various constructions of the period of childhood affect the child's social location, we will examine how child development is socially constructed.

Review Questions

1. How do categorization and characterization contribute to the social construction of the child?
2. Describe how the category of "adolescence" came to be used and what effects children experience as a result of being included within this category. Is there a difference between adolescence and youth? Explain.
3. How does generationing affect toddlers and teens?
4. How do children learn to be helpless? What are the structural determinants for this learning process?
5. Name five groups of children in Canada who are marginalized and explain the impact of this marginalization on their lives.
6. How did government encourage women to rejoin the workplace in the 1960s and leave the care of their children to others?
7. What cultural factors influence the social construction of when childhood begins and ends?
8. How would you differentiate among neonaticide, infanticide, and murder?

9. How does the Youth Criminal Justice Act affect the social construction of the upper limit of childhood?
10. Describe how the legal positioning of a 16-year-old in Ontario can be confusing, and give three concrete examples of this legal confusion.

Discussion Questions

1. Deculturation of some children happened in the past in Canada. Explain why this does or does not happen in Canada today, giving examples to support your explanation.
2. What do you think the lower and upper age limits of childhood should be in Canada? How does your personal culture (family, ethnicity, spirituality, value system) influence your understanding of these age limits?
3. How do you feel about the 1996 case of the pregnant Winnipeg mother being held in custody because of her addictive behaviour while pregnant? Should the state be afforded this kind of authority? Discuss.

3 Developmentally Appropriate Practice

I'll bet that boy's father wishes he had a little girl who finger-painted and wiped her hands on the cat when she was little and who once cut her own hair so she would be bald like her uncle and who then grew up to be seven years old and crowned herself with burs. Not every father is lucky enough to have a daughter like that.

—Beverly Cleary, *Ramona and Her Father*

In the passage above, the seven-year-old speaker, Ramona, clearly knows who she is, even within the context of a society infused with a **gender construction** that places girls in curls and dresses rather than burs and pants. Many of the children with whom we work do not have Ramona's high self-esteem and sense of gender equality. They have been impacted by a rigid **developmental perspective** that prescribes what they can achieve at each age and stage and a gender construction that is equally limiting. The developmental perspective imbues childhood with a mechanical predictability: at age two, the child does this; at age five, the child does that. At the same time, the developmental perspective prompts workers to provide certain play opportunities at certain ages and to take advantage of critical learning opportunities at certain ages. There are, according to this perspective, certain time-sensitive periods for learning and acquiring competencies. In this chapter, we will explore the developmental perspective, its meaning and its strengths, and we will also examine its impact on the social construction of childhood.

Developmentally appropriate practice is the provision of strengths-based supports that meet both the individual and developmental needs of the child. This practice is based on close observation of the child's culture, interests, social location, and overall development. There are two dimensions of developmentally appropriate practice: age appropriateness and individual appropriateness. Age appropriateness refers to an awareness of the general and predictable sequences of development that occur in the physical, socio-emotional, spiritual, and cognitive domains. Knowing this typical developmental sequence helps workers listen to the child effectively, understand the child's play, and plan developmentally appropriate interventions. A second dimension is individual appropriateness, which is grounded in the recognition that each child experiences a unique timing of growth and changes and has an individual culture, temperament, ability, learning style, and family. These individual differences require an individually directed and unique response from the worker. Individual differences are why child-initiated and child-directed interventions are both developmentally appropriate and in the best interests of the child: they match the unique needs of an individual child at a particular time.

Understanding child development entails understanding the child's structural needs and **critical learning periods**, as well as recognizing the strengths and abilities of the individual child at each age and developmental stage. Structural and strengths-based assessment acknowledges that developmental stages are guiding markers only, not strict *requirements*, and that each stage is complete in itself rather than a step on the way to a later stage. When critical learning periods are undermined or when **milestones** have not been reached, appropriate structural and strengths-based interventions may be needed so that the child can achieve optimal well-being. These interventions, designed to meet the individual and age needs of the child, necessitate a revision of traditionally defined developmentally appropriate practice that was informed only by the developmental perspective.

We begin this chapter with a critique of this developmental perspective on the child. A cornerstone of the developmental perspective is the concept that there are three **domains** or aspects of the child to take into account: the physical, the cognitive, and the socio-emotional. In this chapter, we introduce a fourth domain: spirituality, adapted from Medicine Wheel teachings. This fourth domain not only balances the child's other three domains, infusing them with that spirituality or connectedness with Mother Earth, but also balances the child as a whole person with equally important physical, cognitive, socio-emotional, and spiritual strengths.

All four domains include critical learning periods, opportunities for the child to either feel strength and success or experience powerlessness and failure. In these learning periods, the child also internalizes the prevalent gender construction with all of its implications for **sexual orientation** and **gender roles**. At these times, the worker who understands whole child development, critical learning periods, and social construction can support the child's healthy development in all four domains. The worker who follows the developmental perspective, on the other hand, may impede or damage whole child development and certainly will not understand Ramona's observation that "Not every father is lucky enough to have a daughter like that."

Objectives

By the end of this chapter, you will:

- Understand the impact of the developmental perspective on both children and the adults who work with children.
- Identify developmental milestones and critical learning periods and what children need at each critical learning period, particularly as they understand their own gender and their own sexual orientation.
- Demonstrate your understanding of developmentally appropriate practice.

The Developmental Perspective

The developmental perspective on the child views the child as evolving or developing in a natural, orderly progression (in stages). This perspective maintains that particular milestones need to be reached before the child can move from one stage to the next. This perspective was initiated by naturalist and evolutionist Charles Darwin, who based his study "A Biographical Sketch of an Infant" (1877) on the daily logs he kept during the infancy of his firstborn child, William. In these logs, Darwin recorded William's reflexes, first movements, and reactions. He positioned his son as somewhere between a person and an animal, thus advancing his evolutionary theory that people and animals had a common ancestor. From this particular example of one infant, Darwin generalized to all, hypothesizing that child development was linear and evolutionary.

This positioning of the child as an object to be studied allowed Darwin to ignore William's cries in order to record his stamina and vocalizations. He perceived his son as *developing into* a person rather than living as a person. William would become a person later, once he was fully developed, and then his cries (and words) could be listened to and considered. Darwin's thinking about infants was not dissimilar from that of most parents of his time who likened infants to little bunnies, chicks, and kittens. Infants were objects of study rather than subjects, and their growth and survival were precarious. A high infant mortality rate was a fact of life in the late nineteenth century (see Chapter 2).

Evolutionists continued to hypothesize that evolution or development was an organizing principle for childhood, and that all children developed in stages, each stage building upon the previous one. Darwin (1809–82) studied his son William; Sigmund Freud (1856–1939), his daughter Anna; and Jean Piaget (1896–1980), his daughter

Lucienne. Each theorist was a father, and each observed his own child in order to generalize about all children.

G. Stanley Hall (1846–1924), considered to be the first developmental psychologist, was one of the first professionals to study children in a laboratory. Alfred Binet (1857–1911) and Theodore Simon (1873–1961) used a similar laboratory setting to develop cognitive skill tests that defined and bracketed developmental stages. Arnold Gessell (1880–1961) further supported the developmental perspective through several longitudinal studies that compared age-related differences in socio-emotional, cognitive, and physical skills among children.

Lawrence Kohlberg (1927–87) used only males to test his theory of a six-stage, three-level, developmental sequence of morality. At Kohlberg's preconventional level, physical consequences determine what is good or bad: the child avoids what is "bad" because of the punishment factor (fear of being punished). This is a learning stage during which the child is taught certain moral lessons. It leads to a second level, the conventional one, at which the child sees that it is "good" to please or help others even if the action is not rewarded; doing one's duty is seen to be good. Practice at the second level leads to a third, post-conventional level, at which the child comes to understand that what is "right" is a matter of conscience in accordance with universal principles. One stage leads to the next in Kohlberg's developmental perspective on morality.

Note from the Field   3.1

Being Bad

The worker in the Head Start nursery school becomes increasingly frustrated by the toddlers who do not respond when she tells them that their behaviour is "bad." She begins to think that they want to be bad or that they enjoy being bad. Her frustration shows at the end of the day when her voice tone and volume rise. She often feels that she is yelling at the toddlers and wonders if her care is any better or worse than the care provided by their parents. These morally dichotomous terms ("good" and "bad") are part of this worker's spirituality and culture, and she finds it hard to understand why these toddlers, unlike the children she teaches at her Sunday school, do not try to be "good." By the end of a year with this worker and her moral teaching, the children will have understood that they are bad when they do not do what an adult (in this case, the teacher) tells them to do. These children will also be well prepared to comply with the demands of a pedophile who may tell a toddler that he is bad because he is too handsome to resist. An older girl may be told that she is bad because she has asked for it. The pedophile's grooming of victims depends upon their compliance and obedience to adults because their disobedience is "bad."

Perhaps the best-known developmentalist was Piaget (1929), who divided **cognitive development**—the evolution of the organizing and thinking systems of the brain—into a taxonomy of four stages that built upon one another: sensorimotor (birth to age 2), preoperational (ages 2 to 6), concrete operational (ages 7 to 11), and formal operational (ages 12 and above). Table 3.1 provides a brief summary of these four stages of development.

Table 3.1 Piaget's Stages of Development

Stage	Age	Characteristics
Sensorimotor	Birth to age 2	Knowledge of the world is based on senses and motor skills. By the end of this stage, the child can generate mental representations.
Preoperational	Ages 2 to 6	Child learns how to use symbols (words, numbers) to represent aspects of the world, but relates to this world only through his or her own perspective.
Concrete operational	Ages 7 to 11	Child understands and applies logical operations to experiences in the present.
Formal operational	Ages 12 +	Child speculates on the future and thinks abstractly.

Photo 3.1 At the sensorimotor stage the child experiences the colour, texture, smell, taste, and sound of the leaves.

While Piaget's taxonomy is useful for understanding and planning play experiences, it is contradicted by evidence that a very young child may think in all four ways during a single day, even when that child is, in Piaget's terms, in a sensorimotor stage. For example, a young boy may explore autumn by throwing fallen leaves in the air and experimenting with them, hypothesizing the idea of gravity, even though the word is not in his vocabulary or fully understood. Piaget's taxonomy is also challenged by evidence from new imaging techniques and advances in neuroscience. This evidence indicates that infants have both prenatal memories and postnatal recall (Dirix et al., 2009; Fivush, 2011; Rochat, 2012) and can grasp object permanence: "Infants are probably born with an ability to reason, make predictions, and give meaning to objects . . . long before they can deliberately act upon them" (Rochat, 2012: 79). This ability to reason is described by Piaget as only beginning at age seven in the concrete operational stage.

The developmental perspective continues to influence workers' interventions with children and youth. Judges, for instance, might disregard the testimony of prepubescent children who are considered to be only at Kohlberg's level of preconventional morality, or child welfare workers might withhold information from children who are perceived as unable to understand abstract concepts because they are still in Piaget's concrete operational stage. Despite current evidence from neuroscience and the inherent childism in considering children "undeveloped persons," this perspective on children's care and services continues to guide many interventions.

Eurocentrism permeates the developmental perspective. Walking independently and playing independently are considered to be important developmental milestones in a culture in which individualism and autonomy are highly regarded. As Sandra Smidt (2013: 29) observes, "Educators in the developed world promote ideas of self-confidence and self-esteem, separateness and individuality." The child's preferences and opinions are valued over the child's self-restraint and consideration for the needs of others.

This impacts children who are taught to avoid disturbance and discord and blend in with their community of caregivers. An 18-month-old Aboriginal child who lives in a community in which silence is valued, and in which learning happens through close observation of Elders, may not meet these milestones. Also excluded are children raised in bilingual or trilingual families or communities who may understand many languages but may be more reticent to express them to a wider audience. The developmental perspective fails to account for such variations, assessing children of non-European races and ethnicities as "not meeting their developmental milestones" when the assessors use tools based on Eurocentric developmental milestones (Gokiert et al., 2010).

The cultural bias of the developmental perspective is compounded by the flaw in its logic that positions children as underdeveloped or incomplete persons who are developing in a structured, linear progression, with one stage leading to the next. The idea of linear progression makes sense to some extent and certainly reflects human growth patterns. The child coos, babbles, and then says a first word. The child rolls, wiggles and squirms, and then crawls. However, this linear perspective also positions adults as the finished,

Point to Consider   3.1

Meeting Milestones

Caregivers tend to be very concerned about their children's milestones even when they are reassured that the age guidelines around these milestones are historical and cultural. They bring their children for assessment and screening and then worry when tests indicate delays. They fear the label "developmental delay" and want to know how they can help their children to meet or exceed their milestones. They may even push their children to complete a milestone such as "walks on tiptoes" before their children have mastered mature walking patterns. These actions by parents reflect the cultural belief that developmental milestones are universal and innate.

This belief is challenged by research evidence that demonstrates the cultural bias of these milestones (Smidt, 2013: 2–3). Children whose mothers carry them most of the day, for example, tend to toilet learn at least twelve months earlier than children who are not carried. Infants whose caregivers speak to them in several languages tend to develop expressive language later than infants cared for by unilingual caregivers. Children who eat with chopsticks lag in their development of the cylindrical grasp.

Does this indicate that these children are cognitively or physically advanced or delayed? Neither label is valid. The infant who is exposed to many languages develops greater language fluency and increased cognitive functioning (Kuhl, 2011), with evidence of this surfacing at age three or four. The infant who toilet trains at twelve months does so in response to skin-to-skin contact or the mother's body language rather than innate cognitive or physical functioning. The child who eats with chopsticks rather than a spoon develops fine motor skills before the cylindrical grasp. Alberta researchers conclude, "The screening and assessment process can be objective only when assessors are aware of their own ethnocentric views and of imposing their own standards in evaluating people from other cultures" (Gokiert et al., 2010: 37). Milestones change over time and location, and caregivers who understand this flexibility are less likely to choose to have their children screened and assessed.

or fully developed, result. Children are placed in the default position of undeveloped or underdeveloped persons. They are perceived as incomplete and flawed versions of adults, dependent on adults for optimum development; conversely, children who "fail to meet their milestones" are described as slow to develop, delayed, retarded, or abnormal.

This emphasis on linear progression does not take into account periods of stability, consolidation, or natural plateaus in which little to no change takes place in a child's skill level. Nor does it recognize the recurrence of socio-emotional states—a recapitulation of an earlier stage necessary for emotional recovery. For example, a child may return to thumb-sucking, breastfeeding, or cuddling in order to make sense of the birth of a sibling, a transition to daycare, or the sudden absence of a caregiver. **Developmentalists** call this activity "regression," a term that again implies that all child development is linear and aimed at reaching adulthood.

In its emphasis on the achievement of milestones, the developmental perspective takes into account only those environmental forces that directly affect the child: parental caregiving, early feeding, teachers' scolding, and so on. Structural determinants, such as social systems and culture, are not considered—a limitation in scope that ultimately weakens this perspective. Although the developmental milestones of this perspective may prove useful in the diagnosis of specific areas in which the child may need structural intervention, it is important to remember that these milestones are culturally specific and constructed rather than based on objective fact.

The Whole Child

A cornerstone of the developmental perspective is that development occurs in three domains: the physical, the socio-emotional, and the cognitive. In the physical domain, the child develops in stages from sucking to drinking, from crawling to cruising. In the socio-emotional domain, the child develops in stages from egocentrism and a short attention span to an interest in social play and a longer attention span. In the cognitive domain, the child develops from sensorimotor play to formal operational thinking. These three domains of development are interconnected: the cognitive affects the physical and socio-emotional and is, in turn, affected by the physical and socio-emotional. An infant who is not able to roll and squirm will not engage in the exploratory play that is basic to developing language skills; as a result, language skills in the cognitive domain will suffer. On the other hand, an infant whose socio-emotional needs are met and is flourishing will have the trust and confidence to explore the environment and will develop more skills in both the physical and the cognitive domains.

The division of child development into three domains reflects a Eurocentrism that does not include spirituality. The Medicine Wheel teachings describe four domains of the child, each domain coming from a different direction (north, south, east, and west) to make a unified and balanced whole. The fourth domain of spirituality comes from the east to breathe through the cognitive, physical, and socio-emotional domains, connecting the child to the wholeness that is life, the land, the ancestors, and the community (Blackstock et al., 2006). These four domains position the child as complete—a whole person rather than a developing one. The child is a gift from Mother Earth to the community and, as such, is not to be thrown away, rejected, or changed.

The Medicine Wheel is seen as a sacred circle that is present in everything that breathes, in the seasons, and in the stages of life (Gilgun, 2002). This circle represents balance, wholeness, harmony, and equality. If one part of the circle or wheel is flattened or damaged, then the wheel cannot turn smoothly and disequilibrium results. In other words, as Barbara Harris (2006: 123) puts it, "Health means balance and harmony within and among each of the four aspects of human nature: physical, mental, emotional, and spiritual. Over-focusing or under-focusing on any one aspect upsets the balance of the four." As shown in Figure 3.1, the child is in the middle of the four-segmented wheel and develops in all four domains through reflection, listening, action, and communicating. The north domain represents wisdom and understanding, strength, and endurance. The south represents power, learning, personal

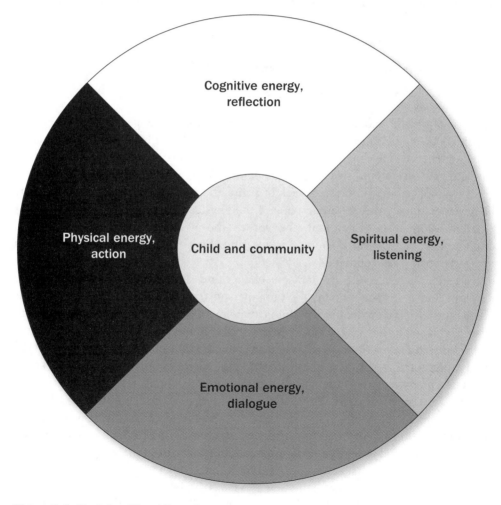

Figure 3.1 Medicine Wheel Domains

growth, and mastery of skills. The east represents connectivity, bonding, and the sense of belonging. The sun sets in the west, which represents uniqueness. All of these domains are interconnected: the child experiences life in all four while simultaneously affecting life in all four. The child, the gift from Mother Earth, is at the hub of the wheel.

When a child becomes distracted, impulsive, addicted to drugs or alcohol, or violent, the Elders follow the Medicine Wheel teachings to bring the child back into the wholeness of life and the circle. The child is placed within a community circle of caring or healing circle that is reminiscent of the Medicine Wheel. The child absorbs the energy of that circle and the strength of the community, past and present, through sacred ceremonies and work with the Elders. This spiritual domain of connection to the earth and to nature has been shown in many studies to have a healing or therapeutic effect on children, whereas removal from the community can break the circle (wheel) entirely.

Patterns of Growth and Development and Critical Learning Periods

The terms "growth" and "development" are often used interchangeably. However, there is a difference in their meanings: growth refers exclusively to physical changes, whereas development refers to changes in all four domains. The infant's body may grow physically, and gain weight and size following a genetically preset timetable, but, because of genetic abnormalities, injuries, or lack of stimulation and nurturance, he or she may be developmentally delayed in any one of the physical, cognitive, spiritual, or socio-emotional domains, or in all four. The worker who understands the patterns of child development, the critical learning periods, and the milestones of development can recognize such a developmental delay.

Development is about simultaneous change and continuity. The child changes or develops, but he or she remains the same person throughout this period of change. The pattern of development in the child can be mapped as a series of questions about where, what, who, and why. The first question the child seems to ponder is "Where?" The child wonders, "Where am I?" "Where is my food?" "Where is the warmth?" The child explores the world, often encapsulated in the mother's breast, first through smell, then taste, then touch. The infant sniffs until the breast is found, latches and sucks, and then nuzzles closer for more. This is the earliest stage of sensorimotor **play**, through which the infant senses the world and moves to find it. Through this play, the infant begins to develop a sense that the world is responsive. In Erik Erikson's terms (see Chapter 4), the child is beginning to develop a sense of trust in the world.

The next question that emerges in the child's developmental pattern is "What?" The child asks the questions, "What is this toe?" "What is this blanket?" "What is this finger?" The infant explores himself or herself in an attempt to discover what the body is and how it feels. The infant inserts the thumb into the mouth, or pushes the finger toward the

Rosemary Gearhart/iStockphoto

Photo 3.2 Toes are tasted, felt, and smelled in the sensorimotor stage.

bottle, or squirms in a wet diaper. The infant is no longer constrained by the womb and now begins to bend arms and flex feet. Gradually, the infant begins to take charge and discover body parts. At the same time, the senses reveal a world of blankets, sunshine or snow, lights that flicker and fade, harsh noises, and throbbing heartbeats. The "What?" question is both asked and answered in every breathing moment of the infant.

As the infant becomes more mobile and is able to roll and then sit up, he or she interacts with the environment more closely. People move into the infant's vision and then fade or disappear; they identify themselves as mother, boy, uncle. In time, the infant grows into a toddler who hears words, makes comparisons, and continues to self-explore. This brings us to the toddler's question "Who?" The toddler wonders, "Who can hold my hand?" "Who can bring me water?" "Who can find my wagon?" The toddler develops a sense of gender, ideas of family, a feeling of race and ethnicity, and a glimpse of friends. This developing **self-concept** is verbalized when the toddler proudly announces, "Me Josh" or "Me big girl." This self-concept widens through exploratory play, parallel play, and then group play as the child develops an idea of who he or she is in comparison to others. The young girl takes note of how caregivers respond to her and her playmates. Are boys responded to differently? Are boys liked? Is the smaller, brown girl liked? The toddler listens attentively to these cues and begins constructing a concept of "who."

It is only much later, after many experiences with persons and the surrounding environment that the child begins to ask the question "Why?" The version of this

> ### Note from the Field   3.2
>
> #### Four Questions
> A youth who is moved to a group home usually asks why: "Why do I have to go there?" or "Why can't I stay home?" The worker can respond by explaining the reasons for coming into care, but this explanation is unlikely to satisfy the young person. It is more helpful for the worker to acknowledge the three preceding unsaid questions of where, what, and who. The worker who remembers the cognitive sequence of where, what, who, and why first answers the three unsaid questions before responding to "why?" The worker's response to "why?" includes the answer (stress at home) as well as the three preceding answers: "We are going to Bravehurst Home near your high school. You'll be living there for the next month as a youth in care so that you can finish the rest of the school year without the kind of stress you've been living in at home. You and I will make a plan for this, but right now let's organize your bedroom, set up your computer, and make sure you have everything you need."

question may be elementary at first—"Why do we have to go?"—but it continues to be asked in many ways and achieves a depth in middle childhood as the challenge, "Why am I not allowed to go?" The child begins to question boundaries, limits, and the socio-political constructs of the environment. The child has moved very far from infancy's narrow focus on the mother's breast.

Growth and development take place concurrently in most infants' lives. When a baby is born, the head is large (one quarter of the body's size), and the brain is close to the surface of the baby's skull. **Fontanels**, or spaces between the bones in the skull, allow the head to be compressed in the birth canal while ensuring that the brain is protected. These fontanels also allow space for the baby's brain to grow further, and they gradually disappear as the small bones of the skull connect together to form the unified skull.

The infant's brain is genetically programmed to produce more **synapses** than it will ever use. These synapses, or connections between individual nerve cells, are formed and become permanent during the first few years of life, affecting the development of vision, speech, and thinking. More than 80 per cent of the major structural changes of the brain happen in the first three years of life (Kuhl, 2011), making this a critical learning period during which the child's developing brain has exceptional plasticity and is open to stimulation. Important windows of opportunity governing cognitive and socio-emotional skills are programmed to close by the end of the first three years; in short, this is a "use it or lose it" period for the child.

The pattern of infant development is **cephalocaudal** (from the head downward) and **proximodistal** (from the midline outwards). The large head of the infant, which requires such care and support, moves first, and then the body starts to roll and squirm. Similarly, an infant's arms move before the hands, the hands before the fingers; the legs move before the feet, and the feet before the toes.

When caregivers recognize and understand these patterns of infant growth and development, and recognize that the early years are a critical learning period, they are more likely to advocate for structural support to ensure the infant's optimal health. Table 3.2 describes these patterns and indicates the requisite structural supports for the infant's optimal growth and development.

Table 3.2 Caregiver and Structural Supports for the Infant

Pattern of Growth and Development	Caregiver Support	Structural Support
Rapid body growth: birth weight doubles in the first five months, and height increases by 50 per cent in the first year	Responsive and consistent care and nutrition to support healthy body growth	Adequate parental leave, financial support, and health care
Rapid formation of synaptic connections in the brain; pruning of unused neurons and strengthening of those that are frequently used	Stimulation through conversation, play opportunities, and movement	Quality, accessible, and affordable childcare and in-home family support
Proximodistal pattern of development: muscles close to the midline develop first	Encouragement to roll, move arms and legs, reach, kick, and squirm	Community infant stimulation programs; adequate community play spaces for infants
Cephalocaudal pattern of development: from the head downward. The head moves before the arms and trunk; the arms and trunk move before the legs	Infant massage; encouragement of kicking, batting with hands, and grasping (using digits)	Parent resource centres and infant stimulation programs in the community
Plasticity of the brain in the first few years of life	Contact comfort, consistency of care and unconditional positive regard	Adequate financial support of caregivers and infants; adequate community child care
Head is one-quarter of total body size; neck muscles are weak; fontanels are still open	Head support for first three months; no shaking or rapid movement of head	Accessible caregiver education provided in a variety of media, languages, and learning modes

Caregivers often worry about an infant's rate of development. They are concerned when an infant "fails to meet her milestones," the developmental markers of critical learning achievements, such as walking or talking. However, caregivers need to remember that these milestones are co-relational: development in one domain affects development in another. The infant who rolls and kicks and squirms is also more likely to put words to this activity because sensorimotor play encourages early language development, or the physical domain affects the cognitive. The achievement of (or delay in) reaching a milestone in one domain may influence the achievement of milestones in other domains. An infant who is immobile and hospitalized, for example, may not meet physical milestones and, consequently, may not meet cognitive milestones regarding spatial awareness. When the child is discharged from hospital and can play with peers, the child quickly catches up and meets cognitive and physical milestones. Similarly, a child who starts to ride a bicycle at age three may interact with older peers and meet socio-emotional milestones earlier than other less mobile children. In this way, one area of development affects the other(s).

The National Longitudinal Survey of Children and Youth (NLSCY),[1] launched in 1994 but now inactive, was one response to caregiver worries about developmental milestones. In tracking how well Canadian children were meeting their milestones of development, it showed that some children reached those markers or milestones earlier, and some excelled in certain domains at an earlier age. The survey also showed which structural determinants most influenced this development. This quantitative data helped both to alleviate individual caregiver worry and to bring the concern about child development to the larger community—the macrosystem or structure on which so much of the child's health and wellness depends.

Gender Construction

Sex is a product of biology: infants are born male or female, and only rarely are they both (i.e., **intersex**). In later life, the child may choose to have his or her sex medically changed. However, the majority of infants of a particular sex grow into adults of that sex and remain so throughout the life cycle. At birth a sex is assigned to an infant on the basis of genitalia. This assignment marks the beginning of gender construction. As Jocelyn Hollander (2002: 474) notes, "Gender is a social institution, not a biological distinction, something that members of a social group collaboratively create, maintain, and enforce." An infant's maleness is socially constructed from the first blue blanket and blue sleepers and tiger toy. A female is socially constructed from the first pink nightie and bonnet and Barbie doll.

Gender construction refers to the process through which children learn the cultural norms, expectations, and behaviours that have been socially constructed for males and females and begin to "do gender." The two sexes are presented as a dichotomy—one in opposition to the other and one inherently stronger than the other. Gender construction produces **gender stereotypes** of strong males and weak females, active males and passive females. These agreed upon or socially constructed patterns of expected behaviour serve to reinforce the relative and dichotomous power of girls and boys. Because gender affects self-concept, peer and family relationships, school performance, and plans for the future, the process of gender construction—or the dominant gender discourse—affects child development. In this sense, gender is something that children *do* as well as something that is *done to* children; in other words, and as identified by the Public Health Agency of Canada's population health project (2011), gender construction is a structural determinant of children's health or wellness.

Even in the earliest stages of a child's infancy, gender construction happens through verbal and non-verbal messaging. "Children are seen from birth as legitimate peripheral participants in local communities of practice of femininities and masculinities. Certain behaviour is encouraged, ignored, praised or emphasised, depending on whether the child is a boy or a girl" (Martin, 2011: 23). Parents may express joy or sorrow when they learn their infant's sex, and their initial reaction can frame their child's emerging gender identity. The parent may express delight: "Oh, a girl!" On the other hand, the parent may smile and say sadly, "Oh, another girl." The newborn does not understand these words but does read the body language and hear the tone and the underlying meaning. The newborn has been experiencing this parent for many months and, literally, knows the parent from within.

Tiffany Field (2007: 148) cites several studies of gender construction as it relates to infants. She estimates that by 12 to 18 months, the infant understands gender

Photo 3.3 Gender construction begins in infancy.

construction and its inherent power differential. One of the studies involves having an infant match images of female and male faces with other objects shown on a computer screen. The infant is given a gender-neutral prompt to do the match and, in most cases, the child matches objects such as fire hats, hammers, bears, and fir trees with the male face. How does the infant learn or absorb this gender construction and sort out the power differential at such an early age? Infants are attentive and watch how other children play and how their caregivers interact with them. They explore their own bodies and later touch other bodies, testing for strength and softness, and searching for similarities and differences. This exploration of self and others results in a rudimentary understanding of gender difference, and the confident toddler will announce, "Me girl!" By now, the dominant gender construction is absorbed. A little girl has learned to be clean and neat and dressed beautifully in order to be praised as a girl. A little boy has been told to be brave and "not a crybaby" in order to be praised. Young boys are urged to climb and run and throw, while young girls are urged to ask for help.

This social construction of and participation in gender roles continues as the preschooler develops an understanding of gender identity, his or her own and that of other preschoolers. The young child easily identifies and begins to seek gender-specific play and play materials. Adults in the child's life, particularly family members, may label this choice of play and play materials as "strong" or "weak and silly." Consider the following case study described by Smidt (2013: 108):

> Leroy is 4 years old. . . . He loves nothing more than to dress up in the clothes in the dressing up box in his nursery. And most of all he likes to dress up in a particular pink dress and drape a purple scarf over his shoulders and totter around in shoes that are too big for him. But he will not do this after lunch and when asked why he explained that he didn't want his mum to see him dressed like that because "it's girly and I'm not a pouf." He seems to fear that his mum will tell his dad.

Leroy wants to explore what it might feel like to be a girl just as he explores what it might feel like to be a knight or a robber. But Leroy has already internalized and absorbed the prevailing gender constructions. He understands that the important adults in his life would disapprove of his gender bending to the girl role, but they would praise his exploring the firefighter role. Gender constructions are solidly fixed in this boy's four-year-old mind, and he recognizes the social disapproval that might occur if these rigid constructions are questioned or transgressed. Sanctions against gender non-conformity begin early in the child's life. By middle childhood, children engage in social or group play, and they tend to form peer relationships with same-gender peers in the ongoing development of gender self-identity. Not only adults but also peers now have the power to denounce play as silly or to support play as fun and healthy. As Karen Wohlwend (2012: 8) suggests, "Gender performances that fall outside hetero-normative expectations and binary gender categories have real and immediate consequences for children in peer and school cultures."

During middle childhood, it is more probable for boys to engage in physical aggression and physically interactive play, following the "boy code" of masculinity practice that pushes them towards extremes of toughness and aggression. Smidt (2013: 58–9) notes that boys tend to gravitate to gun play and fighting, hiding their guns and their fights when socially sanctioned. Judith Jordan (2005: 80) notes that "Shame-based socialization for boys directs them towards being strong in dominant-defined ways: unyielding, not showing vulnerability, and displaying a narrow range of affect." Gender constructions and homophobia combine to discourage boys from public expressions of both softness and nurturance, although this is gradually evolving as more Canadian men take on caregiving careers and household tasks.

In middle childhood girls form peer relationships with other girls and are often themselves victims of **relational aggression** from other girls: rumours, shut-outs, cliques, and **cyberbullying**. Both the female aggressors and the female victims tend to have low self-esteem and often position themselves as vulnerable and weak. They may choose this traditional social construction (girls are weak; boys are strong) while simultaneously acting in a physically aggressive way towards other girls as a means of gaining some relational power and status.

Stress around body image, relationships, and sexuality escalates in the adolescent years when girls are more likely than boys to endanger their health for the sake of body image (e.g., dieting, tanning, etc.); to be diagnosed with eating disorders; to experience internalizing mental health problems, such as depression and anxiety; and to attempt suicide. Girls are three times more likely than boys to be hospitalized for suicide attempts, particularly the 10- to 14-year-olds whose likelihood increases to five times (Girls Action Foundation, Glass, and Tunstall, 2013). While more boys die from suicide, the number of girls who die from suicide has been steadily increasing since 2000. This increase has been attributed to girls' misuse of prescription drugs plus the rise in "choking," a suffocation method which can prove fatal (Kirmayer, 2012: 1016).

When children move into their teenage years, they return to interacting in mixed-sex groups as they continue to explore gender roles and gender relationships. At this time, they may also act upon their sexual orientation, forming sexual relationships with their own sex, the opposite sex, or both. This activity tends to be covert because of homophobia and social sanctions regarding premarital sex, sexual touching, and **contact comfort** (Johnson, 2008). The teen years are characterized by a lack of contact comfort from peers and a lessening of contact comfort from parents and caregivers, who may feel constrained by their children's prepubescent body changes and growing interest in sexuality. This lack of positive physical contact or contact comfort may contribute to the aggression, isolation, and anger that seem synonymous with the teenage years.

During these years, five boys for every three girls drop out of high school (Richards, 2011). Boys tend to engage in risk-taking behaviours such as drinking, fighting, or doing drugs; those who don't take risks may be called "fraidy cats" or accused of being "afraid of the cops." Jordan (2005: 82) notes that boys tend to take a fight or flight approach, either confronting others or running away. Teenage boys are more likely than girls to die from accidents, suicide, or homicide, and they may try out violent behaviour using weapons (Cappon, 2011).

Workers who understand these gender constructions as structural determinants bring this understanding to their behavioural interventions so that the child can begin to understand how a particular behaviour is gendered. Workers can help the child to deconstruct gender as both a structural determinant itself and as being impacted by other structural determinants such as media, class, culture, and legislation. When working with a child with eating disorders, for example, deconstruction may include looking at how females are depicted in the media and how females are culturally positioned as helpless, vulnerable, less than worthy, and body-centric. In the case of a child who is engaging in violent **gang** activity, deconstruction can include looking at how media depicts boys moving in packs and engaging in risk-taking behaviours that are a rite of passage to "being a man." This gender deconstruction helps the child to understand more clearly how gender role scripts can devalue a person and prompt certain behaviour. The worker can present and model positive gender role scripts of strong and caring men and women that challenge current gender constructions.

Group Exercise   3.1

Words of Hate

In this group exercise, each participant is given a blank card on which to write what he or she considers the most disturbing or hurtful word or phrase. In small groups, the participants look at the unsigned and anonymous cards and prioritize them, putting the group's choice of worst word at the top of the pile. Each small group then shares their selection with the larger group.

This provides participants with the opportunity to be shocked, hurt, irritated, and offended by these words of hate. It is important for participants to work through their personal feelings prior to working with children who regularly use such words and attribute different meanings to them. Language changes continuously, and workers need to understand that it is the child's meaning of a word that is important, not the worker's feelings around that word.

Since we initiated this group exercise in 2005, we have found that the words of hate have become increasingly virulent and racist. However, the words of hate most often selected by female-dominated groups have been "fat" and "ugly." This word choice is even more significant when the prevalence of other racist, sexist, and homophobic words in the piles is considered. This is an effective reminder that words commonly considered offensive within a society are not equally offensive to all people, and that other, more body-centric, words may hurt more.

Sexual Orientation

Sexual orientation refers to one's erotic attraction towards, and interest in developing a sexual relationship with, members of one's own or the opposite sex. A **heterosexual** orientation refers to an erotic attraction to, and preference for developing sexual relationships with, members of the opposite sex. A **homosexual** orientation refers to an erotic attraction to, and preference for developing sexual relationships with, members of one's own sex. Heterosexual children may be called "straight"; homosexual boys may be called "gay" or "queer"; and homosexual girls may be called "lesbians" or "dykes." A **bisexual** orientation refers to an erotic attraction to, and preference for developing sexual relationships with, members of both sexes. A child may also decide to alter the expression of his or her sexual orientation, stifling what feels "natural" or modifying it to suit others. A child may experiment with sexual relations with the same sex or the opposite sex or both. The way sexual orientation is expressed changes as the child develops relationships and understands the prevailing social climate. Children who are not heterosexual are referred to as **two-spirited** by First Nations and, increasingly, by other Canadians as well.

Sexual orientation has been described as both genetically determined and as a lifestyle choice; this duality reflects the nature versus nurture debate that dominates the discourse about many spheres of human behaviour. Psychologists, sociologists, and neurologists have not reached a consensus about what causes an individual to develop a heterosexual, bisexual, gay, or lesbian orientation, but leading researchers now agree that there is no evidence that sexual orientation is simply a choice.[2] Many Canadians certainly feel that they have little personal choice about their sexual orientation. According to the *Canadian Community Health Survey*, 1.1 per cent of Canadians aged 18 to 59 identified themselves as gay or lesbian, and 0.9 per cent as bisexual (Statistics Canada, 2009a). These percentages are tiny in comparison to the 10 per cent estimate from the Children's Hospital of Eastern Ontario (CHEO).[3] This wide gap in these statistics reflects the lack of reliable research in this area. The subject of sexuality, sexual feelings, and sexual orientation remains controversial territory in the area of child study.

Just as heterosexual children begin to develop "crushes" on children of the opposite sex, homosexual children begin to develop the same type of crushes on children of the same sex. It is quite common to hear stories of gay and lesbian children who start to develop attractions to people of the same sex and then realize that this attraction is more than a friendship attraction. While this attraction is usually not acted on until puberty, many children may, in fact, experiment with sexual games and role play at a very young age. They play out sexual roles with other boys and girls of the same age, but these typically involve touching, hand holding, and kissing only.

At the same time, even very young children soon recognize and acknowledge the socially dominant sexual orientation, and, regardless of their own sexual orientation, they usually try to conform to the dominant construct of heterosexuality. This is easier to do because the behavioural role models dominate and heterosexuality is more socially acceptable. Boys will talk about being "daddies" and girls will play out being "mommies," with both sexes assuming that their partners are of the opposite sex. Homophobic views also start forming early in life. In a Canadian study conducted from 2007 to 2009, 70 per cent of Canadian high school students reported experiencing homophobic slurs every day, with 10 per cent of these slurs coming from teachers (Taylor and Peter, 2011: 15). For sexual minority children, school is not a safe place: 74 per cent of these children also reported feeling physically vulnerable at school (Taylor and Peter, 2011: 17).

Despite the prevalence of heterosexuality in Canadian society, some children recognize in middle childhood that this doesn't represent who they feel they are. These children will choose to identify with whatever gender attributes are most comfortable for them. Gay and lesbian children will often begin to identify with attributes of the opposite sex; a little girl may dress like a cowboy and play with cars, while a boy may like to dress up in feminine clothing and play with dolls. Sometimes these attributes are closely linked to the same-sex attraction they are experiencing, or they may, as mentioned above, simply be an exploration of others' gendered roles. In identifying with attributes of the opposite sex, these children are, in a sense, experimenting with both gender roles and sexual orientation and creating a third gender that they can identify with that exists outside the conventional norms of heterosexuality.

This is not to say that all children who identify with a third gender will later identify as gay or lesbian. While some children who engage in gender experimentation at a young age do in fact identify as gay or lesbian later in life, many children who later identify as heterosexual will also experiment with gender construction. Such experimentation demonstrates that these children—regardless of their ultimate gender identification—do not feel strictly bound by the social codes of gender and are more willing to accept and identify with experiences and attributes that fall outside the limits of the sexual orientation norm.

Social cues affect every aspect of a child's development. When cognitive excellence is emphasized, for example, a child will see academic work as a positive and will tend to want to read and write at an early age. Similarly, the social cues of sexuality and sexual orientation can shape and influence how a child behaves. Attraction to the same sex is inherently different from the type of attraction that is inculcated in many Canadian families. Heterosexual parents do not always overtly teach that homosexuality is wrong; however, they may covertly and subtly suggest that homosexuality is a second, rather than a first, sexual choice. Author Andrew Solomon had a close relationship with his mother but did not tell her when he was bullied for being gay. When he was asked later why he suffered in silence for so long, he answered, "I felt that the qualities for which I was being tortured would be abhorrent to my mother, too, and I wanted to protect her from disappointment" (Solomon, 2012: 11).

This situation is very different when children are cared for by gay, lesbian, queer, transsexual, or bisexual parents. The number of these couples in Canada doubled from 2001 to 2011 (Gordon, 2013), and a growing number of these couples have chosen to become parents. Their children report that discussing sexual orientation is less problematic for them simply because their parents are positive role models who are open to discussing sexual orientation, knowledgeable about sexual matters, and comfortable with the GLBTQ community (Gordon, 2013).

When a child identifies with attributes that are outside the dominant sexual orientation construct, he or she also recognizes the strong negative social reaction to this identification. It is not uncommon to hear stories from the gay and lesbian community that involve children being socially reprimanded for making choices and engaging in behaviour that is outside the bounds of the strict sexual orientation code. Sometimes the reactions the child experiences are volatile and can cause emotional as well as physical harm to the child. When children exhibit signs of same-sex attraction, this "difference" can alienate and upset family members, teachers, and friends. They may be punished, mocked, or chastised or may become victims of bullying, homophobic "jokes" and slurs, and exclusion by peers (Taylor and Peter, 2011). They may even be thrown out of their homes; GLBTQ youth, for example, make up approximately 40 per cent of all of the homeless youth in Canada (Abramovich, 2013: 387).

These punitive and shaming actions reinforce the social constructs and diminish the developing self-esteem of the child. Because sexual orientation is so much a part of self-identity, the shame and guilt of being different becomes internalized and associated with the self. The child develops a self-concept of being unworthy, isolated, freakish, and may try to hold back, disguise, or hide any expression of sexual orientation at all. Suppression of sexual orientation can lead to lags in developing a viable social reference group and socialization skills. Without this reference group and positive role models, the child may become even further isolated. This isolation can cause the child to spiral into depression and can lead as far as suicidal ideation; GLBTQ children in Canada form a disproportionate percentage of the number of child suicides, with estimates varying from four to eight times the number of heterosexual children who commit suicide (Dyck, 2012).

Sexual activity usually begins with the onset of puberty, although full sexual activity (namely, intercourse) may not happen until adulthood. This healthy sexual activity is part of a child's socio-emotional development and a way for the child to develop a fuller awareness of his or her sexual orientation and sexual relationships with others. Although delay in sexual activity is not itself a risk, confusion as to sexual orientation can delay self-acceptance and self-actualization. Sexual orientation is as much a part of self as cognition, physical ability, and spirituality. To deny or distort sexual orientation is to deny an essential part of the self. Youth who demonstrate their sexual orientation and sexual behaviour in public tend to be heterosexual. They know that they will be accepted. Because of their social experiences, GLBTQ youth are less likely to demonstrate their orientation and behaviour publicly, and the worker may not be aware of the youth's situation. That is why full acceptance and support for diversity in healthy sexuality is so important for the worker to actively demonstrate.

Such acceptance and support are modelled in the First Nations community as described proudly by one two-spirited youth: "The two-spirit being is a higher being and I am supposed to have a higher wisdom" (Barbara and Doctor, 2007: 12). The worker may strengthen structural supports for a child's sexual orientation by doing any of the following:

- celebrating community and national role models with a variety of sexual orientations;
- correcting misinformation and prejudice by sharing current research and evidence;
- using stories, visuals, and media that depict families led by both heterosexual and GLBTQ individuals and couples;
- accepting and validating individual **sexual identity** and sexual orientation;
- challenging homophobia and homophobic "humour"; and
- modelling positive and affirming gender constructs.

Summary

This chapter explores the characteristics of developmentally appropriate practice through a critical discussion of the developmental perspective on the child. We acknowledge that this perspective has strengths. It cautions workers not to teach infants to walk at nine months unless the child is ready to, or to share at 24 months. It reminds workers how interrelated the physical, cognitive, spiritual, and socio-emotional domains are when the infant is starting to babble and explore. The developmental perspective has weaknesses, however, in its linear logic, its incongruence with current neuroscience, its failure to consider the whole child (four domains), and its Eurocentrism.

By recognizing the linear logic as a weakness and by expanding the three domains to four, and so including the spiritual domain, we expand the developmental perspective to encompass the whole child and we ground this perspective in Medicine Wheel teachings. This expanded developmental perspective on the child positions the child as a gift from Mother Earth and as the centre of the Medicine Wheel, connected to community as well as to family.

In the next chapter, we will apply our critical and expanded understanding of the developmental perspective on the child to the subject of attachment. We will ask ourselves how important attachment is to the overall physical, cognitive, socio-emotional, and spiritual development of the child. Our focus will not be limited to the caregiver–child relationship, but will widen to include the child–caregiver–community relationship as well. Specifically, we will examine the importance of healthy attachment to the overall wellness of the child, the self-confidence that Ramona expressed in her pride regarding her gender. This healthy attachment sets the child's life course, a fact that makes it imperative for the worker to intervene when unhealthy attachment is diagnosed.

Review Questions

1. What is the flaw in logic in the developmental perspective on the child? Explain.
2. How did the cultural bias in the developmental perspective form? Is this bias prevalent today? Why or why not?
3. How are the four domains of development interrelated?
4. Describe how patterns of development are both cephalocaudal and proximodistal.
5. Name and explain Piaget's four stages of cognitive development.
6. What are critical learning periods for children, and what happens when these periods are missed?
7. How is development both co-relational and cultural? Explain with reference to walking.
8. What is the difference between sex and gender, and what is meant by gender construction?
9. When do children become aware of their gender, and when do they become aware of their sexual orientation? Explain.
10. How can workers support positive gender roles for children?

Discussion Questions

1. When planning a play area for school-aged children, how does your support for the children's sexual orientation guide your planning process? Do you find this support difficult to offer because of your own sexual orientation or because of your beliefs about the sexual orientation of others?
2. Children who have to flee their home country often suffer developmental delays as a result of this trauma. Their language skills may lag or their social skills may suffer. How can their optimum development be supported when they reach Canada? You may want to visit programs that welcome refugees to your own area and explore the supports that they offer to children on their own and children in families.
3. Consider the developmental milestone of independent toileting. When is this milestone reached, and how does this milestone reflect cultural values? Is it important for children to reach this milestone before they begin preschool? Why or why not?

4 Attachment

You cannot touch love, but you can feel the sweetness that it pours into everything.

—Helen Keller, *The Story of My Life*

When we think of attachment, we may picture a mother in a rocking chair singing a lullaby to her sleeping baby. This is an appealing image, but it does not necessarily illustrate attachment. The mother's singing may be for her own amusement, and the child may be an unconnected part of the musical moment of the mother as she rocks. The child may look into the mother's eyes and see loathing, and may try to cuddle into her body and feel only bitter rejection.

Attachment begins to develop during infancy, when the infant is distressed or feels threatened and the caregiver responds to this stimulus of distress with love, nurturance, and consistently responsive care. The attachment relationship develops over time as the infant and the caregiver interact. The caregiver with whom the infant forms attachment may be a mother, a father, a nanny, an extended family member, or a community group—any caregiver who is attuned to the infant and responds consistently, attentively, and lovingly. This synchronous response provides the infant with a secure emotional base for exploring the wider world.

Because research on the subject is relatively new, the lifelong importance of healthy attachment is only now being fully realized, and it is still undervalued and misunderstood by some workers. Though the impact of attachment on life success is still being researched, much of the evidence points to this impact being deep, dramatic, and sustained. This chapter introduces the key researchers in the field, many of whom are Canadians, along with some of their significant findings.

Early attachment affects behaviour, growth, and the formation of intimate relationships throughout life. Workers must understand how attachment develops and how they can best intervene when symptoms of unhealthy or insecure attachment become evident. The knowledgeable worker can intervene in a structural and strengths-based way to restore feelings of attachment and security and to heal early attachment injuries. This chapter describes some of the most effective attachment interventions.

Objectives

By the end of this chapter, you will:

- Understand the importance of healthy attachment for the child.
- Recognize insecure attachment as well as the specific structural determinants and caregiving behaviours that contribute to this.
- Demonstrate how to intervene effectively with caregivers and children when there are attachment injuries.

The Research

In the early 1930s, Konrad Lorenz (1903–89), an Austrian zoologist, studied the bond that baby chicks formed with their mother and noted that they appeared to be preprogrammed to follow her after birth (Lorenz, 1970–1). Lorenz theorized that the chicks' **imprinting** on their mother—their spontaneous attachment to her as the source of their nutritional needs—could be transferred to another figure. He tested his theory by removing the mother immediately after birth and replacing her with another moving object, after which he observed that the chicks followed the moving object as they would follow a mother. This imprinting worked only if applied in the first week of the chicks' lives, during which Lorenz could imprint himself or a mechanical object, and the chicks would follow. This pattern of imprinting has subsequently been observed by other biologists and environmentalists who find themselves caring for newly born mammals and birds. These newborns imprint on the caring human, attaching themselves easily to the consistent and responsive caregiver.

Harry Harlow's (1905–81) later research with mammals (primarily rhesus monkeys) in the 1960s and 1970s revealed the flaws in imprinting theory and the effects of **maternal deprivation** (Harlow and Harlow, 1962; Harlow and Suomi, 1972). Newborn monkeys that Harlow studied preferred the comfort and warmth of non-lactating, terrycloth mothers over lactating, mechanical wire mothers. The newborn monkeys would literally starve themselves to death in their search for contact comfort and nurturance. Those who were not comforted, and were fed only by a mechanical mother, grew into socially crippled adult monkeys. Exhibiting hostility, aggressive behaviour, depression, and self-destructive habits, they were unable to read social cues or to solve problems and, as adults, they were unable to mate (Kraemer, 1997). Food from a non-responsive dispenser did not replace the emotional benefits derived from contact comfort. Even more worrisome was the fact that monkeys exposed to maternal deprivation for over 90 days (six months in human-growth terms) could not be comforted. Their hostile and aggressive behaviour persisted even when they were systematically treated with an intervention of contact comfort.

The terms "attachment" and "bonding" were coined first by John Bowlby (1969) in his description of the socio-emotional or affective bond that develops between the infant and the primary caregiver. He postulates that all infants instinctively seek attachment with caregivers who provide basic physical needs, emotional comfort, security, and protection. Bowlby also argues that attachment was an evolutionary survival mechanism in that the search for such a connection prompted the infant to seek nourishment from the attachment figure, and likewise prompted the attachment figure to provide nourishment to the infant. Bowlby (1988: 27) defines attachment behaviour as "any form of behaviour that results in a person attaining or maintaining proximity to some other clearly identified individual who is conceived as better able to cope with the world." Bowlby's description of this proximity-seeking behaviour helps to explain why a young child can form an attachment with an abusive adult. The adult wielding abusive control over the child appears "better able to cope with the world" and is able to provide the short-term nurturance or protection that the child needs, while simultaneously abusing the child. Bowlby explains that attachment can be unhealthy but nevertheless gradually becomes the internal working model of **intimacy** for the child. Hence, unhealthy attachment can extend across generations as one insecurely attached caregiver wields power over an infant, producing another insecure attachment.

Vera Fahlberg (1988: 13) explores this interactive dynamic of attachment, describing healthy attachment as an affectionate bond between two individuals and demonstrating through her work with adoptees that attachment affects the child's life-long socio-emotional development: "A strong and healthy bond to a parent allows a child to develop both trust in others and self-reliance. The bond that children develop to a person who cares for them in their early years is the foundation of their future psychological, physical, and cognitive development and for their future relationships with others."

Canadian researcher Mary Ainsworth and her colleagues devised a procedure known as the "Strange Situation" in order to investigate, verify, and classify attachment relationships (Ainsworth et al., 1978). The Strange Situation comprises a series of experimental episodes, each about three minutes long. First, the mother and infant enter an unfamiliar room filled with interesting toys; next, once the infant is settled, the mother leaves the room briefly; and, finally, she returns to reunite with her infant. During these three episodes, the experimenter observes the infant and records the infant's responses to the mother's presence and absence.

The results show that most of the infants seem to be securely attached to their mothers. They relate to their mothers through warm interactions; they use their mothers as a safe base for exploration; they protest and cry upon separation; they show pleasure when their mothers return; they are easy to console; and they clearly prefer their mothers to strangers. These infants are considered to have healthy attachment. However, some infants display a variety of conflicting behaviours, both in the presence of their mothers and when separated from them, that suggest anxious or insecure attachments to their mothers. Through the Strange Situation, Ainsworth develops a taxonomy of insecure attachment, classifying attachment according to degree (from least to most severe) as avoidant, resistant, and disorganized.

Elinor Ames used Ainsworth's taxonomy to identify early attachment injuries in Romanian children adopted by Canadians. These children displayed indifference and hostility to their new adoptive parents as well as indiscriminate friendliness towards strangers, two of the classic characteristics of insecure-disorganized attachment. Her research pinpoints the cause of this insecure attachment to be early maternal deprivation in Romanian orphanages (Ames, 1997). Like Harlow's monkeys, these children had been given dry diapers, bottles of milk, and warm cribs as infants, but they had lacked early emotional nurturance.

Canadian adoption research confirms Ames' findings. Descriptions of "searches for birth mothers," "attachment injuries," and "reunions with birth parents" in the adoption literature (Cech, 2000) clearly signal the deep and long-lasting effects of early maternal deprivation. As Marlene Webber (1998: 72) notes, "The inner lives of those who've been rearranged by adoption have nothing to do with the families who adopt. The drive to seek and hold on to the truth of one's beginning exists only for the people essential to the moment of delivered life."

Although not always working directly with children, Sue Johnson, founder of the Ottawa Couple and Family Institute, studied the long-term damage caused by attachment injuries in individuals who seek to maintain their adult relationships. Using **emotionally focused therapy**, which she developed over decades of working with couples, Johnson (2008: 27) describes the contact comfort needed by adults with attachment injuries: "Love is not the icing on the cake. It is a basic primary need, like oxygen or water. Once we understand and accept this, we can more easily get to the heart of relationship problems."

Attachment research also has been carried out by Diane Benoit and her colleagues at the Hospital for Sick Children in Toronto. In a meta-analysis of three decades of attachment research, Sheri Madigan, Leslie Atkinson, Kristin Laurin, and Diane Benoit (2013: 682) identify the maladaptive behaviours in children that result from insecure attachment and their caregivers' "insensitive, hostile, or rejecting parental behavior" that contributes to this insecure attachment. Their research is hopeful and indicates that "attachment-based interventions can increase caregiver warmth, responsiveness, and sensitivity, as well as promote the development of secure attachments" (Madigan et al., 2013: 685).

Healthy Attachment

Infants will attach themselves emotionally and psychologically to a primary caregiver if that caregiver is consistently responsive and nurturing. This attachment to a source of benefit offers a distinct survival advantage: the attachment figure provides the essentials for life—food, water, and warmth. However, the meeting of attachment needs continues beyond infancy. A bond of trust with a caregiver or a community of caregivers who consistently provide the essentials for life is the basis for an individual's mental model of intimacy, self-esteem, and health. A feeling of attachment answers two questions: "Am I lovable?" and "Can others be trusted to supply my essential needs?" The securely attached child feels worthy of love and is able to trust others.

Sometimes called a "secure-base relationship," healthy attachment is fundamental or basic to the overall growth and development of the child. Healthy attachment provides a secure and dependable emotional base and a sense of emotional safety from which the infant can explore, experiment, and develop the self-confidence, self-reliance, autonomy, and resiliency needed to cope with future stresses. Abraham Maslow (1943) describes this need for a secure and dependable emotional base in his five-level hierarchy of needs (Figure 4.1). He identifies the most basic needs as physiological. Once these needs are met, the next level of needs is for safety and security, followed by love and belonging. Maslow's hierarchy provides a template for the importance of healthy attachment as the foundation of an individual's eventual development of self-esteem at level four and self-actualization at level five (and for self-transcendence, level six, which he added later in his life).

Psychologist Erik Erikson's psychosocial development model similarly complements attachment theory. Erikson (2000) identifies eight stages of psychosocial development, the first two of which take place in early childhood. According to his model, the first stage—in the first year of life—is the critical learning period for developing trust in the world, a sense that the world is safe. The next stage, when the child becomes a toddler, is a critical learning period for independent decision making. Erikson's

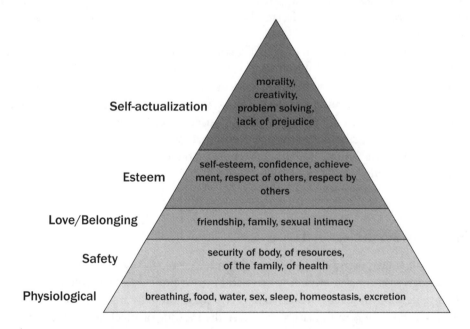

Figure 4.1 Maslow's Hierarchy of Needs

model suggests that without a solid foundation of trust built on healthy attachment the child cannot move forward to the second stage of being an independent decision maker. As the psychoanalyst Donald Winnicott remarked, "There is no such thing as a baby—meaning that if you set out to describe a baby, you will find you are describing a baby and someone. A baby cannot exist alone but is essentially part of a relationship" (qtd in Solomon, 2012: 1).

A healthy attachment is one of the strongest protective factors for a child and can outweigh a constellation of risk factors. Securely attached children who are raised in war-torn countries, in abject poverty, and amid constant chaos can develop into successful, optimistic adults. Their secure attachment outweighs the poverty, stress, malnutrition, disease, and turmoil of their early years. Secure attachment promotes resiliency, is associated with school success, and reduces the risk of depression and **self-injurious behaviour**.

A healthy attachment is also fundamental to the development of communication. Babbling, cooing, vocal interactions, and eye contact with caregivers are the first stages of language development. Infants use this rudimentary language to indicate their need for food, sleep, and comfort, and the attentive caregiver soon learns to respond to this infantile language. Within a few weeks, the infant's cries become differentiated, and the caregiver can recognize what each cry means and can respond appropriately. When this happens, the infant feels heard and begins to understand and imitate the rhythm of conversation. The caregiver will pause and the child will react; the caregiver will hum or sing and the child will respond to the rhythm of the words. This stimulus-response language development depends upon healthy attachment.

In addition, Mary Ainsworth and her colleagues (1978) found that children who were securely attached were able to be more caring and empathetic towards others. Because they were cared for and protected by responsive caregivers, these children felt valued, worthwhile, respected and wanted, and secure enough to feel concern for others. Healthy attachment is thus related to higher self-esteem, openness to experiences and people, and an internal locus of control (Johnson, 2004). The child begins to feel part of the larger culture of the caregiver and gradually absorbs the attitudes and values of this culture. On the other hand, the child with an unhealthy attachment has less cultural identification and affiliation, and so develops poor self-image and low self-esteem.

A healthy attachment prompts the child to want to please the responsive caregiver. This desire to please is a significant motivator for the child to learn and to explore the world. The securely attached child engages in activities such as ball tossing, running, swimming, and reading as a means of further engaging with the caregiver and developing this trusting relationship. The child develops social skills—sharing, co-operation, and negotiation—through play with the caregiver and is encouraged in this skill development; for example, many children would never attempt to swim (or would attempt to swim and drown) were it not for a proud, cheering, and encouraging caregiver. The reciprocity that infuses this relationship is evident, as the confidence with which the child explores the water, the playground, and the slide is nurtured by the responsive support of the caregiver. As each skill is acquired, the child's confidence and feelings of **competence** grow.

A healthy attachment also forms the basis of the child's internal working model of intimacy and intimate relationships later in life. Intimacy alleviates attachment fears and opens up possibilities for acceptance and responsiveness. In an intimate relationship, securely attached adults can expose their vulnerabilities because they already have a secure base and high self-esteem.

How do we identify healthy attachment? Unfortunately, observations such as the following are unreliable indicators even though they are commonly believed to demonstrate how attached and secure a child is:

- "Look how she cries when her daddy leaves the daycare!"
- "Oh, aren't they sweet! They do everything together!"
- "He just lights up when his mama comes into the room."
- "Look you. She's laughin' up a storm. I guess she jus' loves her nana!"

A child's response of crying, laughing, or being silent may or may not indicate healthy attachment. Nor is healthy attachment an inevitable outcome of a relationship in which a child and a stay-at-home parent do everything together. As noted earlier, the mother rocking her child in the rocking chair may in fact hold an infant who is insecurely attached to her.

Healthy attachment can be identified when an infant under stress seeks proximity to and contact with the caregiver, and the caregiver responds with reciprocal body language. Through this harmonious and instantaneous sequence of responses, called **synchrony**, the caregiver achieves a state of **attunement** to the child's needs over time. The caregiver's behaviours of feeding, holding, nurturing, massaging, smiling, cuddling, and talking to the infant reinforce the infant's attachment to the caregiver. And, at the same time, the infant's responses to care, including cooing, smiling, cuddling, and becoming quiet when held, stimulate and strengthen the caregiver's attachment to the infant.

Healthy attachment also can be observed when a young child deliberately chooses interactions that maintain contact with and seek proximity to the caregiver, and that include social referencing. The child seeks out physical contact with the caregiver, turning towards her,[1] gazing at her, crawling towards her, and cuddling into her body. The child gazes into the eyes of the caregiver and, in that reflected loving gaze, begins to develop a sense of self. The child seeks the touch, smell, and sound of the caregiver and is soothed by the feel of her, the smell of her body, or the sound of her voice. The child moves towards the caregiver or reaches out to touch her fingers or hair.

Proximity-seeking is evident when the child deliberately moves into the area occupied by the caregiver or brightens when the caregiver moves into the child's area. The child may turn his or her head at the sound of the caregiver's voice, seeking to meet

Photo 4.1 This boy sees himself reflected in his father and both express joy in their attachment.

her gaze. The proximity of that gaze provides the child with a sense of security and comfort in stressful situations.

In addition to maintaining contact and seeking proximity, the child's engagement in social referencing is a third indicator of healthy attachment. **Social referencing** is the child's action of looking first to the caregiver to decipher cues regarding a new event or a new person in the room. If the caregiver becomes tense, the child reads that cue and then becomes tense or fussy. If the caregiver smiles at the new person, the child relaxes, smiles, and opens up to that person, too. This early learning of social cues through social referencing is a safe learning experience that encourages the child to explore beyond the known and into the unknown in order to distinguish between safe and unsafe situations.

Insecure Attachment

The child's social history and current behaviour may indicate attachment injuries. The worker may assess the extent of these injuries using the Child Behaviour Checklist, Attachment Q-Sort, or the Cassidy-Marvin Preschool Attachment System, all of which are focused on the mother-child relationship (Madigan at al., 2013). The worker may also use a variation of the Strange Situation procedure, particularly with infants and toddlers, to identify their reaction to separation and reunification, and to identify their caregiver's response to these same separations and reunifications.

Separation typically activates the child's need for comfort and security. Infants and toddlers who show no reaction when their parent or caregiver leaves the room may have an attachment injury. However, their reunification with their parent or caregiver is a more reliable gauge. Attachment injuries are likely if the same infant or toddler continues to show no reaction when the parent returns, or the parent shows no reaction, or the parent shows an inappropriate reaction such as mocking or teasing the distressed child.

Insecure attachment has three levels of severity—from avoidant, to resistant, to disorganized. The insecure-avoidant infant has already learned in the first few weeks of life that the caregiver is not to be trusted. When the infant cries, the caregiver does not respond or responds inappropriately. This caregiver is not a safe base, and the insecure-avoidant infant responds in a self-protective way by avoiding or ignoring her. When the caregiver leaves, the infant protests briefly; when she returns, the infant shows little or no signs of pleasure. The infant gradually learns to detach from or avoid the caregiver. As the insecure-avoidant infant grows and becomes verbal, the child continues to show little **affect** when the caregiver comes and goes. The child does not differentiate between caregiver and stranger, kissing and hugging either of them when required, but with little or no enthusiasm. The child may answer "whatever" when asked to choose an activity, clothing, or food. The child develops the self-protective response of detachment to cope with an early attachment injury and an insecure base.

The more significantly affected insecure-resistant infant demonstrates confused behaviour, alternating between anxiety and **resistance**. The infant becomes severely agitated and anxious and may cry continuously when the caregiver is out of the room. However, when the caregiver returns, the infant continues to cry and cannot be comforted, alternately clinging to the caregiver and pushing her away. As the insecure-resistant infant grows and becomes verbal, the child tends not to develop social relationships or engage in social play with peers. The child appears fearful of new experiences and changes playmates often, never developing close friendships or a stable social group. This unconscious and unspoken **strategy** insulates the child from potential disappointment and further attachment injuries.

All insecure attachment is cause for concern; however, insecure-disorganized attachment is the most damaging because of its deep, long-term effect on the child. The insecure-disorganized infant displays very confused and contradictory behaviours in reaction to the chaos and danger posed by the caregiver. Judith Feeney (2005: 45) describes insecure-disorganized attachment injury as "fearful, the most negative attachment pattern." The infant may exhibit intense anger, followed suddenly by a dazed appearance. When held by the caregiver, the infant may show signs of fear and cry continuously, with stiff body and arched back, in a desperate attempt to get a reaction, any reaction. If the caregiver continues to offer no response or contact comfort, the infant may then withdraw. Feeling loss, despair, and helplessness, the infant gives up on life. This emotional withdrawal can result in chemical, physical, and anatomical changes in the brain that can permanently damage the infant, resulting in non-organic failure to thrive, or **growth-faltering**. The infant, like the baby monkey with the mechanical mother in Harlow's studies, receives food but fails to put on weight or become healthy. Children with insecure-disorganized attachment develop socio-emotional difficulties so deeply rooted that any change, even a positive shift to nurturing caregiving, is strongly resisted. Unfortunately, Harlow was correct about the long-term damage caused by insecure-disorganized attachment.

At all three levels of insecure attachment the infant develops a coping strategy that is both defensive and protective: ignore the caregiver and relate on an equal basis with both the caregiver and any random stranger. The infant searches for nurturance from any source, and the toddler may try to leave the room with a stranger or whoever appears to be most attractive at a particular moment. The older child chooses high-risk activities and demonstrates little sense of personal safety. Later, the youth may gravitate to gangs or relationships with other attachment-disorganized youth with similar attachment injuries. This coping mechanism affords a temporary feeling of safety with like-minded peers who also avoid close emotional relationships.

Change in this internal working model of intimacy is possible. However, over the course of early childhood this model becomes less flexible and less susceptible to change (Hamilton, 2000). As a result, some or all of the following behaviours may develop:

- social withdrawal and hesitancy to participate in interactions and activities;
- poor problem-solving skills;
- hostility and aggressiveness towards others;
- controlling behaviours ranging from solicitous caregiving to bossiness;
- lack of respect for the property of others;
- superficiality in relationships and rejection of any affectionate overtures;
- a pervasive lack of trust;
- bedwetting and poor hygiene skills;
- volatile anger, hostility, and cruelty to animals and to other people.

These behaviours may also be observed in deeply troubled children who are securely attached. At times they may vandalize property, for example, despite a secure attachment to caregivers and community. However, it is the constellation of behaviours, and their pervasiveness, that characterizes insecure or unhealthy attachment.

Causes of Attachment Injuries

Attachment injuries happen in the child's microsystem—the intimate relationship between child and caregiver. The infant may not be able to signal needs because of communication delays, brain injury, autistic spectrum disorder, or prenatal exposure to alcohol or drugs, and may cry continually or not at all, sending the caregiver confusing messages that may trigger no response or an inappropriate one. The caregiver may feel overwhelmed by the demands of caring for an infant, may have attachment issues herself, or may also be unable to respond because of mental health issues, postpartum depression, a developmental delay, or addictions. The caregiver may not know how to respond, may not have the affect to respond, or may respond in a way that the infant perceives to be negative. Each time that the infant's need is met with no response or an inappropriate response, an attachment injury occurs. Each attachment injury or wound builds on the previous one; thus, insecure attachment develops.

While it is tempting to focus solely on the child and caregiver in the microsystem as the cause of insecure attachment, there are causes in the mesosystem too. Relatives and the caregiver's partner(s) may make disparaging remarks about the infant, the caregiver, or the relationship between them, and may caution the caregiver not to pick up and soothe her infant. They may call the caregiver inadequate, a "lousy mother." Colleagues, neighbours, health practitioners, friends, and employers may also question or criticize the caregiver's parental capacity. The community may reject the child as an outsider or outcast. These mesosystem determinants may make the caregiver feel inadequate and even more unsure of how and when to respond to her infant. She may pass around her infant from babysitter to babysitter, adding to the infant's insecurity and feelings of fear.

Most important, however, are the structural (macrosystem) determinants which include childism in parental culture, child welfare systems, war and violence, sexism, racism, and socio-economic factors. For example, childism in the prevailing parental culture may endorse harsh discipline as a way to "manage" children. Childism prompts caregivers to ignore, punish, or neglect the child when the child communicates physical or emotional needs through crying, fussing, or moving. This inappropriate, abusive caregiver response reflects childism in the prevailing parental culture and triggers insecure attachment in the child.

War and violence separate children from their attachment figures and from the communities of their birth. Sexism and racism lead to attachment injuries when the newborn reads disappointment in her caregiver's response to her sex or race. The caregiver may regard the female sex as inferior or brown-skinned people as less valuable than white ones. Then there is poverty. Parents living in poverty may be juggling several day and night jobs; they may be forced to move continuously to find affordable housing; they may not have access to quality child care because of the cost; and they may lack healthy peer relationships and recreation. They may not have the time to respond to their child's needs and, even when time permits, their response may be inadequate because there is just not enough food in the cupboard. Poverty is an overriding structural factor that directly impacts the development of healthy attachment between the child and caregiver.

Child welfare policy is another structural determinant of attachment injuries, causing children to be removed from their attachment figures when these persons are assessed as being incapable, abusive, or neglectful. Four particular child welfare processes impact the development of healthy attachment in children: foster care, adoption, intercountry adoption, and deculturation. Some children are able to recover from their separation from caregivers and community through appropriate and timely counselling and support, as well as through their innate resilience. However, other children do not recover, either because of the lack of timely and appropriate supports or because the injuries are simply too deep to bear. Like the child in Yann Martel's novel *Life of Pi* (2001), they drift alone on the ocean of relationships, trying to find nurturance in the temporary caregivers of their lives.

 ## Group Exercise   4.1

Losses

This large group exercise begins with individual work and ends with a large group discussion of separation and loss. In this brief yet powerful exercise, the participants are guided towards a deeper understanding of the losses and attachment injuries children suffer through alternative placements and the deculturation that accompanies them.

The exercise begins with the group leader asking participants to write down the five most cherished people, animals, or things in their daily life. The leader then offers generic examples of friends, parents, extended family members, pets, home, cottage, car, and so on. The leader then pauses while participants try to narrow down their lists to five.

The leader then explains that everyone in the group will have to stay in a retreat for the next month and must forego one of the people, animals, or things on their lists. After a pause, the leader asks participants to look again at their lists and cross out two more people, animals, or things. Each participant now has only two remaining list items. The leader then explains that each participant will begin life tomorrow with only one item on the list. One must be discarded. Finally, the leader explains that all participants must now begin a new life without the last remaining item.

Participants may want to share the name of their last item with the large group. Participants may also want to share their feelings on having to leave behind everything and everyone in their lives. Some participants may have had such experiences in their lives and, if so, their input can guide the large group discussion of losses and what they mean. This exercise not only prompts discussion of foster care, adoption, and deculturation, but also leads to a greater understanding of the depth and expanse of personal loss suffered by the child who must leave behind family, friends, and community.

Foster Care

Removal of the child from the family home breaks the lifelong network of birth family relatives—siblings, cousins, aunts and uncles, and grandparents. This is a traumatic experience for the child. The family may be unsafe, unresponsive, and incapable, but they are the only attachment figures the child has ever known. Because their daily lives continue while the child lives alone with strangers (foster parents or paid staff), this separation becomes even more hurtful (DiCiacco, 2008: 28–30). Regular access visits with the family only add to this grief as the child experiences parents and siblings continuing with their lives, apparently forgetting about the one in foster care.

The foster parents or residential care workers are unfamiliar and unknown to the child, and their cultural dissonance makes them even more suspect. The child usually reacts angrily to placement and then succumbs to a despair that looks like classic depression. Faced with the loss of family, the child catapults through the five stages of grieving—shock and denial, anger, depression, bargaining, and acceptance, with few children ever reaching stage five (acceptance).

A child in foster care experiences an average of seven moves during foster care,[2] a situation described as **foster care drift**. Some children have substantially more moves than this, even in one year, while others, because they are discharged from care, may have only two or three moves in all. These moves happen for many reasons: foster parents may relocate to a smaller home or another jurisdiction; they may become ill; or they may have a family member who is hospitalized and requires additional care. Sometimes they have expertise with a limited age range only, and the child "ages out" of the home. A child may move to reunite with brothers or sisters in another foster home, and then may move again when the foster parent feels overwhelmed by the number of children in the home. Each move is the disruption of a relationship and another perceived rejection. Children who have to move often assume that there is something wrong with them and that they are unlovable. They may feel "not good enough" for the family and may self-identify as "bad kids" who have to be moved. Negative self-worth and low self-esteem compound, with each move making the attachment injury larger, and the feeling of belonging to a family or a community much more remote. If some of the children in the family return home while others stay in foster care, those in care may never overcome their anger and hostility towards their brothers and sisters who get to go home.

Foster care is meant to be a temporary solution to a high-risk situation. It may begin with an emergency home for a few days and continue with many placements in foster homes, staffed group homes, or specialized treatment homes. Children in care start to view caregivers as disposable, interchangeable parts, and they see themselves as all they've got. Webber (1998: 39) observes, "Little wonder kids risk developing attachment disorder. It may start in the womb, but it certainly comes from an early childhood spent like a rubber ball. Being kicked around can, understandably, turn a kid off love." An estimated 90 per cent of children in foster care are attachment-disorganized

© Katrina Brown/Alamy

Photo 4.2 Smiles, sunshine, and rainbows may hide the multiple losses of children in foster care.

(Cicchetti, Rogosch, and Toth, 2006). Although some attachment injuries begin prior to foster care there is no doubt that placement in foster care adds to the injuries.

Foster care separates children from neglectful and abusive family members but also separates them from family members who are potential lifetime sources of care and support. A British Columbia study of children in foster care (Jones and Krak, 2005) revealed that the children identified their birth family as the primary object of their attachment and expressed a wish to find their birth families, despite having suffered abuse and neglect within these same families. This instinctual wish for family and for some secure attachment, even when that family is abusive, neglectful, or emotionally distant, is well documented (Blackstock and Trocmé, 2005), as is the traumatizing effect of multiple placements.

Adoption

Adoption is a process in which the permanent care and custody of a child is transferred from the parent (or state acting as a parent) to an adult who is not the birth parent(s) of that same child. In Canada, there are public and private adoptions, open and closed adoptions, and **customary adoptions**. Adoption from foster care happens through the public adoption system. Customary adoption happens when parents (usually Aboriginal parents) place their baby with a relative or friend in the community who promises to keep the child's birth name and support that child's sense of identity by keeping the child within the community. Private adoptions happen when parents arrange placements of their children to private adopters. Most public and private adoptions are closed and involve no visitation or ongoing contact between the birth family and the child. Open and customary adoptions, on the other hand, can involve some contact between the birth family and the child as agreed to by the adoptive parents.

The secrecy in closed adoption (public and private) ties the relationship into an emotional knot. In closed adoptions, the child's file, the child's birth history, and the location of the birth family are all kept confidential. Adoptive parents may be given a limited **social history** of the child, but they are often advised to keep this history secret. They may tell their adopted child a fabricated birth story, a happy adoption story that conflicts with the child's own prenatal and postnatal memories. This causes the child to begin to doubt early memories and to suffer "genealogical bewilderment" (Lifton, 2009: 48). David Kirschner (2007) describes this disassociation as Adopted Child Syndrome (ACS) with its resulting childhood behaviours including problems with authority, preoccupation with fantasy, pathological lying, stealing, running away, learning difficulties, and a lack of impulse control. ACS has been researched by other psychologists in the adoption research field and has been used in Canadian courts as an explanation for the deviant behaviours of adoptees from closed adoptions.[3]

The fragile relationship between an adoptive parent and child (adoptee) is an artificial legal one. It requires additional nurturance, parenting skill, knowledge of attachment issues, and commitment. The parenting work is well beyond that required to sustain adult love relationships (Johnson, 2008). When the initial euphoria or honeymoon period of adoption placement ends in a week, a month, or a year, the adoptive parent is left at home alone with an unknown and genetically unrelated child who is grieving many losses. The third person in the relationship (birth mother) may have become more real to the child than the actual adoptive parent who provides daily care. As memories of this mother continue to surface, the child may become unresponsive and silent, distant and non-compliant, or angry. Some children have tantrums—lashing out, breaking toys, smearing feces, and running away—while others simply shut down and refuse to eat, talk, play, or sleep.

At the same time, the adoptive mother may be grieving fertility and birthing losses. This woman may have undergone painful, invasive procedures prior to adoption and may have spent a large amount of time and money to adopt this child. The adoptive father or fathers may have spent years searching for a child and being assessed by workers. When the chosen child appears to be angry and ungrateful, the adoptive parent may begin to feel inadequate, rejected, and hurt and may react by slowly pulling away and detaching emotionally and physically. The child may respond to this second rejection from this second caregiver and act out again, sometimes with the same behaviour but more often with a new and equally puzzling one (stealing, lying, hitting). The adoptive parent may pull even further away from the child. Rejection is answered by rejection, and so begins the stimulus-response cycle of insecure attachment.

This doesn't feel good for either the child or the parent who is left to struggle alone with these feelings of inadequacy, depression, and regret. The myth of the happy adoption story is hard to sustain when the child is rejecting the adoptive parent and openly defying rules in the home. Without attachment interventions the relationship between child and parent may deteriorate and eventually break down completely. The parent may ask that the child be removed permanently or temporarily, and the child may be placed in or return to foster care, resulting in a further attachment injury and another loss for the child.

Note from the Field 4.1

When Love Is Not Enough

David and Anne Brodzinsky and Daniel Smith (1998) present the case of an adoptive mother and her seven-year-old adopted daughter, Susan. Susan's first year of life was marked by attachment injuries, and when she was adopted at 13 months she demonstrated stiffness and inability to respond. Her adoptive mother felt that her love could change this, so she destroyed the social history that she had been given by Susan's social worker, hoping that by destroying this written record of Susan's abusive past she could also remove some of its pain from Susan's life. Susan is not grateful and, in fact, resists the overtures from her adoptive parents. Her adoptive mother describes Susan's behaviour:

> Susan never seemed to warm up to us. From the very beginning she resisted being held and comforted. She would go stiff when we tried to cuddle with her. . . even now she doesn't come to us when she gets hurt. . . . . I feel that the only time we exist for her is when she wants something . . . then she gets all friendly and sweet but we feel the falseness. Even after all this time, she doesn't feel that much for us or really care about us. (Brodzinsky, Brodzinsky, and Smith, 1998: 101)

As Susan grew, so did her untreated attachment injuries. Her new parents did not recognize or treat her injuries, so Susan lost her trust in them and did not go to them for affection. Her adoptive mother reacted by feeling hurt and rejected and by withdrawing emotionally from Susan. She labelled her daughter as manipulative and began to blame Susan as the cause of the family's problems. The mother's anger and blaming further reinforced her daughter's mistrust of adults.

continued

Susan's adoptive mother had never had the chance to grieve her own infertility and feelings of loss around birthing. Susan had not had the chance to grieve the loss of her birth mother. These early and primal losses were repressed by both Susan and her adoptive mother and would need expression and validation before the healing and the nurturing of healthy attachment could begin.

The counsellor listened to Susan reconstruct her memories of early infancy through pictures and drawings and supported these memories by telling her some of her real social history. Susan began to understand that she had been a wanted and loved baby, but her birth mother had been ill and unable to care for her. The counsellor also listened to Susan's mother recount her pain and feelings of loss and helped her to tie these feelings to those of Susan and Susan's birth mother. Gradually, Susan's adoptive mother began to let go some of her own grief and disappointment. She was coached in attachment through play, and she began to spend more time playing with Susan. Together they began to rebuild their relationship and to share Susan's birth and real adoption story. Affection and love cannot be taught, but, through the counsellor's attachment interventions in the home, Susan and her adoptive mother were able to develop an emotional bond that grew stronger over time.

Intercountry (International) Adoption

Adopting any child is difficult but adopting a child from a completely different culture, race, ethnicity, religion, and homeland is tremendously hard work, especially when it is done alone. Intercountry adoption involves adopting a child from a foreign country through a private agency. The Canadian adoptive parent must pay from $30,000 to $80,000 for this private adoption process. Despite this high cost, the parent does not receive the lifelong adoption support that is available at no cost through the public system.

In addition, intercountry adoptive parents do not receive the anti-racist or cultural competency training that is provided in public adoptions (Dwyer and Gidluck, 2010; Barcons et al., 2014). Lack of this training makes it even more challenging to parent an ethnically and racially different child, especially when intercountry adoptive parents are told to be colour-blind in their choice of child and to embrace diversity. One adoptive parent from Newfoundland explains, "This isn't going to be such a big deal because all my friends love the baby, my family loves the baby, and they all embrace this black child, and race is not going to be an issue in our community even though they are the only black child in the community" (Dwyer and Gidluck, 2010: 12). Her naïveté and her blindness to the sting of racism are staggering; the impact of her parenting on her baby can only be imagined.

The children adopted from abroad by Canadians experience racism in their adoptive family, neighbourhood, school, and community. They report being targets of daily racial slurs, being called apples, Oreo cookies, bananas, and worse, and they usually suffer alone: "Transracial adoptees must learn how to navigate racialized stigma from parents whose racial status is not stigmatized" (Samuels, 2009: 83). Kevin Minh Allen, an intercountry adoptee, blogs on the group website *Transracial Abductees* (2013):

> Middle-class wives
> can't get enough of these infants.
> So adoptable, adaptable,
> so contractually obligated
> to fit neatly in a grateful paradigm.
> After their husbands hand over the check
> that greases the palms of the minister of interior,
> who dropkicks the orphans over the border,
> these sunburnt women catch them in their gardening hats
> and shine them on their aprons,
> like so many apples in a bowl.

Kevin's anger and pain are palpable: he was dropkicked from his homeland, only to land in the middle-class home of strangers who look nothing like him.

In the documentary *Adopted* (Point Made Films, 2008), the adopted daughter is a Korean "apple in a bowl" with white adoptive parents. She asks to have her eyes enlarged and her hair dyed so that she can look like her adoptive family and her white friends at school. Her adoptive parents are mystified by her request and cannot respond to her. Their racial privilege minimizes a racism that they have never personally experienced. They assume that their neighbourhood welcomes and embraces intercountry adoptees even when their own adopted daughter encounters racism every day. They describe their daughter's experiences as "her burden" and "her journey" and dismiss her descriptions of racism as "teasing" and "kids being kids." They retreat behind the myth of racial harmony and diversity while their alienated daughter speaks bitterly of the "gap of benign ignorance" in intercountry adoption.

There is no doubt that most adoptive parents devote quantity and quality time to their children, particularly those from foreign countries. However, the process itself does not provide these parents with adequate insight into both racism and attachment issues (Cantwell, 2014). Insecure attachment develops when there is denial of loss and birth memories, and the denial of racial and ethnic differences. When parents understand, acknowledge, and affirm these losses and this pain, the child begins to heal and feel validated: "Yes! My memories are real. I can and do remember important people in my life." When the larger community of teachers, neighbours, and friends also affirm these losses and confront racism openly, the adopted child feels supported. Denial and secrecy only leave the child mistrustful, isolated, insecure, and unable to trust or attach with parents.

Deculturation

Culture is intrinsic to identity, and this culture is fostered and affirmed by family and community. Deculturation devalues culture and is an attachment injury that, like sexism and racism, strikes the core of the child's identity. Deculturation is the stripping away of the child's culture and is a necessary part of the intercountry adoption process that brings children from foreign countries to their culturally foreign (to them) adopters (Trenka, Oparah, and Shin, 2006). These children must relinquish their cultural identity and assume the language, religion, and culture of their adoptive parents.

Deculturation happened in the past in Canada when Aboriginal children were taken from their families and communities and put into residential schools where their language, spirituality, and culture were replaced by a foreign (white) culture. Deculturation continues for Aboriginal children today when, like the intercountry adoptees, they are placed in culturally foreign foster or adoptive homes. Beth Brant (2005: 146), a Mohawk writer born in Ontario in 1941, recounts her removal from her community, followed by her daughter's similar removal: "They said it was in her best interests. How can that be? She is only six, a baby who needs her mothers. She loves us." Deculturation is perpetuated through the generations. Children are removed from communities, raised by culturally dissimilar caregivers, become emotionally distanced themselves, do not attach to their own children, and then have their children removed and placed with culturally dissimilar caregivers. Many of the children who are adopted become self-abusive and even suicidal, and others drift into addictions and street life, leaving their culturally foreign adoptive families behind them (Carrière, 2010). An estimated 95 per cent of the Aboriginal children who were adopted in the 1960s (during what is now known as the "Sixties Scoop") left their adoptive parents before they even turned sixteen (Sinclair, 2007: 65).

The histories of Aboriginal children have been recounted in the records of residential schools, foster care and adoption agencies, and Canadian political texts. In his report on Indian and Métis adoptions and placements, Senior Family Court Judge E.C. Kimelman (1985: 185) calls deculturation "cultural genocide" and characterizes the system as one in which "cultural bias is practised at every level, from the social worker who works directly with the family, through the lawyers who represent the various parties in a custody case, to the judges who make the final disposition in a case."

Deculturation is best understood through the storytelling tradition of Aboriginal culture. For this, we turn to Jeanette C. Armstrong (2005), an Okanagan born in 1948 in British Columbia, who tells the story of a coyote trapped in a hallway in a city building. Someone has mistaken the coyote for a dog and let the coyote into the building, not recognizing that the coyote is an outdoor animal, a free spirit. Trapped and cut off from all that is familiar, the coyote becomes fearful, anxious, and disoriented, searching for a way to escape to the outside and return to his pack (community). The coyote finally rides up to the roof in an elevator, and then jumps off the roof rather than go back down in the elevator into a building that inspires such fear. Armstrong (2005: 242) describes "the coyotes hanging around in the cities these days. Nobody wanted them there, so nobody made friends with them, but once in a while they made the papers when they did something wrong or showed up, trotting along Broadway, cool as could be." Here, the coyote refers to the transplanted child moving on the margins between cultures, gaining attention only through misbehaviour, and ultimately turning to death for escape. In this story,

Photo 4.3 A coyote on a rooftop, alone and far from the pack, gets ready to jump.

Armstrong strongly criticizes the removal of children from their birth community and culture, illustrating that, for Aboriginal children, deculturation is an attachment injury.

Garnet Angeconeb is one of the survivors of deculturation who spoke at Canada's Truth and Reconciliation Commission:

> Many of us went through a cultural identity crisis—loss of language, loss of family and community ties, loss of self-worth—to mention only a few of the negative but real impacts of residential school. I myself lived through times of spiritual confusion. I lived through times of anger. I lived through times of cultural confusion. I lived through the disruption of my family relationships. At one time in my life I was ashamed of my culture. (qtd in Rogers, deGagné, and Dewar, 2012: 29)

The Commission heard from hundreds of people who were similarly affected. The long-term effects of separation from community and deculturation were horrific for those who testified and those who could not.

🗩 Point to Consider   4.1

Language and Culture

The Aboriginal Healing Foundation (Chansonneuve, 2005) reminds us that Aboriginal children in residential schools were robbed of their home language. This cultural damage compounded the injuries of removal from family and community and traditions. Today only 15 per cent of Aboriginal persons speak an Aboriginal language.[4] For the non-Aboriginal worker this means that the process of building trust with the child and family will be lengthy. There will be many "first meetings" and many silences. Similarly, many Canadian deaf children who attended

continued

residential schools were told their deafness was a deficit. They were encouraged to lip-read and to speak orally in order to fit in with mainstream, and many today feel caught between the deaf world and the mainstream, while fully belonging to neither. Language and culture are inseparable. When children are stripped of their language, or made to feel their language is inferior, they carry deep scars. Even when a child has only heard birth language prenatally, that child carries the memory of this birth language for life. That is why the loss of birth language for children adopted from foreign countries is so damaging and often holds them back from full use of their expressive language.

Attachment Interventions with the Child

Attachment injuries are less visible than physical wounds, so they are often left to fester unattended. It is easier to focus on the child's presenting behaviours—anger, hostility, and lack of respect, for example. This focus on the behaviours allows attachment injuries to mount, wound upon wound, eventually crippling the child's emotional well-being. A trained and caring worker acknowledges these injuries and contextualizes them, empowering the child to develop a sense of efficacy and **self-control**. The child cannot change the past or past injuries, but he or she can develop an understanding of why these injuries happened.

Work done by the Truth and Reconciliation Commission exemplifies just such an attachment intervention. The focus was not on the **presenting problems** of the adult survivors (addictions, alcoholism, and poor parenting), but on the underlying attachment injuries. Survivors were supported to describe the details of their horrific "care" in residential schools (Rogers, deGagné, and Dewar, 2012). Through the telling and recounting of their past, these adult survivors were empowered to locate their abuse within a government policy and religious belief system that legitimized and promulgated this "care." Understanding these structural determinants led many of those who told their stories to further understand their own attachment injuries and their subsequent problems. From blaming themselves for their own shortcomings, they moved to contextualizing these problems within early attachment injuries caused by policy and belief systems that tore them from their families and placed them with violent, cruel, and abusive individuals.

Attachment interventions such as these demand attentive listening and relationship-building. Each injury and each abuse was listened to and recorded. In the same way, each attachment injury experienced by the child needs to be listened to and affirmed. Trust needs to be established so that the insecurely attached child feels safe enough to express emotion and reveal injuries from the past. The residential school survivors spoke to the members of the commission because they gradually began to trust these commissioners. Similarly, the child speaks to the worker when the worker earns the trust of the child and builds a relationship based on this trust.

The worker's predictability and consistent care are fundamental to this relationship-building. The worker who follows through on promises and consistently attends to the child, listening carefully and working with the child in the child's time, may be able to slowly gain the child's trust. Only with this trust and a secure relationship is the child able to move from silence to speech. It is important for the worker to acknowledge and validate the child's resiliency and strength, ability to survive,

---

📝 Note from the Field   4.2

So Angry

Youth are referred to mandatory counselling and group work when their probation officer, child protection worker, or school principal identifies their "anger management problems." These problems display as bullying, swearing at authority figures, challenging peers and adults, and other aggressive behaviours. Youth live up to their label and typically resist both counselling and group work. They come to counselling armed with silence, sarcasm, taunts, and defensiveness.

The counsellor can introduce a ten-point anger management plan or follow group work programs that focus on anger. The counsellor who recognizes the youth's social history may shift the focus to the underlying attachment injuries. This shift will feel unfamiliar and uncomfortable for a young person with the anger label. However, this shift is essential for long-term behavioural change.

Rather than beginning the meeting by asking for explanations or descriptions of "the problem," the counsellor can shift to the injury, opening with a genuine question that acts as a scaffold or bridge that connects the child to the counsellor:

- I'm stuck on this part of your lifeline: were you living in Richmond or in Wabano when you went to kindergarten?
- I heard you lived with your mom when you were a baby. Is that right?
- I have a little brother on your genogram. Did you have a sister too?
- My records list 11 foster homes. Is that number right?

These questions seek to open up early attachment injuries and engage the youth as a teacher. The youth corrects the counsellor, equalizing the power dynamic at the onset, and the counsellor listens and thanks the youth for each correction. The counsellor learns from the youth, leading from behind as they walk along the path of the attachment injuries that led to anger.

problem solve, and create a life. The worker incorporates as much of the child's own language as possible to keep the dialogue real; for instance, the worker may say, "Yeah, I'm onto that," rather than using professional jargon. The worker may also use crayons and paper, drawing visuals in response to the child's instructions. These drawings can become positive images for the child; for example, the worker can use genograms to map family connections as well as early attachment injuries. When the worker is consistently supportive, the child may gradually begin to trust.

Children with attachment injuries typically describe their family members as "weird" or "crazy." The worker accepts and affirms the child's descriptors and writes them down as instructed. Together, the worker and the child slowly reframe the family. The worker may tell a story about other families or friends with similar attributes that can be seen as positive. The weird sister who changes jobs all the time, for example, can be reframed through a story about a co-worker who does the same thing in order to learn more. This **reframing** does not excuse or rationalize the caregiver's behaviour or minimize the child's pain. Instead, the reframing broadens the child's understanding and expression of early attachment injuries. The worker supports the child in naming the pain and acknowledging its effect, and when the child is ready, the worker can provide support as the child confronts family members and begins a different, more open relationship with past and present caregivers.

Attachment Interventions with the Caregiver

The child's permanent caregiver may be an extended family member, sibling, guardian, parent, adoptive parent, or foster parent. The birth parents typically feel most responsible for their child's attachment injuries. Other caregivers tend to blame the birth parents, and there is some validity to this emphasis on the injuries caused by prenatal and postnatal experiences. However, caregivers can also inflict attachment injuries on the child who is adopted, the child in care, or the child of a relative. When these caregivers recognize how their own attachment injuries impact their caregiving style with the child, work can begin to heal the child–caregiver relationship.

Adults usually resist this reflective work as it generates painful memories of their own attachment injuries, and they certainly resist doing this self-reflective work in front of the child. In the following dialogue the worker (W) meets separately with a mother (M) who appears to be exhausted and increasingly detached from her six-month-old son, Bryan. She expresses her frustration with his crying and asks for a quick fix, a behavioural solution of medication, respite, or a diagnosis of her son's disorder. The worker withstands the urge to be prescriptive and instead engages the mother in self-reflection. The mother resists initially. Her problem is urgent and she wants a solution. However, she begins to make personal connections between her own childhood and that of her son's through a slow dialogue with the worker. It is this memory that will help to repair her emotional bond with her son.

W: Parenting isn't always a choice. Sometimes we just fall into it without thinking much about where it leads. What was it like for your own parents?

M: I don't remember. Anyway, this has nothing to do with my own son and his screaming.

W: That must be hard for you, especially since you tell me you don't have any help or time away from Bryan. I am just trying to imagine what Bryan is trying to say, so that you and I can stop his crying. Sometimes it helps when we try to think about a time when we were babies like Bryan. Did you cry a lot, for instance?

M: I don't know. I don't think so. It was just me and my mom and dad, and no one said I cried a lot, so how can I know?

W: So you were an only child?

M: Yes. My mom had a miscarriage before I was born, but then she had me!

W: A miscarriage?

M: Well, not really. A stillborn. Actually, he died when he was six months old.

W: Oh? Her son died?

M: I never thought about it like that. My parents never talked about it. They never even had a funeral for him.

W: Never talked about it?

M: No. It was one of those things we never talked about: that, and the fact that they had a daughter. I mean, they really wanted a son even though they never had one.

W: Never had one?

M: Well, you can't count my brother. He was only six months old.

W: The same age as Bryan (pause) and now you are at home just like your mother.

M: Oh, she wasn't at home. She never stayed at home. I was always with babysitters—and what a lot there were! I only remember one really mean one though.

While all dialogues do not progress as quickly as this one, the worker's simple reflective statements prompt the mother to recall her own childhood and attend to her own injuries. The worker opens up time and space for the mother to express her anger over a very frightening babysitter who emotionally and physically abused her. This babysitter, and the indifferent parental care she received, added to her attachment injuries. She links the intermittent and sometimes abusive caregiving she received to the concerned caregiving she gives to Bryan. This link is empowering and she begins to feel more competent and confident in her parenting. This is not a quick fix. Attachment injuries linger throughout our lives and are the internal working model for intimacy—the intimacy we have or the intimacy we miss. This mother may need many more meetings before she feels confident enough to respond to Bryan with contact comfort. Her recognition of her own attachment injuries is her first step towards this healthy attachment.

The worker may also want to explore the mother's perception of and feelings towards her son. The worker asks her about Bryan and watches as she describes his behaviours, feelings, and routines. The worker carefully notes the mother's expressive and body language as well as her defensiveness or irritation when asked **open-ended questions**. The worker identifies areas of concern. These may include any of the following:

- expressions of anger about the needs of the child
- depictions of the child as a burden, a friend, or a helper
- negative descriptions of the child as manipulative, clumsy, slow, or stupid
- lack of concern or indifference toward the growth and development of the child
- disappointment in the child and the child's abilities or potential
- vague prenatal or postnatal memories of the child
- limited knowledge of the child's preferences

The mother's expression of feelings about Bryan adds to the worker's understanding of the relationship. When she demonstrates willingness to work on her attachment issues with Bryan, and to confront her frightening and frightened caregiving behaviours, the worker can involve her and Bryan in play-based interventions. These interventions can draw out even further her perceptions of and feelings towards Bryan as well as her own attachment issues. Afterwards the worker can encourage reflection on the play through the use of open-ended questions, silence, and scaffolding supported by video playback or simple recall of the playtime. This prompts the mother to pause and reflect upon her relationship with Bryan. Table 4.1 demonstrates how caregiving behaviour can stimulate feelings of insecurity, fear, anger, and detachment in the child, all of which contribute to insecure attachment.

Table 4.1 Stimulus-Response in Insecure Attachment

Caregiver Behaviour	Child Response
· Withdrawal through physical distance	· Feelings of being unlovable or unwanted
· Focus on toys rather than the child	· Insecurity and isolation
· Distancing from the child	· Detachment
· Ignoring and hushing the child	· Mistrust
· Frightening and erratic behaviours and moods Erratic changes in voice tone, volume, speed	· Insecurity and fear
· Role confusion demonstrated through alternating threats and pleas	· Insecurity and fear
· Laughing at child's distress, teasing, mocking	· Feelings of being unlovable and insignificant
· Withholding toys	· Confusion and fear
· Pretending to leave	· Insecurity and fear

When the caregiver raises her voice or shouts, the child may either mimic this shouting or move away to escape the shouting. When the caregiver distances herself from the play and becomes detached and aloof, the child may either move away or try to get closer to the caregiver. When the caregiver reprimands or scolds the child, the child may repeat this action with a doll or simply hit the doll with a toy. As the caregiver watches and reflects upon the impact of her behaviour on the child, the caregiver may better understand why the child screams, cries, or remains impassive and detached. This insight leads to deeper sensitivity to the child's emotional needs.

Summary

Tracing the development of early attachment between the child and the caregiver or community of caregivers, this chapter explores the actions and contexts that help or hinder this relationship. The importance of the secure emotional base that attachment provides is evident in the contrasting descriptions provided here of the child with a healthy attachment and the child with an insecure or unhealthy attachment. Interventions with the child and the caregiver can help to build secure attachment or to repair the injuries caused by an insecure attachment. So much in a child's life depends upon healthy relationships, and one of the most important bonds can be that between the child and the worker. For this relationship to be healthy, it must be built on congruence, respect, and empathy, as well as cultural competency. This is the subject of our next chapter.

Review Questions

1. When and how does healthy attachment begin?
2. Name three researchers who have studied attachment and their contribution to this theory.
3. Explain how you would work with caregivers of children with attachment injuries.
4. Why is healthy attachment so important for the child's socio-emotional development?
5. Compare and contrast the three kinds of insecure or unhealthy attachment.
6. Which behaviours of a young child indicate that there is a healthy attachment between the young child and the caregiver?
7. What is synchrony? How does it develop between two persons?
8. How do microsystem, mesosystem, and macrosystem determinants impact attachment?
9. Of the four structural causes of attachment injuries, which one do you feel is the most detrimental to the child? Explain.
10. Name three possible interventions that can help to heal a child's attachment injuries.

Discussion Questions

1. How can structural determinants be altered to encourage the development of healthy attachment between caregiver and infant? Are there programs that facilitate such change?
2. Do you think it is possible to heal attachment injuries that occur in the first year of life? What evidence do you have that this is either possible or impossible?
3. Healthy attachment is considered the basis for forming healthy adult relationships. Reflecting on your own experiences, do you think this is true? Why or why not?

5 Relationships

Uncle drummed and everyone sang as Solomon lifted the mask to his face and danced. Beneath their feet the spring sunshine warmed the ground and woke a dormant maple seed. As Solomon danced above, the tip of a root sprouted below and pushed into the loamy earth. "Ahhh," whispered the cedars to each other. "A new beginning."

—Andrea Spalding, *Solomon's Tree*

This scene from *Solomon's Tree* (2002), Andrea Spalding's children's book about a Tsimshian community in Canada, takes place after the Elders ask the young Solomon about the condition of his maple tree, and he shares his grief for his broken, dead friend. The Elders' active listening empowers Solomon to find a pathway to recovery. Solomon watches, learning, as the Elders make a mask from the dead branches. Then he joins in the task and makes a mask to fit his own face. He lifts it and dances, thus finding a new beginning.

In 1940, psychologist Carl Rogers set in motion just such a new beginning for social services when he challenged the traditional dynamic between worker and client. Working *with* clients rather than telling them what to do, he positioned them as equals—as persons with rights who were deserving of respect. Like the Elders in Solomon's community, Rogers led from behind, listening with **congruence**, **empathy**, and **respect**. By listening rather than speaking, he defined in a moment healthy working relationships.

The strength and wisdom of this respectful approach to relationships, with roots in both Aboriginal and Rogerian practice, seems obvious, yet it continues to elude the authoritarian workers who reinforce dichotomous relationships in which one person (the helper or giver) has all of the answers and the power, and the other person (the helped or receiver) can only passively accept help. Authoritarian workers feel validated by their elevation to the superior position of helpers and authorities but, at the same time, they are trapped in their own self-made "helping prison" (Dass and Gorman, 1997: 122–52). They disempower children by putting them into the inferior position of being helped and receiving services.

In this chapter, we will explore the Rogerian worker–client relationship and analogous Aboriginal healing practices. This journey may feel strange and unsettling to those more familiar with authoritarian approaches to children and more comfortable with their own childism. These workers feel they have little to learn from children and much to teach them. They document their meetings with children rather than discover the children they meet with, and they tie up their documentation with confidentiality practices that are often detrimental to these children. They disregard the rights of children and the Rogerian relationship with its rights-based approach. The rights-based approach empowers the child to embrace personal change and move forward in the dance of life. This chapter concludes with a description of how this approach is exemplified in **community capacity building**, through which the child can experience learning without being taught, just as Spalding's Solomon is able to do within a community that cares. If both overt and covert barriers are openly and honestly challenged, community capacity building can include the child as an equal participant and a valued community member.

Objectives

By the end of this chapter, you will:

- Understand how to develop a power-sharing and respectful relationship with children, and how to overcome relationship resistance.
- Identify the components of documentation that can be developed with the child.
- Demonstrate how to plan and participate in a community capacity building activity that involves children as equal and valued participants.

Healthy Working Relationships

In the biomedical, deficit-based approach described in Chapter 1, the worker identifies and assesses the child as being at risk or having problems; in fact, the child is often seen *as* the problem. The worker visits the family home, not to establish a relationship but to collect "facts" or reality bites about the family that provide further evidence against them. The worker speaks *to* the family members rather than *with* them and assesses the family situation, clipboard in hand. Henry Parada (2002: 106) describes this authoritarian power construct: "An assessment is already made, and the purpose of meeting the family is to corroborate the assessment."

The worker represents a larger, more powerful structure with bureaucratic protocols and systems. The worker is the expert who plans the intervention, sometimes in collaboration with the family and sometimes not. The worker bases this intervention on pre-existing assessments of the child, applies the intervention to the child, and then assesses the result. Adjustments follow, and the intervention is reapplied or a new intervention is tried based on the "expert assessment" of the worker. Both the power and the solution lie with the worker rather than the family, who must conform to the dictates of the worker.

The worker may have good intentions and may want to be a helper. However, these intentions and these wants are worker-centred: they are based on the premise that the worker holds the solutions or remedies to the family's problems. Such help is grounded in the worker's control of the situation and is inherently disempowering for the child and family. This approach reinforces the traditional power dynamic between helper and helped and causes the child and the family to feel helpless simply because they have been put into the role of being helped. Cindy Blackstock and her colleagues (2006: 5) quote historian John Milloy in describing the damage done by helpers with "good" intentions:

> Doing "good" is apparently better than doing "nothing" well—and so hangs the tale of the residential school system and the child welfare system too, which could only ever afford child protection (removal of children from their families), rather than prevention activity (building up families). Those good people constantly lobbied for better funding but rarely made any structural critiques and thus they became fellow travelers of a system they did not approve of and earned the ill feeling of those to whom they delivered second-class service.

However well-intentioned, help that is rooted in power and control tends to hurt children and families rather than help them. The child's competence and capability to solve problems is undermined because needing help suggests incompetence. The child's feeling of being in control is diminished because the child is put into the position of being helped by others according to their timetable and direction. The child's helplessness develops as the child becomes increasingly dependent on adult help and resources. Re-victimized by the helping adult, the child feels that he or she has nothing to contribute to the relationship with the helper. With nothing to contribute, some children resist the restricting, limiting "help" being offered and instinctively look for a window of escape. This traditional helping model can be likened to the wheel in a gerbil's cage: it goes around and around as the worker chases the child in circles, gaining little ground.

The working relationship developed within Rogerian client-centred practice is based on mutual respect and shared power and control (Rogers, 1951: 41). The cage is replaced by a level playing field on which the worker is a coach who builds on the child's assets and strengths to secure the child's position in centre field. The worker assumes that the child has the inner strength for healing and problem solving and can be an active and equal participant in the intervention. A respectful sharing of viewpoints and searching for solutions takes place, rather than a struggle for control and domination. More than just a shift in perspective, the **Rogerian model** demands a

© Corbis

Photo 5.1 The soccer coach builds on the strengths and hopes of the players.

complete change in power dynamics in that it is based upon congruence, empathy, and respect, all of which are attributes of power sharing.

Congruence refers to the alignment between words and deeds, between what the worker says and what the worker does. No promises are made about confidentiality, resources, or care that cannot be kept. Empathy refers to the worker's ability and willingness to understand what the child feels and thinks and to communicate this understanding to the child. Respect is demonstrated by the worker's acceptance or unconditional positive regard for the whole child. Rogers (1951) maintains that these three worker attributes, discussed more fully below, are essential to a healthy working relationship between worker and child.

Achieving congruence is not easy because it requires the worker to tell the whole truth to the child and not keep secrets. The worker honestly acknowledges when either the law or agency policy requires that confidentiality be broken, even when this broken confidentiality angers and disappoints the child. Because many of the laws related to consent and confidentiality do not respect the child as a person, this congruence is difficult to fully achieve. Table 5.1 demonstrates the difference between worker statements that are congruent and those that deliberately mislead the child, "helping" statements that do no "good."

Table 5.1 Congruency

Congruent Statements	Helping Statements
When you say "secret," I cannot keep a "secret" because the law sees you as a child. If the secret harms you or someone else, or if it is a secret about abuse or neglect, then the law requires me to tell someone.	Don't worry. Your secrets are safe with me. Tell me everything that happened and I promise that nobody else will know.
I am making notes on what you are saying and I am going to share these notes with you. Then you can sign and date them. Only you, I, and my supervisor see these notes.	I am just jotting down a few notes for myself so that I remember what you have said. These notes are just for me.
The agency does not allow you to see your file until you turn 18. Even then, you will not have access to your mom's current address.	I will put in the request for you but it may take some time. Once you get your file you'll be able to contact your mom.
Your dad is not able to care for you now so you are being placed in a foster home for the next three months.	You are going to a great home with lots of other kids. It's just for a short time until your dad can come by and get you.
The high school cannot re-admit you until you make a commitment to attend every day.	We have decided that you will do a correspondence course. It'll be a lot easier for you than high school.

The helping statements are comforting for the child. The congruent statements, on the other hand, may provoke the child's anger and sadness, and the child may become silent, leave the room, or shout at the worker. However, this congruence is fundamental to a healthy working relationship between the worker and the child as equals and part-ners in seeking solutions.

The second worker characteristic Rogers insists on is empathy, or warmth and responsiveness. These qualities encourage the child to freely express feelings of hatred, envy, remorse, guilt, anger, and resentment, even when these feelings are described by others as wrong, bad, cruel, or shameful. When the child expresses dissatisfaction with parents or teachers, the worker unconditionally affirms the feelings the child expresses and does not respond by arguing or defending the child's parents or other professionals. The worker responds with empathy, placing the child's dissatisfaction within a structural construct. The worker may say, "Exams and tests can be really stressful" or "Social housing is just not adequate for families, and forces them to squeeze into small spaces." Rogers (1951: 41) describes the merits of this empathetic approach: "In the emotional warmth of the relationship . . . the client begins to experience a feeling of safety as he finds that whatever attitude he expresses is understood in almost the same way that he perceives it, and is accepted."

The third crucial characteristic of the Rogerian relationship is respect: the worker's unconditional positive regard for the child as a person, not as a vulnerable innocent or property of the family or social capital (see Chapter 2). Respect is not the same as the overly sympathetic, often patronizing, indulgent praise sometimes heard in adult–child situations: "Oh, aren't they sweet?"; "What an adorable child"; "Kids say the darndest things." Instead, respect entails the worker's caring and appreciation for the child as a unique person. Landon Pearson (2008: vii) describes this deep valuation of the child: "Respecting children goes beyond merely listening to what they have to say. It means hearing their words with your eyes, your ears, your heart, and your undivided attention. It advocates using the voice of children to inform action." The respectful worker is emotionally constant and responsive to the child, matching activity type and level to the child's cues. The worker practises attunement or interactive synchrony, engaging when the child is ready and beginning at the child's interest and developmental level. When the child signals the need to disengage, the worker supports this need and does not impose adult plans, timelines, or solutions on the child. Respect entails working *with* the child rather than *on* the child.

Congruence, empathy, and respect are interrelated, overlapping in a child-centred focus that is very similar to the traditional Aboriginal way of working with children, based on Medicine Wheel teachings. Describing this approach, Jane Gilgun (2002: 68) notes, "The framework assumes trust, mutuality, and reciprocity between young people and the persons to whom they relate." To return to the example of Andrea Spalding's novel, when Solomon's maple tree dies and he is devastated by the loss, the Elders of his community hear him and do not judge his grief as silly, foolish, or childish. Instead, they ask open, respectful questions in order to understand the boy's feelings: "Did your tree have a voice?" and "Did your tree smell nice?" (Spalding, 2002: 17). Solomon's community works with his grief, encircling it with spirituality and a love for Mother Earth. Through the empowering and very physical experience of creating, alongside his community, a mask from his tree, Solomon is able to transform his grief into something more positive that will help him move forward. As he lifts the mask to his face and dances, a new maple tree sprouts from the seed of his old tree, symbolizing the life connection between Solomon, the Elders, the community, and the earth.

In this client-centred, collaborative practice, advocated by Rogers (1951), Ram Dass and Paul Gorman (1997), bell hooks (1994), and Paulo Freire (2000), the key element is mutual respect. Hooks (1994: 54) notes,

> Authentic help means that all who are involved help each other mutually, growing together in the common effort to understand the reality which they seek to transform. Only through such praxis—in which those who help and those who are being helped help each other simultaneously—can the act of helping become free from the distortion in which the helper dominates the helped.

In child-centred practice, the child experiences a sense of emotional and physical safety that encourages further self-exploration and reflection on structural determinants. Freire (2000) calls this **conscientization**, an internal exploratory process in which people develop an understanding of their collective **oppression** through learning about the structural impacts on their lives. Conscientization normalizes personal difficulty, connecting it to difficulties experienced by others who are equally oppressed. Children experience mandatory schooling, curfews, and apprehensions and understand how the structure (education, poverty, foster care, gender roles, power constructs) impacts their daily lives in a country that does not uphold international law as stipulated in the Convention on the Rights of the Child. Children are already primed for conscientization and ready to engage with the worker in this process.

Rogers (1951) notes the impact of boundaries on this process. Agreed-on boundaries circumscribe the healthy relationship between worker and child and help the child feel physically and emotionally secure. When the worker crosses these boundaries, the child begins to feel unsafe and less liable to engage in conscientization. The worker who extends the meeting time, for instance, because the child is upset or wants to play longer in the playroom, is jeopardizing the established limits and safety of the relationship. The worker who needs to be admired by the child and asks the child for praise ("Do you like coming here?") threatens these same boundaries, as does the worker who offers personal affection to the child ("You know what? I really like you. You are my friend.").

Establishing and maintaining boundaries in the worker–child relationship shows respect for the personhood of the child. Because workers influence the lives of children, they are held to a higher standard in fiduciary relationships with children and are solely responsible for maintaining professional boundaries. Subsections of the Code of Ethics for the Canadian Association of Social Workers (2005) prescribe the following worker responsibilities regarding trust and boundaries:

2.2.1 Social workers do not exploit the relationship with a client for personal benefit, gain, or gratification.

2.4.1 Social workers take care to evaluate the nature of dual and multiple relationships to ensure that the needs and welfare of clients are protected.

2.5.1 Social workers avoid engaging in physical contact with clients when there is a possibility of harm to the client as a result of the contact.

2.6.1 Social workers do not engage in romantic relationships, sexual activities, or sexual contact with clients, even if such contact is sought by clients.

This code of ethics is a guideline only, not a legal document. Words such as "romantic" (2.6.1), "possibility" (2.5.1), and "nature" (2.4.1) are inherently ambiguous and indicate the difficulty of enforcing prescriptive codes. The effectiveness of such codes relies on trained workers applying the principles in a thoughtful and ethical way, as described by Brian Wharf and Brad McKenzie (2004: 160): "Our vision of the professional is one who surrenders the desire to control while acknowledging that there are some limits imposed by legislation, by budgets or, increasingly, by time. These professionals welcome the contributions of those being served and work hard to establish relationships characterized by partnership."

Documentation

The healthy working relationship is openly and honestly documented: nothing is "off the record." Every email, telephone call, or face-to-face meeting with a child, child's family, or **collateral** is recorded. For almost a century, since Mary Richmond's *Social Diagnosis* (1917), those who work with children have had the responsibility to document, not only to record their work but also to organize it into specific content areas. The worker writes case notes, daily log notes, progress notes, case management reports, and minutes of meetings, and completes provincial or agency mandated forms such as safety assessments, risk assessments, consent forms, contact sheets, service plans, plans of care, and behavioural checklists. These documents are put into the child's file along with the child's school reports, health records, and psychological reports from collaterals. Table 5.2 indicates some of the documents that children's workers may have to prepare or complete.

Documentation is textually regulated and must fit into prescribed formats. It is considered to be valid although it is socially constructed through the process of transcribing and categorizing. Gerald deMontigny (1995: 64) describes this process: "The text is a mask, concealing the embodied speaker who utters this or that claim. Through the text, social workers can promote their claims as though these were the universal wisdom of the profession in general." The worker who documents takes on the persona of a professional with universal wisdom who can speak for the child. The worker, who may have never met the child before the event, is the interviewer and expert who transforms the child's room into an "unsafe bedroom" and the child's play into "inappropriate behaviour." This categorization is demanded by the agency in the safety assessment: "In all cases, the representation is designed by the conceptual organization of an institutional discourse to which the actuality it represents must be fitted" (Smith, 2005: 186).

In her institutional ethnography (2005), Dorothy Smith appropriated Karl Marx's terminology of "tricks" to describe what happens when the worker translates reality into institutional discourse or documentation. The first trick separates what is said from its context: the child becomes either an acronym or a client. Seven-year-old Mohammed, strong and articulate and a defender of the family through their five years in a refugee camp, becomes M.R. His elder sister, raped at age six, becomes W.R. The child's manner of speech, beliefs, and emotions become secondary to the child's words as "information." A phrase or word from the child is pulled away from the facial expression, the commotion on the street that makes him apprehensive, or the child's sob. The phrase or word, the accent and intonation, are lost in the words on the page

Table 5.2 Types of Documentation

Document	Description	Purpose
Case note	Objective, accurate recording of an event	Document an event (phone call, meeting, home visit, critical incident) Provide evidence supporting risk assessments, affidavits, or service plans
Daily log note	Objective, accurate running record of the day's events at a group home or residential care facility	Provide a foundation for planning interventions with the child
Progress note/ case management report	Record of achievement of measurable outcomes of behavioural interventions	Ensure that interventions are documented and completed and that measurable outcomes have been met
Minutes of meetings	Record of where, when, and who met, what was discussed, and who is responsible for each proposed action	Provide a written record of the meeting and the decisions made during that meeting
Safety assessment	Checklist of immediate (microsystem) dangers to the child	Assess whether or not the child should remain in the home
Risk assessment	Rating scale of risk and protective factors within the child's immediate environment	Assess the likelihood of future maltreatment of the child
Consent form	Signed and witnessed written agreement (to treatment, to share information, to be adopted)	Ensure that the child understands and agrees to share personal information or participate in the particular service or plan
Contact sheet/ Activity log	A list of persons met, as well as the dates and locations of these meetings, activity accomplished, and action required	Ensure that every effort has been made to contact and meet with clients and collaterals and follow up on their input
Service plan	Detailed plan of action including resources to be provided and outcomes to be met	Record proposed plan to ensure the child's safety in the home
Plan of care	Plan for alternative care of the child including timelines, expectations, and planned supports. Plan of care may also include specifics such as dietary restrictions, tutoring needs, religious requirements, and holiday plans	Indicate how the child's current and longer term needs will be met in alternative care. Facilitate collaboration among parents and foster parents, foster care workers, and child's worker
Behavioural checklist	Screening tool for behaviours such as aggression, anxiety, attention deficits, and depression	Provide a foundation for planning behavioural interventions

and may even assume a meaning contrary to the one intended by the child speaker. A mother may say, between sobs, that she once gave her child a spanking. The case note is written as follows: "R.T. admits physical abuse (spanking) of B.T. on March 4, 2013." This admission in the case note, coupled with the mother's struggle with alcohol and chronic poverty, may be enough for her children to be apprehended, removed from her arms and from her home.

The second trick is the categorization of the child according to agency protocol. Agency mandated forms divide the whole child into risk factors, deficits, or domains. The child behaves and the adult labels the behaviour and, in doing so, recreates the child. A parent's self is also categorized to fit the mandate of the agency, whether it be child protection, mental health, or addiction treatment. A parent's choice to live in the woods is described by a worker as "social isolation" and a "risk factor." A Mexican father's struggle to answer questions is recorded as "low literacy level" and a "parental risk factor." Neither the smell of the pine forest nor the warmth of the Spanish language is captured in the documentation. These are impressions rather than facts, so they are not included.

A child's strengths, or those of the parent, are rarely captured because documentation is problem-oriented and is expected to pinpoint problems, deficits, and risk factors rather than strengths. The father's skill in carpentry and cooking is extraneous information for which no checklist line exists. There may be a line called "adequate nutrition" on which the father may fail because there is no milk in the kitchen. There may be a line called "living room safe for toddlers" that the father may also fail because he has left his hammer or sandpaper on the rug. The father's culinary and carpentry skills are not relevant and are not recorded.

The Ontario Risk Assessment Model (Ontario Ministry of Community and Social Services, 2000) demonstrates this second trick. This model presents 11 risk decisions with set timelines, plus a requirement that the worker rate the caregiver on a Risk Eligibility Spectrum. There is no Capability Spectrum or Asset Checklist. At the first meeting, the worker must rate the caregiver from 0 to 4 on the CG4 (Caregiver Report 4) as follows:

0   Very accepting of the child
1   Limited acceptance of the child
2   Indifferent and aloof to the child
3   Disapproves of and resents the child
4   Rejects and is hostile to the child

Most caregivers have at some time acted in all five ways towards their children. A caregiver may resent the crying child early in the morning and be very accepting by mid-morning. If the child breaks a treasured gift, the caregiver may appear hostile or indifferent to the child. A caregiver may move from 0 to 4 and back again in one morning! The worker interviewing the caregiver might see any one, or several, of these manifested feelings and write a case note to justify the rating. This rating is extremely important in determining the future of the child. If the caregiver's manifested feelings score high (3–4), then the child's place in the home may be in jeopardy and the child may be apprehended.

The third trick is making the child believe in the documentation rather than the reality of his or her daily life. The child who is labelled as a "slow learner" or as having a "behaviour problem" begins to act according to what has been recorded (see Chapter 1). The child takes on the attributes of struggling to learn or acting out. The document describing an event, a family dynamic, or a behaviour gradually becomes more real than the actual event, family dynamic, or behaviour. If the documentation describes "dysfunction," then the child begins to act out dysfunction every day so as to make the documentation seem more accurate.

Christie Barron (2000: 48) describes her review of the files of Canadian young offenders: "The files contain massive amounts of information, ranging from youth risk assessments and custody reports to case management reports and daily program logs, providing a valuable source for understanding how authorities interpret the youth's behaviour." Note Barron's deliberate wording. These very full files are a source for understanding "how authorities interpret the youth's behaviour"—which is to say, the institutional construction of the youth's behaviour using the three tricks just described. When Barron meets some of the young offenders whose files she has reviewed, she encounters a very different reality. During her meetings with the young offenders, they do not behave in the same way as they are portrayed in their files. The agency-centred reality in the young offenders' files does not include the youth's own photos, personal notes, and journal entries, evidence of their strengths that do not fit into the prescribed notion of documentation.

Barron describes the difference between the young offenders and the documentation, a dichotomy that affirms the power and control issues inherent in agencies and the lack of power of the children and youth. Yolanda Lambe (2009: 22), former research director of Youth in Care Network (now Youth in Care Canada) notes, "When a youth has a behavioural problem it all has to be 'chemical imbalance'; it has to be something wrong with the brain, not something wrong with their environment, or their resources that they're receiving, or their support." Workers know the power of their documentation as a basis for medicating children. They know that their documents can be **subpoenaed** by the courts and used by judges as the basis for life-changing decisions for the children. In this way, workers who document become judges rather than witnesses to the child's healing, morality enforcers rather than morality models of the honesty, empathy, and congruence called for by Rogers.

Documentation is expected to be professional, honest, and accurate. This is tested when the people named in the document are encouraged to read documentation and verify its accuracy by signing it. When collaterals are asked to approve and sign a document they are empowered by this request. In this way, documentation can increase the likelihood of their collaboration because they are, at least, informed of the plan and,

---

👥 Group Exercise   5.1

Hot Docs

Hot Docs is the name of the Canadian international documentary film festival; it is also an apt title for this large group exercise on the power of documentation. Objective and accurate documentation is fundamental in the preparation for meetings with children and families, meetings with collaterals, court statements and **affidavits**, and advocacy work.

This exercise begins by the group leader asking participants to watch a brief (five-minute) video clip and case note what they see. Afterwards, volunteers are asked to read their case notes aloud. The leader notes on a white board or flip chart paper which words seem to be subjective and which facts seem to be inaccurate. This leads to a group discussion on the challenges of note-taking, the subjectivity in witnessing an event, and the bias in recording. Participants are then asked to relate this to the three tricks described by Smith (1998). This exercise concludes with the group development of a guide for effective documentation.

---

at best, are part of this plan. The child also has the right to see and read all documentation pertaining to him/her, although few children are aware of this right, and fewer still access this right. Those who do read their own documentation feel empowered by this process and better equipped to work collaboratively with their workers.

Workers who fail to document professionally and accurately do not share their documentation with children, families, or collaterals, and their duplicity often puts themselves and the children whom they serve at risk. Their documents are riddled with inaccuracies, vagueness, and half-truths. They may write things like, "a couple of times" or "could have been on Thursday," and they may use these vague notions as the basis for their interventions. They intervene because "it feels right" rather than because their collaborative planning is documented and approved by the children, caregivers, and collaterals who are involved.

The format of documentation continues to change. Today most documentation is word processed and **encrypted**, and then either stored or forwarded to a supervisor or collateral for final approval. The professional requirements for documentation remain the same: honesty, accuracy, and objectivity. Documentation that misleads or tricks the reader, as described by Dorothy Smith, does irreparable damage to the children and families who are documented. The child-focused worker uses a documentation checklist (Table 5.3) to verify the integrity of all documents in the child's file.

The child's file contains this documentation and is secured in a locked cabinet or on an encrypted USB flash drive. Workers, other than the child's worker and supervisor, are typically allowed access to this file only on a "need to know" basis. When a particular

---

Table 5.3 Documentation Checklist

❑ Notes completed, signed, and dated within 24 hours of any intervention, incident, or meeting. All amendments and corrections also signed and dated.

❑ Indicates exactly what has been seen and heard—nothing more and nothing less.

❑ Concrete and accurate with no imprecise, relative words such as "tall," "small," "dark," "many," "normal," and "some."

❑ Assumptions or opinions prefaced with qualifiers such as "appears to be" or "seems" (e.g., Hibo appears to weigh between 50 and 52 kilos.).

❑ Conclusions supported by evidence or direct quotes (e.g., The boy seemed angry as he punched the wall six times before refusing to sit down.).

❑ Formal language in the third-person used. Slang, jargon, and expletives used only when included in a direct quote.

❑ Context provided for direct quotes in order to fairly represent the circumstances in which the words were said.

❑ Acronyms followed by the bracketed original word.

❑ Participants identified by first and last names and complete addresses.

---

document is removed from the file, this action is noted on the summary sheet, and a photocopy of this document is kept in the file until the original is returned. The summary sheet lists the child's name, address, date of birth, physical description, family, other household members, medical history and doctors' names, medication, allergies, school, part-time jobs, referral source, and the titles of all of the documents in the file. A dated photo of the child is usually attached to the summary sheet. The child's file is retained for a specific number of years as dictated by agency policy or college codes of conduct. Some files, such as adoption files, must be kept for the lifetime of the child. Other files are kept for only seven years after the child reaches the age of majority.

Confidentiality

Confidentiality prevents the sharing of information without expressed and signed consent. The capacity to consent and the rules of confidentiality are determined by legislated age limits, both upper and lower. These age limits vary among the provinces and territories; even within an individual province or territory, professions and colleges dictate varying age limits for consenting to service and interventions. This variation and complexity can confound workers who are trying to explain to children why confidentiality cannot be guaranteed because of lower or upper age limits (see Chapter 2). In Ontario, for example, the child welfare system requires children aged 7 and older to provide written consent to being adopted, and children aged 16 and older to provide written consent to leave the foster care system. Both consents, one at age 7 and one at age 16, have life-changing effects. In the first instance, the child consents to severing all ties with all members of his or her family of origin, including extended family. In the second instance, the child consents to losing all child welfare services, which include counselling, housing, financial support, and educational funding, among others. That these consents are required and are considered valid—one at age 7 and one at age 16— demonstrates the variation in age determinants of capacity for consent in Ontario.

The adults in the child's life—guardians, parents, or the state acting as guardian— typically have first rights of consent. When a child approaches a worker without parental knowledge or consent, this action is considered to be **implied consent** to treatment. However, the law generally supports parents and guardians who forbid counselling of their minor children,[1] except under extenuating circumstances; this law takes precedence over agency practice and all codes of ethics. This is why workers usually try to obtain **express consent** from the adults in the child's life unless danger to the child may result from doing so. A child's safety could be jeopardized, for instance, in cases in which the parent is alleged to be an abuser. If the parent is informed that the child has sought help, the parent may further harm the child. Federal law also recognizes **mature minors**, children who are considered to be able to fully understand the implications of service or treatment. In most provinces and territories, mature minors can consent to non-therapeutic treatments such as termination of pregnancy, blood donation, cosmetic surgery, and provision of contraceptives (Rozovsky, 2003).

Point to Consider   5.1

Infant Consents

How do infants consent to interventions? They are not yet able to speak, write, or understand a consent form. As persons they have a right to withhold or grant consent, but this right is assumed by adults who consent on their behalf. The child-focused worker needs to reflect on these questions prior to assuming this consent:

- Would this infant consent to being physically examined by a stranger?
- Would this infant consent to being placed in a stranger's home?
- Would this infant consent to giving up breastmilk in favour of bottled formula?
- Would this infant consent to not seeing sisters and brothers, aunts, uncles, and cousins for the next month?

While the infant's safety and care is the worker's primary concern, attention to these questions affirms the infant's right to consent, and the worker's responsibility in understanding and speaking on behalf of the infant in assuming this consent.

A child may be monitored by many different people, such as a child protection worker, foster care worker, family physician, psychiatrist, teacher, sports coach, and foster parent. The child protection worker is trying to collect evidence; the foster care worker is allocating a per diem rate for the child's daily needs; the doctor is treating the child's injuries; the psychiatrist is assessing the child's mental health and perhaps beginning therapy and/or medication; the teacher is planning the child's upcoming test; the sports coach is wondering whether or not the child can make the next out-of-town sports meet; and the foster parent is wondering how to access information about the child's family history, health, or school records.

Photo 5.2 Does this infant consent to leaving a parent?

Legislation related to consents and confidentiality restricts the information available to each of these professionals and **paraprofessionals**. Psychologists, psychiatrists, doctors, child and youth workers, social workers, parole officers, and early childhood educators are guided by their colleges and associations and their codes of ethics and are often caught in ethical dilemmas posed by conflicting agency, union, and association or college rules. In addition, and probably more important for the child, each person has vital information about the child that can be shared. But they may not share this information, and one of them may function as a gatekeeper for the child's life, retaining all of the information about the child and choosing which information to provide to which person.

Sometimes, to ensure the child and family's confidentiality, agencies, associations, colleges, or unions may prohibit the sharing of information about the child with the foster parent. As a result, the foster parent has only limited information on which to base daily decisions around caregiving. Child welfare agencies operating within the same city may be restricted by agency policy and may not even be allowed to share information with a worker at another agency in the same city who is investigating the abuse of another child in the same family. This inability to share information can seriously jeopardize the safety of the children in this family.[2] The counselling records of parents can be shared with child welfare workers only with the parents' consent; without this consent, the worker needs to apply to the courts. Child abuse registries that list child abusers operate in some provinces and not in others, and access to these registries is limited. There is no national child abuse registry in Canada, although the government occasionally expresses an interest in developing one.[3] Confidentiality can result in a failure to recognize the child's rights, and the child receiving inappropriate and poorly timed services or even being put in an unsafe situation.

Children have very little privacy in their lives. They attend meetings in which adults talk about them rather than to them, which leads children to assume that all adults talk about them without them. They expect that their workers will tell their secrets, thoughts, and feelings to their parents, teachers, and group home staff. When their workers talk about confidentiality and consents, most children are skeptical and few believe that workers abide by the rules. Children assume that confidentiality means that adults know all about them and they know nothing about the adults. Children whose questions have not been answered because of "confidentiality" weigh their own experience against the worker's explanation of confidentiality. A congruent and child-focused worker might explain confidentiality in this way:

> You may have heard about confidentiality or seen this word on one of the forms. Confidentiality is like privacy. Confidentiality means that what you say to me is private and I am not allowed to repeat it to your parents, teachers, or anyone else. If I repeat your story to someone else without your permission, I am in big trouble. There is only one exception. If I think that you are in danger or at risk, or if I think someone is hurting you, I have to tell my supervisor or the police or the authorities.

This child-focused explanation can be followed by specific scenarios or applications of confidentiality:

- If you tell me you are not going to school any more, will I tell your parents?
- If you tell me that your brother keeps punching and hurting you, will I tell anyone?
- If you tell me you are sad and lonely, will I tell your teachers?

When the child understands these applications and feels confident in this understanding, the worker introduces consent forms. Each signed consent form allows the worker to talk to one specific collateral. The child needs to know that the worker cannot speak to any of these collaterals without this signed consent form (express consent). The child can then decide who can be given information and how this information can be shared.

As this explanation and signing of consent forms continues, children are simultaneously aware that they can check out their workers online, find out their workers' home addresses, past work experience, and publications. They can also email friends to assess their workers, and they may post these ratings or assessments on social network sites along with a witty review of their meeting. Children going into foster care know that they can email or call their families from school or a friend's home, far away from the watchful eyes of their foster parents and workers. Children know all of this during the worker's explanation of confidentiality, and children wonder about the importance and the relevancy of these consent forms.

That is why the explanation of confidentiality, boundaries, and privacy, along with the old and cumbersome consent forms, needs to change. Each agency will decide how to manage these changes, but it is certain that change must happen. Otherwise, workers lose credibility and the first meeting begins with skepticism and mistrust. Confidentiality, boundaries, and privacy are increasingly important simply because children are caught up in personal disclosures online all the time. The conversation about confidentiality needs to include privacy issues and what this means to the child. Children generally appreciate cautionary tales because they know intimately the dangers of online exposure both as exposers and those being exposed.

Relationship Resistance

Many of the children with whom we work have attachment injuries (see Chapter 4) and resist relationships with adults, particularly the strangers who come and go from their lives. Adults have consistently lied to them, let them down, or hurt them, so they are unlikely to seek out adults or knock on the door of a worker or counsellor. Relationship resistance is an understandable coping strategy for children who have been battered by previous relationships with adults who control and hurt them. These adults have been and may continue to be the context for the child's daily life.

Steve de Shazer's categorization differentiates **visitors**, **clients**, and **customers** of worker interventions. In de Shazer's (1984) terminology, a child is the involuntary visitor who is brought to the worker or some social control agent who holds all of the power. The child may be forced to participate in an intervention by parents who want a solution, child welfare workers who want a disclosure, or a parole officer who wants behavioural compliance. The child is the visitor who is compelled to be involved.

This forced involvement leaves children feeling powerless or disempowered. They may fear or mistrust the worker, or feel hostility towards the worker because of the worker's race, ethnicity, age, gender, or sexual orientation. They may have had previous negative experiences with adults and authority figures and may believe that workers don't listen and won't help. They may be influenced by media portrayals of workers as suspect or their family's distrust of both the system and those in authority. Children who are being bullied, abused, or neglected bring all of these feelings, plus the fear of foster care, to the relationship, and they often deny their original disclosures when workers ask them for details about the abuse or violence in the home (Trocmé et al., 2003).

A child may gradually become interested in being a client and receiving some limited services. However, only when the child is a willing and voluntary customer seeking out services can there be a collaborative working relationship. Rogers (1951) concurs with de Shazer's description of the customer being a willing and equal participant in the healthy working relationship. This equalization of power or empowerment of the child is essential for the child to shift from feeling powerless as an involuntary visitor, interested in service as a client, then in control of the relationship as a customer. Jake makes this shift from visitor to client when he takes control of the silence in Note from the Field 5.1. He may remain a client until the worker shares power with him and he becomes an equal participant or customer.

> ## Note from the Field   5.1
>
> ### Shifting Control
>
> Jake is sitting in the meeting room when I arrive. His hood is pulled over his baseball cap, his body sprawled over the chair. He grunts in answer to my first few questions and then shuts down entirely. I let the silence settle for several minutes. Finally Jake asks, "Can I leave now?" This is the opener that I wanted. Now that Jake is the questioner, he can take some control. Now this first meeting begins to feel promising!

The yawning chasm of silence between Jake and the worker feels uncomfortable. This silence is ambiguous and the worker can only speculate on its possible meanings:

- Leave me alone. Don't bother me.
- I don't trust you. I don't trust strangers.
- I'm watching you and listening.
- I don't understand a single word you say.
- You can't make me speak. I will be silent until I choose to talk.
- You mean nothing to me. You are boring and I will try to ignore you.

While this silence is ambiguous in meaning, it is also powerful, and the silent child controls the meeting. Relationship resistance clearly demonstrates the child's power, and the child-focused worker affirms this power and control rather than trying to break or undermine it by threatening, cajoling, or coercing the child to speak. Jake is the involuntary visitor who needs this affirmation of power at a meeting that he has clearly not asked for in the first place. With his question Jake assumes more control and he moves from being a visitor to being a client who wants a response. This is a pivotal moment: the door is ajar and the worker may slip through to make a connection by responding with warmth, empathy, and an acknowledgement of Jake's power. The worker may respond, "I know you don't want to be here, but you and I are stuck together for an hour. Is there something you'd like to work on since you're here anyway, or do you just want to wait out the hour?" At some point, in this meeting or in subsequent ones, Jake may feel empowered to become a customer and join with the worker in a healthy working relationship.

Sometimes the child does not break the silence to ask a question as Jake did. The child expects the worker to lose interest and shuffle papers, or lose control and order the child to speak or leave. It is confusing when the worker does not lose interest or become authoritarian and controlling. The worker may try to understand the meaning of the silence and say, "I understand why it is hard to trust a stranger, particularly an older person like myself. Take your time. Only tell me things when you are ready." The worker may then make some non-threatening comments that invite engagement, such as, "I see you've brought your backpack. You know I have almost the same one. Sometimes it feels a bit too small though. What about yours? Does it hold everything you need?"

An informal chat about sports, weather, movies, or video games, a self-deprecating humorous story, or an offer of food or drinks can reduce the pressure of keeping silent and increase the possibility of the worker understanding the meaning of this silence. The worker's respect, humour, warmth, and courtesy can defuse some of the child's resistance and help to equalize the power in the relationship:

- I'm having a snack attack. Would you like a granola bar?
- I don't have any coffee but would you like to choose a herbal tea? I'm having some.
- I think I'm getting a cold. Would you like a cup of hot cocoa?
- What kind of fruit do you like? I'm going to have an orange.

The intimacy of sharing granola bars, herbal tea, cocoa, or a piece of fruit can defuse relationship resistance and give the child some space and time just to talk over ordinary things: favourite snacks, drinks, or fruit. The child may also suggest different snacks to the worker or show a preference for certain snacks. Rather than plunging directly into the "problem," the worker and the child can spend some time relaxing, eating, and talking together. Food and drink can serve as a **metaphor**, a way to relate to a problem or issue:

- Do you ever get hungry like this in the middle of the day and just need to eat or leave the classroom?
- Herbal tea makes me feel peaceful. What about you?
- I guess we only drink cocoa in the wintertime. Did you do this last January too?
- Oranges are funny, sometimes sweet and sometimes a bit sour. Have you met people like that?

Alternatively, the worker can ask the silent child to be the expert:

- I'm stuck. Has this ever happened to you—the silent treatment?
- I need your advice. When your friends won't talk to you, what do you do?
- Silence sometimes makes my mind wander. Does that happen to you too?
- I'm probably way off base, but are you trying to say something to me?

It is important for the worker to remain upbeat and positive and continually affirm the child's capabilities by involving the child in the relationship and affirming the child's control.

This is difficult to do when the child launches verbal assaults. These can include offensive, hurtful, and rude remarks, laughter, and racist, ageist, homophobic, or sexist language. Verbal assaults are launched to undermine or derail relationship work, unhinge the worker, or simply sabotage (and end) the entire meeting. Workers can feel under attack, their confidence dented by the way the child is acting or speaking. It is important not to engage defensively or offensively with verbal assaults but to respect the child and listen to the underlying message. Each verbal assault tells a story, and it is this story or history that needs to be heard and understood.

- The child may say, "You really look stupid in that long skirt." The worker listens attentively to the words: "stupid" and "skirt." The worker may respond, "Do skirts seem stupid to you?" Alternatively, the worker may respond, "What could I wear that would look less stupid?"
- The child may say, "You're a real weirdo." The worker listens attentively to the word "weirdo." The worker may respond, "I am guessing that something I do is scary. What can I do to help you feel more comfortable?"

These responses demonstrate the worker's attentive listening and genuine desire to understand and join with the child. These responses are neither defensive nor offensive. There is no attempt to self-protect or to verbally assault the child. The focus is clearly on engagement.

Verbal assaults can be accompanied by equally offensive and rude body language. The child may roll her eyes, sneer, stick out her tongue, or get right into the worker's personal space. The child may put her feet on the worker's desk or knees, kick off her shoes, sit in the worker's chair, finger the worker's briefcase or personal effects, or try to crawl onto the worker's lap. Children and youth intuitively perceive what pushes the worker's buttons whether that is fingering a family picture, kicking a plant, or simply zoning out.

Once again, the worker contextualizes this body language, listening to it and trying to hear and understand the message underneath the language. If the worker reacts with irritation, sarcasm, or anger, the child or youth reacts similarly and ramps up the assault. This can become a control game that the worker always loses. A wide-angle lens shows that the child loses too, but this wider focus is missing in control games. The worker who pays careful attention to these non-verbal messages responds with interest and empathy and a desire to engage with the child:

- Are you angry with my plant?
- This colour seems to interest you. Why is that?
- Rolling your eyes tells some people that you're bored, but I think you are actually interested in what we're doing. I think the eye roll is just a nervous tic. Am I right?
- Do family pictures annoy you?
- How often do you stick your tongue out every day? How does that work for you? Would you be able to stick out your tongue more often if you tried? Let's try!

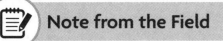

Note from the Field   5.2

Still Here

High staff turnover in group homes teaches youth not to form relationships with the staff, even those who appear to be concerned and caring. Youth know that workers are apt to come and go frequently, and they hear the staff longing for their weekends away from the "home." This adds to the young person's low self-esteem and feelings of being unwanted.

Alex was a veteran of the child welfare system, having graduated from a number of foster homes to this group home. She had seen 14 workers come and go over the last 8 months, and she was skilled at breaking new workers. On my first night shift Alex rolled her eyes at me, flashed her tongue ring, and said loudly, "What cage did you crawl out of?" Whenever I walked into the room she would point at me and laugh, "Look at that!" All my attempts to connect with her were met by sneers, guffaws, and swearing. During the December holidays, Alex was the only resident left. After her chore was done she hung back in the kitchen and said, "I suppose you want to hear about how I got here." When I replied, "Only if you want to tell me, Alex," she left the room. The next morning she was quiet. I made a lame joke about the eggs and she almost smiled. After that we developed a joking banter. She had a wicked sense of humour, and her droll commentary on everyday situations made me laugh. We rarely disagreed as she tended to keep a low profile during my shift. I was into my eighth month at the home when I went into the common room to shut off the lights. Alex was texting. We started talking about a recent television episode when Alex interrupted, "How come you never ask me how I got here?"

"I guess I figured you would tell me what you wanted when you wanted. I trust you to do that Alex. You know what you're doing."

She smiled at me then. After a few seconds she said goodnight.

When she moved out on her sixteenth birthday I gave her a card and signed it with my name. Underneath I wrote, "still here." Alex came back the following month, maybe just to check if I was telling the truth. She told me her story then, and it was similar to the one in her social history but radically different to the ones she had told the other girls during her stay in the home. We talked for a few more hours and I asked her to come back to visit. She did.

Each question assumes that body language is within the child's control. The worker suggests that the child take even more control. The worker may suggest that the child increase or decrease the body language and record the reactions. The worker may suggest a time trial: record the eye rolls every hour or every evening. Experiments such as these affirm the child's control over body language, and can be a starting point for a working relationship in which the child takes control of other issues and problems in daily life.

Alex taught me so much about myself —what my "buttons" were, how to de-stress, and how to deal with my own anxiety. I am eternally grateful for these lessons as they have helped me to deal with relationship resistance. Most children and youth do not want to be counselled and shun adult concern as an intrusion into their lives. Most do not want to have any sort of relationship with an older worker like myself. Compelled to come to my office, they skillfully express their resistance through silence, verbal assaults, and body language. My role is to understand and respond.

Community Relationships

The community is the mesosystem in which the child lives, attends school, forms friendships, and engages in play. The geographic boundaries of this mesosystem may be wide and may include a distant school and a faraway sports field. However, the child is a member and stakeholder in this community that may nurture and value the child, listening to the child's needs, opinions, and observations, or disregard and dismiss the child, valuing only adults and considering the child as unimportant, even annoying.

Community capacity building is a process of building on individual and community assets that begins *inside* the community. Community members identify a focus or need: food assistance, safety in the neighbourhood, or an after-school program, for example. Next, they map their community's assets and strengths as this mapping will be the foundation of the capacity building process, and lastly, they design a plan.[4] The focus of this process is on capacity building *of* the people, *by* the people, and *for* the people in the multiple levels of the community. The external (to the community) professionals participate in the process but do not direct it. They may provide resources if asked, but their participation is short-term, unlike the long-term participation and vested interest of community members. Community capacity building is a new name for the traditional community-powered process of neighbours helping neighbours. When a school burns down in a community, the local residents get together to decide what to do to either rebuild it or relocate it. When a family moves into the neighbourhood, bringing violence and criminality with them, the community members meet to strategize how and when to speak to the family to change their behaviours or, at least, reduce their impact on the community.

Community capacity building has developed in reaction to traditional modes of community development: short-term programs and targeted interventions by external professionals. In these well-entrenched approaches, public funds are directed towards specific groups within the community, such as young single mothers, low birth weight infants, children with language delays, and teens at risk of suicide. Professionals deliver the programs to those community members who are identified as "at risk" by other professionals. The programs are evaluated by the participants who usually respond positively to the support, snacks, free childcare, and other benefits. However, when the funding dries up, the programs end, the professionals leave, and the community returns to its former state.

This top-down approach is the opposite of the bottom-up approach taken in community capacity building—an approach in which the ideas, opinions, and expertise of professionals and community members have equal value when decisions are made. Those who know the community best on a daily basis are seen to have pertinent

Photo 5.3 Community capacity building begins inside the community.

information, opinions, and observations. In addition, they have a vested interest in the welfare and future of their community and will live in their community long after the professionals have left. Glen Schmidt (2012: 11–12) evaluated community child welfare projects in British Columbia and noted that the projects that survived were those that were driven by community volunteers and those engaged in train-the-trainer projects in which learning was shared. The projects that ended when public funding ended were the projects designed and led by external consultants.

This does not discount the expertise of professionals. However, community capacity building channels this professional expertise through the ears of the community. Professionals are involved as equals rather than as assessors, planners, and funders— "office-bound, rules-driven, at arm's length from parents, families, and communities" (Barter, 2009: 275). In Ken Barter's project in the Chalker House neighbourhood in St John's, Newfoundland, for example, the professional worker simply listened for the first year, sitting in kitchens and playrooms, while the residents spoke of their dreams and hopes as well as their frustrations. Long hours of this kind of attentiveness in non-traditional settings (kitchens, yards, and sidewalks) resulted in the development of relationships and long-term projects that were important to and driven by the residents of Chalker House rather than by the professionals.

In this **collaborative practice**, professionals move away from the traditional **silo approach** of working in isolation with families who are marginalized and rarely interact with the mainstream. Instead, they work collaboratively with families, other professionals, and stakeholders in the child's life. Leadership is shared. In a study of Aboriginal community capacity building, the researchers noted "the flexible role of each individual and the contribution of expertise at the right time. In other words, individuals took the 'lead' based on the ability to do what was required to advance the work" (Fletcher, McKennitt, and Baydala, 2008: 28). Table 5.4 delineates the difference between community capacity building and community development.

Table 5.4 Community Capacity Building

Traditional Community Development	Community Capacity Building
Directed and driven by professionals	Directed and driven by community members
Professionals are the majority	Community members are the majority
Top-down approach	Bottom-up approach
Community as project site	Community as home
Focus on measurable outcomes that are required by funders	Focus on process and developing social relations among people in the community
Short-term funded projects	Long-term sustainable development
Focus on deficits and problems to be fixed	Focus on assets and strengths
Focus on welfare	Focus on justice and power sharing
Silo approach	Collaborative approach
Increases social division as only certain projects are funded	Increases social cohesion as decisions on projects are made collaboratively
Reliance on market forces or public funding	Self-reliance

In community capacity building, the personal becomes political as real change happens on a community level. People in the community share stories and make connections. Through their involvement with the community-building project and with one another, they realize that their ideas are important. Parents actively participate in these projects because they know that other community members value their talents and strengths. As they participate, they develop a sense of pride and belonging in their community, as well as relationships with other parents, neighbourhoods, and the professionals working alongside them. Their commitment to the success of their community and their community-building project develops.

Schmidt (2012), Barter (2009), and Ray DeV. Peters (2005) describe communities that work collaboratively to build the capacity of all community members, children and adults alike, to live better lives. Projects and programs such as the Neighbourhood House project in Victoria, BC, the Chalker House project in St John's, Newfoundland and Labrador, the Whole Child Program in Whitehorse, Yukon, and Community Holistic Healing Circles lower the numbers of reported child abuse incidents and raise health and wellness rates for children (Barter, 2005; Deslandes, 2006). Community capacity building becomes a key protective factor if children are to have healthy relationships with one another and with adults—relationships that value the contributions of all community members.

An example of this approach at work in Ontario is Better Beginnings, Better Futures, a community capacity building project that was started in 1991 in eight Ontario neighbourhoods. All of these neighbourhoods had been the subject of previous government interventions in which much funding had been spent with little improvement. Peters (2005: 173) describes the resulting mood in these neighbourhoods: "local residents viewed government programs and social services with skepticism, suspicion, or hostility."

Better Beginnings, Better Futures began by asking community residents to map their community's needs in order to identify sustainable and long-term projects that they could operate and manage. Because the project's organization was bottom-up rather than top-down, the eight programs have continued to operate beyond the funding period. Quantitative data (Peters, 2005) supported this long-term success on the Ottawa site: 10 per cent decrease in cigarette smoking by mothers; 20 per cent increase in "excellent health" of children as rated by parents; and more timely immunizations of children. In 2008, qualitative data from this site (Jenkins, 2008) documented the enhanced relationships among children, families, and workers, and a better sense of community among all of those involved. One community member remarked, "The program offers more help and on longer term and with a constant follow-up which makes us feel more important and valued" (Jenkins, 2008). Another commented, "There is no bureaucracy" (Jenkins, 2008). In the same year, all eight Ontario sites were evaluated and a cost-benefit analysis was applied. It was estimated that each child who participated in Better Beginnings, Better Futures for four years saved the province $983 per year in publicly funded services (Roche and Peters, 2008: 21).

The child who participates in such community capacity building saves public dollars but, more importantly, this child develops a sense of citizenship and community. Because the child's contribution is valued equally with that of other community members, the child develops a sense of self-worth and belonging that both protects and empowers the child. The child begins to feel that local community members care and watch out for the child's safety and success. At the same time, the child feels responsible for the safety and success of other community children, those who are also involved in community capacity building. With two feet solidly on the community base, the child is empowered to innovate and to help others over time, confident in the strengths and power of the community.

Barter's (2009: 279) description of the Chalker House project encapsulates the asset-focused energy of community capacity building, an approach that is "not about change but innovation, not about welfare but justice, not about wielding power but discovering it, not about programmatic 'fix-it' approaches but about distributive collaborative approaches, not about programs and services that are rule- and procedures-driven but about programs and services that are vision- and value-driven."

Summary

This chapter examines the components of a more beneficial working relationship between the worker and the child. In this relationship, the worker, traditionally viewed as the helper, becomes the learner and the child becomes the teacher. The conventional power dynamic is reversed so as to create a more equal relationship based on the Rogerian tenets of congruence, empathy, and mutual respect. The worker is bound by legislation that regulates the information that can be shared, the services provided, and even whether the child can be served at all. The ongoing worker–child relationship is widened through community capacity building to include all of the community who supports the child. How this healthy working relationship unfolds is the subject of the next chapter, which provides a guide for the first worker–child meeting. Valuable tools—genograms, sociograms, and lifelines—will be explored, as well as potential dialogues, agendas, and financial supports for the family. More importantly, you will learn how to use these tools and your current skills more effectively to convert interviews into meetings.

Review Questions

1. Define a healthy working relationship between worker and child, and describe the components of this relationship as formulated by Carl Rogers.
2. How can a worker's good intentions get in the way of a healthy working relationship?
3. Name ten documents that a worker might have to prepare or complete when working with children.
4. Why is documentation so important? Give three examples of this importance.
5. How do the guidelines for effective documentation protect against the three tricks described by Dorothy Smith (1998)?
6. What are some of the causes and signs of relationship resistance?
7. Identify three ways in which a worker can overcome a child's relationship resistance.
8. Describe the process of community capacity building.
9. Which relationships are built and sustained through community capacity building and why?
10. How does the child benefit from community capacity building?

Discussion Questions

1. According to Carl Rogers, healthy relationships are built on congruence, empathy, and respect. Reflect on healthy relationships, both past and present, in your own life. Do they follow the Rogerian model? Explain using specific personal examples.

2. Angelina is a 14-year-old student with straight A's in school. She is also on several sports teams and has a wide circle of friends. Angelina comes to you because she is pregnant and wants you to arrange an abortion. She does not want anyone, especially her parents, to know about this. In responding to Angelina, how would you deal with issues of confidentiality and consent?

3. Acronyms are used to keep recordings brief for both the writer and the reader. Some common acronyms used are TM (telephone message), TC (telephone call), BM (birth mother), SP (service plan), LOC (length of contact), FP (foster parent), MH (mental health), PHN (public health nurse), and DOB (date of birth). Initials are also used to replace full names. Read the following case note and highlight any words or phrases that may mislead or trick the reader. Then rewrite the case note so that it resembles the minutes of a meeting, trying also to keep the case note brief.

26/01/08 10:40 a.m.
Visited T.R. as arranged on 12/12/07 per SP. T.R. is sleepy and is obviously still having drug problems. House still very dirty. Sufficient food but no jars of baby food as required by SP. Baby X (DOB: 10/08/07) sleeping in crib beside T.R.'s bed. Unwashed baby bottles still in kitchen sink; obviously she's overwhelmed by baby. T.R. admits to smoking joint one week ago. House stinks of cigarettes, and beer bottles lined up at back door. T.R. claims that ex-partner has not visited since New Years. TC to supervisor confirms that PHN visit confirmed for tomorrow at 11:00 am. Informed T.R., then left. LOC: 15 mins.

6 The First Meeting

I spent the first day picking holes in paper, then went home in a smouldering temper.
"What's the matter, Love? Didn't he like it at school, then?"
"They never gave me the present."
"Present? What present?"
"They said they'd give me a present."
"Well, now, I'm sure they didn't."
"They did! They said: 'You're Laurie Lee, aren't you? Well just you sit there for the present.'"
"I sat there all day but I never got it. I ain't going back there again."

—Laurie Lee, *Cider with Rosie*

We laugh when we read about Laurie Lee's misunderstanding of the teacher. Then our laughter subsides. Did the child misunderstand the teacher, or did the teacher misunderstand the child? Was the child's first day at school ruined because a teacher did not communicate effectively? Like Laurie Lee, the children who come to us sometimes leave our first meeting saying, "I ain't going back there again."

The first meeting is the first time the child sees us, and our energy, warmth, and focus may entice the child to work with us. We may meet the child in a drop-in centre, on the sidewalk, or in a shelter, or at a spontaneous meeting in response to a crisis. Beforehand we take time to reflect. Informed action based on reflection, education, training, and sound practice principles is called **praxis**. Praxis is more likely to be helpful than an impulsive reaction based on sympathy or emotional reactivity.

When the meeting is scheduled in advance, we have more time for praxis. There is also time for a file review, preliminary resource scan, telephone intake interview, consultation with a supervisor, and reflection on this combination of information. Previously completed assessments, case notes, school and health records, and diagnostic material can be evaluated for validity and reliability.

This first meeting or face-to-face encounter, whether or not in the home, is the beginning of a relationship. The worker tries to learn as much as possible from the child about the child's home culture. If the worker signals disinterest, disengagement, or bias, the first meeting will likely be the last. On the other hand, the worker may convey empathy, openness, and a willingness to listen to the child. If so, the child will understand that a relationship is beginning, and the child may choose to enter into this relationship.

This chapter describes how to engage the child, and possibly the child's family, in that first meeting. We will explore guidelines for the home visit as well as the practical applications of these guidelines. We will identify tangible structural supports for the family. We will learn how to co-construct **genograms**, **sociograms**, and **lifelines** as part of this empowering process in which the child uncovers capabilities and skills for daily living.

Objectives

By the end of this chapter, you will:

- Identify the key elements in both praxis and cultural competency.
- Understand the power dynamics that differentiate meetings from interviews.
- Demonstrate how to conduct the first meeting with a child, and with a child and family, both in the agency and in the child's home.

Praxis

Workers who react to children with punishment, manipulation, coercion, assessment, and judgement defend their reactive thinking on the grounds that their heavy caseloads, meetings, and excessive paperwork give them no time to reflect on their actions and respond appropriately to children. The bureaucratic and reactive climate in agencies and services, plus the demands of paperwork, does constrict reflection on practice and often shuts it down completely. As Michelle Lefevre (2010: 21) explains, "Being bombarded with the emotional pain and distress of children and their families and required to make complex, finely balanced decisions without time to reflect or adequate supervision may also be evoking defences in practitioners which prevent them from responding."

Workers also cite structural barriers to reflection such as overriding child welfare legislation, confidentiality requirements, and agency protocols. They rarely cite the covert barriers of their own bias, insecurity, and fear—an unwillingness to relate openly and equally with the child and to give up the powerful position of expert. This powerful position is not one that encourages self-reflection on authoritarian and reactive practice. Self-reflection can be uncomfortable. It leads to questions, challenges, and criticism, which, in turn, suggest change in the structure of the agency and the practice of the worker. This is praxis: action based on reflection.

Praxis stimulates active confrontation of structure, practice, and theory. Praxis checks unbridled theory that has no foundation in practice and practice that continues year after year without any foundation in theory. Jennifer White (2007: 226) defines praxis as "ethical, self-aware, responsive and accountable action, which reflects dimensions of knowing, doing and being." These interrelated and overlapping dimensions of knowing, being, and doing are also the three dimensions of working with children and youth.

Knowing child development theory and research, legislation, policy, and theoretical models of practice correlates with knowing oneself or self-evaluation (being). The worker examines personal practice and confronts personal bias, fears, unmet needs, and lack of ethics and integrity. This active self-evaluation tests interpersonal skills such as empathy, congruency, caring, and friendliness with each child and within each meeting. The worker then evaluates each meeting for both its theoretical underpinnings and its practical effect. The worker draws on both practical (doing) and theoretical (knowing) knowledge plus knowledge of oneself (being) in this evaluation. This is painful but necessary work.

Praxis works at the intersection of this knowing-being-doing model (Figure 6.1), and confronts both the "knowing how" or practice and the "knowing that" or theory. "The analytical interpretive process ('doing') that this involves requires careful attention to subjectivity and bias so should be informed by research, theoretical perspectives ('knowing'), ethical standards, and rigorous self-reflection ('being')" (Lefevre, 2010: 167). This is illustrated in Figure 6.2 as a wheel or circle in which reflection challenges theory that informs action. Action then inspires reflection on the theory that underpins it. This reflection in turn confronts or challenges what is known, adding to this knowledge or theory, and changing future action.

Reflection is also described as **mindfulness** or "purposefully paying attention to the present moment with an attitude of openness, nonjudgment, and acceptance" (Hick, 2009: 4). The mindful worker is not defensive and does not try to justify practice. Instead, the mindful worker watches how theory does or does not work in direct practice and tries to understand the reasons for this. David Brazier (2013: 117) explains that "mindfulness

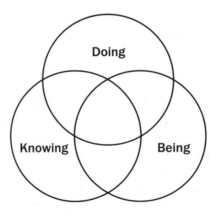

Figure 6.1 Praxis

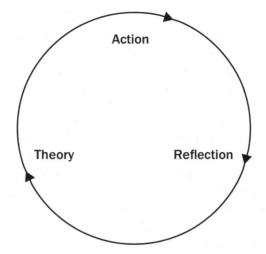

Figure 6.2 Reflection

in its original Buddhist context had much the same import, to remember and apply the teachings, or to hold fast to what one knows, including the fruit of both present and past experience and observe how it works out in practice in one's direct experience."

Paulo Freire (2000) challenges workers to be mindful and to commit to revolutionary and transformative practice. He defines praxis as "reflection and action upon the world in order to transform it" (2000: 33). This transformative work of creative reflection and critical inquiry uncovers new meanings in interventions, or draws out the meanings that were always there. It is the opposite of reactive and prescriptive action that blindly follows policy, protocols, and assessments. Praxis is responsive rather than reactive, and Carl Rogers (1980: 115) describes praxis as an essential prerequisite to working with children: "The feelings the therapist is experiencing are available to him, available to his awareness, and he is able to live these feelings, be them."

Group Exercise 6.1

Mindfulness

This large group exercise uses guided imagery that is common in most mindfulness courses. It is intended to challenge the preconception that mindfulness is instinctive and easily acquired. This exercise begins with the group leader asking participants to focus on their bodily sensations and their thoughts while they listen to this guided imagery. At the same time, the leader puts a slice of apple on a napkin in front of each participant. The leader then begins to speak slowly, leaving a distinct pause after each statement or question.

continued

"Think about your feet. Are they flat on the floor? Are they comfortable? Is your back curved or straight? Where is your head in relation to your neck? What are you looking at right now? Is the apple slice the same colour as the napkin? Touch the apple with your fingertips. Think about your hand moving with your arm to do what your brain commands. Now pick up the slice. Is the slice heavy? Smell it and try to identify the smell. Feel the skin. Is the skin smoother than the flesh of the apple? Does the skin smell more now that you are holding the slice? Are there any spots on the skin? Take a small bite and hold it in your mouth. What is the texture—rough, floury, syrupy? Chew the apple in your mouth. How does the texture change as you chew? Does the apple taste juicy, sour, or sweet? How do you know when to swallow what you have chewed? Does swallowing the apple satisfy you or make you want more? Are your fingers sticky from the apple? Where are your hands right now? Is your back curved or straight?"

The group leader signals the end and asks participants to put down the remainder of the slice, shake out their hands, breathe, and relax. The leader then asks participants to reflect on the exercise and any change they noticed in their level of awareness. Finally, the leader asks how mindfulness can impact sensitivity to the feelings of children and families.

Cultural Competency

A worker meeting a child for the first time may see someone whose culture is similar to his or her own, or a child whose culture is dramatically different, even antithetical to the worker's. Each child brings a personal culture to the first meeting. How a worker responds to that personal culture is determined by that worker's level of **cultural competency**.

Culture has an enormous influence on who and what we are—on every action and decision that we take and every relationship that we enjoy (Cech, 1991). The construction of our own culture begins from the moment we are born and continues to develop through family life, travel, social interactions, ability level, socio-economic status, religion, and our exposure to violence and war. In other words, our culture is multi-faceted and always changing. The child carefully constructs a personal culture and experiences it as unique and different from the culture of family and others. This personal culture is tied to self-worth: if society values the child's culture, the child feels valued, and if society misunderstands, ridicules, or hates the child's culture, the child feels marginalized and diminished.

Each child's culture is unique. Brothers and sisters may appear to be very similar in mores and traditions; however, their individual interpretations of family culture make them behave in slightly different ways as they develop their own unique cultures. One child may embrace the religion of the family, while another child rejects it. One child may absorb the pacifist norms of family behaviour, while another child chooses more aggressive norms and values.[1] In addition, the child's culture changes continuously through exposure to different religions, customs, peers, and life experiences.

> ## 🗨 Point to Consider   6.1
>
> ### Cross-Cultural Factors
>
> The Negotiating Resilience Research Project developed by Michael Ungar (2008) of Dalhousie University demonstrates the cultural bias that permeates many communities. This project examines resiliency factors of children aged 13 to 15 years who are in transition between two (and sometimes more) culturally distinct worlds. One child with a physical disability is being educated among able-bodied children; one Aboriginal child lives off-reserve in a largely mainstream urban environment; one multi-ethnic child negotiates her identity in an ethnically diverse community; and a child refugee without family is situated in a family-based community. Ability, spirituality, ethnicity, race, family, language: all these and more are components of culture. The children in this study try to fit in with other children in their respective communities while still holding on to their own distinct personal cultures, but they are met with systemic cultural bias in each of these Canadian communities.

If the child's culture is both unique and continuously changing, how do we learn about it? Surely by the time we learn about a child's culture, that culture will have changed! How can we expect to be a cultural expert about so many individual cultures in a family? And how can we achieve cultural competency in a worker–child relationship when we do not know what the child's personal culture means to the child?

The answer to all of these questions is simple: we must listen to the child, who is the expert in his or her own culture. We can learn about the child's constantly evolving culture from the child, using our own culture as our reference point and acknowledging that every word, action, or behaviour of the child is filtered through our own cultural bias. The child is our doorway to cultural competency, and cultural competency is the essential framework for the first meeting and the beginning of a healthy working relationship. So, we listen.

Achieving cultural competency does not entail knowing everything about the culture of the child, but it does involve being mindful of one's own culture. When the worker intervenes with a child who is in the program because of "obesity," for example, the worker filters the concept of "obesity" through his or her own personal cultural bias. What does obesity look like to the worker and how does the worker describe it? Does the worker even consider obesity to be a problem? Think of the variety of culture-specific descriptors for obesity: "overweight," "healthy," "fat," "disgusting," "curvaceous," "well-rounded," "full figured," and so on. Each of these descriptors reflects personal bias. Understanding and acknowledging this personal bias enables the culturally competent worker to understand and support the child's view of obesity.

Personal bias is constructed over years, through life experiences, and it affects the worker's appreciation of the child. A bias towards small children, for instance, may prompt the worker to remark, "Isn't she too cute? I just love that little girl. I'm going to bring her out some little shoes the next time I visit." Another child in the family who is tall beyond her years may get little or no attention from the same worker. Bias thus causes the worker to favour one child over another and appreciate one family member more than another.

Bias can also cause the worker to misinterpret the child's messaging. The worker may value close body proximity, for example, and seek to be physically close to the child and family and to share their personal space. When the child steps back or rejects this physical proximity, the worker may experience this as a rejection and may perceive the child as shy or fearful of adults. Another worker may view the child's direct eye contact as disrespectful and challenging and may perceive such a child as bold and aggressive. The worker who is culturally competent is aware of personal bias and the multiplicity of possible cultural behaviours and so is less likely to attribute the wrong meaning to the child's cultural mores.

Bias can be even more evident in the worker's response to a family's cultural values. In many cultures, the family comes first, and family members feel that attention to the individual, particularly to a child, is insulting. "Think about the family and not about yourself" may be a family maxim. This extends to keeping family matters private, respecting family elders and their wishes, and putting the needs of the family first. The culture of the worker and the agency, however, may value individuality, which could cause the worker to complain, "How can they be so selfish? Why don't they see that their child's needs should come first?" The worker can thus culturally misinterpret the family's means of caring for the child and may describe the child's frequent babysitting chores, for example, as inappropriate or even abusive.

Culture not only affects the family's relationship with the worker; it also affects who in the family participates in this relationship. While some Canadians value independence *from* the family, others value interdependence *within* the family. Some families may expect parents to come to a meeting with the child, some may expect the child to come independently, and some may expect all extended family members to be involved. Calvin Morrisseau (1998: 90) describes this respect for extended family members, even those who are no longer alive: "When we understand 'all our relations,' we will know our ancestors are just as much a part of us today as when they were physically walking Mother Earth. In this sense, we are never alone. Our relations are still present to help us." This Aboriginal belief in the importance of all family members, living and dead, is a belief that is held by many non-Aboriginal Canadians too.

Privacy is another value strongly affected by culture. A child who values personal and family privacy may be silent and guarded in relationships with strangers, and may avoid personal disclosure. The child may be especially guarded with a worker who is culturally different. The child may perceive such a worker as a government trickster who is trying to deceive or ensnare the child. When the worker tries to establish a warm and caring relationship, the child may interpret this as an invasion of personal privacy, an insult rather than an invitation. The child may avoid a warm handshake or greeting and may prefer to call the worker by a last name or as "Teacher Sue" rather than as "Sue,"

Blend Images/Shutterstock

Photo 6.1 Each child brings a unique culture to the worker.

for example. Workers who are biased towards the Dr. Phil style of casual openness, in which intimate thoughts and activities are discussed and shared with strangers, may describe these children as distant and closed or fearful of adults, or they may interpret this cultural value of privacy as a possible indicator of interfamily child abuse.

The most detrimental bias in a healthy working relationship is expressed in the worker's bold assertion, "I have no bias. I treat everyone the same." This **monocultural bias** leads the worker to treat every child and family the same as the worker and the workplace. They are expected to conform to worker and workplace culture rather than vice versa. This may prompt the worker to threaten the family: "If you don't co-operate, we'll have to amend the service plan." Other workers, confronted with a family culture they do not understand, may impose their monocultural bias on the family: "They need to be told what they're doing wrong; otherwise, we'll take their kids away. They need to learn what we do in Canada."

What *do* we do in Canada? Traditional approaches to counselling are white, male, Eurocentric, and middle-class in origin and practice (see Chapter 3) and alien to those who are not white, male, Eurocentric, and middle-class and who, as a result, avoid counselling, even when their children's behaviour appears problematic. They may believe that, because of their language or their cultural beliefs, their concerns will not be heard or understood by the worker who counsels them. They may not reveal their family situation for fear of being misunderstood, of being judged incompetent, or even of losing their children.

👤👤 Group Exercise   6.2

Welcome to My Home

This large group exercise begins with pair-sharing and ends with large group sharing to create a webbing map of cultural components. In this brief yet powerful exercise, the large group discusses the components of personal culture, why each culture of each person in the group is so distinct, and how cross-cultural miscommunication can happen.

The exercise begins with participants pairing up with participants that they do not know well. The leader then prints on the board some components of a home visit: rules in the home, rooms for visitors, food and drink, other people in the home, pets. The leader explains that each participant will offer an overview of these home visit components prior to the other participant visiting the home. The leader explains that this overview will be brief (five minutes) and may involve questions and answers.

At a signal from the leader, the exercise begins. In five minutes, the leader signals the participants to switch. In this way, both participants have the opportunity to describe their homes to each other. After an additional five minutes, the leader signals the pairs to stop for a debriefing.

At this point, the leader collects the components of the home visit from the pairs. These components may include rules and mores, customs, manners, beliefs, and lifestyles. Then the group leader asks pairs to identify whether their home visits were identical and, if not, what made them different. These differences are added to the webbing map of cultural components that is emerging on the board in front of the large group. Finally, the leader asks which specific components might prove problematic or puzzling to others. Those components are then circled on the board. This exercise not only prompts discussion of cross-cultural misunderstandings but also leads to a greater understanding of the depth and expanse of personal culture.

Another dimension to this lack of trust is the bias of the child and of the child's family. This bias has been carefully constructed over many years. A grandmother who has experienced 85 years of the social construction of her culture, for example, may resist the worker in an instinctive strategy to protect her grandchild and her family culture. The grandmother may have had previous negative experiences with educational and social welfare systems and may assume that workers are not to be trusted. "They are just part of the system," she may think. "They say they are here to help, but really they're just here to catch us and get our kids into the foster homes." She may refuse to let the worker into her home, refuse to talk to the worker, exhibit anger and verbal hostility, deny the existence of any problems, attribute blame for family problems to someone or something else, miss scheduled appointments, or openly threaten the worker.

Such resistance is to be expected. A stranger from another culture who challenges the family's way of life and their love for their child may be experienced as a threat, regardless of how sensitively the worker begins the relationship. One of this grandmother's cultural values may be that children must respect their elders. Confronted by a grandchild who does not respect her, interrupts her, or even dismisses her, she may feel ashamed, hurt, or angry. She may feel culturally obligated to teach her grandchild how to behave, and so she may hit or spank her grandchild and shout a warning. The grandchild may express anger, distrust, or hatred of that grandmother, but that grandmother is still a part of the child's life, past, present, and future.

The worker's culture, on the other hand, may prescribe very different attitudes towards elders and towards spanking. In such a situation, the worker is required to investigate the grandmother as a potential abuser of her grandchild. However, before intervening with the grandmother, the culturally competent worker pauses, acknowledging both personal bias and the bias of the grandmother. Just as the construction of the grandmother's culture has been lengthy, so is the deconstruction of this culture a long process. The culturally competent worker recognizes this fact in planning interventions that are culturally appropriate, long-term, and respectful of the child and family.

Cultural competency entails awareness of personal bias and how it affects our acceptance and understanding of the culture of others. Each child and family who arrives for the first meeting with a worker comes through the door bringing a specific personal culture. This culture may bear no resemblance to what the person's skin colour, name, or religious affiliation suggests. *All* counselling is multicultural in that all individuals think and behave according to their own personal culture and, as Bob Shebib (2007: 303) notes, "within-group cultural differences may actually exceed between-group differences." This cultural distinctiveness of everyone involved needs to be acknowledged at the first meeting

Note from the Field   6.1

Why Don't You Like My Kids?

Emily has started working in an ESL nursery school program and she really enjoys the diversity of children and parents. After a few months in the program, however, she notices that the mothers still have not accepted her and seem eager to leave when they collect their children. She asks Maria, her supervisor, about this and is surprised by the response. Maria has assumed that Emily does not like the children. Further discussion reveals a cultural misunderstanding. Maria holds, cuddles, and hugs the children, unlike Emily who is aloof, more verbal, and less physically responsive. The children and their parents interpret this as Emily's dislike for them and their response is to imitate her aloofness and to stay away from her whenever possible.

of worker and child. The honest acknowledgement of the dissimilarity between the two participants begins a dialogue that positions the worker as the learner, listening carefully to the child who has the personal cultural knowledge fundamental to building relationships with others. The child becomes the cultural expert rather than the one being helped.

Meeting or Interview

A "meeting" implies a relationship of some equality. There may be a chairperson and a minute-taker, but the persons who are present usually are considered to be equals. We have a family meeting and each member of the family expresses an opinion or makes a recommendation. We have a community meeting and neighbours discuss what can be done about a proposed change in the community. Sometimes there are minutes taken of a meeting, and these minutes are shared with everyone at the subsequent meeting and approved (or not) by them.

On the other hand, an interview is a way to collect facts. It is an "us-and-them" activity. We interview an author to gain insight on a recently published book. We interview a criminal to gather evidence. We interview an applicant for a job to decide whether this applicant is suited for the job. On the basis of the facts gained at the interview we make a decision, assess the risk, or form an opinion. The person giving the facts is in one position (usually subordinate, but not always), and the interviewer is in another position. An interview usually reflects a power imbalance.

The worker makes the crucial decision whether to "interview" or to "meet with" the child. Deciding on the action of this initial contact determines whether or not the child engages with the worker, feels safe, and is motivated to communicate feelings and intentions to the worker. The worker who interviews places the child in the inferior position of being scrutinized or examined. The worker shares information with the child only when the child is deemed to be "ready for it" or "able to understand." The worker decides when the interview will begin and end, and the child cannot choose to leave. If the child does decide to walk out of the interview, the child may be apprehended and runs the risk of being placed in a foster home or institution.

The worker who meets with the child affirms the child as an equal participant. The agenda is jointly agreed on and approved. It may even include a written agreement such as the one below between Walid and his worker, Heather. This simple agreement is jointly approved and any changes to it must be made jointly by both Walid and Heather.

This meeting between Walid and Heather takes place in a playroom, but first meetings may take place in an agency meeting room, detention centre, restaurant booth, home, sidewalk, or hospital waiting room. I once met with a lone mother and her daughter for the first time in a vast, empty lecture room for a hundred people. Too often the surroundings of the first meeting convey the power of the agency and the worker. Big office desks, hard chairs, two-way mirrors, and interruptions are threatening and reinforce the powerlessness of the child and family. The worker's body language may be saying, "I want to help," but the meeting space says the opposite.

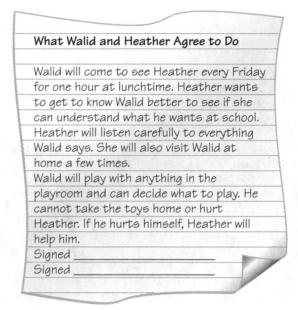

What Walid and Heather Agree to Do

Walid will come to see Heather every Friday for one hour at lunchtime. Heather wants to get to know Walid better to see if she can understand what he wants at school. Heather will listen carefully to everything Walid says. She will also visit Walid at home a few times.
Walid will play with anything in the playroom and can decide what to play. He cannot take the toys home or hurt Heather. If he hurts himself, Heather will help him.
Signed _____
Signed _____

Figure 6.3 Sample Agreement

This power dynamic can change at the first meeting by the worker making sure that the large and threatening space is converted to a comfortable, private, and more secure one. The restaurant booth can become a cozy place to talk when the worker speaks quietly and orders food and drinks that are comfortable and familiar for the child and last for an hour. The sidewalk can become an open and relaxed meeting place if it is the child's home turf; the worker follows the child's lead because the child knows best where to sit and where to go for a quiet talk. In an agency or waiting room, the worker has even more opportunity to soften the edges and the mood of the space. Cozy comfortable cushions, chairs pulled together, and attentive concern for the child's comfort can convert an otherwise sterile room into a safe haven. If tables are pushed out of the way, there may be space on the carpet for conversation. If the lights are dimmed rather than glaring, the blank, beige walls will soften.

The worker is part of that space and the worker's body language can be threatening and confrontational, or comforting and open. The worker who is positioned in a lower chair, or even on the floor with the child, is immediately less intimidating to the child and the family. When eyes meet eyes on a level plane, there is more chance to communicate freely than when eyes look down from five or six feet to a child lying on a blanket on the floor. If the worker cannot squat, then the worker can pull together two chairs so that, in the sitting position, eyes still can meet eyes. If the worker pauses to consider the child's feelings and is willing to meet the child at the child's physical level, rather than looking down at the child, some of that fear, trepidation, and power imbalance can be reduced.

Equally important is an open, comforting body posture that communicates safety without the barrier of a desk, clipboard, briefcase, or paper. During the first meeting,

Photo 6.2 Eyes meet eyes and smiles connect as this worker learns from the child.

recording materials such as paper and pen, laptop, and recorder are obstacles to the relationship, whereas crayons and paper can be used together to build a relationship. A record (case note) of the meeting can be jointly drawn or written, and then can be signed. This keeps the focus of the meeting on relationship-building before information-gathering.

Engaging the Child

The worker is a stranger who does not touch the child's body, hair, or clothing without the child's consent. Even when the child asks to be touched, the worker uses professional judgement before responding. If the child asks to be picked up or held, the worker can hold the child briefly, squat down to the child's level, or engage the child in comforting talk. Each response demonstrates respect for the child and the child's personal space, as well as appropriate "stranger behaviour" with children. The culturally competent worker reads visual cues from the caregivers and the child as to the level and type of physical interaction that is appropriate to meet the child's comfort needs. The worker sits close to the child while respecting the child's personal space and need for movement.

One preschooler asked repeatedly to sit on my lap in the first meeting. Her request was neither a spontaneous response to an established relationship nor an immediate need for contact comfort, but a consistent and learned response to the sexual abuse she had suffered. She was used to being seen as an object of sexual pleasure for adults, and her behaviour had been groomed in this fashion. She routinely made this request to all of the adults in her home. While I understood the source of her anxiety and fear, I also understood that acceding to her request would only strengthen her belief that all adults took pleasure from her tiny body and that she was an object to be used for pleasure. Providing a lovely child-sized chair for her and having that chair close to mine gave her some feeling of safety, while still acknowledging that she was a separate person with a story to tell and a unique self to be respected.

The worker's clothing also sends a message in the first meeting. The worker who wears loose, uncluttered clothing and appropriate footwear can squat, run, play, jump, and move with the child. Children who drool, spit, or vomit can be held comfortably. Infants can be soothed rather than annoyed by dangling jewellery, rough textures, or accessories. The worker's clothing keeps the focus on the child's comfort rather than the worker's hair, jewellery, or fashion statement.

Vocal tone and rhythm are generally more important than words. A high-pitched tone, raucous laughter, or machine-gun speech (a fast-paced volley of words) loaded with agency jargon can frighten the child (and everyone else) and exacerbate the child's stress. Too often, the worker is the loudest person in the meeting. The worker who modulates tone, rhythm, and accent can create an aural comfort zone for the child. The worker puts aside both professional jargon and "baby talk" and uses appropriate and simple words that echo the words of the child. The worker is speaking to be understood rather than to coerce, mislead, impress, or intimidate the child.

Gestures can comfort or threaten. They are more forceful than words and are easily misinterpreted. A gesture such as offering a chair to everyone but the child, for example, both disrespects and disregards the child. This gesture forces the child to sit or climb on a caregiver or to sit on the floor. Offering a chair only to the women in the family and ignoring the grandparents or elderly members of the family is equally insulting. Then, there are the workers who arrive at a first meeting carrying their coffee cups. The worker drinks throughout the meeting, oblivious to the lack of refreshment for the child and the family. If a worker cannot talk or listen without a drink, perhaps the child feels the same way. These forms of behaviour transgress basic etiquette and consideration for others; after all, providing water as a bare minimum for everyone in the room is just common sense. Regrettably, these insulting gestures are all too common and can prevent any relationship-building in this first meeting.

This first meeting is an opportunity to listen respectfully to the words and the body language of the child by being silent and attentive when the child is speaking and following the child's lead; appropriating the child's words whenever possible; and offering a bathroom break to a child who is squirming or bouncing on the chair, a blanket or warm coat to a child who is shivering, or a tissue to a child who is sniffing. The respectful worker attends to the safety and security needs of the child and takes time to become acquainted with the child, listening to the child attentively and trying to read the child's body language and words. The worker also acknowledges how hard it is for the child to be at the meeting:

- I'm glad you came up to see me today. How can I be of help to you?
- I know that your teacher has sent you here for an hour every Wednesday. It must be a real drag to spend extra time after school with me. How can I help you to get back your time?
- I know that your parents told you to come and see me because of your grades. What do you want done about your grades?
- The staff asked me to speak to you about vandalism, but I am wondering who did all the damage in the recreation centre. Are you good at detective work? Do you know if the person left any clues?
- We have an hour to spend together today. How would you like to spend that hour here?

These types of introduction convey the message that the child owns the time. The child is in charge of the agenda for this meeting, and the worker is primed to listen. The worker assumes that the child is competent and can actively engage and look for solutions.

The child is the expert on the presenting problem as well as potential solutions. The child may have seen many other workers and has some clear ideas on the most useful direction for this first meeting. The worker can acknowledge and support this expertise so that the child is empowered to advise the worker on the meaning of the problem, potential solutions, and the roles and relationships in the family. The key is to acknowledge and respect the child's input through open-ended questions:

- Can you think of anything else I should do differently with you?
- What other things did your counsellors do with you that turned you off?
- You say they really bugged you. What did they do that you didn't like?

Even very young children intuit when the worker is genuinely interested. If the worker is just making conversation and faking interest, the child will not respond, or may respond with the same level of superficiality as the worker. When the worker meets the child as an equal and looks to the child for information, advice, or expertise, the child tends to respond. The worker's genuine interest in the child is conveyed through open-ended questions:

- Are you really able to draw caricatures of your teachers? I would like to see some of the ones you've drawn.
- Did you sit through the entire film without leaving? You have more concentration than I do. I left after 20 minutes. Can you tell me how the film ended?
- Was the candy under the bed really attached to the carpet? How did you eat it that way?
- Wow! That family holiday sounds like a wild trip! How did you manage to survive it?

| | **Group Exercise** | **6.3** |

Children at School

This small group exercise is best done in groups of three to five people. In this brief yet powerful exercise, the small group discusses how to engage an older child. One member of the group volunteers to play the older child, and the other members play the team that is meeting the child for the first time.

The exercise begins with the volunteer stepping away from the group to prepare an improvised script for the child based on one of the following instructions:

- You have been suspended from Grade 5 for three days because you witnessed a bullying incident at school and did not report it. Both the bullies and the victim are classmates and friends of yours and you are not going to implicate them.
- Your best friend in Grade 8 has been having sex with your current boyfriend so you trashed her locker and posted gossip about her on a social media site. You are two months' pregnant and have told no one about this.
- You are in Grade 12 and have been cutting yourself for the last year as a way of coping with your father's pressure about getting good enough grades for university. You have been to two different psychiatrists about this already and you are on heavy medication now.

At the same time, each team is given one of the corresponding instructions:

- Jeremy, 10 years old, has been suspended from school (not the first time) under the anti-bullying policy.
- Emma, a 13-year-old student, vandalized a classmate's locker and posted hate mail about her on a social media site.
- Amal is suspected of selling drugs to other Grade 12 students and has been diagnosed as possibly bipolar.

When the team is ready to begin the meeting, they call in the volunteer child and engage in dialogue for five minutes. At this point, the leader stops the action of all the small groups and begins a debriefing by asking questions such as the following:

- How did the team initially engage the child? Was this successful?
- From the child's perspective, how could the team have equalized the power construct right away? Did the team appear to be accusatory?
- What strategies work best to begin a meeting?

Table 6.1 Making Meetings Work

Competency	Achieved
Attend first to the child's comfort and feelings of safety.	✓
Affirm the child's strengths, capabilities, experience, and expertise.	☐
Stay in the moment. Be attentive to silence and body language.	☐
Follow the child's lead. Be the learner.	☐
Use appropriate (to the child) language that is mutually understood.	☐
Use scaffolding, questioning, or paraphrasing to ensure that you understand.	☐
Seek and accept corrections, changes, and guidance from the child.	☐
Speak with the child, not at the child.	☐
Be playful and stimulating. Have a sense of humour.	☐
Include collaterals only as agreed to by the child.	☐
Make notes and share these with the child.	☐
Follow through on commitments made during the meeting.	☐
Start on time. End on time. Do not cancel meetings.	☐

Table 6.1 provides a quick checklist for workers at the first meeting.

Empathy and respect are basic to any honest working relationship. However, so often this is lacking in worker–child relationships. I remember working with a child in a group home who remarked about her former worker, "She didn't even know my name." The worker had misread the file name and never checked with the child about her correct name. That hurts.

Genograms, Sociograms, and Lifelines

The billion-dollar alternative (foster) care system in Canada is not cost effective. Children are abused within the system (see Chapter 4); less than half graduate from high school; and a substantial proportion of those who leave the system become either homeless or are housed in mental health facilities, addiction treatment centres, or prisons. Statistics from M.O. Fechter-Leggett and K. O'Brien (2010: 207) confirm this: "Former foster children have lower educational achievement; higher rates of unemployment and underemployment; are overrepresented in the homeless; have higher rates of arrest and conviction; and suffer from more mental health issues such as PTSD, depression, and substance use than the matched comparison groups of non-foster children."

The attachment injuries inflicted on these children before being apprehended and after being placed in alternative care can be compared to the attachment injuries that are at the root of presenting problems brought to the worker by families and children who are still living together. The worker who is able to depict these injuries through the use of genograms, sociograms, and lifelines is better able to support the child's (and family's) healing. These pictorial representations trump words at a first meeting when visuals and body language speak more clearly than lengthy explanations of agency policy. Drawing and dialogue help to bring the worker, child, and family closer together even when all of the family members are not physically present.

The genogram is a pictorial case note of family relationships that shifts the child from family-less to family-full. When asked about family, the child may initially respond, "I have no family" or "I am on my own." This is not a lie. This is contextually true for the child. The child may feel alienated, abandoned, or dispossessed by family; as a result, the child states that he/she has no family. "Family" brought the child to this point, and "family" can't help now—so the child's statement may realistically express all of these negative feelings about the concept of family.

The worker affirms the child's statement by encouraging the child to construct a genogram on a serviette, notepad, or a large piece of flipchart paper. The child controls and directs the genogram, deciding who to include and who to exclude. The first picture on the paper is the child (a circle or a square) with the child's age on the inside and the child's name underneath. Then the genogram unfolds, with the worker drawing and the child spotting any mistakes, correcting lines of connection and names, and adding people as they are remembered. The child directs the worker, and the worker configures dates from the child's memory of "two years ago" or "when I was eight." Most children can recall and name one person from their family. At subsequent meetings that one person may become two because the remembered person is now married, has a child, or has a parent. Slowly, a family emerges as uncles appear, grandparents surface, and a long forgotten and much disliked stepfather is given a name. With these remembered names come memories, painful and joyous, as well as feelings of familial connection. Each direction from the child is affirmed during a slow and gentle dialogue filled with empathy and support such as this one between the worker (W) and child (C):

C : I don't have any family.
W: Okay. I will put you alone in the middle with your age inside: 14, right?
C : Yeh, and I guess you better put in my brother Paul.
W: Okay. Is Paul older or younger?
C : He's 22 now. He's not the oldest, though. Ray is. He's 23.
W: Right. We can draw them both, too. No sisters, right?
C : Yeh, I have a little sister but she's with my dad.
W: And what's her name?
C : Celine.

W: Is she much younger?

C : She's only eight. I don't see her much, though. Really, she's just my half-sister; her mom was my dad's girlfriend before she took off.

This 14-year-old child begins this first meeting with the statement, "I have no family." That one declaration is a very brave and painful assertion by a child who has survived alone and is still surviving without family. However, in less than a minute of dialogue directed and controlled by the child, a family has emerged on paper. The child identifies five family members: two much older brothers, a younger half-sister, a step-mom, and a dad. These five family members may not be the most important ones for the child and they may have been sources for many of the child's problems. The really close ones may emerge later: an aunt, a grandfather, a half-sister who lives far away. But the structure of the family is emerging, and the lines of connections can literally be seen by the child and the worker together.

This dialogue may prompt the child to talk about family, if only to correct the worker who is drawing the genogram. The child directs the telling of a story that becomes increasingly visual and rich with detail. This shared case note—the geno-gram—slowly becomes filled with the emotions, nicknames, and attitudes of family members, potential sources of problems and sources of solutions and supports, too. A dialogue between the worker (W) and child (C) during the co-construction of the genogram may sound like this:

C : That is my Aunt Martha. She was always bossy with me.

W: I'll write "bossy" beside her name.

C : Yeh, that's right. She used to call me "lazy."

W: I'll write that beside you and put "M" in brackets so we remember where that came from: Aunt Martha. Were there any other names?

C : Just Tony. He called me his "princess."

The child sees the genogram emerge on the paper, much like a picture of family life. There may be a pattern of leaving the family. Dad's girlfriend leaves; mom leaves with a new partner; an elder sister leaves home to live on the streets. Other members of the family do not leave but stay to care for one another. Why do they stay, and what gives them the strength to survive the loss of another family member when that person chooses to leave the family? Alcoholism may have permeated the lives of several gener-ations; however, there may be one aunt who is not an alcoholic. In her case, what made the difference? Why did she not become an alcoholic? What can be learned from her pattern of problem solving? Did she seek outside help? Did she get a job? Did she have a stable love relationship? What made the difference?

This is not a story about a distant national hero or a character in a movie. This family relative who solves problems and who breaks the pattern is a relevant and valid role model for the child and, unlike all of the other strangers in the child's life, this

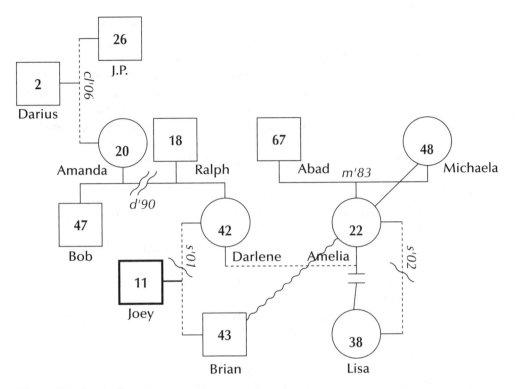

Figure 6.4 Joey's Genogram

relative is physically linked to the child for life. Finding a family is finding a potential source of support as well as the potential source of the problem.

Consider Figure 6.4. Joey is the 11-year-old son of Darlene (42) and Brian (43). Darlene and Brian have been separated (one slash mark) since Darlene moved in with Amelia (22). Joey spends his weekdays with his father, Brian, and spends his weekends with his mother and his mother's partner, Amelia. Joey also has a close relationship with his older stepbrother, Ralph (18).

Joey identifies five people for his genogram: himself, his mother Darlene, his father Brian, his stepmother Amelia, and his stepbrother Ralph. His mother adds the other people. When Joey sees her add these other people to his genogram, he begins to ask questions about Bob, Darlene's first husband. He asks if his mom knew then that she liked girls. Joey and his mother begin to talk about relationships while they look at his genogram, and their conversation reveals that Joey has been bullied at school because of his "weird moms." His school problems emerge from the homophobia he experiences there, plus his confusion over his mom's apparent change in sexual orientation. This subject was taboo at home where Joey was perceived as being too young to know about sex. This put him in the disempowered position of having some, but not all, of the information that he needs for his daily life. The genogram helps to fill the gaps in his information. He may not fully understand his mother's sexual orientation, but he now feels closer to his mother who assures him of her love.

There are many genogram models, all of which have similar characteristics of simplicity, clarity, and literacy. The genogram is truly an open book if it is co-constructed honestly by the child and the worker. It is meant to be read easily by the child, the family, and the workers who consult the genogram in the child's file many years later. There are no words on the genogram except the names of family members. In this way any child can read the genogram even when linguistic or literacy barriers exist. The following are guidelines for a simple, child-directed genogram:

- Females are represented by circles and males by squares. The age of the person is put inside the circle or square, and the name of the person is put under the circle or square.
- Genograms are read from left to right, the oldest child in the family being furthest to the left.
- A solid line denotes a close relationship, and a dotted line denotes a distant relationship.
- A double solid line indicates a very close relationship, and a squiggly line indicates tension in the relationship.
- Separation is shown by one slash mark, and divorce by two.
- Pregnancies are indicated by a triangular shape.
- Death is indicated by an X and a date of death.
- The genogram itself is signed and dated.

Co-constructing genograms, sociograms, and lifelines helps to develop and establish an equal power dynamic between worker and child in the very first meeting. Instead of the child looking for answers from the worker, the worker looks for information and direction from the child. This equalizing of power creates a positive and optimistic problem-solving environment.

Sociograms depict the child's social networks or community and are particularly helpful for children who feel unsupported, disliked, and alone. Once again, the child is placed at the centre of the sociogram, and friends are recalled and added by the child. A dialogue between a worker (W) and child (C) during the co-construction of the sociogram may sound like this:

C : I don't have any friends at school, so it's no big deal.
W: So when it's lunch you usually eat alone, right?
C : Yeh, Ahmed joins me sometimes. But he isn't in my class.
W: Ahmed?
C : Yeh. He was at my last foster home.
W: Are there any other kids from that home at your school?
C : Simon's there, but he's in the baby class. His sister, April, is in my class.

W: Do you ever eat lunch with her?

C: Are you kidding? She's a complete loser. She always wants to sit with me on the school bus, but I tell her to get lost.

W: You do?

C: Yeh. She bugs me when I'm on the bus.

W: I guess you'd rather sit alone?

C: Marshall sits with me and we make all kinds of noise. We drive the driver nuts!

The drawing of this sociogram reveals that the child with no friends actually has at least four immediate social connections: Marshall, Ahmed, Simon, and April. More children will be added to the sociogram, some from past foster homes and others from the current home and school. Teachers, neighbours, coaches, and bus drivers may be added too. The child watches these social connections emerge on the sociogram and feels the influence of these connections as well as the support they might offer.

Older children appreciate the lifeline, life path, or life river. This can be drawn as a winding line or a straight one that begins at the child's year of birth. Events that are significant for the child are noted on the line. This pictorial representation of life events supports **autobiographical reasoning** and the construction of life narratives, as well as memories of resiliency and problems solved. A dialogue between a worker (W) and a youth transitioning out of foster care (Y) may sound like this:

Y: I've been in care all my life, and now I'm getting kicked out of care.

W: It feels like that—getting kicked out?

Y: Yeh. Have to move out by the end of June. Then where do I go?

W: Let's work on that. Help me out here with a lifeline. You were born in 1996. You came into care in 2005 when you were nine, right?

Y: I guess so. But before that—how many aunts and uncles and stepdads?

W: Let me plot it on your line. You lived with your mom for six months until 1997. Then you lived with your aunt for three years until she left Alberta. In 2000, you moved back with your mom. Then you stayed with an uncle for a year (2001). Then you moved back with your mom and step-dad in 2002. Wow! You were on the move a lot and you still kept up with your class. It looks like you did really well in Grade 5 when you were in your foster home.

Y: Yeh. It is pretty amazing when I think about it. Grade 5 was a good year!!

W: Then your foster mom got sick and you had to move to Medicine Hat.

Y: That was horrible.

W: When was that?

Y: Right at the end of Grade 8. No wonder I wouldn't go to high school.

W: Yeh. You did really well in Grade 8. The teachers wrote so many great comments on your school report that year. You played soccer too.

Y: I forgot about that.

The co-construction of the lifeline reminds this youth how adversity has been overcome, problems solved, and challenges met. The youth moves from hopelessness to hopefulness as a new chapter of independent living begins. The youth recognizes a pattern of moving and a pattern of overcoming obstacles. Lifelines graphically represent these patterns and offer hope for the future.

Engaging Caregivers

Caregivers include parents, foster parents, guardians, extended family, siblings, and adoptive parents—all those who provide daily care and nurturance for the child. Their investment in and attachment to the child varies, but they all have intimate knowledge of the child whom they care for every day. Sometimes they are the ones who provide long-term or lifetime care for the child, and sometimes they provide only a few months of daily care. In both cases, it is important that they are fully involved with planning for the child's optimum care. The worker's role is to inspire and maintain that engagement. When the first meeting is over it is the caregiver who provides the care, not the worker, and it is the caregiver who decides upon the volume, shape, tempo, and style of this care. The child-focused worker recognizes that a homemade and shared plan of care is more likely to succeed than one that is imposed by an outsider.

The best place to engage caregivers is in their home, a place where they feel comfortable and in control. Agency offices and meeting rooms are a poor substitute. Home is also the context for the child's daily life and can provide clues to the child's functioning within the family dynamics. The worker hears the sounds in the home, smells the cooking, sees the unwashed laundry, and feels the mood. The worker sees where the child sleeps and eats and plays and where the child is not allowed to sleep, eat, and play. Sometimes a parent's office is strictly off limits. Sometimes the dining room is only used for company. Sometimes a television is the only piece of furniture in the living room and all the meals are eaten on the floor in front of the television. The home is a stage on which the child and caregivers play out the drama of daily life. This stage either supports or undermines the child's daily care.

The worker prepares for a home visit by following these five steps:

1. Identify preliminary objectives for the visit and potential areas of challenge and cultural differences. Assess personal bias in engaging with the caregivers.
2. Note names, relationships, and identified family and child assets or strengths, and prepare a preliminary genogram.
3. Do an online search for potential sources of family support in the caregiver's community, and list these sources with contact information.
4. Collect identification tag or card, mobile phone, needed agency documents, plus any materials that can be left with the family. Practical materials (baby carrier, learning toy, diapers) are always preferable to reading materials.

Point to Consider 6.2

Child Carers

Child carers provide care and support on a regular basis to another family member. Their feeding, cleaning, bathing, and personal care responsibilities to a family member are essential to the maintenance of their family. Most child carers provide less than 20 hours of care per week, but an estimated 8 per cent provide over 50 hours of care per week (Butler and Hickman, 2011: 108). A Vancouver study (Charles, Stainton, and Marshall, 2012) revealed that 12 per cent of high school students are child carers, and it is estimated that there is one child carer in every Canadian classroom (Action Canada, 2013: 2).

These children tend to hide their caregiving role and their family's problems from others. They may resent their chores at times, but their resentment is counterbalanced by their intense loyalty to the persons they care for and their family. Street smart and mature, compassionate and caring, they have little patience and even less time for the pranks and play of their peers. They have few (if any) structural supports. They are too young to qualify for provincial or territorial caregiver funding. If they ask authorities for help, they risk being taken from their families, which would leave family members without any care. However, exhaustion and stress may also lead to their dropping out of school or becoming ill themselves because of their caregiving responsibilities.

5. Provide the visit details (address, telephone number, time and length of visit) to a supervisor, and ensure that this supervisor is apprised of any safety concerns.

Upon arrival at the home, the worker parks facing outwards for prompt and easy exit, and then quickly surveys the immediate vicinity of the home. The worker may park several blocks away in certain districts, and may check the apartment corridor before knocking on the apartment door. Baby, the heroine of Heather O'Neill's (2006: 7) *Lullabies for Little Criminals*, describes her Montreal neighbourhood: "That neighbourhood looked the worst in the morning. The street was empty and there was vomit on the sidewalk. All the colourful lights had been turned off and the sky was the color of television static." Despite the lack of food, the rats, the squalor, and the drugs, her father Jules walks Baby to school every morning. Outside the school they "gave each other seven kisses for good luck" (O'Neill, 2006: 7), and then he rushes home to shoot up more drugs. Her tone and choice of words, her resilience in the face of poverty, neglect, and abuse, are evident. A few minutes checking the vicinity of her home would enlighten any worker who wanted to get to know Baby.

The worker who gets these few minutes on the child's street is lucky. Before knocking or ringing the doorbell, the worker listens carefully for any sounds of animals, television shows, doors banging, or children crying. If no one opens the door, the worker phones the residents to let them know of her arrival. If there is no answer, the worker leaves a message with the expected time for a return visit. If the person who opens the door appears to be intoxicated or drugged, violent or suspicious, the worker leaves immediately and does not enter the home. If the person does not allow the worker to enter, the worker identifies herself and her mandate. Child protection workers have full authority to enter without a warrant if there is suspicion that a child is at risk, while other service workers may have to return later with a child protection worker.

The worker enters the home only when there is an assurance of safety: no weapons, no violent persons, and no unleashed animals within the home. The worker identifies herself and her mandate again, and then introduces herself to each family member. The worker's position is that of a visitor, a stranger in the home, and the caregiver sets the tone. If the caregiver stands when the grandmother comes into the room, the worker also stands. If the family members take off their shoes in the home, the worker does the same. These signs of respect demonstrate an acknowledgement of the family culture.

The children in the home may hide from the worker, try to hug and kiss the worker, distract the caregiver, or dominate the meeting with their cries. The caregiver may react angrily to their cries or feel compelled to ignore them, fearing the worker's disapproval for turning towards the children and away from the worker's questions. Caregivers usually feel judged by the worker and respond in different ways: anger, antipathy, defensiveness, and antagonism. They may express anger because of past negative experiences with workers, agencies, the system itself, or other power and control agents and agencies. Alternatively, they may express antipathy towards the worker and a general reluctance to tell their story to someone who appears to offer nothing. Some caregivers are defensive regarding their caregiving and clearly articulate their previous efforts to get supports or respite. Others have prepared a list of demands and express exactly what they want. In addition to these responses, there are a myriad of cultural responses to worker intrusion, ranging from anger to friendliness.

The worker anticipates these reactions and acknowledges them before beginning the meeting, affirming the caregiver's authority in the home and prior experiences with workers and agencies. One lone mother I visited was working full-time outside the home in addition to parenting her nine children. She had schedules written in Arabic on her kitchen wall. They were as clear and well-constructed as any genogram from the case files. Her strength in organization was immediately evident to me and, when I praised her, her very tired eyes sparkled.

During this first brief meeting the caregiver watches the worker's body language; this includes how the worker gets to the home, where the worker parks, whether the worker rings the bell or knocks on the front door, where the worker chooses to sit, what the worker eats or drinks in the home, and what the worker wears. Some workers leave their coats on during the entire visit, while others wear their religious beliefs

Note from the Field   6.2

The Power of Laughter

Humour opens, oils, and sometimes accelerates the planning process. A moment of shared laughter can defuse tension, reduce stress, and kick-start that essential working relationship. This is indicated in the following dialogue between a worker (W) and caregiver (C).

C : She throws tantrums at home whenever I ask her to do anything—eat breakfast, take off her snowsuit, turn off the television. She's hit me, I don't know how many times, with anything she can find. She is sitting over there playing quietly now, but that never happens at home!

W: That often happens here.

C : What does?

W: Children play with the toys quietly, whereas at home they scream and shout at their parents.

C : Is that true?

W: Yes. Lucky for me because I'm not wearing a helmet today and that doll could really hurt my head.

C : (Laughs) You really wear a helmet?

W: (Laughs) No. But it sounds like you need one at home.

around their necks or dangling from their ears. This sends out a very loud cultural message to the family and certainly establishes clear and rigid boundaries. The worker's cultural and boundary messages impact the relationship with the family and any interventions that the worker may attempt.

One family that I worked with was more impressed with my mode of transportation than with any of the resources that I suggested. Because I took the bus to their home rather than a car, they welcomed me with warmth and friendliness. They had never owned a car, so taking a bus positioned me closer to their culture than previous workers, and they opened up to me more easily. Telling me which bus to take home and the schedule of that bus positioned them as the smart ones, the ones with the information. They felt in control of the situation not only because it was their home but also because they knew more about the neighbourhood (and the bus!) than I did. I looked to them as a source of genuine and tangible information, first.

As a result of this positioning, each member of that family began to tell me a story about the family and their role in the family. Each member of the family had a presenting problem that involved another member of the family and each demanded an urgent solution, perhaps one that I had brought in my briefcase or that I could impose on them from my position of authority. But my briefcase had no magic pills, and my authority in their home would be temporary at best. The family member they identified would still be their parent, brother, or sister long after I had left the family. The solution lay within their family already and together we worked to locate it.

I listened carefully to their narratives. I watched as the parents looked at me, occasionally at their child, and never at each other. I watched the brother slip out of the room to "do homework," and then watched as he slipped out through the kitchen door and into the street. I saw the crowded bedrooms and the empty cupboards in the kitchen. I watched and listened, and I asked them questions that affirmed their strength and reframed their current problems as transitory challenges they could meet and overcome:

- How do you make sense of what is happening? What does it look like to you?
- How would you like your family to function?
- What works, even for a while?
- Are there times when things seem better than now?

When only one person spoke I tried to engage the others in the meeting:

- Thanks for all the information. You are really working hard here. Maybe somebody else should take it for a while.
- Well, I think I understand your view. I'm going to need everyone else's for this work. Who's up next?
- You really have a good grasp of the situation. What can the rest of you tell me?
- That took courage to speak first. Now you can relax and listen to what the others have to say. Who's next?

Patterns of communication began to emerge while they offered their solutions.

Triangulation is the most common pattern in families, with the child being the buffer between caregivers, two siblings, or a parent and a sibling. Siblings talk about each other to the child, but never talk with each other. Similarly, caregivers talk to the child about each other, but never talk to each other. Sometimes the worker is caught up in triangulation as parents ally with the worker and against the child. I also noted familiar areas of conflict over school, bedtime, chores, or friends. I observed that some subjects were simply not discussed, and certain absent family members were never mentioned. These patterns of triangulation, conflict, and avoidance formed the delicate pathways that the child walked every day in the home.

The worker maps these triangulation patterns and notes significant words and phrases. A sample case note of a first meeting with the Cross family (Figure 6.5) shows three caregivers in this home: Loretta, Mamoud, and Mrs Ibiza. Loretta and Mamoud are married, and Mrs Ibiza is Mamoud's mother. She speaks Farsi but cannot read English, so Mamoud explains the case note to her. They correct the worker, adding the correct age of Mrs Ibiza, and they question the triangle, offering further information about their relationships. Loretta adds to the two quotations attributed to her. Mamoud

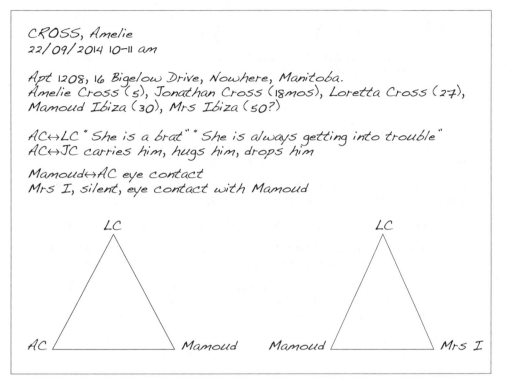

CROSS, Amelie
22/09/2014 10-11 am

Apt 1208, 16 Bigelow Drive, Nowhere, Manitoba.
Amelie Cross (5), Jonathan Cross (18mos), Loretta Cross (27),
Mamoud Ibiza (30), Mrs Ibiza (50?)

AC↔LC "She is a brat" "She is always getting into trouble"
AC↔JC carries him, hugs him, drops him

Mamoud↔AC eye contact
Mrs I, silent, eye contact with Mamoud

Figure 6.5 Home Visit Case Note

explains why he looks accusingly at his stepdaughter Amelie during the meeting. All of their explanations and questions are added to the case note before Loretta, Mamoud, Mrs Ibiza, and Amelie sign it. This affirms their lead role in the caregiving and the planning process.

With their lead role comes the responsibility for developing solutions that work for both the children and the family as a whole. The worker listens to their solutions and their hopes, affirms their capability and expertise, and encourages them to share their expertise and life experience. If Loretta identifies a bullying problem in the family, for example, the worker can ask her to recount her own experiences with bullying. She may talk about being bullied when she was a child, describing how she felt and how she reacted. This helps the worker to contextualise her caregiving. This also helps Amelie to understand that her mother was once a little girl with experiences and expertise from which she can learn. In the end, the worker and the family construct a new and more hopeful narrative that is culturally appropriate for their family.

The worker also identifies those structural determinants that impact the caregiving. These may include federal, provincial and territorial, municipal, and Band subsidies (Table 6.2), food bank support, and benefits. Caregivers do not always use these subsidies, supports, and benefits effectively or to the fullest degree. A worker in British

Table 6.2 Federal Programs for Children, 2013

Aboriginal Head Start initiative provides supplemental learning programs for children and parenting courses for their parents.

Adoption Expense Deduction is a tax deduction for parents who adopt children to help them recover eligible costs associated with the process of adoption.

Canada Child Tax Benefit (CCTB) is a tax-free monthly payment made to eligible families to help them with the costs of raising children under 18 years of age. The CCTB may include the National Child Benefit Supplement (NCBS) and the Child Disability Benefit (CDB).

Canada Education Savings Grant (CESG) provides grants to Registered Education Savings Plan (RESP) contributors until the beneficiaries reach the age of 17.

Canada Prenatal Nutrition Program (CPNP) provides support for "at risk" pregnant women.

Child Disability Benefit (CDB) is a tax-free benefit for eligible families who care for children under the age of 18 who have a severe and prolonged impairment in mental or physical functions.

Children's Arts Tax Credit lets parents claim up to $500 per year for eligible artistic, cultural, recreational, or developmental program expenses paid for each child who is under 16 years of age (under 18 if the child has a disability) at the beginning of the year in which expenses are paid.

Children's Fitness Tax Credit lets parents claim up to $500 per year for eligible fitness expenses paid for each child who is under 16 years of age (under 18 if the child has a disability) at the beginning of the year in which expenses are paid.

Community Action Program for Children (CAPC) provides funding to community groups who deliver programs for children from birth to six years of age who are deemed "**at risk.**"

Family Supplements are provided by Employment Insurance to low-income families to raise the replacement level of lost income while parents are on parental leave.

Federal Child Support Guidelines ensure that family support obligations are respected.

National Child Benefit Supplement (NCBS) is a tax-free monthly payment made to eligible families for each child who is under 18 years of age.

Paid maternity and parental leaves are for parents covered by Employment Insurance (EI).

Universal Child Care Benefit (UCCB) is a monthly payment of $100 per child made to all families who have children under six years of age.

Columbia commented, "A grandmother explained that she chose to avoid asking for needed services because she was afraid that the Ministry would become involved and apprehend her grandchildren from her" (qtd in Bennett and Sadrehashemi, 2008: 27). Almost half of those who need food bank support never go to a food bank. Over half of mothers who are entitled to parental leave under employment insurance also do not claim this benefit. There are many reasons for this reluctance to claim subsidies, supports, and benefits:

- distrust of authority and authority figures such as police officers, child welfare workers, teachers, and health visitors;
- cultural and family pride, and the desire to remain independent;
- illiteracy and the inability to read and understand forms;
- inability to speak either French or English;
- lack of telephone;
- lack of online access; and
- lack of transportation.

The worker who identifies subsidies, supports, and benefits must also ensure access to them. The worker may arrange for a translator or cultural interpreter to assist with completing forms or a drive to a food bank, toy lending library, or family resource centre. This practical support engages caregivers in a genuine way, and extends the first meeting by prompting conversations that happen away from the home. Caregivers often share their memories, opinions, and feelings from the back seat of a car and disclose secrets during the drive that they would never disclose at home. Practical support converts structural determinants into assets for daily life, empowering caregivers to seek solutions.

 Note from the Field   6.3

Practical Supports

Behaviour problems, too many activities, clutter, poverty, and overwhelming chores can drain the physical and emotional resources of a caregiver. When the worker offers agency pamphlets or lists of government supports, this often seems to add stress rather than reduce it. A well-informed and respectful worker offers practical supports instead. Rather than teaching bedtime routine, the worker sits with the caregiver during that hour before bedtime. The worker quietly helps with the bathing or reading, firmly discourages loud or boisterous play, and talks with the caregiver after the child is in bed. Quiet conversation happens naturally in the early evening as the child sleeps, as it does when the worker and the caregiver sort through food in the kitchen, discarding the food that may be harmful for the child. The caregiver explains which fresh vegetables the children eat, and the worker suggests where to find these vegetables at low or no cost. Practical supports, encouragement, and shared parenting stories build relationships and lighten the caregiving load.

Summary

Preparation through reflection is fundamental to a successful first meeting. From an understanding of the power dynamics that differentiate meetings from interviews, you learned how to prepare for a meeting with a child or a child and family. You learned how important your body language, tone, and attitude are in conveying your empathy and respect for the child. You also learned how to use genograms, sociograms, and lifelines effectively in this first meeting. Much depends upon your listening to the child: the gestures, the play, and the silences. This listening is a skill that will be explained in the next chapter as we explore autobiographical reasoning and the slow and deliberate construction of the child's narrative.

Review Questions

1. What is praxis and how is it similar to mindfulness?
2. How are knowing, being, and doing connected?
3. Name three ways in which a meeting is different from an interview.
4. What are the five steps a worker takes to prepare for a home visit?
5. Does everyone have personal bias? Explain, giving examples.
6. Name five aspects of family culture that must be considered in developing a healthy working relationship with a family.
7. Why might you choose to co-create a genogram rather than a lifeline with a young child?
8. What can be learned during a home visit?
9. Why would a family not welcome a home visit? Suggest three ways you can begin a home visit when encountering a family's initial resistance to your visit.
10. Name five potential sources of financial assistance available to a lone mother of an eight-year-old child who is in an after-school daycare program. The mother is working full-time outside the home but does not earn a living wage.

Discussion Questions

1. Have you ever reacted to a child's behaviour and then regretted your reaction? How might praxis have changed your intervention?
2. Draw your own genogram and then share your genogram with another student. What questions did that student ask that caused you to adjust or reconsider your genogram?
3. How might you introduce yourself the first time you meet a child or youth? Write down two introductions you might use, one with a six-year-old child and one with a 15-year-old youth. Now test your introductions the next time you meet a child.

7 The Child's Story

Grown-ups never understand anything by themselves, and it is tiresome for children to be always and forever explaining things to them.

—Antoine de Saint-Exupéry, *The Little Prince*

A personal narrative develops and evolves as one experiences life and immortalizes segments of this life in memories. Each new experience becomes part of this life narrative, while some experiences are altered or discarded along the way. Telling the life narrative to others helps one to reflect on experiences and make sense of one's life in the larger relational context.

When people relate family anecdotes or tell about experiences that reveal unusual twists and turns of relationships, they put these anecdotes and experiences into a structure or story. When listeners react to those stories with pity, anger, or joy, the storytellers observe such reactions and adjust their stories accordingly. The next time they tell their stories, they may leave out events, embellish them, change the names or dates, or put someone else or some other feature at centre stage. In this way, our stories evolve and develop just as people do. A toddler tells a story quite differently when she becomes a preschooler and adjusts her story again as an adolescent. These stories become part of her always-evolving life narrative, which, in turn, begins to reflect her self-image and self-concept as it is shaped and moulded by the surrounding structure.

Each member of a family has a personal story within the family life narrative. A father who experiences his child's first steps interprets this experience quite differently than the older sister who watches these first steps. For the father, this event might be like a miracle in his life, the moment at which his son begins to walk. For the sister, this might be a moment to fear, a moment in which her little brother takes over the attention of her father and begins to get into all of her toys. The same family story, told by different members of the family, sounds quite different as each member tells it. Like witnesses at the scene of an accident, each person sees the same accident but each sees only certain elements of the accident and experiences these elements in a personal way. Each witness tells the story from a personal perspective and through the window of his or her personal culture.

As the family evolves and as each member of the family grows and develops, the family narrative also evolves. Sometimes one unresolved problem piles on top of another, interfering with the narrative until the entire family narrative becomes problem-saturated. The family forgets about the good times, and the problem-saturated narrative becomes the dominant family narrative. Structural determinants are not identified and seen as oppressions. Instead, the family begins to own these oppressive structural determinants, absorbing them into the family problem. At this point, the family, or one member of the family, may turn to a worker for help with a presenting problem.

The worker uses the AHA! Method to listen to the pain and sadness of the problem-saturated story. Structural determinants contextualize the story; these determinants are questioned and confronted. Specific challenges and problems are named and externalized as metaphors, and the story is re-authored, name by name and experience by experience. The child and the family begin to move forward from a problem-saturated family narrative to a more positive one.

Objectives

By the end of this chapter, you will:

- Recognize the difference between a "story" and a "narrative" and how auto-biographical reasoning creates this difference.
- Understand how to listen to the child's narrative using the AHA! Method.
- Identify the many underlying problems beneath the presenting problem.
- Demonstrate how to support the child's narrative through externalizing the problem and identifying it as a metaphor, contextualizing, and re-authoring.

Autobiographical Reasoning

As one grows and develops, a life narrative evolves. Each experience is a story of its own; when compiled and edited, these stories become the life narrative. These stories may be internalized and never told, or told much later, once a sorting process has identified the roles of the people in the story and the emotions behind the storyline. On the other hand, the story may be told right after the experience. As the story is told, it evolves. Each listener, each storytelling context, and each storytelling experience impacts the story. Each one of these stories—told, retold, and untold—becomes part of the life narrative.

Young children tend to tell stories about events in terms of what the people in the events look like. A young child may describe a teacher as a "witch" and a neighbour as "grandma." The child calls the neighbour "grandma" because the child associates the neighbour with grandmotherly qualities and physical characteristics. The child calls the teacher "witch" because of her harsh words and demeanour. This "mistake" is not lying or deception. This form of description is simple preconventional morality at work (see Chapter 3). The young child uses morally dichotomous terms that reflect a simplistic morality of "good" and "bad." As Harvard professor John Gibbs (2014: 42) observes, "Young children's tendency not to keep in mind intangible or subtle considerations means that their moral evaluations tend to be absolute and inflexible."

Some of the child's stories, and some parts of the stories, are already metaphorical. Fantasy figures such as the good fairy, Santa Claus, dragons, and witches are blended together with the family dog in these stories, and all of the characters in the stories are considered to be equally real. The child demonstrates skill at engaging these fantasy figures with the real people or animals in each story. This skill also reflects the preoperational reasoning of the young child. Like Piaget's daughter Lucienne, the afternoon does not exist when the child is napping (see Chapter 3). The teacher lives in the school; the family dog may talk to the child at night; and there may be a monster under the bed.

School-aged children develop concrete operational thinking while they are developing complex language skills and a deeper socio-emotional understanding of people. They begin to reflect on the motivations of others and to see morality in less dichotomous terms. The "bad" and "good" of the young child are replaced by "seems to be mean" and "sometimes okay" of the older child. The child begins to construct more complex stories that reflect a deeper understanding of other people's motivations as well as a growing self-awareness. Fantasy figures deemed to be childish or silly are replaced by **avatars** and movie stars.

School-aged children also begin to try to connect the past events of their lives to the emotions surrounding these events. They sift through their memories, already faded by time, keeping some and discarding others, depending on whether these memories support their current ego identification. Neil Sutherland (2003) calls these random memories "the winds of childhood" and suggests that they are only glimpses, especially when the winds are from infancy or very early childhood. Children use these winds to make sense of the present or to adjust their present self to the remembered self. This reflective process is called autobiographical reasoning, and it usually begins in middle childhood when stories, past and present, are contextualized by emotional and moral reasoning.

An angry 12-year-old girl may look at her baby pictures and see only scowls on her tiny face. The pictures may remind her of the toddler tantrums she has often been told about by her parents. She begins to see herself as an inherently angry person, and anger becomes her narrative. Similarly, a lonely 12-year-old boy will look at his camp pictures and only remember how much he hated camp. He will mentally discard the pictures of himself laughing with his bunk buddies. He will see the pictures from camp as further evidence that he is himself friendless or unsociable or different.

Loretta Hostettler/iStockphoto

Photo 7.1 The lifebook records memories but she chooses which memories to keep.

Michael White (1989, 2007) developed the theory that people's lives are actually shaped and organized by their life narratives. He believes that individual stories not only mirror the past but also shape the future as the child reinterprets the past through these stories. The angry girl sees her past as being full of anger and sees only one future for herself—a future full of bitterness and anger. The lonely boy will push away classmates who call on him or ask him to join the team. He will see these friendly overtures as phony and shallow because he is now convinced that he is destined to be friendless.

A family whose **dominant narrative** is that they are all "losers" may only remember and recount their stories of failures and problems. Happy moments, family celebrations, jokes, and laughter are discarded, suppressed, or minimized. This dominant narrative of "losers" is repeated so many times and over so many years that everyone in the family now knows it, believes it, and behaves accordingly. The family gets stuck in its problematic narrative and the members mould themselves and their experiences to fit into this narrative. If someone in the family has brief success, it is not celebrated. Instead, this success is seen as an aberration and a reason to turn away from that person until that person has another failure. The dominant narrative requires this reaction and causes the family to feel too discouraged to move forward or to change. The family may feel that they can never succeed and can never alter their narrative of being "losers."

This dominant narrative tends to be generated from the dominant person in the family. If the family structure is hierarchical and patriarchal, the father may construct the dominant narrative of his daughter and may repeat this narrative until the daughter and everyone else in the family believes it. The father may repeat a problem-saturated story of his daughter, carefully constructing the dominant narrative of the daughter as "stupid" or "idiotic." This same story and these same terms are repeated by the family power figure (in this case, the father) until the dominant narrative is believed and ingrained and perpetuated, or at least not contradicted, by all of the members of the family, including the daughter, who now identifies herself as "stupid" and "idiotic."

This is a symbiotic process. The autobiographical reasoning of each member of the family both contributes to and is affected by the dominant family narrative. In this patriarchal family, the narratives of the less powerful members of the family are often not expressed, or, if they are expressed, they are not accepted. The brother, who no longer lives in the home, may not contribute to this dominant narrative of his sibling. This brother may have some very important and illuminating stories to tell about his sister, and his more positive stories could contribute to a richer understanding of her behaviour. However, because he no longer lives at home, his voice is neither recognized nor accepted, and his sister's narrative is untouched by his contribution.

Another daughter in the family may have absorbed the dominant narrative that she also is stupid. She puts aside memories of successes and achievements and instead remembers only failures. Moments of success at school are either forgotten or dismissed as exceptions or aberrations. She may say, "I've always sucked at school" and may not accept a tutor or an extra study class on the grounds that the dominant family narrative shows that such interventions are always unsuccessful. This maladaptive narrative is constructed incrementally over the years and reinforces the negative self-concept of that daughter, eventually becoming an obstacle to her health and wellness.

Many children construct life narratives that are negative and problem-saturated through this process of autobiographical reasoning. Their parents have repeatedly told them (or perhaps only once and it sticks!) that they are clumsy, so "clumsy kid" becomes a persona in the older child's narrative. A sister may have taunted the child with the nickname of Plain Jane, so "ugly me" becomes the child's dominant persona. Without anyone in the family to interject and offer happy stories and memories, the child may begin to reason that life has always been unhappy or problematic. An eight-year-old boy may say, "I've never been good at sports." A 13-year-old girl may say, "My sister and I have always fought." The child believes this narrative because it has been carefully constructed through autobiographical reasoning and it has been supported and verified by the dominant family narrative.

Structural oppression supports the narrative. Racism convinces a child that his race is tainted, unworthy, and insignificant. Ableism oppresses the child with cerebral palsy, describing her struggles to play sport as clumsy, futile, and weak. Cultural beliefs about poverty tell the child in a poor family that he is a failure and that his mother is lazy or stupid because she is not rich. Sexism convinces girls who like to build engines that they are "weird." Structural oppression, when not countered by community or family culture, continuously affects the child's autobiographical reasoning.

There are those who are able to counter structural oppression and an inherited negative narrative. A child may singlehandedly defy racial oppression while other family members accept it. A child may embrace the power of her gender and challenge gender constructs accepted by the family. A child may see a structural determinant such as ableism as a challenge and a problem that needs to be solved. For example, Jason Kingsley and Mitchell Levitz challenge ableism in their book, *Count Us In*, in which they describe their experiences as persons with Down's syndrome. Despite medical advice to institutionalize them, despite exclusion from schools, committees, and sports activities, Jason and Mitchell have become advocates for the message that "people with disabilities *can learn*" (2007: 27, emphasis in original). They challenge the structural determinants and the inherited narrative to construct a more hopeful narrative for themselves, which they are now able to share with others.

Children need to make sense of their lives, past and present, and so they engage in autobiographical reasoning. When they tell their stories they also conduct a backward search for memories that support their dominant life narrative. Memories are not so much retrieved as rewoven. The memories that do not fit either are not retrieved or are shaped to fit, rewoven into the dominant life narrative. Threads are added, weaving is tightened or not, and the tapestry emerges. Because children want to experience their own intentions as "good," their rewoven stories justify their behaviours as being the only possible way to act in the circumstances; in other words, they "did good."

A 10-year-old girl who has not seen her father since she was a toddler and who really misses fatherly love and attention needs to make some sense of that absent father and manage her own feelings about him. She also needs to make sense of and incorporate her mother's story of her father as an irresponsible and uncaring man. She suppresses her warm and intimate memories of her father; she may bury these memories so deeply that they are temporarily forgotten. They are certainly not retrieved for her dominant narrative. She begins to reason that her father abandoned her because he really did not care about her, a reflection of her mother's story of the uncaring husband and a way to deal with her own feelings of abandonment. She incorporates that story into her life narrative to make sense of the past and the present. If her father reappears in her life when she is a teenager, she probably will reject him because of her carefully shaped narrative. Her autobiographical reasoning tells her that her father is not to be trusted.

The adopted child needs to make sense of having been relinquished by her birth parent, so may gradually assimilate a social construction that mothers who relinquish their children are bad mothers who abandon their babies. She may also assimilate her adoptive parents' story that they "saved her" or "chose her," which implies that her birth mother was hurting her or did not choose her. This feeling of rejection is too much for any child to bear, so the child carefully constructs a story in which her birth mother was bad and her current caregivers (her adoptive parents) are good. This story becomes problematic as the child tries to reconcile being both chosen (wanted) and bad (she is her mother's daughter, after all). Should she eventually contact her birth family, her dominant narrative becomes further compromised. The child may be left with attachment injuries (see Chapter 4) and a feeling of betrayal by all of the significant adults in her life. This feeling of betrayal has huge socio-emotional consequences as she struggles to make these contradictory, constructed stories fit into her dominant narrative.

The child's narrative formed through autobiographical reasoning represents three lives: one that has been lived; one that has been experienced; and one that is being told. The life lived is what actually happened. The life experienced consists of the images, feelings, sentiments, desires, thoughts, and meanings acquired through living that life. The life being told is shaped by the structural context, the dominant family narrative, the contributions of others, and the cultural conventions of the storytelling. Out of all of these threads comes the child's narrative. As the worker carefully listens to this spoken narrative, the worker also attaches meanings and interpretations to the stories, and these spoken interpretations and silent responses contribute to the evolving co-construction of this narrative.

The Importance of Listening

There is a popular mythology that children are always listened to by adults. It is commonly suggested that adults spend too much time listening to children and that adults should teach children not to interrupt. This socially constructed myth is the subject of many parenting advice books.[1] The deconstruction of this myth requires only a short period of observation. Watch what happens when children talk to adults. In the home, children are told to wait, to listen, and to be quiet. When parents or caregivers do talk to children it is often to correct them, teach them, or control them. Sometimes they are ignored, sometimes misinterpreted, and often marginalized: "Not now!" or "Save that for later." In school, children are told to listen to adults before speaking. Students' speech is circumscribed by adult dictums and often limited to responses. If there is a student discussion or debate, this speech has boundaries and marks are dependent on adherence to these adult-set boundaries. Speaking about behaviours and feelings is typically confined to therapeutic settings, counselling, and social skills groups.

One of the largest studies of listening to children was conducted in Swedish child psychiatry sessions. This study (Cederborg, 1997) revealed that the 19 therapists (workers) spoke during 37.5 per cent of the sessions, parents for 56 per cent of the sessions, and the children for the remaining 6.5 per cent of the time. Workers have the language skills, authority, and comfort with the conversational process to construct and control the dominant narrative. There is no space in this conversation for children to speak, except to confirm or deny the dominant narrative, so children's voices and stories often are not heard. A Canadian boy in foster care spoke to Fay Martin (2003: 267) about the effect of this situation on his life: "Do you have any idea how hard it is to be always watched and never seen? To be constantly analyzed and never understood? That right there, that's loneliness."

Photo 7.2 The multi-tasking adult has little time to listen and no time to hear.

Michael White and other narrative therapists have championed clinical, educational, and community approaches for listening to the child's narrative. In Michael Ungar's story of Christine (2006: 8–11), he describes her teacher's active and affirming listening and how this affects Christine: "[He] listens as Christine tries on her new identity as social activist, educating her educators about the realities of today's youth. Mr Makhnach gives her space to speak, to play the expert rather than the problem kid." Mr Makhnach takes time to listen. He co-constructs the narrative with Christine through his active listening and, as a result, Christine begins to believe in herself and to actively engage in school.

When a teacher, parent, or worker asks the child to journal, have a chat, or describe an event or a feeling, and the adult really takes the time to actively listen or to read the journal, the child may initially feel very uncomfortable. If the adult persists, the child may begin to trust and may respond with a tentative story. When the adult affirms rather than judges or scolds the child, the child may continue that story. This listening without interruption or interpretation is crucial for the child: "We need to empower children such that they can tell of their experiences within the context of interviews that acknowledge the distinctions between life as lived, experienced and told" (Westcott and Littleton, 2005: 153).

The worker who actively listens is open and unbiased rather than directive and judgemental. There is no hidden agenda of trying to convince the child to make a particular change in direction. Instead, the worker is trying to understand the truth from the child's perspective. This attentive listening is empowering for the child because the child is the expert on the story and controls its shape and content. The child is the teller, not the one being told (how to behave, what to do, where to go). Every time the child tells the story, the emotions around the story change, as the power of the story begins to dissipate. This repetitive telling of the story to a safe and supportive listener can alleviate its emotional impact and bring relief to the child.

The power of this listening process is described by Carl Rogers (1980: 154). His colleague conducted a research study on visual perception that involved interviewing students regarding their visual perception history, their reaction to wearing glasses, and so on. The researcher listened to the students' replies with interest but made no judgements or comments on their replies. When the research interviews were completed, a number of the students returned spontaneously to thank the researcher for all of the help he had given them. Although he had not given them any overt support or direction whatsoever, he soon realized that his active and interested listening was seen by these students as helpful, even though his intent had been to gather information rather than to help. The impact of active listening on the participants' lives was enormous!

At the beginning of term, my graduate students do a half-hour assignment. They listen to two stories on film, one told by a 10-year-old girl and one told by a 12-year-old boy. Their reactions to the stories and their attentive listening are filmed, and they are given a mark on the basis of their filmed listening. Their only instruction is to listen attentively to the stories as they would in their professional capacity as workers.

My students bring to this exercise several years of curriculum work incorporating the theory and practice of attentive listening. They have already acquired many listening skills: how to focus on the client, lean forward, demonstrate empathy, and keep their body language open and comforting. Yet over half of the students fail this assignment! This result shocks them and rivets their attention towards the material in this chapter.

The 10-year-old girl tells a story about being sexually abused by her father. Although none of my students speak, their body language speaks volumes. Some bodies convey shock, disgust, anger, horror, and uneasiness; others convey sympathy and a desire to stop the story and comfort the little girl. If this were a real interview rather than a video, their body language would prompt the girl to feel guilty, ashamed, diminished, and unworthy. The girl would probably either stop telling her story or change her story, if only to comfort and re-engage the adult listener.

The girl's story is immediately followed by the boy's story. The 12-year-old boy tells a story about doing poorly in school. Without words, many of my students convey disinterest in this story, and some even convey disgust at the boy's weakness in the face of such a seemingly minor problem. Compared to incest, who really cares about poor grades? Their minds appear to wander, and they appear to be out of step with the boy's story. As a result, in a real interview setting the boy would begin to feel ashamed, diminished, and unworthy. The boy would probably either stop telling the story or change the story, if only to elicit support and attention from the adult listener.

Because the mark is based on filmed evidence, the students do not complain too loudly. The film corroborates their mark. After several screenings, the students begin to be able to identify and evaluate their own body language, their expressions and their posture. They see that flicker of disgust and disinterest in their eyes. They soon grow to understand the effect that their body language has on any interaction with a child.

So the first and most important lesson is accepted: listening to a child is a skill. It is a learning process for the worker and it can be an empowering process for the child. Watching Elders work with youth in a healing circle is enlightening. They are usually silent as they listen with their bodies and their minds. They tune into the thoughts of the youth as well as the others, past and present, in the circle. While we cannot pretend to be Elders, we can learn from them. Barbara Harris (2006: 125) reminds us, "Traditional learning processes are holistic. . . . Learning and healing go hand in hand, and that learning is based on watching, listening, and doing."

Group Exercise   7.1

Telling Left from Right

Most people feel that they are active listeners, particularly when their daily job involves listening. This large group exercise dispels this myth in a few minutes. The large group stands in a circle, and each person has a pen. The group leader first asks if everyone knows the difference between left and right. A show of hands usually confirms that everyone does know left from right.

The group leader then explains that a story will be read slowly. Each time the participants hear the word "right," they must pass their pens to the right. Each time the participants hear the word "left," they must pass their pens to the left. Then the group leader slowly reads the following story:

"Most children know that the right thing to do when there is only one cookie left is to share what's left with the right friend. But what if there are three cookies left and four friends? Who knows the right thing to do? If it's left to some right-thinking children, they will share what's left. But others will think, 'Right! I'm not sharing, no matter how many cookies are left.'"

When the pens are returned to their "rightful" owners, the participants can discuss why, even when they are told which words are important, it is still difficult to attend to the story, to listen and pick out the words. How much harder is it when the child speaks and all of the words that are spoken are potentially important!

Gerry Fewster (2002: 18) cautions, "However simple it seems, listening to another human being may be one of the most difficult tasks that we will ever embark upon. And, for most of us, listening to one of our children may border upon the impossible." Now the real work of change can begin for the students. I call this an AHA! moment, which is the precursor to being open to learning the **AHA! Method**. Now we can begin to Affirm, Here and now, and always be Authentic (AHA!) when listening to the child's narrative.

The AHA! Method

Listening is not an easy process. The AHA! Method guides this listening so that it is affirming, in the here and now, and authentic, leading to mutual understanding or the "Aha!" moment. The worker who affirms the child's pain, misery, and loneliness does not try to change or minimize these feelings in an effort to make the child smile. Instead, the worker affirms and validates these feelings, whatever they may be, and however disturbing, disgusting, or odious they may seem. There is no judgement here. Instead, this affirmation says that the child's feelings are important and that the worker respects and values these feelings. This non-judgemental affirmation of the feelings behind and in the words encourages the child to share more of these feelings with the worker.

A girl may tell the worker, for instance, that she is afraid her hospitalized mother will die. This is not the first time that she has told anyone about her fear. Her only mother is dying! She has lived this fear, then reflected on it and recounted it during sleep, play, and at school. She has said the words so many times and in so many ways to relatives, friends, and other professionals. When she has expressed her fear that her mother will die, however, her relatives and friends have misinterpreted, minimized, or even laughed at her emotions. In an effort to make her smile or make her feel better, they have offered her advice, fantasy, or lectures:

- You're not really afraid, are you? Your mom is in the best hospital in the city.
- That's just silly! It's so silly to be afraid.
- That doesn't make sense. Your mom is going to get better.
- I'm sure you don't mean that. You're a big brave girl.

Through these replies and these reactions from adults, the girl begins to doubt her own feelings and to be unsure of how and when to express her feelings. She learns that she is weak or simple-minded, making her unable to understand her mother's health situation. Most of all, she learns that her darker emotions, such as fear, are not to be expressed because these emotions are usually wrong and will be met with sarcasm, derision, or advice. It is safer for her to keep these emotions bottled up inside and not express them.

The worker who uses the AHA! Method affirms the child's expressed emotion rather than soothing, changing, or dismissing it. The worker asks questions only to clarify the emotion, not to lecture, dismiss, or blame. The worker is a curious listener, affirming and clarifying strengths whenever they appear. This affirmation supports the girl as she begins to trust her own feelings and as she gains a new sense of emotional knowledge, control, and responsibility. Fear and uncertainty about her mother's dying are replaced by feelings of her own competence and strength in expressing this fear. The worker's affirmation assumes that she is strong and competent and controls her own life narrative.

John Gottman (1997: 69–70) provides a personal example of the power of this affirmation. On a long airplane flight with his two-year-old daughter, Gottman realized that he had packed his daughter's favourite toy, Zebra, in the checked luggage rather than bringing Zebra on board. When she asked for the toy he explained this luggage situation slowly and carefully to his daughter. His daughter rejected his lengthy and careful explanation. She turned away from him and began to sob loudly. She continued to ask for Zebra, wailing and moaning, and the other passengers started to look at Gottman in disgust.

Even more agitated, he tried a different strategy. He stayed in the moment to hear his daughter's pain. He focused on the words and the emotions behind them as expressed by his daughter's gestures, posture, pauses, tone, cadence, and expression. What he now heard in his daughter's wails was loneliness; she was missing the comfort of Zebra. When he affirmed this feeling of loneliness to his daughter and expressed empathy, she immediately quieted and, within a few minutes, soothed herself to sleep.

© Radius Images/AllCanadaPhotos

Photo 7.3 Hearing the feelings behind the words means taking time to really listen.

The worker checks out the child's emotions before affirming them. Does the girl fear her mother's death, or does she dread it? Gottman asked his daughter if she felt lonely because Zebra was in another part of the airplane. He didn't tell her that she was lonely; he asked her. When the child identifies and names the emotion, the child is the controller of the story and the emotion. The worker listens and affirms the emotion expressed by the child. This affirmation in turn strengthens the child's self-esteem as the child takes charge over the emotion by naming it. Rogers (1980: 142) summarizes this skill of affirming: "It includes communicating your sensings of the person's world . . . frequently checking with the person as to the accuracy of your sensings and being guided by the responses you receive. You are a confident companion to the person in his or her inner world."

The child who is telling the story watches the worker's eyes, body, and comfort level for cues on how to change the story or when to stop the telling. A worker's raised eyebrows, slight frown, or drifting attention may cause the child to withhold parts of the story or to change the remembered events. Dana Fusco (2012: 37) notes, "This 'being present with' itself is of value to young people who too rarely find adults willing to just be with them. Most good practitioners understand intuitively that a young person will rarely respond if they feel like the adult(s) has a hidden agenda." Being "here and now" with the child is where the worker needs to be, not mentally planning the upcoming intervention. When the child says that homework is difficult, the worker listens to the sadness and frustration but does not race ahead to planning potential tutors, eye tests, study areas, cognitive assessments, and teacher consultations. The worker listens attentively to the child's body language and all that it discloses. By staying in the moment, the worker demonstrates respect for the child and authentic interest in the child's story.

The Rogerian worker–child relationship (see Chapter 5) is based on the worker's being authentic, honest, and congruent. Authentic listening is central to the AHA! Method. The worker does not fake interest in the child but is genuinely curious, interested in knowing more about the child and about the story that the child is telling. The worker listens carefully to the child's body language, the child's silence, and the sound of the child's words. The worker's total presence conveys genuine curiosity and affirmation, a powerful combination that supports the child's telling and prompts the child to tell even more. This means reflecting the story back to the child in a positive and curious way. The child tells the worker about an everyday event, then lapses into silence. The worker reflects on the everyday event and may ask, "What are you feeling now?" This genuine question expresses the worker's interest in knowing. In answer to this question, the child may express an emotion or thought about the event. The worker may then reflect, "Where does that come from?" This is an authentic question that expresses the worker's interest in what the child sees and feels and thinks about those things. This authenticity supports the child's role as the teller and the one in control of the life story.

Children spot pre-scripting, dishonesty, and pretension very quickly. They see it reflected when the worker says to them:

- "I know how you feel." This intimate understanding of feelings around a child's past devalues the child's story, dismissing it as a common experience.
- "That's just what I would do." This fake attempt at an alliance denies the fact that the worker is an adult in an office in an agency while the child may be living on the street, for example.
- "You can take as long as you like." This fake attempt at an alliance contradicts the schedule agreed upon at the beginning of the meeting.
- "How are you?" This rhetorical question effectively shuts down dialogue.

The authentic worker listens attentively, sharing accurate and current information if and when it is needed and as it can be received. This information-sharing is just as important as the information-withholding demanded by confidentiality. Both are ethical requirements of any worker who listens to the child's story. The worker who does not have accurate information is ethically bound to find this information and transmit it accurately to the child. The following are some examples of accurate information that children may need.

- Child abuse is an abuse of power and is wrong. Adults do not have the right to hurt children just because they are bigger and more powerful than children.
- When a child is abused or assaulted it is not the child's fault.
- There is alternative care for children. If you cannot live in your own home with your own family, you do not have to live on the streets.
- Mental illness is not contagious.
- Death is part of life. It happens. Wanting someone to die, or wishing that person dead, does not cause that person to die (or to get sick).
- You are not ill because you are evil or bad. Illness happens to people.
- Poverty is not your fault. There are many children in Canada who live in poverty. Their parents may work very hard, but they still live in poverty.

Because the child may have heard contradictory information for many years, these facts may not really register with the child or be accepted. Child abusers, for instance, may have groomed the child for years with the tale that abuse is the child's fault because the child is the seducer. The worker needs to repeat the facts in different ways, check that the child understands and absorbs the information, and then listen carefully to ensure that this accurate information is integrated into the child's narrative. If not, the worker needs to repeat the information in another way until it is fully absorbed and integrated into the narrative.

Countertransference

The AHA! Method of listening to the child's story helps to elicit emotions underneath the story—the anger, sorrow, pain, and feelings of loss and betrayal. The worker who tunes into these emotions from the child's frame of reference supports the child in naming and articulating these emotions and what they evoke. This can be painful for the worker as well, especially when the worker is feeling emotionally fragile or vulnerable, when the worker personally identifies with the child's pain, or when the child's story evokes a worker's repressed personal memory. Michelle Lefevre (2010: 135) explains, "Listening to such painful materials may be very stressful personally and emotionally for practitioners, however. It might re-evoke thoughts and feelings stemming from their own difficult earlier experiences; this may cause them to stop listening or be too much for their current level of emotional capacity or resilience."

At such moments the worker may cross that boundary of the healthy working relationship and appropriate the child's emotions or countertransfer. **Countertransference** is an interactional or symbiotic process in which the child's narrative stimulates the worker's unconscious and dormant thoughts, emotions, and psychic memories, and the worker responds by projecting these same thoughts, emotions, and psychic memories onto the child's narrative. Neither the worker nor the child plan for or consciously want countertransference to happen. They are usually not even aware that this process is taking over the child's narrative and changing it. The worker may project guilt onto the child and the child conforms, reshaping the narrative to match the worker's sense of guilt. Similarly, the worker may project anger and fear onto the child, reshaping the narrative into one filled with anger and fear.

The obvious detriment is that the child's personal narrative changes as the child slowly begins to feel responsible for the worker's guilt, anger, and fear. Fewster (2002: 19) describes this worker–child countertransference simply: "As we look after them, so they must look after us." Because this process impedes the child's development of a more hopeful narrative or **re-authoring**, the worker needs to be aware of and guard against the subtle power of countertransference before using the AHA! Method to listen to the child's story. Being aware of both countertransference and one's own emotional wellness can help to prevent this process from damaging the child. This is why most workers make use of supervision or work in treatment teams rather than alone.

In the following example of countertransference, the worker (W) appears to be listening to the child (C) but is actually processing personal emotions and projecting these emotions onto the child.

C : I've always known my mom didn't want me.
W: Oh, that's not true. Every mom wants her baby. She just might not have had the resources to look after you.
C : You mean she couldn't look after me?
W: Maybe. But she loved you.
C : Hmm . . .
W: How do you feel knowing that?
C : Well, I guess I could answer her letter then. Maybe I owe it to her.

The worker crosses the boundary of the working relationship very early in this meeting, shutting down the child's exploration of feelings of loss, rejection, and betrayal. The worker insists that all mothers love their children. This may be a careless remark reflecting popular "mother mythology," or it may come from the worker's own attachment injuries, guilt, or anger. Whatever the source, the worker projects this personal belief onto the child, compounding the complexity of feeling that the child has expressed. Now the child must add the worker's emotional baggage to this complexity. Confronted by the reflecting team or the supervisor afterwards, the worker may defend this early boundary crossing as an empathetic response or an emotional scaffold for the child's telling of the story. However, the silencing of the child's story (and the emotion within it) amply demonstrates the real damage caused by countertransference.

It is natural to have feelings of despair, hopelessness, sadness, anger, shock, blame, embarrassment, or sympathy when hearing a child tell a story. These human reactions are engendered by the child's story, and they can be used constructively in the listening process. Being aware of these reactions is the key to active listening. The worker tries to distinguish between his or her personal feelings and the child's feelings, both of which are evoked by the child's story. When the worker is self-aware rather than defensive, the worker can internally name and distinguish these feelings while the child is speaking. The worker can name sorrow and be aware that this sorrow comes from an abiding concern for the child, a recognition of the story's sadness, or a memory of a similar event in the worker's own past. This recognition and naming of feeling allows the worker to use that feeling constructively and consciously. This process of exploring feelings in the story (listening and telling) is continuous and helps to prevent countertransference from impeding or infecting the child's re-authoring of the narrative.

Externalizing

Parents, caregivers, or teachers typically describe the presenting problem as the child's problem or even the child himself or herself. This reflects a century of practice in which "therapists were universally locating and privatizing problems inside the client's body—thereby creating a culture of the docile, disembodied, unaffected, relational subject" (Madigan, 2011: 17). Linking the child to the problem also links the child's self-identity and self-esteem to the problem. A boy may self-identify as "a bad kid" or "a drinker." His family may repeat this label, supporting it with several problem-saturated stories of the many times he drank excessively. Ram Dass and Paul Gorman (1997: 60) describe this phenomenon: "In comes Mary Jones, hurting real bad. As she sits across the desk she suddenly becomes Mary Jones, 'schizophrenic.' With a flick of the mind, we've turned a person into a problem."

Externalizing places the problem outside of the child. The problem is the problem, not the child, and can be identified or named as a metaphor. When the problem is "out there" rather than within the child, an emotional distance is created that frees the child temporarily from the problem and allows the child to examine the problem from the outside. The child becomes a problem solver rather than a problem or a failure. The child can change, lose, forget, or remove the externalized problem from its current position of power. This emotionally distant relationship decreases the stress and conflict over who is responsible for the problem. It stops the **blamestorming** that problems often trigger, with one person assigning blame to the other in a spiral of accusations. Instead, the child can begin to look at the problem from the outside, as can other members of the family. The problem can also be solved!

The presenting problem may be chronic absenteeism from school. Descriptions of this problem will vary according to the person's relationship with the problem in the past and the present. An older brother who enjoys school may describe his little sister's chronic absenteeism from school in this way: "She never goes to school." His sister may describe her absenteeism another way: "I never go on Fridays because Fridays suck." Her parent may present quite a different picture of the problem: "She's only missed a few days this term. I don't know what the big fuss is all about." The worker may say to the older brother, "How do you think your little sister sees her absence from school?" Or the worker may ask the child, "What do you think your mother knows about your attendance at school?" Asking one family member to relate the problem from another family member's point of view expands the understanding of the problem and creates a shared understanding and a shared responsibility for solving the problem. On the basis of this shared understanding and responsibility, the problem is externalized as a metaphor that is chosen by the child, or the child and the family, and reflects their understanding of the problem.

An older child may describe getting drunk on the weekends, joy-riding with friends, and being grounded by parents. The worker listens attentively, using reflective statements and **paraphrasing** to find out more about these events and the feelings that they evoke. The child may use words like, "high," "wicked," "crazy," or "messed up." One word may continue to recur in the storytelling, and the worker and the child may agree to use this recurring word as a metaphor for the presenting problem. "Crazy" has been convincing the child to get drunk on the weekends.

By putting the problem outside of the child and positioning the problem as an externalized metaphor, the child can now be seen as a person. So Jordan is no longer a drinker or a drunk; Crazy is interfering with or controlling Jordan and convinces him to do "bad" things. Crazy is making Jordan sleepy, stealing the money from his bank account, and upsetting his parents. A question for Jordan's parents might be, "What has Crazy told you to think about your son?" Jordan and his parents are affirmed as strong persons who are capable of confronting problems, and the reflecting questions affirm this strength: "When have you been able to withstand Crazy? How have you been able to beat him in the past?" These identified strengths are potential assets for combatting the problem. Jordan can take time away from Crazy, manage Crazy, or just tell Crazy to go away for a while, at least until he graduates from high school. Jordan and his parents may be able to tackle Crazy together. After all, they have survived as a family in spite of Crazy and the suffering that Crazy has caused.

On the other hand, Crazy may be associated with a peer group that Jordan prefers to his parents. Jordan may opt to stay with Crazy and his peer group. He may leave his parents, physically or emotionally or both, to spend more time with Crazy. His parents are then left with many options, one of which is to bring Jordan and Crazy to an addiction specialist who is more familiar with Crazy and more able to work with Jordan to reduce his dependence on Crazy. Because Jordan has externalized the problem he may be less likely to see his parents' concern as a personal attack and more likely to see their concern for him as a concern about Crazy.

Michael White demonstrates how to use this externalized metaphor in his classic story of Sneaky Poo (1989: 10–11). The parents express frustration and anger over their son's apparent encopresis or lack of control over his bowel movements. The boy is equally frustrated and anxious. Both the parents and their son decide upon the metaphor "Sneaky Poo" to describe the problem that sneaks in to interfere with their

Note from the Field   7.1

Be Direct!

Rogerian techniques such as paraphrasing and reflection may not be appropriate with families whose cultural values dictate more direct confrontation. These families may feel that non-directive techniques (paraphrasing, reflection) are sneaky and deceptive. Take the case of Clement and his son Peter. Clement brought Peter to the worker for help because Peter's graduation from high school was in jeopardy. During the meeting, the worker used reflective statements and paraphrasing in an attempt to understand this school situation from both Clement's and Peter's points of view.

Although Peter became increasingly more responsive during this meeting, his father became increasingly irritated. He interrupted the worker several times, asking what the point of the questioning was when it was obvious that Peter was simply not applying himself in school. The worker in turn became irritated with Clement, judging Clement to be an authoritarian rather than an **authoritative** parent with little concern for his son and with little patience or interest in the process.

However, Clement's personal culture valued directive statements rather than the non-directive ones used by the worker. This cultural clash stopped the meeting in its tracks. Clement and Peter left before their hour was over, and Clement vowed not to seek outside help again. When a cultural clash is minimized or ignored rather than articulated and affirmed, the child or the parent may shut down completely and stop communicating. The cultural clash may result in this being the first and last meeting with the child.

family life. This problem has started to take control of their family. By identifying this power dynamic through creating a metaphor, the family can look at the power dynamic and begin to regain control over their lives. It is no longer the boy who is the problem. In fact, the boy is an interesting and much loved person. The real problem is Sneaky Poo. Now the boy, his parents, and the worker think about ways to deal with Sneaky Poo together. Externalizing helps the child and his parents conspire together to trick Sneaky Poo into leaving, and they eventually eliminate it (pardon the pun) from their lives.

Contextualizing

The systems approach, developed by Urie Bronfenbrenner in 1979, provides a structure in which the worker can contextualize the narrative. The worker can situate the child's life narrative, and each particular story told by the child, within the ecological environment that impacts the life of that child. Bronfenbrenner describes this ecological environment as a set of nested structures extending far beyond the immediate experience of the child, each nested structure inter-related and connecting with the other, and each indirectly influencing the life of that child (see Chapter 1).

Contextualizing situates the child's narrative within a larger social construct or structure. This structure can both create the child's problems and support the child's solutions. The child's life narrative of addiction, vandalism, truancy, and violence can be contextualized within societal bias, support, funding, legal interventions, and culture. This context not only places the narrative within an explanatory macrosystem but also suggests potential solutions within that structure. The worker who contextualizes the child's narrative understands this dual role of the structure. Structural oppression, for example, impacts the child's ability to participate in placement decisions when the child is being placed in a group home. At the same time, this oppression can be challenged through the office of the children's lawyer, a challenge that is empowering for the child and one that may result in a more appropriate placement than another group home.

The worker contextualizes the story of a girl who meets with him because of her shoplifting arrest. She tells her story and, as the worker listens attentively, she adds more details. The girl talks about her need to fit in with her friends, all of whom are middle-class. The girl's family is struggling financially and the girl cannot afford designer jeans. Shoplifting is her solution and her gateway to her peer group. She talks about the sexy, peer-approved clothing and, as she talks, she begins to question both the gender construction and the economic disparities between herself and her peers. The worker supports this structural contextualizing, adding information when asked. Contextualizing shoplifting does not diminish or eliminate the girl's responsibility for this illegal act, but it does place shoplifting within the oppressive social construct of her gender group that requires young girls to dress in certain ways.

Contextualizing is an empowering process that redefines the child's story within a structural framework. Media messages encourage children to drink alcohol, for example, as a gateway to adulthood and as a way to be socially acceptable. Contextualizing alcohol consumption helps a boy who drinks to see this as an effect of structural determinants and structural oppression, rather than as a personal deficit or weakness that is genetic and can never change. This boy may oppress others because of his alcohol-saturated narrative, while at the same time he is equally oppressed by media messaging, peer influence, and an inability to gain entrance to "adulthood" without drinking alcohol. Multiple oppressions combine to keep the boy disempowered despite his fleeting moments of getting drunk and feeling powerful. Similarly, the girl who shoplifts does not use phrases such as "gender construction." However, in describing her need for peer-approved clothing, she begins to understand where the messaging for the clothing originates, and she feels her own power in challenging this messaging.

A young child may not fully understand socio-economic and political ideologies. However, this child does understand the feeling of powerlessness that these structural determinants engender. The worker's empathy, reflective statements, and open-ended questions can situate the child's story within the context of these socio-economic and political ideologies. In the following dialogue between the worker (W) and the child (C), contextualizing empowers the child to begin to consider structural change. The worker is not in a high school every day and is curious to know what this context feels like for the child. The worker's genuine curiosity leads the child to try to make some sense out of his problem (truancy) within its larger context (power and authority).

W: I know several other guys who've skipped school. They tell me it's boring.
C : Yeah, it sure is.
W: I haven't been to a high school here. What's it like?
C : You don't have any control. All day long they tell you what to do.
W: They?
C : The teachers, the secretary, the principal. You got no power, no nothing.
W: No nothing, yeah?
C : It's just how it is.
W: And that's okay?
C : Yeah, I guess so. I guess that's boring, too, just to accept.
W: What wouldn't be boring?
C : Maybe to run my own school, plan my own classes, be my own man . . .
W: Could you do that? Would that be allowed?
C : I knew a kid who did that.
W: Yeah, how did that happen?

Contextualizing is a way for the child to understand that the situation or problem is not always a reflection of personal psychological, developmental, or moral deficits. Instead, truancy can reflect the child's resiliency in the face of adversity. The worker opens up this discourse, prompting the child to both identify and challenge structural oppression and to form meaningful solutions that really work within the child's life. This empowering process supports the child's position as the controller and the director of change. The child is responsible for the change, not the adults.

Re-Authoring

Children naturally link together the events or stories in their lives according to a theme. The theme may be failure, and events or stories are told and re-told to support the story of a child failing in school, friendships, family life, or sport. The theme may be ugliness, and the stories all illustrate how ugly the child is, regardless of the clothes or the situation. When the dominant narrative supports this negative perception and problem-focused connections, any strengths or positive stories are suppressed, minimized, or forgotten.

Re-authoring creates the possibility of change. The child's past, present, or future can be reconfigured and remembered differently. The child can link together the events or stories that are uplifting or positive to form an alternate more hopeful narrative. Re-authoring is an opportunity for the child to remember and recount these positive events—in short, to own them. The child recalls moments of strengths and personal assets that helped to resolve difficulties. As each moment of strength is recalled, the child feels more and more empowered. Success builds upon success.

The worker encourages this re-authoring by prompting the child to reflect on the past and explore its multiple layers. An angry girl, for example, may be asked about being hurt as a toddler, "When that happened to you, did you feel anything else?" She may insist that she felt only anger at the time. Gradually, however, she recollects and shares other emotions such as sorrow, distress, and loneliness. Each emotion is explored with the worker, and memories of loneliness and sorrow resurface, as well as the girl's skill at managing this sorrow and loneliness. A story of anger begins to evolve into a story of resilience and strength in the context of early childhood abuse. Re-authoring reconfigures the memories, as well as the current feelings attached to these memories, into an alternate narrative.

To elicit memories of skill and strength, the worker may use the **miracle question**, a question that was developed by family therapists Insoo Kim Berg and her husband, Steve de Shazer. The miracle question asks what life could look like without the current difficulty. This question brings the child back to a remembered life before the difficulty or forward to a potentially less difficult life. The miracle question acknowledges the strength of the child in imagining and creating solutions.

The child has been living within the problem so long that a different problem-free life may be difficult to envision and the child may not have an immediate answer. Similarly, this may be the first time that a brother or sister has been asked for input about the situation, so that brother or sister may also need time to reflect before responding. The first family member may suggest a solution that appears to be muddled or confused. The worker draws out the details of the potential solution, encouraging that family member to paint in these details. Sometimes no one can envision a solution or even remember an exception or a positive memory. They continue to talk about the problem because this is the most familiar and comfortable subject for them. They are heavily invested in the dominant family narrative and the **homeostasis** that this narrative brings to their family. A solution means change and change is hard.

In these difficult moments, when a solution seems too hard to envision, the worker can ask **exception questions** that elicit descriptions of situations or moments when the family narrative was not problem-saturated:

- Can you remember a time when you were feeling different from the way you do now?
- Tell me about the times when you felt less angry about all of this.

Exceptions contain the seeds of solutions because they prompt feelings and emotions that have been suppressed or forgotten. Once an exception is identified, the story around the exception can be remembered and further developed. The specific exceptions are less important than their layers of meaning and messages for the child. Each layer begins with details. The details are vivid and concrete. They are also fluid; they expand and contract as more details are added and some are discarded. Slowly the child is able to re-author a positive narrative that is quite different from the problem-saturated narrative of the past.

📝 Note from the Field   7.2

Lazy Girl

A 15-year-old girl from Scarborough, Ontario, came to my office because she was not attending school regularly. She played her assigned role of lazy girl well, arriving late and saying little. Over several meetings, we discovered a mutual love of slam poetry. She told me that about a year ago she had gone upstairs to show her mom a poem she had written, and her mom had responded, "Have you done your homework?" She didn't repeat her "mistake" and kept her poems to herself now, retreating into a story in which her parents despised her for her failures, and she despised them for their middle-class values.

The parents have one story for her, and she has another one. When the daughter rejects her parent's story of school success and entrance to college or university, she may be labelled argumentative, rebellious, or defiant. She may in turn call her parents mean or controlling. Her story may lead her to run away and may cause her parents to pull back emotionally just when their emotional support is needed.

Each story makes sense to the teller, and each story is vastly unlike the other. There is heartbreak and loneliness beneath each story. The parents long for their little girl who talked to them and shared her poetry with them. The girl misses the parents who believed in her and cheered her on in life. When the parents and their daughter told me their individual stories, I listened. When the silence prompted a response, I empathized and tried to enlarge my understanding of the story. The parents and their daughter in separate meetings confirmed their feelings of grief and loss as they mourned the death of their relationship.

Yet they continued to come to see me. When they felt ready to share their stories with one another, the stories merged. The daughter affirmed her hard work and her power. The parents affirmed their caring and their love. By this time, there was a safe space for listening. Courageously, the girl and her parents began to construct a re-authored narrative in which the girl was talented and her parents supportive. The girl began to listen to her parents' worry and anxiety, and she started to be grateful that she was loved.

The Re-Authored Narrative

Externalizing, contextualizing, and re-authoring are used simultaneously with the AHA! Method. Externalizing, for instance, helps to contextualize. Simple externalizations, such as getting rid of anger, help to affirm and contextualize the child's temper or anger. This anger can be seen on its own with all of its memories, feelings, and emotions, or it can be seen as a legitimate response to an oppressive structure. Contextualizing anger is part of the child's gradual reclaiming of both the problem and the potential solution, or the re-authoring of the narrative.

A common difficulty with older children is skipping school. Parents may identify their child as lazy, sly, deceptive, or worse because the child skips school. The child may describe skipping school differently. The worker does not know if skipping school is a reaction to school, the people in it, classmates, teachers, or a cry for freedom and the lure of the streets. The story of skipping school belongs to the child who alone lives that story. The parents may guess, as might other family members and the worker. Only the child knows, consciously or not, what is really driving the action.

The worker gradually elicits the story from each member of the family, as well as their feelings around the story. The child listens and adds some detail. A problem-saturated story spills into the room. The story generates blamestorming as each person in the family blames the other. The presenting problem may be truancy but the real problem is much more.

The worker supports the re-authoring of a new narrative through first externalizing the truancy, using the child's suggestion of "Headache" as the metaphor.

Having Headache stops the child from getting out of bed to go to school. In describing what Headache does, the child tells stories about school failure, boredom, bullying by older students, and a teacher who sometimes yells. All of these details build a picture of the Headache that stops the child from attending school.

The worker, the parents, and the child begin to contextualize Headache. Through active questioning the worker finds out that Headache is worse before the child gets to the schoolyard. Then, Headache actually stops the child from going to the school door. Once the child turns around and walks towards the park, Headache gets lighter and weaker and eventually goes away completely. The schoolyard has been identified, with all of its terrors, loneliness, and alienation.

The worker uses exception and miracle questions to pinpoint days when Headache does not hurt as bad; the child's strengths in resisting Headache when it starts; previous school experiences that were positive; and previous neighbourhoods in which the family lived. One parent remembers a favourite teacher, and another parent recalls the child's previous classmates at a birthday party. The child remembers a tutor and a school award from the past. Together these memories and feelings weave into a re-authored narrative full of hope, promise, and optimism.

The re-authored narrative offers choice: a new school, a new neighbourhood, a different class, a friend in the class, a supportive teacher. There are now many choices and many potential solutions to Headache. Having control of this expanded menu, the child chooses to discard Headache and walk a different walk. With the clear memory of past strength and present friends, the child is now in control and feels empowered to take charge, and the child is supported in this scenario by a positive adult role model within the school, a new route to school, and family concern and support. The worker congratulates the child and the family in finding their own solution and their own re-authored narrative.

Summary

This chapter introduced you to the AHA! Method of listening to the child's story. How this story changes shape through autobiographical reasoning and how it changes into a re-authored narrative through externalizing and contextualizing were also explained in this chapter. When you understand the changes that take place as the child speaks about emotions, experiences, and memories, you also begin to understand the difference between the presenting problem in the story and the actual problems that lie within or beneath the story. The presenting problem is usually a behaviour. The meaning of that behaviour is different for the worker, the child, and the family of the child. Our next chapter will explore how these multiple meanings unfold during play in the child's choice of play materials and play episodes. As we listen to the child's language of play, we will take another step towards understanding how children construct meanings in their lives.

Review Questions

1. Do children lie when they tell stories about their daily life? Give examples to support your opinion.
2. Explain how autobiographical reasoning works with children.
3. What is a dominant family narrative, and how does this affect the child?
4. Do adults typically listen to children's felt emotions? Why or why not?
5. What is countertransference and how can a worker become aware of this happening?
6. What are the three parts of the AHA! Method, and how would you put them into practice?
7. How might a worker show authentic curiosity in the child's story?
8. Describe the use of a metaphor in externalizing.
9. Why is contextualizing so important when listening to the child's story? How might you contextualize a child's story about being bullied in school?
10. What are the steps in re-authoring, and why is this so important for a child who feels overwhelmed by the presenting problem?

Discussion Questions

1. Recall one of your own life events that included other members of your family. Ask each family member to describe the same event to you. Are their descriptions similar? What do you conclude about yourself, your family, and each member of your family from doing this exercise?
2. Sutherland describes "winds of childhood" and suggests that the child sifts through these winds in developing a life narrative. Which winds of childhood have you discarded in your personal narrative and which have you kept? What influenced you to make these decisions? Do you feel you may have lost the veracity of your narrative through this process?
3. Use the AHA! Method to listen to someone telling a story. What part of the method was most difficult for you? Did anything surprise you when you used this method? How did the person telling the story react to your active listening? Did the person find your body language and use of silence helpful or not?

8 Listening to Play

I tried to teach my child from books,
She gave me only puzzled looks.
I tried to teach my child from words,
They passed her by, oft unheard.
Despairingly I turned aside, how shall I teach this child, I cried?
Into my hands she placed the key. "Come," she said, "and play with me."

—Anonymous

Toys are the words of children, and play is their grammar. Children express their ideas, opinions, stories, and feelings more easily and naturally through play than through written or verbal communication. A toddler acts out frustration by crushing paper boxes. A preschooler tries to make sense of her parent's discipline by scolding or spanking her doll. Play provides a common language for the child's evolving life narrative, and the worker creates a respectful context for this language of play by shifting from words to toys, from language constructs to **play episodes**. The worker attempts to hear, understand, and interpret the child's play episodes in order to understand and explore the ideas, memories, and feelings of the child.

Play is an ideal healing intervention with children because it is such a familiar and natural part of their daily life. It is not strange and does not come from the world of adults. Play is a way to express emotions and gauge the impact of that expression on others. As Jason Jent, Larissa Niec, and Sarah Baker (2011: 30) put it, "It is a safe arena to explore and practice emotions they have observed in others or have experienced themselves." Children can let go of their anger by punching clay, banging drums, breaking bubble wrap, and bashing puppets. They can relax through making music, dancing, painting, and pouring water. They can express grief, loss, and sadness through puppet play and drama. They can revisit their fantasies, dreams, and memories when they touch wind chimes, sift sand, crumple tissue paper, string together beads, and braid wool.

Play heals children because of its holistic quality: the child's mind, body, spirit, and heart are involved in each play episode. Unlike physical therapy directed at one body part, or cognitive-behavioural interventions directed at the child's cognitive response to stimuli, play as a healing intervention involves the whole child. Play works in the same holistic way that is described in the Medicine Wheel teachings and traditional means of healing.

We will begin by differentiating play from play as an intervention (**play therapy**). Workers observe, supervise, and engage in play, but only certain workers build on the theoretical foundations of play therapy to unlock the child's deeper intrapsychic struggles through play. Some workers engage both the child and the caregiver in this play; others meet with the caregiver separately; and others use play therapy effectively with adults. This multiplicity of applications expands play therapy beyond crisis intervention and **trauma** work, and into those meetings in which children explore their feelings, memories, fears, and fantasies.

Objectives

By the end of this chapter, you will:

- Understand the meanings within play and how the child unravels these meanings.
- Identify the components of witnessing play in the playroom.
- Recognize indicators of trauma in play and respond appropriately to these indicators.
- Demonstrate how to use play effectively as an intervention with children.

The Function of Play

Play is activity that is usually pleasant and voluntary, or chosen by the child. Playing the piano is play until it becomes forced and compulsory practice. Throwing a ball is play until it involves the stress and routine of baseball practice. It is this freedom and choice that characterize play for children, and it is this same freedom and choice that are increasingly absent from much of the "play" in the child's life today.

Play is pleasant and voluntary but it is also essential to the development of physical, cognitive, and social skills and the understanding of the complexity of life. Children figure out how their bodies work and explore the limits of their strength, skills, and agility through stretching, climbing, running, toddling, grabbing, pulling, and pushing. They run until they are exhausted; then they feel their hearts pounding. They jump over and into puddles and streams until their shoes are soaked. They throw leaves into the air until their arms ache. They slide over ice and snow, feeling the difference in friction, and testing their limits. They also imitate the meanings of their daily life by acting out their fears, problems, and relationships. They try to make sense of their world through acting out going to school, making food, playing doctor, winning and losing.

They hand out papers and pencils to their friends and make them sit at desks just as they have seen their teacher do in a classroom. They put plastic food in a toy refrigerator just as they have seen their babysitter do, expressing themselves through words and gestures and watching the reactions of their play partners, caregivers, and onlookers.

While adults plan their play, the play of children is spontaneous and unplanned. It simply happens. Children see the paint, the water, and the box, and they paint the box. They watch friends climb up the rocks and they run to join them. Play is absorbing and experiential, and children usually do not make any ongoing interpretations of their play or links between individual play episodes. A child may occasionally wonder aloud, "Why did I do that?" However, a child rarely interprets individual play episodes or reflects on the motivation behind a particular choice of play material.

Play is a way to relate with others, to see what other children do when they are bitten, pushed, hugged, or ignored. It is said to progress in stages that correspond to the child's cognitive, physical, and socio-emotional development (Piaget, 1929; Russ, 2004; Schaefer and Kaduson, 2006). The infant is said to engage in solitary play, exploring his or her own self as well as people and objects within easy reach. But even infants watch other children, their eyes tracking the faces of others. "Two six-month-olds will look, smile, and point at one another. Over the next few months, infants laugh and babble when with other infants" (Kail and Zolner, 2005: 213). The toddler is said to engage in parallel play. Each toddler watches the other, and each watches what the other toddler is doing. Older children engage in group or social play with other children, interacting and sharing play materials and play spaces, and learning social skills such as turn taking, negotiating, decision making, leading, and following rules. However, a child may engage in solitary, parallel, and group play all on the same day. A child may kick a ball in the yard, and then kick the ball alongside a friend who is skateboarding. The two children may then join other friends to kick the ball in the yard or skateboard together. Children of all ages engage in solitary, parallel, and group play, using this play to explore and develop their skills and friendships.

There are many different kinds of play, each with several functions, and each of which involves the whole child—spiritually, cognitively, physically,

Photo 8.1 Social play is a chance to interact, negotiate, and share.

Denis Kuvaev/Shutterstock

Table 8.1 Play, Function, and Theory

Kind of Play	Function	Theory
Gross motor/ psychomotor	Build eye–hand and eye–foot co-ordination; test physical limits; develop strength, agility, and balance	Developmental Kinesthetic
Group	Develop and test social skills and relationships; practise co-operation and competition; experience failure and success; develop problem-solving and negotiation skills; develop language skills	Object relations Attachment
Solitary	Develop self-awareness and self-confidence; replay memories, dreams, and experiences as part of autobiographical reasoning and healing	Psychoanalytic
Parallel	Develop social relationships and understanding of others; learn how to accomplish tasks	Object relations
Creative	Reflect upon actual experiences; express memories, feelings, and emotions; develop self-awareness and self-knowledge; communicate trauma	Psychoanalytic
Role	Understand how others behave and the meaning of family and friends; communicate trauma	Family systems Object relations
Free	Act out emotions such as anger, fear, hatred, despair, loneliness; understand consequences of actions	Cognitive-behavioural

and emotionally. A child who kicks a ball may seem to be engaged in physical play only. However, positioning the ball and strategizing the trajectory of the kick involves cognitive function; playing with others involves social skills and communication; and the achievement of the goal involves personal growth, success, and failure. Any play— arguing, drawing, swimming, playing doctor—can have many functions and meanings, which makes the worker's role in understanding these meanings so important. The worker observes play not only to keep children physically safe but also to ensure their emotional safety and emotional healing. The above table (Table 8.1) summarizes several kinds of play, their functions, and the theory that attempts to explain these functions.

Play as an Intervention

Play as an intervention is called "play therapy." It is sometimes confused with other therapies such as pet therapy, dance therapy, art therapy, and riding therapy, some of which are legitimate and helpful, while others lack professional status and accreditation.

Because of this confusion, play therapy has also been critiqued as a fraud and a pretense, a false therapy created by early childhood educators who crave some professional legitimacy. Play therapy has also been associated with puppet play, prompting some puppeteers to call themselves "therapists." The word "therapy" suggests that only certified therapists, doctors, psychologists, or psychiatrists are allowed to use play therapy. Workers with extensive training and empathic understanding of children hesitate to "do" play therapy because they are not qualified therapists. They confine themselves to planning, supervising, and controlling play rather than observing and participating in play as a healing or therapeutic intervention. They may recommend play therapy and advocate for this service, but they also know that funding prevents most children from ever participating in the play therapy that is offered by therapists.

At the same time, workers recognize that play is an ideal healing process with children because it is a natural and familiar part of their lives. They recognize that play can be a way to understand children and support their healing. Rather than simply planning, supervising, and controlling play, workers who observe every choice of word, play material, space, and silence can situate their observations within the theoretical framework of play therapy. Garry Landreth (2012: 11) offers a comprehensive definition of play therapy as "a dynamic, interpersonal relationship between a child and a therapist trained in play therapy procedures who provides selected play materials and facilitates the development of a safe relationship for the child to fully express and explore self through play." His definition reminds workers of the importance of training as well as applying this training thoughtfully in the playroom.

The underlying assumption of play as an intervention is that children will play through their conflicts, difficulties, trauma, and feelings and arrive at a resolution that is psychologically satisfying to them. It is their recognition of the meaning of the play that is healing. They self-heal through play, and the worker affirms and supports this ability to self-heal and to work through personal memories, trauma, problems, and challenges towards a re-authored narrative. Eliana Gil describes this self-healing in the case of Wilson, a preschooler who watched his eldest brother beating to death his middle brother. Wilson plays out the event as he recalls it. Gil provides support and reassurance, plus the materials in the playroom that Wilson needs to re-enact the murder of his brother. This re-enactment begins in silence and ends with Wilson finding his voice. Gil (2010: 90) concludes, "Children know what they need to do to self-repair. Wilson . . . went from a passive position (as a child who could not move) to an active position (as a child who could retell what he had seen without feeling a debilitating loss of control)." Throughout her relationship with Wilson, Gil provides the empathy and affirmation that encourages Wilson to unfold memories and take control of his painful past.

The worker who uses play as an intervention follows the child's lead, affirming the child's strengths and capabilities. Bruno Bettelheim (1987: 40) describes this self-healing as a process in which the child takes responsibility for finding solutions: "The most normal and competent child encounters what seems like insurmountable problems in living. But by playing them out, in the way he chooses, he may become able to cope with them." Virginia Axline (1969) recorded this self-healing by Dibs, a preschooler who was labelled by his teachers and parents as unsociable and mentally defective. He was headed for institutionalization prior to Axline's intervention. She unlocked his genius as well as his pain, and her pioneering work is a template for play intervention today. Commenting on Dibs' self-healing through play therapy, Axline (1969: 23) writes, "When he plays freely and without direction, he is expressing a period of independent thought and action. He is releasing the feelings and attitudes that have been pushing to get out into the open." Both Axline and Bettelheim point to respect for and belief in the child as the foundation for play-based healing.

This is also the foundation of the healthy working relationship between worker and child (see Chapter 5), but there are differences. The worker who chooses play as an intervention has extensive theoretical knowledge that supports this choice. The worker–child relationship is singular, not group, and unfolds in a carefully designed playroom that supports healing and the therapeutic relationship, rather than pure relaxation or the expending of energy. The play itself is healing rather than relaxing. This is not the play that children do to find out how their bodies work or to develop their psychomotor skills: swimming, skating, running, or skipping. It is not the play children do to engage with other children: soccer, video games, or hockey. Nor is this spontaneous or reactive play that happens when a child tries to catch a bubble or kick leaves into the air. The play is focused on unlocking the *meaning* or the motives and intent within the play. The intrapsychic world of the child is the focus rather than the child's ability to catch and throw or play a co-operative game.

The Playroom

The playroom is specific to working with an individual child to unlock memories, unblock trauma, and heal injuries. This room must be safe and stable enough to ground the child, yet unsafe enough to unlock repressed memories, trauma, and pain. This combination of safety and risk is essential.

The safety of the playroom is conveyed by its size, appearance, and boundaries. The playroom is small and designed for one child and a worker or a child and caregiver and a worker. A room that is 12 feet by 12 feet is an adequate size, although a smaller space can be used. A larger space is not conducive to observation or interaction and can create yawning gaps between the worker and child.

The playroom is orderly and calm. The materials are arranged attractively and neatly on accessible and open shelving. They are in the same spot each week, and this order and predictability conveys an important message of safety. The child does not have to search for the dragon. It is on the shelf in the dragon's designated spot. The playroom is the antithesis of the chaos in many children's lives. This safe space with lowered lights, comfortable chairs, and little or no external noise allows the child to say the unspeakable and express the inexpressible. There are no windows and no onlookers, critics, or audience, although there may be a supervisor or caregiver observing the playroom from behind a two-way mirror.

Boundaries are the third component of this safe space; boundaries in this space define the child as controller and director of play. The child decides what and when to play. The child may select one toy, drop it, then go to the next toy, drop it, and so on until all of the toys are scattered in the room. The child may move, hide, bury, or throw figurines. The child may choose to paint, then model clay, then play in the sand table, then play with puppets, all in rapid succession. Boundaries are reinforced through the natural course of play:

- no hurting—only pretend hurting
- no taking toys home

The worker may add, "If I think that you are not safe or someone else is not safe, I have to tell someone." When the worker states this rule, the child often asks if parents are going to find out everything that is said in the playroom. The worker is honest and direct and uses the child's words to establish the privacy and confidentiality of the relationship. The child can tell the parents about what goes on in the playroom, but the worker does not do this unless the child is at risk of being injured or abused. Once again, the child usually tests these boundaries in order to verify the worker's congruence. The child is free to toss up the sand, to throw the dolly against the wall, to knock over the cradle. The worker does not rush over and scold the child, nor does the worker rush over to sweep up the sand. In the playroom, the worker does not disapprove, scold, or intervene.

The worker is more intent on the meaning within the play than the cleanup of the room. This response may puzzle a child who is expecting a reprimand or a scolding. The child may become confused, even angry at this upset of homeostasis, and may increase the volume of disequilibrium, throwing more sand and scattering more toys. This testing of the boundaries of the relationship can include questioning, playing with and discarding toys, or trying to leave the room. The following is a dialogue about boundaries between the child (C) and the worker (W):

C : Can I take one of these teddy bears home?
W: No, the teddy bears stay in the playroom.
C : *plays out aggression and anger with the bear*
W: It seems really hard for you when you want the teddy bear and can't take the bear home, but all the toys stay here in the playroom. The bear will still be here in the playroom when you come back next week.
C : Can I stay longer today to play with teddy?
W: No, you are staying only for one hour.
C : *rolls on floor and kicks*
W: I'll help you know the time to go home by reminding you five minutes before the hour ends so that you will know that your playtime is almost over.

These clear boundaries create a safe space in which feelings and emotions can be expressed. Axline (1969: 15) describes this space:

> The play therapy room is good growing ground. In the security of this room where the child is the most important person, where he is in command of the situation and of himself, where no one tells him what to do, no one criticizes what he does, no one nags, or suggests, or goads him on, or pries into his private world, he suddenly feels that here he can unfold his wings; he can look squarely at himself, for he is accepted completely; he can test out his ideas; he can express himself fully; for this is his world.

Each playroom meeting lasts one hour. The worker explains this and shows the clock or timer to the child so that the child knows that the full hour belongs only to him or her and to no one else. The worker asks the child to close the playroom door, a thoughtful and deliberate request that lets the child know that the door is not locked and that the child is the doorkeeper. The child can open and close the door at will.

Note from the Field   8.1

The Runner

What does the worker do when the child is a runner? In a room with no locked door, how does a worker ensure the safety of the runner? These questions are often asked when setting up the playroom because the open door is an enticing part of this playroom, particularly for a child who has been confined, restrained, or chased by adults.

There are three parts to the answer. The first is that the playroom is in a building that typically has a waiting room, corridors, heavy exterior doors, and other impediments to running out into a dangerous parking lot or street. If there are no impediments, some can be added, such as a second adult or a buzzer system on the exterior door. The second part to the answer is that being chased may be an established part of the child's culture. Whenever the child has run, the caregiver has chased the child. In the playroom, the child is confused when the worker does not chase the child. When the worker consistently does not chase the child, the behaviour of running is gradually extinguished, particularly when there is a positive reinforcer (play materials) for not running. The third part of the answer is the playroom itself. The security, warmth, and attractiveness of the playroom naturally counterbalances the discomfort, uncertainty, and confusion of running. When the worker confidently and consistently implements all three parts of this answer, the running gradually diminishes, fades, and then stops.

Some children initially run out of the room into the corridor with the expectation that they will be chased and reprimanded. They may repeat this action many times until they understand that they won't be chased, punished, or scolded for running away or opening the door. When this trust is established over several sessions, most children choose to stay in the playroom for the entire hour.

Risk is equally important in the playroom and is provided through play materials that can be used in any way the child chooses. Sand can be spilled, water can be poured, paint can be touched, and clay can be smashed and pulled. The heads and arms of the dolls can be torn off, pounded into clay, or drowned in the water. The materials are sturdy, plentiful, open-ended, and carefully selected to match the child's perceived needs and to act as a symbol or metaphor for specific memories, feelings, or unresolved trauma:

- keys, locks, rope, and handcuffs provoke feelings about bondage and freedom;
- sunglasses, puppets, masks, hoods, microphones, mirrors, and phones encourage the child to speak anonymously;
- puppets with movable mouths encourage the child to verbalize memories, thoughts, and feelings;
- sensory materials stimulate sensory memories and blocked traumatic events;
- bottles, baby blankets, cradles, potties, and soothers prompt feelings around trust and attachment;
- magical wands, play money, dart guns, treasure chests, and plastic bottles of "poison" stimulate expressions of anger and desire.

These simple play materials fall into three categories: "art," "aggression," and "anywhere." This is not art to fill an hour or a file folder. This is expressive art to unlock an emotional need or feeling. Children who do not dare to speak about their indescribable pain and anger can make their pain visible through art. Gluing black objects on paper, painting a family picture of one person, drawing a self-portrait with a face and no body, arranging a sand tableau of broken dolls: all of these creative expressions convey feelings and horrors that children may not be ready to communicate with words. The puppet talks about abuse, not the child; the puppet cries, not the child; and the voice in the microphone discloses troubling or traumatic events. Art materials speak for the child so that the child can maintain an emotional (and safe) distance. Carl Rogers' daughter Natalie (Rogers, 2000: 2) describes how she uses the expressive arts in her work as a psychologist: "using the emotional, intuitive aspects of ourselves in various media . . . going into our inner realms to discover feelings and to express them through visual art, movement, sound, writing, or drama." The variety of art materials matches the expressive needs and interests of the child, the boundaries of the playroom, and the comfort level of the worker and may include paint, modelling clay, sand, playdough, water, paper, velvet cloth, spiky pinecones, wooly puppets, green clay with a peppermint smell, shiny rocks, drums, and silver crinkly paper. What is created is not important here. What is important is the emotion that is experienced and expressed during the creative process.

The second category is "aggression." This category includes blocks, toy guns, handcuffs, locks, keys, ropes, rubber knives, masks, puppets, inflatable punching bags, hammers, people and animal figurines, beanbag chairs, drums, and pillows. These materials elicit the child's feelings of powerlessness, anger, and hurt, and invite the child to act out remembered injuries, pain, and violence.

The third category of "anywhere" includes props that the child can customize to reflect family dynamics and intrapsychic losses and crises: stroller and doll, bendable doll, rag doll, kitchen furniture, plastic food and dishes, cars and trucks, medical kit, school kit, backpack, suitcase, lunchbag, and phone. The bendable doll, for instance, may be given a name of a sibling and put inside the play fridge or locked inside the suitcase.

© Beau Lark/Corbis

Photo 8.2 Deliberate choices make this play space a battleground of emotions.

These three categories intersect and combine. The child can pound, squeeze, and hammer clay as a way to express anger and aggression. The child can bury animals in the sand and cover the sand with water, making a muddy grave for the animals. The child can handcuff the rag doll. The categorization of play materials does not suggest separate areas or separate activities but reminds workers to include materials from "art," "aggression," and "anywhere."

Arranging these materials prior to a session with an older child requires some adaptations. An easel can be set up with an abundance of paint and collage materials. A recorder can be added to the microphone. A beanbag chair can replace toddler-sized chairs, and a play kitchen can be reshaped as a cafeteria or coffee shop. The figurines and puppets remain. In my experience, when older youth are given a choice of play materials, they choose soft teddy bears before action figures. The comfort of many play materials dubbed "childish" prompts inclusion of soft toys. Youth may initially survey the playroom and conclude, "This place sucks" or "I don't paint." However, the appeal of fantasy figurines, puppets, art materials, and role play is strong, and older children pick up the phone, shove the dragon into the potty, and happily handcuff the dolls together, exploring feelings, thoughts, and memories through these open-ended materials.

The Sand Table

Central to every playroom is the sand table. It is large enough to hold the **tableaux** that the child creates, and the sand in it is deep enough for the figurines to be buried, water added, and muddy mixtures to splash up to the sides. Near the sand table is water, as well as carefully selected figurines or miniatures. These figurines are sturdy enough to be bent, drowned, thrown, and buried. Although some workers have hundreds of figurines, too many can be overwhelming. A careful selection of figurines arranged neatly on a nearby shelf is a more attractive incentive for the child to create tableaux in the sand table. Categories (Table 8.2) again provide a guide to acquiring and arranging the figurines.

The figurines can be used as symbols or metaphors for people, emotions, or events in the child's life. The black policeman figurine may not look like Alec, the child's father, but may have a quality (stern face, uniform, slim build) that reminds the child of his father. The figurines can depict emotionally charged events and emotions and say the words that the child may find frightening to say. Sheila Smith (2012) used the sand table in her classroom to elicit narratives from students who found it difficult to tell their stories. She describes one student, Abel, who is so engrossed by the tableau he creates at the sand table that he tells Smith, "My body does the story." She reflects, "Abel inhabits his story. From inside his world he is each of his characters. . . . Abel is embedded in his sandworld" (Smith, 2012: 48).

Figurines work like metaphors in Michael White's narrative therapy (see Chapter 7). They provide that necessary safe distance between the child and the emotion or problem. The child can control the figurines and can decide where to place the figurines and what to make them do. The figurines can depict traumatic events and allow the child to explore the emotions that surround these events. Grandma does not have to go away. Grandma can stay or be magically brought back in a big tractor. In this

Table 8.2 Figurines/Miniatures

Family groups	Multi-ethnic mommies, daddies, babies, elderly men and women
Occupations	Police officers, fire fighters, doctors, nurses, clergy, soldiers, judges, teachers, students
Wild animals	Lions, tigers, elephants, bears, crocodiles, snakes, eagles, deer
Domestic animals	Horses, dogs, cats, cows, birds
Buildings	Apartment buildings, schools, churches, houses, garages, hospitals, forts
Transportation	Cars, fire trucks, police cars, ambulances, school buses, minivans, taxis, tractors, bicycles, strollers, scooters, planes, military tanks, boats, motorcycles
Fantasy	Poison bottles, wizards, ghosts, witches, dragons, knights, dinosaurs, warriors, kings, queens, monsters, castles, fairies, treasure chests, flags, gold coins, fences, twigs and branches, shiny rocks, feathers, wings, gates

way the child can test out solutions. What would happen if Grandma came back? What would happen if we buried Grandma?

A young boy, for instance, may choose a dog as a metaphor for himself. This dog may fall into a big ditch that the farmer has made or into a deep hole dug in the sand table. The dog may try to get out of the hole without success. The other animals may come around the hole and laugh at the dog. Then the child may decide that the dog can fly out of the hole. What makes the dog fly? The dog decides not to listen to the other animals but only to himself, and so he discovers wings and jumps over them all. This is the child's narrative and the child's solution to bullying. The child creates a tableau at the sand table and he also creates the solution to his story. Play is an alternative way for the boy to re-author himself from being a victim of bullies to being a controller of the situation.

A castle or a pit in the sandbox can hold misery and despair, hopes and dreams that cannot find expression with words. The child can build and decorate, using specific colours and textures to convey the feelings that are too terrible or strange to express. This is the stage on which battles are fought, figurines are buried and resurrected, and the drama of daily life unfolds. In Dennis McCarthy's (2012: 72) words, "Worlds are made and unmade with apparent ease, yet with a profound effect on the child. With the flip of a hand an orderly world can be turned literally upside down."

Axline (1964: 114) describes Dibs' use of the sand table: "Then he turned toward the sand, dug a hole with his hands, and buried the soldier. On top of the mound of sand he placed a toy truck. Without a word, he made this graphic statement to dramatize his feelings." Dibs repeats this sand table tableau in several sessions as he begins to uncover his thoughts and feelings, all of the emotional hurt he has experienced in his family life. Elizabeth Newson (1992: 104) describes similar work by an older child who announces that he is going to "muck around." He chooses two cars—a police car and an ambulance—and throws them into the sand table with the words, "That's my world!" Newson identifies the strong message in his deliberate choice of these two specific cars, as well as in his decision to throw rather than place the cars.

The sand itself is both familiar to the child and enticing. Like a blank sheet of paper, it invites the child to create images and worlds on it. Unlike paper, however, it offers depths for digging, tunneling, and hiding figurines and expressed emotions and stories, much as black paint covers paper. The use of sand is a deeply satisfying and pleasurable physical experience that involves feeling, touching, mounding, tunneling, and simply making patterns on and through the sand. Children who work their fingers through the sand or mould the mud get in touch with their bodies and their feelings in this very kinesthetic experience. The child may remove the sand, scooping it out, or may mix the sand with water, moulding and mounding sand when it is wet. The child may arrange tableaux in the sand or may actually sit in the sandbox, feeling the texture and the safety of the sand. Sand is therapeutic and healing of itself. McCarthy (2012: 78) notes, "Many children never move away from the sand . . . Others mono-focus on the sand for a time and then suddenly notice the room around them as if it had not been there before. Such is the magnetic power of the empty box."

The worker actively observes the sand table and the healing that happens within it. The worker witnesses the stories and the disclosures of thoughts, emotions, and injuries and provides the child with the reassurance that this play is being witnessed: "You are throwing the sand over the knight." These affirmations reassure the child that the worker is attending to the play, witnessing it and reflecting on it. The worker does not interpret or interrupt the play and is mindful of the child's direction in the play, being more intent on understanding the meaning within the play than the cleanup of the room.

Observing Play

Adults organize play and supervise children as they play, managing their disputes and conflicts. Adults try to keep play spaces safe so that children are not injured, and they are largely responsible for supplying safe play materials and safe play spaces. When a young child is injured during play, the adult supervising the play is usually seen as responsible for the injury, even when the injury is perpetrated by another child. This adult account-ability converts free play into supervised and controlled play and engenders **learned helplessness** in children who do not manage, control, or direct their own play. When injuries happen or when conflicts arise, children become accustomed to turning to adults for nurturance and solutions rather than turning to themselves or their peer group.

Because of this increasing accountability, adults become accustomed to managing, interrupting, and interpreting play. They tend to interrupt play when children present aggressive, angry, or defiant behaviours: frowns and tears do not fit into the social construction of childhood or play. They twist the negative into a positive to make children's play more optimistic: "Look at the dragon—he's smiling now!" They may coax children to play with one another co-operatively: "Play nicely now!" Or they may stop competitive play entirely. They feel compelled to exert their authority and inject their wisdom, and they may interrupt play to admonish a child: "Get down now!" They may also change the direction of play to make it more pleasurable for themselves: "Put that away now because we are going to do a puzzle."

Adults also feel compelled to interpret play to demonstrate their authority, wisdom, or concern. They may attribute qualities to certain children based on their play: "Ooo, isn't she strong!" They may attribute emotions to certain children: "He looks scared, doesn't he?" They may also attribute motivations for play: "I think they want to hurt her." These interpretations of play are based on the structural context of play, the adult's cultural bias and understanding of play, and the child's own verbal and body language. One adult may see play as fun, while another adult sees the very same play as risky and dangerous. One adult may see the child as competent and social, while another sees the child as manipulative and aggressive.

These adult interruptions, modifications, interpretations, and observations change play and cause children to hide and suppress their negative, aggressive, or sad feelings in play. They also learn to hide their feelings about their playmates in an effort to "play nicely," and they learn to mould their play to suit the emotional needs of the adult. This play is stressful and can cause the child to tantrum, yell, scream, or hit. Play as a therapeutic intervention can also cause stress for the child, prompting the child to tantrum, yell, scream, or hit. The difference between these seemingly identical reactions during play is that the first indicates a reaction to adult control, supervision, and assessment. The second indicates a reaction to that intrapsychic stress the child feels when struggling for emotional understanding and control.

Training and supervised practice are necessary prerequisites to effectively observe or witness play without tainting it with personal emotion and bias, and without interrupting, controlling, or interpreting it. The trained observer is a witness who is curious about the intrapsychic meaning within the play in addition to the meaning of the play. The observer recognizes that play has a meaning for the child, and this meaning is far more important than the adult meaning attached to play. The observer is watchful and does not stop the flow of play, for this would stop the meaning for the child.

The observer actively watches play episodes, those deliberate and focused units of play that are time-limited with a definite beginning and end. The length of each play episode depends on many factors, such as the child's age, interest and motivation, and the attractiveness of the play materials. Drawing a picture can be described as a play episode that may last a few seconds or longer. McCarthy (2012: 26) explains the brevity of these play episodes: "The child will say something quite profound in his play and then leap away the next moment into silliness, not as avoidance, but because of the river-like flow of experience in which he still lives." The observer who misses that brief play episode during which the child speaks through play misses a crucial part of the meaning of that play; in short, the observer misses the child's message. McCarthy (2012: 31) goes on to describe the observer's responsibilities: "To witness actively is to be ready to jump in as needed, to engage in the child's play playfully, accepting the seeming dichotomy of the serious and the banal. To empathically accept the complex and contradictory emotions and impulses in the child and to not attempt to resolve them is essential, albeit very hard."

This observing or active witnessing is contingent on several elements. At the foundation is the Rogerian relationship in which the worker is congruent, empathic, and respectful of the child, working with the child rather than on the child (see Chapter 5). Equally important is the free play that is directed and controlled by the child in a safe playroom. The safety of a trained observer who does not interrupt or interpret and the safe grounding of the playroom provide a stage on which children can play out their emotions, dreams, fantasies, and trauma without fear of being rebuked, chastised, cheered, or minimized. Caregivers who watch this play on video or from the other side of a two-way mirror often ask, "Why didn't he tell me?" or "Why doesn't she do this with me?" The answer lies in the safety provided by the observer in the playroom. There are no interruptions or interpretations. There are only observations. As McCarthy (2012: 29) summarizes, "Our witnessing it is a crucial piece of both its appearance and its resolution. And our knowing it has meaning is even more important than knowing what that meaning is."

Barbara Sobol (2010) describes her work with four-year-old Natasha B. who had been raped by her older brother. Barbara and Natasha worked together for many years in the playroom. Natasha chose art, sculpture, and dance to unravel her trauma and find her voice. Over the years, she developed an interest in the arts: "During the intense sessions of dance, Natasha poured out deeply felt emotions, so much so that she was both exhausted and unburdened. In the wake of these experiences, she was able to make an eloquent painting that expressed a deep and lucid implicit sense of self" (Sobol, 2010: 259). Natasha healed herself in the playroom through the support of Sobol's active witnessing. Canadian artist Ingrid Johnson tells a similar story. Sexually abused by her babysitter's husband, then by her own stepfather, Ingrid withdrew further into her own dream world. In adolescence she too found her voice in art, poetry, and music in the playroom, and today she tells her story of survival through her poems and songs.[1]

Trauma Work

Children such as Natasha and Ingrid who suffer abuse, neglect, or trauma often blot out whole days or months of their lives. Sometimes they cannot remember years. Jurek Becker, who was interned as a child in Ravensbuck and Sachsenhausen concentration camps, speaks of the effects of this forgetting: "Without memories of childhood, it is as if you were doomed to drag a big box around with you, though you don't know what's in it. And the older you get, the heavier it becomes, and the more impatient you are to finally open the thing" (qtd in Miller, 2005: 84).

Becker is describing trauma and **post-traumatic stress disorder** (PTSD). Trauma is an enduring adverse response to a life-changing event such as the loss of family, injury, isolation, bullying, abuse, rejection, neglect, domestic violence, terror attacks, accidents, torture, or war. The child may not be directly involved in these events but may see them unfold. Although those who are directly affected are clearly the hardest hit, a child does not have to be in the direct path of a disaster to feel its impact. Children who survive school shootings may not see the shooter but they witness the devastating effects of the shots.

These life-changing events, whether witnessed or experienced, may not prompt trauma. Some children live through them and adjust to them, while other children react differently. They do not continue on with their lives. They block their response and disconnect with the memory of the event, burying it deeply and hiding it well, dragging it around as Becker did. Peter Levine and Maggie Kline (2007: 4) describe how trauma "overwhelms us, leaving us altered and disconnected from our bodies. Any coping mechanisms we may have are undermined, and we feel utterly helpless and hopeless. It is as if our legs are knocked out from under us." The child may feel helpless and disempowered for a year or a lifetime; in fact, even a single day may seem like a lifetime. Trauma can be acute or slowly evolving and complex, but in all cases trauma severely restricts the child's potential and the possibility of forming relationships. Gurvinder Singh and Judi Fairholm (2012: 352) describe trauma as a "genetic imprint that reduces the children's ability, as they grow into adulthood, to cope with stress." This pinpoints the long-term damage of trauma and the possibility that those who suffer from its effects can unconsciously transmit their suffering to their own children.

When these life-changing events happen in an infant's life and the infant is unprotected, trauma can be both global and lifelong; in other words, trauma affects all four domains and lasts for a lifetime. Infant trauma has "a disproportionate influence on brain organization and later brain functioning" (Perry and Hambrick, 2008: 40) because of the stage of brain development in infants. The infant's reaction to a life-changing event can be screaming or crying, but these screams and cries are unlikely to elicit an appropriate response, especially when caregivers are unaware of the event. The infant's cries cannot be understood, nor can the infant talk about the event to either caregivers or counsellors. The infant has to manage the event internally with (as yet) unsophisticated coping strategies. Because these coping strategies are largely undeveloped, infant trauma is unlikely to be healed later in life.

Toddlers and older children rarely self-identify as "traumatized" or disclose their trauma to adults. Instead, they communicate through any of the following coping behaviours:

- Aggression and violence
- Impulsivity and defiance
- Silence and withdrawal
- Attention-seeking and acting out
- Substance abuse
- Self-injurious behaviour

James Anglin calls these "pain-based behaviours" (2003: 111). In his study of children and youth in ten residential treatment programs in British Columbia, he uncovered pain-based behaviours and frustrated workers who reacted to the children's pain with yet more pain: punishment, isolation, withdrawal of privileges, and restraint. Most workers saw only the behaviours. They used the *Diagnostic and Statistical Manual of Mental Disorders* (DSM) to assess and classify these behaviours and then tried to physically or chemically restrain these children or place them in an alternative care treatment facility. Other workers tried to manage, control, or modify the behaviours. Some workers were punitive, sarcastic, or controlling, and they engaged with children through escalating power struggles. Their reactions validated the child's trauma and added to the child's feeling of being unsafe with adults.

Close observation of play can uncover the trauma beneath pain-based behaviours. Repetitive play episodes or obsessive-compulsive rituals repeated joylessly each time the child is in the playroom may indicate trauma. Monisha Akhtar (2011: 93) describes "the child's displeasure in play and yet being unable to stop." Akhtar (2011: 89) also observes abrupt stops in play or "frozen modes of behavior" as other indicators of trauma. In other words, when children stop their play abruptly and switch roles, their "frozen mode of behavior" may indicate trauma. When they joylessly and mechanically repeat a play episode, they may be unfolding their trauma before the active observer.

This observation is not easy. A worker's gesture, word, play material, or sensory stimuli can inadvertently unlock trauma and trigger escalating changed behaviour. The worker may lift her hand in a certain way that unblocks the child's memories of trauma. The worker may use a word that a former abuser favoured. The worker may wear body cream or aftershave lotion that evokes a sensory memory of pain. The child who reacts to this trigger with an abrupt change of behaviour cannot verbalize the stimuli and is unlikely to be able to articulate the memory. However, the child's reaction is often explosive: "It is as if there are invisible triggers attached to internalized traumas that can set off an explosion without a moment's notice, and sometimes attached with slow-burning fuses that can be lit unknowingly and that will result in a detonation some time later if the tell-tale smouldering signs are not detected and respected" (Anglin, 2003: 110). Larry Brendtro (2004: 9) recounts a reaction to restraint from a youth in care: "If you put your hands on me I'm breaking your neck, you know what I mean? A few people grabbed me and tried to put me in my room and I just smashed them. . . . I've been grabbed all my life. You know what I mean? It just turns me right off when someone touches me."

Unlocking repressed memories of trauma is scary and upsetting for the child. The worker responds by seeing the chaos and struggle as an opportunity for both the child and the worker to deepen their shared understanding of the trauma. The worker may hold a toddler until that child stops thrashing and is able to self-soothe or self-regulate. The worker may quietly sit on the floor beside a youth who is yelling until the youth is able to breathe normally. **Co-regulation** can take half an hour or more. This quiet

---

Point to Consider   8.1

PTSD and PTG

Reaction to trauma is individual, and not all children who experience trauma suffer from post-traumatic stress disorder (PTSD). Some children who experience trauma actually experience **post-traumatic growth** (PTG). After the traumatic incident, they develop closer relationships with others and have a renewed desire to help others. Their life philosophy seems to change and they experience a new sense of maturity or wisdom. These children begin to understand their daily life in a new and more meaningful way, and some also develop an interest in religion or spirituality. These changes are reported by children who have experienced trauma, leading researchers (McElheran et al., 2012; Glad et al., 2013) to conclude that not all of the effects of trauma are detrimental for children. Through these life-changing experiences some children actually discover their own resilience and strength and develop new ways of relating to others.

time is needed before self-regulation can begin. When the child is soothed and his or her heartbeat slows, the child is usually tired from the expenditure of emotional and physical energy. This is the time for reflection and quiet.

The worker may simply say, "You did good" or "I'm tired too." The worker may ask, "Can you remember what happened?" When the child feels safe enough to unlock some small piece of the trauma, the worker responds with quiet concern and care. As each piece is unlocked, the child checks the response. If the worker reacts with disgust or shock, the pieces are put back safely inside the child. Stacy Klapper and her colleagues (2004: 149) note that "following the child's lead ensures that therapy will not push the child into painful or retraumatizing material too quickly." The child leads and the worker follows.

Participating in Play

The child's invitation to the worker to participate in play marks an abrupt shift in the worker–child relationship. The child is ready for a deeply shared experience with the worker, and the worker is now trusted not to scold, direct, criticize, interpret, or shape the play. Both the worker and the child get ready to feel the emotion of the play episode as they perform a role within the play.

The child is the director of this play episode, reversing the traditional power construct in which the child's creative expression is channelled according to the dictates of adults. The child assigns roles to the worker, and the child decides when and how the play episode will evolve. Participating in play takes many forms. Participating may be an extension of empathically observing play by gesturing at certain times during the play. The child may glance at the worker and see the worker's rapt attention or smile. This attention or smile provides the comfort and safety for the child to continue the play. It may also cause the child to abruptly stop or change the play, fearing the worker has seen too much.

Participation may go beyond gestures and into responding to a question, demand, or action. The child may say, "Tie my shoe" or "Bring me water." The worker may respond with an empathic and reflective statement such as, "You want more water for your paint." Alternatively, the worker may respond with a simple observation, "Your lace is undone and you are wondering how to tie it up again." These responses indicate thoughtful and affirming participation rather than helping reactions that undermine the child's self-confidence. Participation in play does not mean doing things for the child such as mixing paints, setting up scenes, or dressing a puppet, actions that undermine the child's self-efficacy and control. Axline (1964: 15) stresses the importance of this supportive participation in her story of Dibs: "I wanted him to take the initiative in building up the relationship. Too often, this is done for a child by some eager adult."

Participation may also mean playing a role in an unfolding drama. The worker responds synchronously to the child's role assignment so as to maintain the play and reinforce the child's position as director and controller of the play. The child with a puppet may throw another puppet at the worker. The worker assumes the puppet's persona, conveying a willingness to participate in the puppet play. The child may tell the worker to "be the baby" in a car driving drama. The worker lies down on the floor and curls up like a baby. The worker does not question the play episode or ask the child about the kind of baby, the age of the baby, or the name of the baby. The worker does not offer suggestions or ask for a different kind of play; nor does the worker ask the child what to say or how to say it. These questions are interruptions that impede the emotional flow of play and the play script.

Jim Wilson (2005: 90) describes a play therapy session with a six-year-old girl who is brought to see him because her parents are going through a divorce and are concerned about their daughter's behaviour. Both the little girl, Clara, and her mother take part in the play therapy in the playroom. The mother's goal is to know how Clara is feeling about the divorce. Her preconceived expectation is that Clara will go to the figurines in the sand table, or role play the mother, or beat out her anger with the drums in the corner. Wilson convinces the mother beforehand, however, that Clara must choose, control, and direct the play and that they (Wilson and the mother) must follow her direction. Clara tells Wilson and her mother to be quiet because they are going to play school. Clara takes up a piece of chalk and goes to the blackboard in the room, assuming the role of teacher. Wilson and the mother immediately sit down with books and role play being students who are reading and writing. Clara (teacher) accepts questions from her two students and Wilson (student) puts up his hand. Clara tells Wilson to stand and allows Wilson to speak. Wilson stands and asks the teacher what parents should do when they are going through a divorce. The teacher (Clara) explains to her student (Wilson) that parents should focus on fun things rather than divorce talk. She tells student Wilson that children are tired of being asked questions about divorce all the time. In this way, Clara the teacher conveys her message clearly to her mother and to the worker. She can speak in her role as teacher because the other two play participants are in place and in role.

The worker stays in the assigned role while continuing to reassure the child of both empathic attention and understanding. When Clara's lesson is over, Wilson might say, "School is out." This reflective statement demonstrates to Clara that he has witnessed her move to another part of the playroom to begin another play episode. He does not stop or impede her play; nor does he intrude upon her play. He reflects back to Clara his attention and engagement. Clara might respond, "School is not over for you. Stay in your chair. You're a bad boy!"

Reflective and empathic statements capture the child's strengths. The statements might be verbal or non-verbal body language. In both cases, these statements support the child's mastery of play. A worker who is told that the painting is blue may respond, "Yeah, that's blue." This response affirms the child's knowledge. Similarly, the worker who actively observes a child wrestling with the lock on a pair of handcuffs, trying several methods in succession, may remark when the handcuffs release, "There, you opened them!" The worker puts words to the child's accomplishments. The worker respects the child's strength and does not take over play or provide solutions that the child has to discover. When the child asks, "How does this work?" the worker responds, "Hmmm, I wonder." This positions the worker as a participant in the play, following the child's lead.

Elizabeth Newson (1992) reflects on the effectiveness and power of play with a 12-year-old boy. This angry young boy actually tied her to the play structure and then left the room. She accepted his action and participated in the play rather than reprimanding or scolding him and in this way was able to earn the boy's trust. Newson (1992: 105) "was rewarded a week later when Jack asked for 'a talk' and proceeded to discuss his history and anxieties in a way that she had never achieved with him in two years of social work."

Understanding Play

The meaning within the play may be obscure to both the child and the worker and may be difficult to uncover, unravel, and identify. The worker needs to identify patterns in the play and decipher the important messages within the play. Michelle Lefevre (2010: 149) describes the skills that workers need to do this work: "The skills required for this move beyond perception and memory into an ability to sift information so as to work out what may be important and to identify patterns." The worker who tries to understand this play in the context of the other personal, cultural, familial, and developmental information about the child may feel overwhelmed. A template can aid in this understanding; in this case, mapping or webbing is ideal. The play episode can be webbed to all of its possible meanings. One might be correct, several may be correct, or none may be correct. Through reflection and discussion with a supervisor, the worker can sift through these meanings to uncover those that match more closely to the child as understood by the worker. Figure 8.1 provides an example of this webbing.

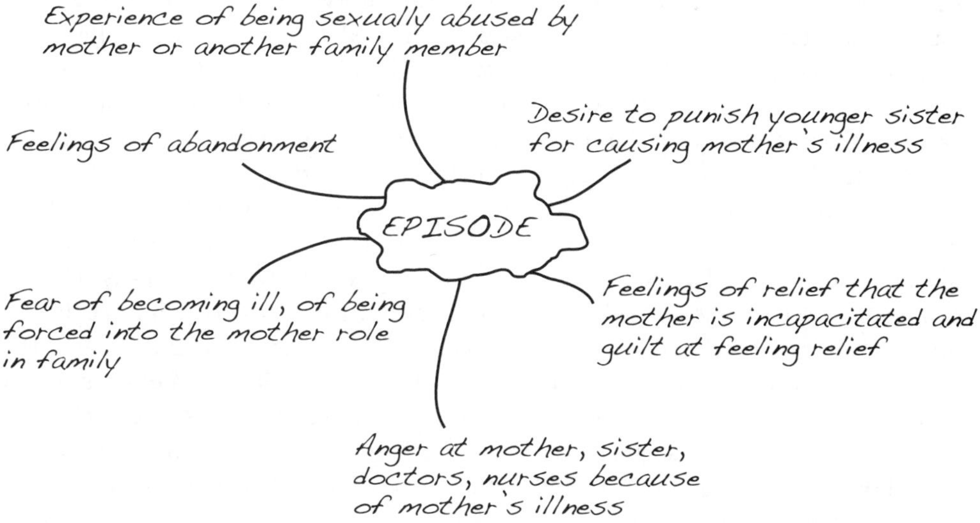

Figure 8.1 Webbing a Play Episode

This figure depicts the worker's attempt to understand a girl's 30-second play episode. The girl has been brought to the playroom by her mother who has cancer and is worried about the effect of her illness on her daughter. The particular play episode webbed here involves the girl giving the rag doll an injection in her upper leg. During this episode the girl appears to be intently scowling and tense. The worker observes this play episode and, after the play session is over, uses webbing to try to unravel the many possible meanings of this play episode. Certain meanings are seen as most likely, and the worker checks these out with the child. The worker may ask the child how it feels to give the needle or to get a needle. Alternatively, the worker may simply state what is happening: "You are giving dolly a needle." In either case, the child does the correction, while the worker listens carefully to the body and verbal language of the child. The child may cover up the doll, scowl at the doll, push the doll's legs apart, or stand on the doll. The child may give the injection a new name or description: "poison," "needles to help people to get better," or "just what she deserves." These verbal and gestural clues help the worker to focus on a couple of meanings or on a single meaning.

In understanding play, the worker is guided by many theories of learning, development, and relationships. No single one of these theories can explain the whole child or the whole play episode, but each theory helps to unravel the many messages within these play episodes. **Psychoanalytic theory** understands play as a vehicle through which the child makes sense out of repressed memories, dreams, fantasies, and the unconscious. The child can play out the conflict between superego and id so as to gradually develop the ego strength necessary for self-reliance. Anna Freud (1935) and Melanie Klein (1965) demonstrated this superego–id conflict almost a hundred years ago (1921–45) when they applied psychoanalytical techniques in their work with children, using play as a substitute for the free association work done during psychoanalysis with adults. Instead of saying a word to a child and then asking the child to freely associate another word with it, they placed materials in front of the child and observed how the child used the materials in play. Referring to the need for analysis, or the close observation and understanding of play, Klein called this strategy "play analysis." Like Anna Freud, she made minute notes on the child's body language and verbal language during the play episodes that she constructed and observed.

Axline (1964) also applied psychoanalytic theory, using play with children to uncover their repressed memories, fantasies, and emotions. She describes Dibs' feelings of anger, shame, and alienation that came out during play and the conflict between Dibs' id and his superego. Dibs resolves this conflict through his play as he gradually acquires control of his ego or self: "He had learned how to be himself, to believe in himself, to free himself. Now he was relaxed and happy. He was able to be a child" (Axline, 1964: 214).

Another way to understand Dibs' play is through the lens of **family systems theory**. This theory explores the boundaries, communication lines, life cycle, and dynamics of the family as a whole unit or system. The role of family members is to keep this whole unit intact and healthy rather than for each member to pursue individual goals. The behaviour of one family member affects the whole system, and the system is only as strong as its weakest member. Through this lens, Dibs' play can be understood as his way of making sense of the patriarchal structure of his family, as characterized by his father's emotional distance. The dynamic of a distant and disappointed father, frustrated mother, and idealized sister plays out in the sand table. Dibs calls on memories of a gardener who cares for him, a grandmother who believes in him, and children in the daycare who sometimes play with him. These memories contrast with the current harshness of family life as he is experiencing it before and after the play sessions.

Equally important is an understanding of **cognitive-behavioural theory**. Cognitive-behavioural theory suggests that all behaviour is learned and purposeful; it holds that the child learns to self-regulate behaviour through play. Play becomes a way to act out aggression safely and look for more satisfying and less exhausting ways to express anger and stress. The child learns to self-regulate behaviour rather than relying on external controls such as the lock on the door and the isolation of the bedroom. Axline (1964: 156) observes of Dibs, "He was learning through experience that feelings can twist and turn and lose their sharp edges. He was learning responsible control as well as expression of his feelings. Through this increasing self-knowledge, he would be free to use his capacities and emotions more constructively." Free from the locked room and the icy and disapproving stares of caregivers, Dibs learns to manage his own behaviour more constructively through acting out this behaviour with figurines. He learns how he can interact with other children in more productive ways. He learns to assert himself and to reclaim his identity within the family, and he begins to speak to his parents rather than yelling, crying, or refusing to speak.

Donald Winnicott (1953) offers the lens of **object relations** and attachment theory which suggests that we relate to other people based on expectations formed by earlier relationships, or our internalized object relations. Play is a way to explore these early

---

Point to Consider   8.2

The Canadian Association for Child and Play Therapy

In 1986, the Canadian Association for Child and Play Therapy instituted the first certification in the world for play therapists, a multi-year certification process involving field practice, study, and lectures. Subsequently, the Canadian Play Therapy Institute began training programs in play therapy. By the 1990s, Play Therapy International had formed, and today counsellors, social workers, nurse practitioners, and child welfare workers incorporate play therapy techniques into their work with children and families. What began as an intervention used solely by therapists, psychologists, and psychiatrists with very young children is now an intervention used by workers in many fields with multi-faceted goals and a multiplicity of techniques.

relationships with significant caregivers. Winnicott's focus is always the child's relationships to others and what these relationships, or object relations, mean for the child.

The worker who observes the child from a psychoanalytic framework may focus on the child's dreams and fantasies and the meanings that these have for the child. A family systems worker may provide family figurines and dress-ups that correspond to the child's family and may focus on the child's role within that family. The cognitive-behaviourist notes the presence of certain behaviours and provides materials that relate specifically to these behaviours. The worker grounded in object relations theory is sensitive to attachment injuries and how these play out during the session. The worker's understanding of theories orients the way the worker observes, understands, supports, and affirms the intrinsic meaning of play for the child. This is humbling work, as Winnicott (1953: 89) observes: "The significant moment is that at which the child surprises himself or herself. It is not the moment of my clever interpretation that is significant."

The Three Stages of Play

Play interventions usually progress in three stages from relationship-building to the chaos and struggle stage and, finally, to resolution. The child may play through one or two stages, then stop or withdraw. The child may also play through all three stages in a short six-month period. Alternatively, the child may remain at the first stage for several years, going back and forth, and taking time to settle into that stage.

The first stage is that of relationship-building between the worker and the child in which the child develops trust in the worker and a sense of safety in the playroom. This may be the first time that the child has encountered an adult who simply listens and does not try to teach, correct, question, punish, or make demands. The child needs time to adjust to this new equal power construct and feeling of freedom. If the child chooses to sit all alone in a corner of the room for several sessions, the worker attentively observes the child and responds to

Photo 8.3 Comfort and security help relationships build.

© Christina Kennedy/Alamy

any cues or expressed needs. The worker may pick up a puppet who makes friends with the child, and then introduces the child to the other puppets, encouraging the child to dialogue in the puppet play. The worker may show the child a figurine and ask the child if that figurine looks like her teacher. Alternatively, the worker may offer the child several figurines and ask the child to choose one that looks friendly, mean, or angry. This directive approach is dropped as soon as the child chooses to engage in play. A dialogue between the child (C) and the worker (W) may proceed like this:

C : What does this (toy) do?
W: This toy can do many things. Toys can be whatever you like.
C : Why is this (toy) here?
W: This toy is here because I enjoy playing with it.
C : Why do you keep that broken one (toy)?
W: I know it is broken, but I still enjoy that toy and I want to keep it.

In the second stage—chaos and struggle—the healing journey begins. This second stage evolves naturally from the child's acceptance of the worker and trust in the relationship, and it only happens when the child is emotionally relaxed and ready to really engage in play. In this second stage, the child enters into fantasy play that externalizes the pent-up emotions and memories of the past, and the child may return to the original painful event or incident. A 10-year-old boy may curl up on the couch like a baby or begin sucking his thumb or a bottle. An older child may begin talking like a baby, using infantile expressions and babbling. The child may act out, draw, scream, or play out remembered events or the current family dynamics. The child plays out struggles and wages battles with figurines or puppets. At the beginning, there is no winner. Soon, however, the fighting becomes more intense and organized, and a winner (the child) emerges.

In the termination or resolution stage, the child re-authors the narrative and changes direction or behaviour. This is a new beginning as well as an end to old habits, behaviours, or ways of relating to others. The homeostasis or equilibrium of these old behaviours is broken, and the child grieves this loss before moving forward to a re-authored life. The worker reinforces and affirms the child as an integrated and strong person and reminds the child of the progress that has been made. The focus is on the strengths that the child has demonstrated and the changes that have occurred. At this stage, the child may decide to tell parents or caregivers about the playroom sessions. The child may deliberately do this telling in front of the worker when the session ends as a way of demonstrating strength and control over confidentiality. The child watches the surprised reaction of the parent and, in this reaction, develops a renewed feeling of confidence.

Involving Caregivers

Caregivers also benefit from play and are often stimulated by the playroom to begin their own self-exploration. Adult interventions are beyond the scope of this text, but the adults in the child's life benefit as much as the child from the opportunity to engage in play therapy simultaneously with their child (Landreth, 2012). When caregivers engage in play therapy in separate sessions, they begin to understand and make meanings out of their own thoughts, feelings, memories, attachment injuries, and their own care-giving. This simultaneous play in a separate playroom can restore and heal caregivers, giving them strength and renewed confidence in their caregiving. McCarthy (2012: 67) explains how two mothers are drawn to play therapy through their children's sessions:

> The mother of the adopted Russian child entered treatment in part because seeing the sand and its potential use stirred things up in her that she could not push down. For her the sand's blank potential provoked memories that she had finally to confront. Another woman with whom I worked spoke of how simply walking by the empty box upset her. When I invited her to make a scene in the empty sand box she burst into great sobs.

Caregivers may also choose to be involved through actively observing their child from the other side of a two-way mirror. The mirror provides a safe emotional distance from which to actively observe play without becoming physically involved or feeling responsible for controlling or disciplining the play. Caregivers need this emotional distance in order to consider their dominant family narrative and their child's role within that narrative. Their observations and understandings of their child's play are then reflected by the worker who supports them in their deepening understanding of their child's behaviour.

Wilson (2005: 95–7) tells a story about using the two-way mirror to involve parents in such a process with their son, "the boy who lost his laugh." This little boy, Alan, had been identified as a bully at school and was brought to play therapy because his parents saw him as aggressive. Alan initially acts out this dominant family narrative, throwing toys and trying to break them. Once he has built a healthy working relationship with the worker, however, he begins to act out his sadness more than his aggression. On the other side of the two-way mirror his parents begin to see their son more objectively as a very sad boy who is unable to smile. He is no longer a bully or aggressive. He is a child who has literally lost his laughter. Their son is their only surviving child; their first child, a daughter, died shortly after her birth, and the parents' grief has become the dominant family narrative. Because the parents observe this sadness themselves, they take charge of the change process and are invested in it. They are now able to see what Alan needs, and what they as a family need, too. They are able to plan, control, and direct an intervention to rediscover their joy and laughter.

Caregivers are a necessary part of the child's healing through play. They have the task of reintegrating a more powerful child into the family, a child with a re-authored narrative who may react differently to family dynamics, norms, and rules. Their family narrative needs to accommodate this more hopeful and optimistic child, and the family members need to shift to make room for this changed member of their family. This upheaval and change to old family patterns and structure is difficult and cannot be done without the wholehearted investment of the caregivers. They are tasked with enacting this change in the home so that the child feels safe and secure.

Both the child and the family may resist the end of the play sessions. This resistance is both a resistance to change and a reluctance to work on integrating new roles into the family dynamics. The worker supports the child and the family to move forward independently by being consistent with the message. The play in the playroom is over, and the family can reconnect in six months (or 12) to share their new narrative of hope and progress.

Summary

In this chapter, we learned how to listen to children as they tell their stories, express their feelings, and unlock their trauma through play. Our listening becomes more acute when grounded in an understanding of psychoanalysis, family systems theory, cognitive-behavioural theory, narrative therapy, and object relations. Play in the playroom evolves through three stages: relationship-building, chaos and struggle, and resolution. Through these three stages we struggle to understand the meaning within the play, using webbing to plot possible meanings, and then checking these out with the child.

When children move their play online we listen acutely to their stories, feelings, and trauma, and we respond supportively and sometimes protectively as they encounter virtual threats to their safety and security. Our listening demands a digital skill set with a different language and grammar that lets us participate in a shifting digital landscape. This skill set is described in our next chapter as we listen online, participate in gaming, and engage in e-counselling with children who inhabit an online world that is unfettered by the boundaries of the playroom.

Review Questions

1. What is the difference between supervising children at play and actively observing and witnessing play?
2. Name seven kinds of play and the functions of each.
3. Describe five theories that are fundamental to play therapy.
4. What is meant by self-healing, and how does the worker facilitate the child's self-healing?
5. What are the key elements in designing the playroom?
6. How are play materials chosen? Give five examples of play materials in each of the three categories and the reasons for choosing them.
7. Why does the sand table work as an effective intervention when children are suffering from trauma?

8. What are the indicators of trauma during play, and how might the worker support the child's expression and unblocking of trauma?
9. Name the three stages of play therapy and describe what is happening for the child at each stage.
10. How might play be used with caregivers, and how might they benefit by watching their children in the playroom?

Discussion Questions

1. Reflect upon your favourite kind of play as a child. Who supervised the play? Was it solitary play, parallel play, or group play? What did you learn from this play?
2. Design your own playroom. What elements do you think are most important? Would the room have a window? Include lighting, wall colour, and floor cover in your design, and then make a list of the materials you would include in your ideal playroom.
3. Play has been used as an intervention with high school students and older children who are experiencing difficulties in their lives. How could you use play with a 15-year-old boy who was engaging in self-injurious behaviour? Describe the play materials you might use as well as your theoretical approach.

9 Listening Online

Imagine a highway with no speed limits and no guard rails, where vehicles have no seatbelts and faulty brakes, and drivers (many of them underage) are constantly distracted—that's the Information Superhighway.

— Raffi Cavoukian, *#lightwebdarkweb*

Canada's children are among the most connected in the world, perhaps because federal policy since the mid-1990s has consistently tried to maximize Internet penetration into homes and schools.[1] Ninety-eight per cent of Canadian youth are online every day (Mishna et al., 2012: 63).[2] Similar statistics abound on children's gaming, Internet surfing, and mobile phone use, but these statistics seem to become obsolete once they are posted, as the number of users and consumers of digital technology increases exponentially. In Canada, we may safely assume that most, if not all, of the children and youth with whom we work are digital natives. The amount and focus of their digital interactions will vary according to their social location, but all children and youth play, work, study, and socialize in a digital world.

Digital media refers to the technologies that children and youth use to connect with one another, including mobile phones, game consoles, tablets, and laptops. Through these technologies children and youth can network, blog, email, game, download music and upload videos, text, tweet, and communicate globally in an instant, and their expectation is that everyone else can do the same.

These expectations are not always met by those frontline workers and care providers who are less comfortable with technology. They react rather than respond, trying to curb and control the power of children's digital literacy rather than affirm and support it. Their discomfort is fuelled by their fear of the rapidly changing digital world, an unknown that prompts them to make dire predictions of potential danger, digital traps and temptations. These dangers are largely unidentified and unexplored because of insufficient research: **netnography**, or research on digital natives, is still developing and involves only those children and youth who are part of an **e-tribe** or online group with similar interests.

What is known is that the speed of communication, its global reach, and its simultaneous layers of fact and fiction affect working and social relationships, privacy and confidentiality, and the trust that children develop in others. This impacts all of our interventions with children and youth, whether or not our interventions are online. Canadian musician Raffi warns us to be wary of these online interventions, and he dedicates his cautionary tale to Amanda Todd, an early victim of online bullying.

In this chapter, we will explore the world of digital natives so as to better understand how children and youth think, respond, behave, and play in this digital world and what methods of communication and intervention work best for them. We will identify pitfalls and problems as well as certain groups of users, those who benefit most from the digital world and those who are most at risk within it. We will also describe how and when to work with children and youth online through **e-counselling**, an intervention that has already proved to be highly successful.

Objectives

By the end of this chapter, you will:

- Understand the impact of digital technology on the thinking processes, social and working relationships, and communication styles of children and youth.
- Identify benefits and pitfalls of online communication.
- Demonstrate digital strategies for structural and strengths-based interventions.

Digital Literacy

Digital technology was available in the 1980s, with email and e-bulletin boards being the most heavily used functions. In 1993, the Web (World Wide Web) opened up and soon became the network for speeding up both the dissemination and retrieval of information. The children of the 1990s grew up racing along its global stretch, jumping into online groups and connecting with others in new and creative ways. Some of these children are now the young workers who easily navigate the Web alongside today's children and youth. Both these workers and the children and youth they serve are called **digital natives**, a term coined by Marc Prensky (2010) to refer to those who were born into the world of digital technology.

Although there are diploma and degree courses in computer science, and computer courses in every high school, digital natives acquire their digital literacy mainly through experience. In January 2013, seven-year-old Zora Ball became the youngest person to develop a mobile game **app**. She created a video game app using Bootstrap programming language.[3] Her parents had provided her with the space, time, and resources to develop digital literacy, and they encouraged her enthusiasm for video games and programming. Zora confidently imagined and created her app in the same way that other children imagine and create a tower or a castle out of building blocks. She is one example of how very young children are confidently exploring the evolving world of digital media, learning through **trial and error** as well as help from others. There is no static body of knowledge from which to learn about the continuous updates, diverse interfaces, and security alerts of digital and online technologies. These children explore manually rather than through user manuals.

Trial and error combines with **social learning** or learning from others. Trial and error is the method that children use when they learn the functions of their friend's newly acquired tablet or phone. They pick it up, press buttons, and watch what happens. They do the same thing when they

Photo 9.1 Learning how to use digital technology through trial and error and social learning.

help their parent upload music, click onto new sites, or move the mouse into unknown areas. They explore and rarely pause to read instructions or warnings. Daniel Hillis (2011: xxx) describes this seamless interaction of computers and humans, "That is the real impact of the Internet. By allowing adaptive complex systems to interoperate, the Internet has changed the way we make decisions. More and more, it is not individual humans who decide but an entangled, adaptive network of humans and machines." Spike Jonze's 2013 film, *Her*, depicts this seamless interaction between the main character and his personal computer. Together they imagine and design social situations and problem solve when these situations turn sour. Interaction becomes entanglement, however, as the main character develops attributes of the loner as described later in this chapter.

This entanglement of humans and machines and practice on those machines is often done through social learning as children and youth explore their own and their friends' new devices. They both instruct and learn from peers. Sugata Mitra's early (1999) hole-in-the-wall computer experiments with children in India (see Chapter 12) confirm the efficacy of this method of learning. In Mitra's experiments, street children develop their digital literacy through social learning and the trial-and-error methods that they use on a computer screen that is embedded in the hole in the wall on their street.

A similar experiment was conducted at the same time in several American low-income areas. Hopeworks 'N Camden began in 2000 as an initiative to engage high school dropouts with learning through open access opportunities to play with and explore digital technology.[4] These opportunities were open to all youth in the area, including those attending school (which made up about 30 per cent of the youth) and those who had left school (which made up a much larger 70 per cent). The participants in Hopeworks 'N Camden taught one another how to create personal websites through social learning and trial and error as they engaged with each other to learn the software and create the sites. Those who managed to set up a personal website were invited to stay at Hopeworks and instruct paying customers. This led to part-time and full-time jobs for these youth as well as social networking on other issues. Carol Thompson, Jeff Putthoff, and Ed Figueroa (2006: 319) studied this collaborative digital work at Hopeworks 'N Camden and found that the youth gained self-esteem, communication skills, and problem-solving skills and were empowered to take on the roles of mentor, presenter, and web designer: "As they gain experience, they not only help each other, but also occasionally participate in finding new ways to solve small problems . . . because the focus is on relationships rather than digital technology."

Digital literacy is complex and not confined simply to knowing how to use a particular software program or a particular app. Digital literacy includes using and experimenting with changing modes of digital technology, multi-tasking or multi-processing digital input, and differentiating between digital fact and fiction.

Using and exploring changing modes of digital technology requires both cognitive and psychomotor skills. Children and youth use their critical thinking skills of logic, reasoning, and problem solving when they surf the Web, text and tweet, upload and download, create websites and videos, and configure apps. They also use their fine motor skills as they type, text, and tweet in an easy flow or manipulate the mouse to point and click. There is increasing evidence that using digital technology has enhanced both the fine motor and visual tracking skills of child users (Barnett et al., 2012).

Both the hole-in-the-wall experiment and Hopeworks 'N Camden demonstrate that this first skill is honed through practice, and this practice happens through open access to digital technology. In urban areas in Canada, this access comes more often through small digital devices and big digital domains supported by almost universal Internet access. Children and youth can practice their digital skills anywhere from the bus stop to the park. Their daily practice fine tunes their peripheral vision, problem-solving skills, digital fluency, and eye–hand co-ordination (Small and Vorgan, 2011: 96). A 2012 Canadian marketing survey found that Canadian children use digital technology twenty minutes more each day than their adult counterparts (Duong, 2012). While this may seem inconsequential, these twenty minutes add up to an extra 120 hours of digital practice per year and a resulting digital fluency that rivals and often supersedes that of adults.

Photo 9.2 This digital native chats online, listens to music, and games simultaneously.

The second skill in digital literacy is a skill set that includes adaptability, creativity, and parallel processing or multi-tasking. This skill set is essential for navigating the continuous flow of evolving websites and interfaces. Digital natives text while browsing websites; email while talking to real or virtual friends; and game while listening to music or chatting to another online gamer. Digital technology encourages this parallel processing, prompting children to take pictures, upload them, combine them with music or text, and send them to friends or share them on a social network site, for example. Each of these actions involves learning and using a variety of apps, moving across several sites, changing from one site or device to another and incorporating new interfaces in an easy flow.

This constant evolution of apps, interfaces, and sites also creates positive stress that sparks enthusiasm, creativity and problem solving. As children and youth see and experience change all the time online, they feel energized and empowered to take risks and seek change, learn, and be creative in their responses. Linda Jackson and her colleagues (2012) studied close to 500 child gamers and found that they were more creative than children who were not gamers. The non-gamers were slow to role play characters, act out situations, and imagine ways over and around obstacles. Another longitudinal evaluation of children's video game play (Russ and Dillon, 2011) demonstrates its positive effect on creativity. Unlike previous generations exposed to television, a medium that is neither interactive nor energizing, children and youth who are engaged in interactive digital technology have control of the interface and are expected to change both themselves and the medium. They are not watchers: they are participants.

The third skill in digital literacy is learning how to differentiate between digital fact and fiction. Since the advent of the Web, there has been a continuous uploading of information of all kinds, which has resulted in more online documentation than anyone can ever read, more videos than it is possible to view, and more music than we'll have a chance to hear. Because of this flood of documentation and information, art, music, and video, digital literacy now requires the skill of scanning several texts simultaneously rather than reading or viewing in depth. There are pause and stop buttons on the videos and prompts so that ads can be skipped. Missed videos can be recorded and watched later, or watched in bites rather than swallowed whole. Nicholas Carr (2011, 65) observes, "Once I was a scuba diver in a sea of words. Now I zip along the surface like a guy on a Jet Ski."

Similarly, particular pieces of text can be highlighted, cut, and pasted elsewhere. There are programs that attempt to curtail this cut-and-paste activity, but it is increasingly difficult to trace the path of text and track plagiarism. In a sense, digital technology makes copyright obsolete as videos, music, and text, in *Wikipedia* fashion, become the common property of everyone. This scanning of text, videos, and art that combines with cut-and-paste activity is neither simple nor rote. This is creative cut-and-paste that is combined with expressive language, uploaded photos, and graphics. The language used to weave text, videos, and music together is new and loaded with abbreviations, emoticons, acronyms, and **memes**. There is no time online for lengthy sentences or repetition, and tiny mobile devices do not encourage lengthy text conversations. Instead, brief and pointed phrases (thx, LOL, U2) are increasingly the norm.

Digital technology democratizes information through accepting input from all. Anyone can say anything: publish a book, paper, article, review, or blog online. Unfiltered information with embedded advertising is mixed with equal amounts of gossip and rumour. Fact and fiction blend just as real friends merge with virtual posers and bullies. This volume of information with its various sources, some credible and others anonymous and questionable, makes it increasingly difficult to differentiate between digital fact and fiction. Digital natives are left scrambling to find the truth, and they are primed to doubt anything and everything that is posted on their screens.

JuliAnna Ávila and Jessica Zacher Pandya (2013: 3) describe this aspect of digital literacy as "skills and practices that lead to the creation of digital texts that interrogate the world; they also allow and foster the interrogation of digital, multimedia texts." The American charity Invisible Children launched their Kony 2012 campaign with a 28-minute YouTube video depicting atrocities committed by Joseph Kony and his Lord's Resistance Army. The video had 26 million viewers on the first day and become the fastest growing viral video of all time. However, it took less than 24 hours for the first child to question the facts in the video and upload a homemade video in which he presented contradictory information. This child's video response, in turn, unleashed a flurry of comments and critiques as children and youth tried to verify the factual content of this campaign.[5]

Digital literacy has been described as a "ladder of opportunity" (Livingstone and Helsper, 2007) that begins with general information seeking, increases to include email and games, expands to downloading and texting, and broadens to include all interfaces. This ladder of opportunity has rungs at each step. Initial understanding of the technology and its possibilities breeds the confidence to climb but the speed of climbing depends upon both interest and access. Children living in poverty tend to have less access to the highest rungs of the ladder because they have less access to mobile phones, wireless, and high-speed Internet. This economic divide is gradually decreasing, however, as devices become cheaper and wireless high-speed Internet becomes more common in public spaces.

Constant Connectivity

Children and youth today socialize more with their peers because of their constant connectivity or continuous relationships through texts, tweets, and emails. Rather than taking a bus for an hour to see a friend or phoning a friend to leave a message, a child is only a click away from having an online conversation with a friend from school, an aunt or sibling, or a teammate. This conversation may be visual, vocal, text, or a combination of all three. Digital technology brings friends and relatives closer to a child who is constantly connected.

Real and virtual friends with similar interests also form groups or social networks and connect to exchange ideas, get information, learn, play games, and share personal stories. Mobile devices connect children with their parents and friends, virtual friends, and wannabe friends, all of whom are expected to stay connected and respond instantly. This constant connectivity means that one is always on, able to connect with others, and equally at the call of others. As William Deresiewicz (2011: 312) puts it, "A constant stream of mediated contact, virtual, notional, or simulated, keeps us wired in to the electronic hive."

This constant connectivity of the "electronic hive" is sometimes described as being shallow and short-term: texts and tweets are not as personal and deep as face-to-face conversations and lengthy meetings. Studies have shown, however, that texting and email actually encourage more in-depth conversations and richer friendships (Willoughby, 2008), and longitudinal research (Valkenburg and Peter, 2009) confirms this. While younger children use digital technology to play games and do their homework, older children use social networking sites mainly to deepen and extend their existing relationships and, less often, to form new relationships. They engage in lengthy and ongoing conversations with their friends, exploring new ideas, asking questions, and exchanging information, gossip, rumours, photos, and news.

Online relationships are two-way and usually interactive. A child's post on a social media site may not provoke a reply, but the post is read by someone else who thinks about the post, and then considers it or disregards it. Blogs expect comments; online petitions demand e-signatures; and tweets about flash mobs, protests, and gatherings invite social and political involvement at every level. There is evidence that children and youth are more politically aware and sensitive to global issues because of this connectivity and that they are more inclined to take part in political action that involves other children and youth. They are able to mobilize other children and youth through social media such as

Facebook, Twitter, Instagram, and Foursquare and involve them in a project, protest, or event. Although Canadian 18-year-olds are reluctant to vote at polling stations during elections, they are not shy about expressing political views online, and they regularly vote in online polls on various issues from celebrity haircuts to seal hunts.

Social media is used to organize **flash mobs**, groups that assemble to perform an action (dance, protest, song, theatrical event) and then disappear, as well as **crowd-sourcing** and **crowdfunding.** Crowdsourcing is a way to solicit ideas, resources, and services from the larger crowd, and crowdfunding focuses on finding funds for particular projects that cannot be as quickly funded through regular donations or loans in real time.

This constant connectivity has a price. Ian Jukes, Ted McCain, and Lee Crockett (2010: 4) argue, "There is so much going on from text messages to Internet videos to music to cell phone calls to brightly coloured flashing websites to instant messages that a person's mind is constantly skimming and skipping to keep track of it all." This digital traffic has resulted in what Linda Stone describes as continuous partial attention: "It is motivated by a desire to be a live node on the network . . . To be busy, to be connected, is to be alive, to be recognized and to matter."[6] Continuous partial attention is an auto-matic impulse, quite different from multi-tasking which is conscious and planned. This may be a neural change, a disorder, or simply a new skill in neural processing that is irritating to those who are habituated to longer and more focused attention.

A second price paid for constant connectivity is the decreased unconnected time. Children and youth today have less private offline time simply to be alone and enjoy solitude and lone pursuits. Andrew Keen (2012: 193) calls this constant connectivity "digital vertigo" in his book of the same name, and he laments, "our uniqueness as a species lies in our ability to stand apart from the crowd, to disentangle ourselves from society, to be let alone and to be able to think and act for ourselves." The influence of peers is greater than ever before as peers are everywhere and in every moment.

As both children and their caregivers become increasingly more connected to a virtual world than a real one, there is less real time and space to connect. Caregivers are literally missing in action. In her book, *The Big Disconnect: Protecting Childhood and Family Relationships in the Digital Age*, Catherine Steiner-Adair (2013: 11) notes,

> We complain about kids' love affair with tech, but children—even those who love their screens and smartphones—describe in almost identical ways a sense that their parents are virtually missing in action, routinely either engaged in cell phone conversation and texting or basking in the glow of the computer screen with work or online pastimes.

Children ask their parents questions only to see these parents texting or checking messages on their mobile phones while acknowledging their children's questions with a blank stare. At the same time, caregivers look across at the child eating dinner, recog-nizing by the earbuds that the child is connected to music or another conversation rather than to the caregiver. Constant connectivity sometimes leaves children and their caregivers feeling really unconnected.

Point to Consider   9.1

The Hurried Child

David Elkind's *The Hurried Child* was first published in 1981. This book chronicled the crammed lives of children in Western countries, children whose parents rushed to move them ahead faster and faster. Parents were eager to help their children to learn more and make the most of every minute through after-school activities, Saturday games, and enrichment classes. Elkind (1981: 3) wrote, "Today's child has become the unwilling, unintended victim of overwhelming stress—the stress borne of rapid, bewildering social change and constantly rising expectations." This warning from over thirty years ago seems trivial in the digital world where children are rushed online by tweets, texts, games, alerts, and news flashes that demand their instant attention and connection. The tyranny of the moment means that children today are hurried through their childhoods well beyond Elkind's imagination and dire predictions.

Loners

Digital natives are portrayed as loners, geeks, and social outcasts who socialize only with their machines. Videos, music, and comedy shows popularize this stereotype. Online and offline suicides of loners who are gamers also support this portrayal. One such loner was Brandon Crisp of Barrie, Ontario. Brandon spent most of his time alone with his XBox 360. When his parents took his XBox away from him, Brandon ran away from home. His lifeless body was discovered over three weeks later in a nearby wood, and media pundits immediately labelled his death as a suicide. Later investigation ruled Brandon's death accidental. He was not suicidal but was simply a loner whose connection to his video game was intense and personal.[7]

Loners like Brandon who play virtual games for hours every day are the same loners who avoid playing real games with friends and socializing at school. This technology provides them with another play medium. They have few or no school friends, and they tend to have computers in their bedrooms (Acier and Kern, 2011). They tend to have limited or no parental supervision and close family relationships. Their parents seem to live on the other side of the digital divide and have neither interest nor insight into their children's online world. Brandon Crisp's parents, Steve and Angelika, speak on camera of their bewilderment over his gaming. They are perplexed by their son's fascination with video games and they have never gamed with their son: "I never knew how much it meant to him," his mother admits. They call their son's favourite video game "just a game" and find his interest in gaming to be "unbelievable" (*Fifth Estate*, 2009).

There is usually a lack of trust and closeness between these loners and their families, and certainly there is suspicion on both sides of the divide. Loners tend not to ask their parents for advice about specific sites or games, and they may become entrapped in escalating levels of illegal activity. Valerie Steeves (2012: 19) notes, "Interestingly, the teenagers who did share the details of their lives with their parents were the ones who were not routinely monitored. Trust in this case was mutual; the parents trusted their children to behave appropriately and the children responded by providing them with access to their Facebook page." Loners tend to keep the extent of their online activity hidden from their parents and not seek digital support from their parents. Mitra (2013), long a proponent of digital literacy and the social learning that it promotes, observes, "There is a myth that computers make children more isolated and antisocial. Computers don't do anything of the sort. We, the adults, do, by giving children access to the Internet alone in their rooms with tiny devices. We ask for trouble and we get it."

Just as gamers can be very sociable when they play games with both real and virtual friends, so all online loners are not gamers. Some loners do not play video games and do not really interact or connect with either real or virtual friends. They drift from one virtual world to another, rarely staying with any one site, one idea, or one person. They may not even surface to get a glimpse of reality and real friends. They are the ones who walk into walls, people, and traffic while texting or surfing. Like those children and youth who do not choose to socialize with peers or family, these loners may fall into daydreaming, escapism, depression, and worse. They may become unable to differentiate between reality and fantasy, and they are easy prey to risks that are suggested to them by others (often loners themselves) online.

Loners can become dangerous to themselves and to those beyond their family when they engage in risky activities online. While these risky activities are legal, they are also damaging, and these loners inflict harm on others, those they know and those that they know only online. They become **trolls,** throwing out rumours, misinformation, diatribes, falsehoods, and gossip as they cyberbully (see next section). They may offer false merchandise or false promises to other children who do not have the experience or the financial acumen to handle their continuous and carefully crafted online temptations and scams. Risky loners may seduce others into meeting with them, running away with them, or harming themselves online for everyone to witness.

Loners also engage in illegal activities when they become hackers and downloaders, unblocking porn and gambling sites with questionable content. They can become posers and scammers, using borrowed identities or false credit cards, and their illegal activity comes with huge costs for themselves and their parents. According to a 2011 study among Quebec youth (Acier and Kern, 2011), these kinds of risky loners are often clinically addicted to the Internet. In the terms of the study, they exemplify pathological, excessive, compulsive, and problematic Internet use.

Their physical health is equally at risk because most of their daily activity involves sitting in front of a screen. They tend not to use mobile devices, preferring to be inactive in the solitude of their bedroom. They lack the exercise that is so essential during childhood. Just when their large and small muscles, sense of balance, strength, and psychomotor skills are developing, they do not exercise or engage in activities that hone these skills. As a result, their physical growth can become as compromised as their emotional health and mental well-being.

Bullies and Trolls

Embedded advertising, social media, and online groups ask for personal information. Children and youth, even those with multiple online identities and pseudonyms, become accustomed to sharing this personal information, most embarrassing moments, worst moments, and true confessions. Keen (2012, 23) notes, "Social media is the confessional novel that we are not only writing but also collectively publishing for everyone else to read. We are all becoming Wikileakers." This is a culture of disclosure that invites and encourages personal revelations and connections.

Users of digital technology rarely check the privacy policies of online sites, and it is even less likely that children and youth read through the legalese of these privacy policies. The Office of the Privacy Commissioner of Canada offers some guidelines, a graphic novel for tweens and teens (Social Smarts), and a presentation package for teachers,[8] but there are few real solutions offered for understanding Internet privacy policies. What is private instantly becomes public, and children who are not aware of this soon have their private lives exposed to the world. When the everywhere is online and anonymous, and when both users and abusers can adopt virtual identities, the right to privacy is often disregarded.

Children know about privacy from the time they are toddlers. Their play often has a private or hidden nature, and that is a big part of the fun. Children sleep in tree forts, hide in closets, develop secret codes, and play hide-and-seek. They have secret handshakes, nicknames, and secret adventures with their best friends. Wendy kept Peter Pan a secret from her parents, and there is an implicit rule that the childhood world of fantasy, fun, and play is private and adults are excluded. J.M. Barrie, the writer of Peter Pan, knew that. When he transgressed this privacy and played pirates, redskins, and brigands with the young Llewelyn Davies boys, he paid the price of social exclusion from the adult world. He was shunned and ostracized from adult activities, divorced by his wife, and ultimately excluded from the Llewelyn Davies' household.

When best friends share secrets there is trust involved. Children see their best friends every day and know them well. When these best friends betray their secrets there are repercussions and sometimes the friendship ends. Online friends are different. They can have virtual identities that may be deliberately misleading and anonymous, and they can disappear from the virtual world in an instant after exposing their best friend's secrets.

This online anonymity tends to be encouraged by adult gatekeepers—parents, caregivers, or guardians—who fear for their children's online safety. They often advise their children to assume fake names and different email addresses that give them some protection from stalkers, bullies, and sexual predators. Children find it relatively easy and fun to create and use these multiple identities, mailboxes, and online accounts. Twelve-year-old Zak writes, "I have a YouTube account. I use it to upload videos and watch lots of different types of clips. But when I was getting my YouTube account, I said I was 37 years old, 'cause you have to be much older than 11 to have an account" (*Kids and Media*, 2012). Pseudonyms and identities that are chosen by the child are empowering; they make the child unafraid to ask an expert, email a television personality, or challenge a prime minister. In his study of digital natives, Don Tapscott (2011: 131) describes 11-year-old Niki: "She could talk to whomever she wanted, find out whatever she wanted, and be who she wanted to be, without interference from parents or other adults." Online pseudonyms project personalities, attitudes, or behaviours that children may desire or emulate: prettypony@hotmail.com portrays quite a different persona to warlord@hotmail.com. Children and youth can portray themselves as beautiful, 50 years old or 15, boy or girl, transsexual or queer, just as they always have when they dressed up in costumes, played with puppets, and acted out scenarios. Digital technology expands the stage of this role play, and the costuming is endless. Pseudonyms and online identities act as masks and costumes, allowing the child to try on opinions, attitudes, and behaviours to see which ones are pleasing and which ones invite derision or **unfriending**. Online friends (and strangers) are the audience: "Self-surveillance and peer-surveillance are critical to the possibility of those empowering aspects of presenting oneself and forming an identity" (Regan and Steeves, 2010: 158). When children and youth encounter certain reactions, they can alter their attitudes or behaviours. They may even drop an attitude completely and try on another one to see the reaction.

This is fun, creative, and imaginative dramatic play at its best. It is also risky and depersonalizing, even dangerous, at its worst. As children develop these multiple online persona, the comfort level with deception begins to increase, while the feelings of personal accountability start to decrease. Cyberbullying can result.

When real and virtual friends tell secrets and expose these multiple personalities, behaviours, and attitudes, the exposure remains forever online for everyone to see. Unlike the tracks to the tree fort, these digital footprints cannot be easily erased. The child's personal information, photos, and daily movements are seen, tagged, and commented upon by an ever-enlarging circle of persons, most of whom are not actual best friends. This creates a digital social identity "composed not only of the data elements this person contributes voluntarily, but also of the elements that other people contribute and collect about him or her" (Palfrey and Gasser, 2008: 41). The photos and stories are there for classmates and their parents and for future teachers, employers, colleagues and college admission officers. The traces are open to cyberbullies, marketers, and potential sexual predators who troll the Web. John Palfrey and Urs Gasser (2008: 19–20) observe of a 16-year-old girl, "Although she can change many aspects of her personal identity quickly and easily, she may not be able to change certain aspects of her social identity. The net effect of the digital age—paradoxically—is to decrease her ability to control her social identity and how others perceive her."

Children are bullied online and also bully others. They know the power of the send button. "In our hyper-visible age all it takes is a camcorder and a Skype account to actually destroy someone's life" (Keen, 2012: 53). Children and adults using online identities to hide their own names can post secrets and lies about others. This anonymous posting can become cyberbullying, which includes **flaming** and flame wars, griefing, trolling, and hate speech. Cyberbullying carries less physical punch than being beaten up in the schoolyard but more emotional punch because of its wider spread in both space and time.

Initially it was thought that cyberbullying was largely anonymous and done by strangers, those loners previously described. However, research indicates that at least one-quarter of cyberbullying involves close friends of the person who is being bullied; in other words, cyberbullying is an extension of already existing friendships. In addition, at least one-quarter of bullies are also victims (Mishna et al., 2012: 64). A study of cyberbullying among British Columbia children and youth (Law et al., 2012: 670) concluded that cyberbullying or relational aggression is mainly "reciprocal banter where each participant becomes both the target and the perpetrator." Sixteen-year-old Amanda Todd of Port Coquitlam, British Columbia, described this banter very differently in the video she posted prior to committing suicide. Her video went viral and exposed how devastating cyberbullying had been in her short life. Shortly afterwards, in 2013, similar cyberbullying led to the suicides of 15-year-old Todd Loik of Saskatchewan and 17-year-old Rehtaeh Parsons of Nova Scotia (Todd, 2014).

The traditional gatekeepers, authorities, and protectors of children's privacy are adults. Parents, guardians, caregivers, and teachers are expected to keep children's secrets confidential; in fact, workers still use confidentiality forms (see Chapter 5) and coach children as to what should be kept private and what could be shared. These same adults encourage multiple identities and anonymity online, ostensibly to protect the child's privacy.

Some adults do try to block certain Internet sites in the home computer and limit children's computer use. Other adults try to teach net safety and **netiquette**. In a 2012 Canadian survey of children, "Many of our participants told us that parental monitoring is the price of admission; unless they give their parents their online passwords and 'friend' them on Facebook, they are not allowed to use networked devices" (Steeves, 2012: 16). However, these safeguards are redundant now that computers are mobile devices that are small enough to fit into a child's pocket. In 2006, Internet access from mobile devices such as smartphones, tablets, and gaming devices overtook Internet access from computers. Mobile devices that connect parents to their children also convey and hold personal information. External restrictions, even Nova Scotia's recently enacted Cyber Safety Act (2013), do not stop privacy invasions, deception, and cyberbullying.

Children and youth can be seduced, manipulated, exploited, and programmed by embedded ads, posts, and contests. They can stumble onto porn sites, download music and videos illegally, and get involved with posers who entrap them. Teacher

Ellen Seiter (2005: 98) describes how this happened during a classroom study of 8- to 12-year-old gamers:

> When I first looked at the Neopets site, I was stunned at the embedded advertising, and the commercial audacity of some of the schemes for gaining points. When the children in my class looked at the site, they primarily see opportunities for victory, fame, and fortune in a fan community. After some reflection on why our reactions were so different, I realized I should ask the children straight out why they thought Neopets existed. To my surprise, all the students gave the same answer, more or less: Neopets was just the cool idea of a lone individual who wanted to share the fun.

Like the children in Seiter's class, adults are also seduced, robbed, and exploited online. However, children seem to be more trusting of the world and less tainted by life experiences simply because of their age. They are more digitally adept than older adults, but perhaps less adept at filtering fact from fiction, truth from fantasy. Some children may indeed see a video game being the work of a friendly individual who is just as fun-loving as they are.

Online Interventions

Some workers persist in discounting digital technology. They disparage digital expertise and mock the users. They answer emails but often do so well beyond the 24-hour netiquette rule that requires an email to be answered within a day. They stick to their forms and handwritten case notes, their bulky files, and their morning meetings. Their reactions to children and youth are as dismissive as those of workers who base interventions on their experience rather than their insight.

Other workers embrace their role of digital immigrants and actively learn from and support digital natives. Their genuine interest in digital technology opens up opportunities for strengths-based and structural interventions. Workers who develop a baseline comfort level with digital technology are poised to practise netiquette as they respectfully dialogue with children who are already habituated to answering texts and emails promptly and checking their accounts regularly. Following the ladder of opportunity metaphor, these workers can begin to climb the ladder to meet the child on each rung, perhaps asking for guidance along the way, but always affirming that the child's digital culture deserves to be respected rather than shut down, ridiculed, or restricted.

Digital technology does not necessarily empower children or engage them, and it is not a panacea for disinterest in school, poor social skills, or inability to focus. If used positively by a child-focused worker who is comfortably climbing the ladder of opportunity, digital technology can be a stimulating way to engage children in activities that prompt them to learn more, engage actively with others, and advocate for structural change. Technology does not replace the worker, but it is a mechanism by which the worker can join with children and youth in interventions that are empowering, structural and strengths-based. Thompson, Putthoff, and Figueroa (2006, 328) note, "We have often endowed technology with magical properties rather than looking at it as a tool. The answer to the failure may be found not in the tool, but in the relationships that can be built around its use." If we focus solely on digital technology rather than the relationships that it facilitates and fosters, we miss out on opportunities to cross the divide and truly engage with children and youth in their online space.

Finding that first point of connection for a working relationship or **joining** can happen when the worker shows an interest in the child's phone or game rather than trivializing it or shutting it down. The child may be expecting the worker to say, "Put away your phone" or, "You can't play that game here." The worker's interest may catch the child off guard, causing that momentary disequilibrium that is essential to making change. This interest may lead to larger conversations around gaming, texting, and tweeting. The child may begin to feel more comfortable talking about real and virtual friends, multiple online identities, aggressors and problems, time wasters and threats, and a host of other challenges in the digital world.

Joining can also involve gaming together. This is a chance for parallel play, as well as an opportunity for the worker to tune into the child's language and emotions. The child's choice of avatar may be random or may be just as significant as the child's choice

Group Exercise 9.1

Online Forums

This large group exercise begins with the group leader's description of online forums as spaces for children and youth to gather and exchange ideas, thoughts, and feelings, and feel the comfort of peer support. The leader then walks the large group through one of the online forums from Table 9.1. The leader asks the following questions:

- Is this forum appealing to children and youth?
- What information and links are offered?
- What are the privacy safeguards?

After this general discussion the participants divide into small groups, with each group looking at a forum of their choice, either from Table 9.1 or from their own forum menu. Each group uses the same three questions to guide their discussions. Each group leader then summarizes the findings of the group and reports back to the large group. The online addresses of these forums are then compiled in order from the most to the least useful ones for Canadian children and youth.

of metaphor in narrative therapy. The avatar can personify the child's problems, fears, and anxieties, and the play can involve acting out these same problems. In addition, the worker is likely to lose the game, which puts the child into the power position of winner.

Some games present platforms for dialogue and the exploration of sensitive issues. Depression is one such issue, and the video game *SPARX* (*Smart, Positive, Active, Realistic, X-factor Thoughts*) has been shown to help youth who are struggling with depression. Gamers are given a choice of avatar with which to explore seven provinces. Each province provides a menu of cognitive behavioural strategies to combat the gnats (gloomy, negative, automatic thoughts) of depression. The avatar moves from province to province, gradually developing both the weapons and the confidence to combat depression. When *SPARX* was field tested with 187 youth, all of whom had a diagnosis of depression, *SPARX* proved to be just as effective as face-to-face counselling. It also sparked a greater participation rate because children chose to play *SPARX* rather than meet with a counsellor (Merry et al., 2012).

The worker may also provide a link to supportive apps and free e-counselling sites so that children and youth can connect with qualified counsellors and health resources. Table 9.1 indicates some of these free e-counselling sites and apps that are currently available.

E-counselling is most appropriate for those children and youth who do not have the time, transportation, or money to travel to an agency to meet with a counsellor or talk to a worker. E-counselling means that children do not have to beg others for

Table 9.1 Online Resources for Canadian Children and Youth

Kids Help Phone (KHP)	Professional phone and e-counselling service for youth. Forums also available.
The Jack Project at Kids Help Phone	Specific to youth mental health and well-being, this site is not interactive, but offers resources, symposia, and campaigns in which youth can participate.
Youthspace	Live chat, youth forums, and e-counselling for persons under 30; texting available only within BC.
Path of the Elders	Video teachings of Elders and video games.
Mindyourmind	Interactive online health tools (games, forums, blogs) for youth struggling with mental health issues.
Mindyourmood	Phone app that provides an easy way to record emotions and moods on a daily basis, tracking changes and shifts.
Circle of 6	Phone app that stores contact information for six trusted friends. Pressing a button sends a help message to these friends along with the child's GPS location.
RespectED: Violence and Abuse Prevention	Interactive games, videos, and programs like "Stand Up 2 Bullying."
iCouch	Phone app that tracks thinking and emotions every day.

a ride or bus money, explain why they are late for dinner, miss after-school sport, or fit in a meeting with a counsellor over their lunch hour at school. No one sees them going to counselling, and their meetings can be truly private. E-counselling offers children and youth an accessible and affordable means of support and encouragement, and it empowers them to take personal responsibility to attend meetings online in their own time and space. Faster linked supports for children and youth who are ready for change—"customers" in Steve de Shazer's terminology (see Chapter 6)—means that they do not have to wait for an appointment, group meeting, or referral to another agency. When capable and knowledgeable workers can provide e-counselling in the child's time and child's space, the results can be powerful.

Online meetings can also feel more comfortable and private for a child who is fearful, shy, withdrawn, or depressed, or a child who is reticent to discuss personal issues with a stranger. Meeting online can actually disinhibit the child. The screen serves as a barrier or mask, similar to the puppet used in the playroom (see Chapter 8). A keypad and screen provide the distance, time, and privacy to recall frightening, embarrassing, or traumatic events without having to watch a worker's reaction.

An example of how online work can be disinhibiting is Kids Help Phone (KHP), one of the supports in Table 9.1. KHP is available both by phone and online, and supports are offered all day and every day in both mediums. Most children and youth prefer the online counselling: two-thirds of users report that they are too nervous to talk with someone over the telephone about their problems, and over

Note from the Field   9.1

E-Counselling

How does the worker convey empathy, respect, and congruence through typed words? Workers who counsel online lack that physical presence and body language of nodding in agreement, leaning forward attentively, or smiling in acknowledgement. There is no modulation of the voice or softening of the facial muscles to convey empathy. There are only typed words to convey the Rogerian relationship. These words are typed quickly without edits and cannot be easily retracted, said slowly, whispered, or emphasized. Every word becomes imbued with meaning, and this meaning is sharpened by font (style and size), expression symbols, bold, underline, emoticons, and punctuation. The following worker (W) and youth (Y) online dialogue illustrates this. The worker appropriates the font, language style, and acronyms of the youth right away in order to join with the youth and convey empathy. This helps to establish a working relationship in which the young person (Jacob) can begin to feel safe enough to tell his story.

continued

> W: Hello, Jacob. Thank you for connecting with me and completing your social history. You identified the issue you are having with establishing and keeping relationships, and today I am hoping you can expand on this so that we can work together on some strategies. How does that sound to you?
>
> Y : **Great!!!** But I have some ??
> W: OK – go!
> Y : R U GLBTQ?
> W: Yes............ ?
> Y : Have U worked with Q-guys?
> W: Multi XXXX
> Y : Hmmm. Burnt too many XXX by Qguys. OMG, hurts.
> W: Expand.
> Y : U ready?
> W: Go!
>
> At this point, Jacob writes a page of text, loaded with acronyms, capitals, boldface, italics, bracketed feelings, and other textual cues that paint a clearer picture of his presenting problem. This prompts the worker to explore meanings; responses that end with a question mark convey the need for more information. Throughout this exchange, the worker affirms Jacob's strengths and his ability to seek and identify solutions.

half state that they prefer typing online to talking on the phone about their problems (Haner, 2010).

Counselling online or e-counselling can be synchronous or asynchronous. Synchronous work happens in real time and may be accompanied by voice-over-Internet Protocol services (e.g., Skype, Google Talk), which allow the child and the counsellor to both see and talk to each other. This can happen only when both the child and the worker have this digital capability and bandwidth. Synchronous work involves the child typing in questions or remarks and the worker typing back immediate responses to these questions or remarks. The worker who offers synchronous e-counselling is careful to respond rather than react, as one would in texting, and to role model respectful online communication (netiquette), responding with empathy and without the usual body language that accompanies it. As Steiner-Adair (2013: 20) notes, "Technology is redefining the fundamental cues, content, and cadence of our communication and the improvisational, uniquely human dimension of connection." While this kind of communication feels immediate and real, it can also feel pressurized and stressful as both the worker and the child type and read, forming the cognitive and emotional content of their statements simultaneously. There is no time or space to edit, delete, or retract, and a single word can cause the child or youth to log off, to literally and metaphorically leave the room.

Asynchronous e-counselling allows a pause between posts and replies, time for reflection on the previous meeting, rereading posts and replies, and linking to other supports between meetings. Asynchronous e-counselling happens when a child asks for counselling, and the child is given an answer to this request. The usual time gap is one business day. When the child is assigned a worker, the worker then sets up a schedule so that the child knows when questions will be answered, responses will be sent, or other supports offered.

E-counselling is offered by both freelance workers who operate from their own websites and agency workers operating from agency websites. To offer e-counselling, the website typically has the following features:

- password protection and encryption facilities to ensure confidentiality and to prevent external and internal online intrusion;
- the ability to securely store all client–worker communication; and
- secure payment methods for accessing the service (if payment is required).

The website usually offers general information about the agency and/or the worker, as well as information about the scope of the counselling relationship including timelines, frequency of communication, and rules for cancellations. A child with acute and urgent problems who wants frequent daily contact with a counsellor, for example, would be redirected to a crisis line, local child protection agency, or child mental health service. Once a child or youth chooses to participate in e-counselling, the young person provides and receives detailed information about this participation. This includes the need for a secure and safe place to participate, one that is away from distractions, strangers, and noise. Confidentiality is a key concern for children and youth participating in e-counselling (Haner, 2010: 5). They often fear that peers or adults who break confidentiality will cause even more pain and stress in their lives.

Point to Consider   9.2

Crossing the Digital Divide

The digital divide is sometimes called a generational divide, with the young being the natives and the old being the immigrants. The natives know the culture and are comfortable within it, while the immigrants struggle to fit into the new land. An early landmark study of the digital divide in Israel (1998–2000) demonstrates how young and old can cross that divide and learn from each other. Researchers paired young children (average age of nine years) with seniors in a retirement home. The children were entrusted to teach the seniors computer skills so that the seniors could create their own digital lifebooks. Each child was paired with a senior, and each pair worked together for 10 two-hour meetings. The teacher–learner relationship empowered the children who taught the seniors. Most of the children developed a close bond with their senior students. One child observed, "I had a lot of emotional difficulties this year. But my old lady listened to me and fixed my head. Each meeting with her was like walking into a beautiful land" (Aphek, 2000). Both natives and immigrants learned much about each other and about digital technology over the 20 hours, and some pairs continued to meet well beyond the end of the project. This landmark study inspired two teenagers in Ottawa, Ontario, to start Cyber-Seniors in 2009. In Cyber-Seniors, high school students teach computer skills to seniors in a retirement home. Similar intergenerational projects are happening in high schools across Canada.

Digital Storytelling

While video games provide opportunities for parallel and group play as well as dialogues on sensitive issues, some children may prefer to do their own reflective work or journaling alone in their own time and space through digital stories that incorporate their artwork, music, photographs, and words. Digital storytelling through blogs or e-journals helps children and youth to make sense of the important aspects of their daily life, as well as the memories that resurface through the process. This autobiographical reasoning (see Chapter 7) is work that must be done in constructing personal identity, a sense of uniqueness in the world.

Digital technology takes the reflective power of a personal diary a step further in allowing children and youth easy access to their peers. They can share their findings and meanings with other children and youth who share similar challenges and are also seeking solutions. "Through the multimodal sense-making of digital storytelling, youth create new meaning as they are pushed to talk, think, and engage in identity play" (Nixon, 2013: 43). Children and youth can join with others to exchange ideas and explore structural determinants and assets, encourage one another, link to potential sources of support, and identify avenues for structural change. Feedback from peers expands digital storytelling into a larger dialogue around race, culture, ethnicity, gender, and sexual orientation. These complex issues become more real as children recount how the intersections of race, class, gender, and age impact their personal stories. "A narrative account of how a fight on the first day of middle school affected Solomon, for instance, became a tool for critiquing and questioning the ephemeral influence of violence within the school community" (Garcia, 2013: 111).

Digital storytelling provides a current example of how the personal is political. When children tell their stories online they become engaged with others and with the structural issues that impact all children and youth. This engages them politically, even before they are old enough to vote in civic elections. Michael Wyness (2012: 197) explains, "Children can become part of a global civil society of pamphleteers and political activists, their membership conditional on Internet access rather than age-related political rights." Through online blogs and forums children share their stories with virtual communities of adoptees, animal rights activists, children in care, and environmentalists. Sharing their stories may lead to activism and online petitions and protests, as well as learning more about structural supports and assets.

Children and youth can decide whether or not to join these online debates and groups, and whether or not to make their blogs and stories public. They can invite in some friends or make their blogs totally open. Their blogs are increasingly winning mainstream attention. One mother-daughter blogging team, El and Jae, even compiled a list of the top ten best kids' blogs on their own blog, *Eljae* (2012). As El and Jae note, some of the best blogs were written by six- and seven-year-olds. Their words were limited, but the photos and artwork that the children included on their blogs reflected their feelings about family, friends, and school. Steven Johnson (2011: 29) remarks, "The screen is not just something you manipulate, but something you project your identity onto, a place to work through the journey of your life as it unfolds."

Digital storytelling happens through e-journaling, blogs, forums, and social media sites, and can be a tremendous form of peer support for children and youth. When the shooter at Virginia Tech took the lives of 32 victims on April 16, 2007, mobile phones were jammed. Youth connected on social media sites to check on the safety of their friends from high school and, within minutes, postings appeared: "I'm okay." After similar tragedies around the world, social media sites provide a way for family and friends to check on the safety of others, and to offer their own words of support (and condolences) to others. Online communities assemble faster and easier than do those contacted by phone, mail, or car, and are able to offer support, fundraising, news, and updates at times of crisis.

Summary

Fears and predictions do not scare away Canadian children who continue to interact with digital technology in their daily lives and become more and more adept at tailoring this technology to suit their needs. The fears of cyberbullying, sexual entrapment, and stifled creativity have changed to a realization that digital technology can also expose bullying, provide sexual information, and enhance creativity and communication. Although adults sometimes perceive video gaming and social networking as time-wasters, Markus Kummer (2012: 8) advises that "getting involved will allow parents guardians, educators, and other trusted influences to keep children and young people out of harm's way."

In this chapter, we learned how to get involved and develop a baseline expertise from which to climb up and join children and youth in online dialogues. Children and youth are increasingly more comfortable online, and workers who want to work with children and youth need to meet them in their comfort zone. Like the parents of Zora Ball, we need to empower children to explore digital technology within the safety of our positive online involvement as described by Raffi (2013: 4): "harnessing our Net inclinations to create a culture of true connection." Digital natives see unlimited possibilities in an open future, and workers who join them in exploring and searching for new ways to relate can empower children to find their own unique solutions.

This is particularly important when we intervene in a behavioural crisis. Workers can impose adult solutions that reinforce adult control, but these solutions fade quickly. Real and sustained behavioural change happens when workers meet children in their comfort zones and try to understand the meaning and role of behaviours. This empowers children to take responsibility for their behaviour and its impact. In the next chapter, we will see how children and youth can control and manage behavioural change in a way that works for them in their daily lives and lasts beyond their childhood.

Review Questions

1. How is digital literacy acquired?
2. Explain the three skills of digital literacy.
3. What are the advantages and disadvantages of constant connectivity for children and youth?
4. Why do parents and guardians encourage online anonymity, and what are the pitfalls of this anonymity?
5. Name three microsystem factors that are common to online loners.
6. How has the understanding of privacy changed for children and youth today?
7. How did the advent of mobile technology impact the traditional role of adults as gatekeepers?

8. Why might children and youth prefer e-counselling to meeting with a counsellor at school or in an agency?
9. What is the difference between synchronous and asynchronous online counselling?
10. Describe three strategies for establishing a healthy working relationship online with a child or youth.

Discussion Questions

1. Reflect upon your use of digital technology. Which online forums and websites do you frequent? Do you contribute to blogs or participate on social networks? How has your online activity changed in the last year? Does this online activity interfere with mindfulness?
2. Have you ever been the object of cyberbullying or felt vulnerable in an online space? How did you handle this? Are there safeguards for children and youth that you would suggest to protect them from this situation?
3. Why might some workers resist working online? Would this be your preferred mode of working? Explain, using examples.

10 Understanding Behaviours

Huckleberry was cordially hated and dreaded by all the mothers of the town, because he was idle and lawless and vulgar and bad—and because all their children admired him so, and delighted in his forbidden society, and wished they dared to be like him.

—Mark Twain, *The Adventures of Tom Sawyer*

An onlooker may see a behavioural crisis that seems to arise from nowhere: a screaming, kicking child lashing out at an adult; a shy, quiet child who suddenly rages; an ordinarily compliant youth who turns on his teacher and swears. These crises look and feel scary for everyone, particularly for the child who is lashing out, raging, or swearing. However, not one of these crises simply erupts. Each crisis is a symptom of a previously untended behaviour, feeling, or structural antecedent. Each one is an early warning system, a call from the child to the surrounding adults to pay attention. This scary behavioural crisis, if managed properly, can be a learning opportunity for everyone who is involved and can result in substantial structural and behavioural change.

In this chapter, we will explore both internal and external causes of children's behaviour that is commonly described by adults as "acting out." We will look at traditional ways of managing this behaviour from spanking to physical and chemical restraints to incarceration. Each of these methods locates the child as the cause of the behaviour, and each method demands that the child change. Each method can prompt short-term behavioural change, while possibly causing further long-term damage and a spiral of escalating unwanted behaviours.

We will consider a more time-consuming behaviour management method, that of understanding the role and meaning of behaviour in the life of the child. This structural and strengths-based method draws on Aboriginal child and youth socialization practices that have worked well for centuries. These practices position the child as a person with rights and responsibilities to the community in the present and to all those who have gone before, too. While the Elders in the community provide guidance, the child is responsible for personal behaviour management within the community. This premise radically changes the adult–child power dynamic, equalizing power, with the child assuming more power and responsibility for behaviour. This method assumes that the child is a competent person and citizen who is capable of contributing to the community.

Behaviour is the child's way to communicate, feel powerful, and learn, and when behaviour changes so does the child's method of communication, feeling of empowerment, and level of learning. What appears to be negative behaviour may be a sign of resiliency or positive adaptation to a negative environment. There is no blame involved, only an understanding of both structural issues and antecedents that frame the behaviour. Sometimes structural change in the community is needed more than changing, containing, or punishing the child's behaviour. Structural change is not as cheap or as quick as some methods, but it often results in the child's choosing to learn and to adopt new behaviours or to adapt to existing ones.

Objectives

By the end of this chapter, you will:

- Understand how behaviour is socially constructed and what role behaviour plays in the life of the child, the family, and the child within that family.
- Identify the strengths of both traditional and structural interventions.
- Demonstrate an understanding of how you can intervene when there is a behavioural crisis.

The Social Construction of Behaviour

Behaviour is socially constructed to be either positive (asset) or negative (deficit). It acquires this meaning or value through the social location of the person who reports on the behaviour and categorizes it as either positive or negative. If this person has power, the label carries tremendous weight, both for the child who is labelled and for those interacting with her or him. If the person who reports on and categorizes the behaviour has little or no power, the label will be questioned, ignored, or rejected. The child may be the reporting agent: "Wei-lee hit me!" In this report, the child's tone indicates a negative categorization: the child labels the hitting as a negative behaviour. However, the child has little or no power. The child's report, categorization, and label are not greatly trusted or perhaps even believed to be true. The adult may dismiss the report and respond, "Stop whining."

The reality is that adults have the social location of authority and are the primary reporting agents and punishers of behaviour. They have **coercive power**. They categorize and label behaviour, sometimes constructing it only to fit their needs. An adult observer of a child who is studying, attending school, and being polite constructs these behaviours as positive behaviours or social strengths because these activities usually please adults. The child who is engaged in the behaviour of studying, attending school, and being polite may construct these same behaviours as negative: boring, meaningless, and self-defeating. One child may value the behaviour as positive, while another child values that same behaviour as negative. Some children may socially construct tantrums, whining, and hitting as powerful and effective communication skills, whereas most adults construct these same actions as negative behaviours. Some children (and some adults) construct their outdoor play as fun and positive, whereas other adults see the same play as aggressive, dangerous, and negative. The value of particular behaviours, and their negative or positive attributes, is socially constructed.

Photo 10.1 Is this child abuse or meaningful family work?

These social constructions become behavioural norms that are enforced and reinforced by adults. Children learn compliance to these behavioural norms at an early age. If they appear cheerful and compliant to adults, adults reward them. Even if they only pretend to be interested in the lesson, the teacher rewards them. Using this system of rewards in this way is **classical conditioning** of behaviour. On the other hand, if children express their negative feelings honestly, adults sometimes silence or belittle them. Using this system of punishers is also classical conditioning that teaches children to hide their feelings, particularly their very raw feelings, behind the mask of compliant behaviour.

Social construction of behaviour is both cultural and co-relational. In an affluent society in which education is free (such as Canada), reading is socially constructed as a positive behaviour for children. In a less affluent society in which children are part of a family struggling to get enough to eat, paid work is socially constructed as a positive behaviour for children, and reading is considered an independent and selfish behaviour that does not help the family. This social construction of behaviour is cultural, changing over time and across social groups and societies to reflect gender, race, class, ethnicity, and socio-economic status. Behaviour takes place in this cultural context, against a backdrop of family norms, parenting practices, and attitudes to children.

Is it negative behaviour for a child to interrupt adults? In the past in Canada, interrupting was considered negative behaviour, and the child was punished for it. Currently, many in mainstream society construct this behaviour as a positive behaviour—a sign of the child's confidence, high self-esteem, and communication skills, particularly when the child interrupts with a clever statement. At the same time, many ethnic, cultural, and racial groups in Canada consider interrupting to be negative behaviour on the grounds that interrupting adults is disrespectful and rude. A child in one school in Canada may be praised for interrupting adults; in another school, the child may be punished.

Is one child teasing another child of about the same age negative behaviour? In Canada, teasing used to be viewed as behaviour typical of children. If the teasing created an uproar, punishment was meted out to both the teaser and the teased (or sometimes only to the child who was teased because the child's reaction constituted the uproar). The teaser was told to stop being bossy, and the teased was told to stop whining. Sometimes both children were sent to their rooms or given a job to do together. Today youth may use teasing or put-downs as a form of humour and a way of relating with their friends, but their teasing may also be constructed as bullying. The teaser (bully) is scolded or redirected and, in some cases, suspended from school.

Social construction is co-relational or contextual: much depends on where behaviour happens and whom it affects. Some kinds of behaviour considered positive in the home may be considered negative at school and vice versa. Roughhousing, for example, may be seen by adults as aggressive behaviour in school, and may even lead to the child's suspension from school. However, in that same child's home, roughhousing may be the norm, as family members typically speak and laugh loudly and touch one another frequently (hugging, jostling, and wrestling). The person who succeeds in categorizing and labelling behaviour is the person who holds the social power and who is the acknowledged "expert"; usually, this is the adult with authority.

Parents and caregivers easily describe the "negative" behaviour of their children: tantrums, whining, destruction of property, alcohol and drug abuse, self-harm, aggression, swearing, truancy, non-compliance. An overwhelmed, dispirited, and frustrated parent may describe the child's crying, whining, and tantrums as evidence of a developmental delay, the other parent's lack of parenting skills, or the child's intractable temperament. Brothers and sisters may describe this behaviour differently. They may describe the tantrums as attention-seeking or "spoiled" behaviour. They may see the whining as childish and as a sign of "how really dumb my brother is." However, the whining child may see the whining as a necessary means of getting adult attention in a chaotic home.

An older child may seem aggressive and hostile, and she may act out her emotions through the theft, destruction, or vandalizing of property. The worker may label the child's behaviour as **conduct disorder** or persistent, anti-social activity that violates the rights of others. The parent may describe this behaviour as threatening, criminal, and violent, and may describe the child's group of school friends as a "gang." The child may describe this behaviour as innovative and strong, a valid response to a problem-saturated world, and a rite of passage in the neighbourhood. The child may see the vandalism as "no big deal"; to attain status or membership in the group, property must be vandalized, sacrificed, or stolen (see Chapter 12).

Some criticize such an understanding of the social construction of behaviour as a rationalization—an excuse or justification of the deviant or bad behaviour of the child. This presupposes that behaviour has an absolute value by adults' standards and that this behavioural value does not change. However, social values do change. Asking a young child to sit still in school on a hot, sunny afternoon also can be constructed as deviant behaviour. Should the adult be punished for this deviancy? The child who refuses to sit still for some length of time can be seen as assertive and mature. Should the child be rewarded for this refusal? As we have seen in the above examples, the value and meaning of behaviour change for each person and each situation according to that person's point of view. Table 10.1 presents six behaviours. Three behaviours (skipping school, stealing, hitting) are typically seen as negative, while the other three (reading, playing baseball, attending school) are seen as positive. However, this social construction changes according to the location of the person who labels the behaviour.

In each of the above examples, different social constructions come to bear on the child's behaviour. Truancy (skipping school) feels positive for many children and can be

Table 10.1 Six Behaviours and Six Labels

Behaviour	Negative	Positive
Reading	Avoiding work and responsibilities at home; wasting time; being selfish	Improving literacy and learning more
Playing baseball	Avoiding work and responsibilities at home; wasting time; being selfish	Exercising and developing psychomotor skills; being a team player
Attending school	Avoiding work and responsibilities at home; failing to help support the family; being selfish	Improving literacy and learning more; preparing to join the workforce
Skipping school	Missing valuable class time; missing socializing with classmates; failing to be responsible	Avoiding bullies and boredom; avoiding feelings of failure; being self-motivated and creative
Stealing	Immoral and disrespectful of others and their property	Acquiring the necessities for daily life; being resourceful
Hitting	Hurting others	Self-protection and self-assertion; being strong

an opportunity to explore new neighbourhoods, activities, and friends, but truancy also means that they miss potentially valuable learning offered in the classroom. The worker who rigidly constructs truancy as bad or deviant social behaviour may regard the child's alternate explanations simply as rationalizations. However, a worker who understands those differently constructed meanings as co-relational and culturally sensitive sees each child's explanation as just that: his or her social construction of behaviour.

Causes and Antecedents

Causes of behaviour are complex and often difficult to identify. There may be multiple guesses from several adults, including teachers, parents, relatives, and others. Sometimes the child is asked to guess, "What made you steal the money?" The child may attribute physical conditions such as boredom, hunger, or fatigue, or feelings such as anger or depression. The child may frame this response to suit the questioner, to elicit sympathy, or to evade consequences. The child may also be engaging in guesswork.

Causes can include the child's inner characteristics, the conditions in the microsystem and mesosystem, experiences and relationships, and structural determinants. Each has a part to play in causing or prompting behaviour. The child who stole the money may have a mental health issue, may be hungry for a chocolate bar, may be influenced by neighbourhood friends, or may be impacted by societal violence and immorality. Events that directly precede or trigger a behaviour are known as **antecedents**. The antecedent of the theft may have been the cashier's absence from the cash register and the ease with which the theft could be accomplished.

The child may be aware of some of these causes and antecedents or may behave spontaneously without being aware of any of them. This spontaneous behaviour can feel frightening and distressing and can contribute to the child's low self-esteem and learned helplessness. The behaviour controls the child and the child feels increasingly out of control. When the child's becomes aware of causes and antecedents, the feeling of control gradually returns. The child may choose to modify, stop, or increase a particular behaviour, and may come to understand how to do this by modifying, stopping, or increasing either the cause or the antecedent. This is not a simple process. There are many adults who still behave spontaneously and without reflection. They may be labelled quirky, free-spirited, or creative, but their lack of control over their own behaviour negatively impacts all of those around them.

Behaviour usually is attributed to the child's internal characteristics or temperament. When the child misbehaves, the adult infers that the child is spoiled, aggressive, disordered, or destructive. When the child fails to comply, the adult may pathologize the child as having a conduct disorder, developmental delay, or a mental health issue. If the child steals, the adult suggests that the child is immoral, deceitful, or dishonest. This attribution of behaviour to the child's personality or temperament or inadequate morality equates the behaviour with the child.

Behaviour is also attributed to microsystem factors that affect the physical condition of the child, such as fatigue, hunger, sickness, or boredom. Feed the child and the behaviour changes. Let the child nap and the behaviour after the nap is different. Get the child out of hospital and the child will become gentle and compliant. Changing the immediate physical conditions in the microsystem is typically easier than changing internal characteristics.

Mesosystem factors are also seen to cause behaviour. A child's teacher or class size may seem to be a cause for the child's non-compliant behaviour. Stress in the neighbourhood or loss of a neighbourhood friend may seem to be a cause for the child's depression. Frequent moves and lack of transition time from daycare to home may seem to be causes for the child's aggression or anger.

Note from the Field   10.1

Kwiky-Mart Parents

Fourteen-year-old Tran was brought to counselling by his parents, a couple who ran a Kwiky-Mart convenience store while caring for their four children. Tran was responsible for caring for his younger brothers and sisters after school and for helping at the Kwiky-Mart on weekends. Recently, however, he had been disrespectful to customers and had even started skipping school. When he talked to his parents, he used street slang that they barely understood.

The school counsellor had called Tran's parents and suggested they go for family counselling. She also reminded Tran's parents that they had missed the last two parents' nights at the school and had not been regularly signing Tran's homework. This was very shaming for them and they used the word "ashamed" several times when explaining Tran's behaviour. They said that they had come to Canada for their children's education, and they valued teachers highly. Tran barely spoke during the first meeting and, when he did, he used short phrases and expletives. His parents wondered if he was in a gang or doing drugs; both suggestions had been made by the school counsellor.

My next meeting was with Tran alone. After a few moments of awkward silence, I asked him about his ball cap logo. That started him talking about his favourite show, *Trailer Park Boys*. He was also a big fan of *The Simpsons* and *South Park*. He seemed to be a veteran of television-watching after school and on weekends. Since coming to Winnipeg at age eight, Tran had been exposed to thousands of hours of watching irresponsible and irrational parents on television, probably more hours than he had already spent watching and listening to his own parents. Tran had started to see his own parents as weak and stupid, and his behaviour echoed those of his television heroes who always outwitted their parents. By exploring these media images together, we eventually came to a clearer understanding of how different his hard-working parents were from the parental prototypes on television. Tran started to talk about how much he respected his parents' struggles, and we both looked for ways for him to show them that respect.

Addressing the structural issues is far more difficult; structural issues are seen as "political" and "beyond our scope." Gerald deMontigny, a former child protection worker in British Columbia, was chastised many times for his structural advocacy (1995: 42): "If I outlined that a client's problems were the effects of social factors, such as unemployment, poor housing, exploitative landlords, racial harassment, or unsupportive social workers, I was understood as rationalizing the client's failure to cope." The structural approach demands worker advocacy and real change in the structure. It also demands understanding structural causes of behaviour rather than penalizing and blaming the child.

Antecedents or precipitating factors such as illness, death, bullying, taunting, or violence are easier to pinpoint because they happen just before a behavioural change. The child can begin to recognize and understand antecedents by mapping behavioural outbursts and then looking at the events or circumstances that contribute to the outburst. Applied Behavioural Analysis (ABA) considers these antecedents or precipitating events when analyzing why the child behaves in certain ways: change the precipitating event in order to change the behaviour. Antecedent, Behaviour, Consequence (ABC) is another method of behavioural analysis that suggests changing antecedents or triggers in order to change the behaviour.

One winter afternoon when I was on the bus going home, a man got on the bus with his three small children. The bus was crowded so he sat beside me with his youngest child on his lap. The two other children sat behind me. They started kicking the back of my seat, first slowly, then harder. I turned around and glared but my stern glare had little effect on them. The little girl on his lap started whining and thrashing, her winter boots knocking slush against my sleeve. At the end of a long workday, I found myself becoming more and more irritated. Finally, I turned to the father and said, "Excuse me, but could you ask your children to stop kicking my seat?" He didn't respond at first, so I nudged him again. Then he turned to me and apologized, "I am so sorry. I will. We're on our way home from the hospital and my wife—their mother—died. I just don't know what to do."

This was a moment I will never forget. It was the start of a relationship. I listened while he talked all the way to his bus stop. I thanked him again for sharing with me and for teaching me such an important lesson. His story seemed at first to be one of antecedents: mother dies, father cries, and children misbehave. However, this was a story about the importance of structure. While the trigger was traumatic and life-changing—the loss of a wife and mother—the structure that framed this loss needed to be understood to clearly see both the behaviour and the possibilities for behavioural change.

The man told me about his family's arrival in Canada three years ago and how hard it had been to face the first winter. He told me that he had been a doctor in Ghana and was now a cleaner in the hospital in which he had hoped to practise medicine. Then he told me about the remedies for his wife that he had not been able to get in Ottawa, the ones that he felt certain would have saved her life. These structural impacts were crushing him. His innate resiliency and that of his children were flagging. Over the past six months his usual self-contained and purposeful behaviour had changed. Even before his wife died he had started drinking, a behaviour he feared would get worse. He felt powerless to help anyone, least of all his own children. Now his wife was dead, too, and he as a doctor had been unable to save her. The structural impact on this man and his family was immense.

Changing the antecedents would have been easy. His children were tired and needed sleep. His children were hungry and bored after 10 hours in the hospital and many months of visiting their mother. His children were sad and angry. Change the antecedents by offering sleep, food, and change in stimulation, and the irritating behaviour (kicking the seats) stops.

Most behavioural interventions, such as ABA or ABC, suggest changing, eliminating, or applying antecedents or consequences in order to change or end the behaviour. However, all of these behavioural antecedents reflect larger structural determinants. Bereavement counselling might address the family's immediate loss (antecedent) but this counselling would not change the behaviours within the family or address those structural factors of poverty, underemployment, and racism that put this family at risk of falling apart. The father, devastated by the loss of his wife, would need tremendous support and caring for him to be able to summon enough strength to tackle these issues.

Motivation

Why do children and youth behave in certain self-defeating and self-destructive ways? Understanding causes and antecedents helps the worker to understand the origins of this behaviour, but the worker also needs to understand the underlying trajectory or what motivates the child. Lev Vygotsky (1997), like Albert Bandura (1997), theorized that all learning is social or experiential. Like many others before him, Vygotsky considered the infant a blank slate or tabula rasa on which learning happens through the experiences of life. The infant associates cause with effect by pulling a string attached to a mobile, kicking a blanket, cooing at caregivers, or mouthing a toy. When this movement produces a reaction, the infant begins to feel a sense of personal power with movement and continues to explore. When the environment reinforces this sense of power through repeated experiences, the infant feels empowered to continue learning or acting on the environment. To paraphrase Vygotsky's theory, behaviour is motivated by interactions with the environment. When a behaviour is rewarded, the child repeats the behaviour. When a behaviour is punished, mocked, or ridiculed, the child changes the behaviour. Rewards and punishment can motivate behaviour.

However, some behaviour is neither rewarded nor punished; this behaviour tends to be ignored. Behaviour motivated by the need to communicate feelings tends to be ignored, minimized, misinterpreted, or dismissed. A child may be trying to communicate love; the caregiver seeing and listening to the behaviour may see and hear only roughhousing and try to ignore it. Others watching the behaviour see a variety of emotions, such as anger, loneliness, or grief. A parent imposing a curfew or insisting that the child finish the homework may be trying to communicate love, but the child may ignore the parent's behaviour, hearing the restrictions only as the parent's lack of faith, disapproval, anger, and mistrust.

Children sometimes try to communicate their need for homeostasis by destabilizing the family. They engage in risky or negative behaviour designed to capture the parents' attention and pull the family together. Rivka Yahav and Shlomo A. Sharlin (2000) describe a boy who routinely breaks the rules at school the morning after his parents argue with each other. The boy describes his behaviour as a way to get his parents together at the principal's office, to get them talking to each other again. Yahav and Sharlin also describe a young girl brought for help because of her frequent headaches. The young girl describes how her headaches help to draw her parents together to focus on something besides their very fragile relationship.

A girl may start to use alcohol as a way to feel closer to family members, to gain acceptance among her peers, or to gain status in the family. As a young child, she may have started emptying the beer bottles left lying around in her parents' home. The beer in the fridge, the logos on the wall, the bottle marks on the furniture—all of these are environmental indicators of family culture. Her drinking may be a point of pride, a talent, that she can drink more than any of her friends, or that she can "hold her liquor." She may be drinking because everyone she knows does that. On the other hand, she may drink to escape the anger and misery in the home, or as a way of avoiding criticism and failure in social interactions.

She may be described by her worker as being "in denial" about the drinking. This denial itself may be a positive behaviour, a way of expressing her acknowledgement that her behaviour is harmful, but is the only option she knows for coping in a harmful world. Or she may be terrified that she already cannot stop and has no idea how to get off the track. Seen this way, denial is a protective factor—the drinking itself a sort of skill that the girl has developed. She may not conceive of it in terms of failure or of risk. In the short term (and she still is young), the behaviour has provided an answer to particular stresses she has experienced. This is not to validate alcoholism or to say that drinking is developmentally appropriate or to rationalize the girl's behaviour of drinking alcohol. But her behaviour also needs to be understood in terms of *her* meaning of drinking and her motivation. Her behaviour is a form of communication to be taken into account.

Behaviour may also be motivated by a need to gain some power in the disempowered world of childhood. Children want to feel some power over their lives. When they feel powerless in everyday life because of their social location, they look for opportunities to show their ability and competence and to prove their power. With those first words, "Me do," the toddler tests the limits of personal power and competence, pushes and pulls, toddles, then runs and explores. Erik Erikson (2000) describes this as industry versus inferiority; Abraham Maslow (1943) describes it as the need for self-esteem and achievement. Disempowerment begins at the same time as those first words are spoken and continues through a series of humiliations and put-downs, time-outs, curfews, and restraints on a child's independence and learning. The child learns that only children are hit, ignored, and humiliated; adults do not easily put up with this cruelty. Children in homes in which adults do put up with being hit, ignored, and humiliated learn that this behaviour is part of daily life and that adults cannot protect them or even protect themselves.

When they are in a powerless position, children react in various ways. Some consider their category to be unchangeable and deserved. They learn to hide their own emotions and to put on other emotions that please the adults who are in control; in other words, they learn to meet the emotional needs of adults. Others socially withdraw and adopt self-destructive behaviours that confirm their categorization of vulnerable and inferior. They try to break themselves, venting their emotional pain on their own bodies over which they do have a degree of power. Such neural stimulation, however negative, can become addictive, each hurt reinforcing the last one.

Other children and youth may become aggressive towards adults, protesting, "Stop treating me like a child!" They may externalize their frustration by finding someone smaller to bully or an object to steal or to break. They may hurt another child. They may tear down an old shed that does not belong to them. They may engage in drug use, bullying, sexual promiscuity, and stealing—behaviours that satisfy a need for power and acceptance. Most of these activities also involve physical changes in the neurology (stimulation of the amygdala) that become quickly attached to the impulses of the brain stem. In other words, these behaviours become addictive. Michael Ungar (2006: 7) notes, "Bullying and other problem behaviours as diverse as drug use, sexual promiscuity, and truancy all are attractive to adolescents because they satisfy the youth's need for power, recreation, acceptance, or a sense of meaningful participation in his or her community." This meaningful participation may be non-participation or escape into a community of friends in which the child has place and power.

Prepubescent girls or tweens, for example, are routinely disempowered by gender constructions of bodily beauty. No matter how hard they try, the impossible beauty of the models

© Loretta Hostettler/iStockphoto

Photo 10.2 Motherhood is a powerful place to be when you are young and marginalized.

eludes them. Add to that a school system in which girls begin to slide academically, and consumer messages in which clothing and makeup trump personality and intelligence, and many prepubescent girls begin to feel very powerless. The girl is neither a little girl nor a woman; she is somewhere in between and feeling insecure and lonely. However, sexual pleasure may feel like love and may bring both pleasure and prestige. Motherhood may seem like adulthood, and the power to have a baby is a power that brings attention and status. So a tween may engage in risk-taking behaviours that promise her that sense of power (motherhood) in her life when she becomes a young mother.

In Michael Ungar's Negotiating Resilience Research project (2008), the researchers on the team interview children who have engaged in various kinds of risky behaviour. These children include:

- boys in a Palestinian refugee camp who pledge to protect their camp;
- seven-year-olds in Pakistan working in light bulb factories;
- prepubescent girls in Turkey hooking silk rugs all day and every day;
- First Nations children who live on the land rather than attend school;
- child soldiers in Sierra Leone.

Their behaviours are described by the children themselves as rational and responsible ways to contribute to family and community, rather than being a burden. Each child assumes personal responsibility for getting basic needs met both for self and for family. In reflecting on this project and his other work with youth, Ungar (2007: 131) asks, "After all, what do we have to offer these children that they don't already have on their own terms? Power? Control? A sense of belonging? A meaningful role in their communities?" This question speaks to the understanding of behaviour as power. Only when children feel empowered in their lives can they take charge of themselves and choose to modify their behaviour.

The children in Ungar's research project may choose to modify their behaviour when they are offered empowering structural options such as culturally appropriate education, health care, and stability. Structural options such as a school for which already struggling parents have to pay is not empowering, nor is a curriculum that is imposed rather than culturally appropriate. Empowering structural options might include school in which the child is paid to attend, a political peace movement to which children can make a real contribution, or a curriculum that offers skill acquisition appropriate to the local environment. These structural options could release children from the stifling oppression of hard labour and combat, oppression that offers moments of power in exchange for childhoods of misery.

Punishment and Restraints

Mary Vandergoot (2006: 150) suggests that "the assumption that young people don't understand the difference between right and wrong and must be taught is behind many punitive reactions to a child's delinquency." These punitive reactions begin with hitting and spanking and continue through to incarceration. While the number of incarcerated youth is declining, the hitting of children remains legal in Canada.

Section 43 of the Criminal Code of Canada allows parents and other adults in a position of authority to physically discipline children between the ages of 2 and 12 in order to "teach" or "correct" them: "Every schoolteacher, parent or person standing in the place of a parent is justified in using force by way of correction toward a pupil or child, as the case may be, who is under his care, if the force does not exceed what is reasonable under the circumstances" (Criminal Code of Canada, Section 43). This physical discipline or correction is constrained by age limits (2 to 12) and rejoinders such as "reasonable" and "by way of correction." Instruments such as wood planks and belts are not allowed, nor is slapping the child's face. Discipline must be reasonably applied to restrain, control, or express disapproval of certain behaviours. It cannot be applied randomly (for no reason) and cannot be excessive. This section exempts adults from prosecution provided their attempts to discipline their children follow these guidelines. This defence of reasonable correction has been in the Criminal Code of Canada since 1892 and provides a solid social and legal basis for this section.

However, language is as variable and ever-changing as the people who use it. While the majority of discipline probably does not result in physical injury of the child, there is a clear connection between spanking and physical abuse. In other words, "reasonable force" has a wide variety of meanings. Andreas Jud and Nico Trocmé (2013: 3) found that 75 per cent of substantiated (proven) physical abuse incidents in Canada are described by parents as "discipline." Their research concurs with earlier findings from the Canadian Coalition for the Rights of Children (2011: 11). The more often a parent spanks, the more severe the spanking tends to be. When parents injure their children, these parents are not charged with assault or arrested; they may be given family support instead. Sometimes their children are brought into foster care until the parents learn to be more reasonable in their use of punitive discipline. The Canadian Coalition for the Rights of Children (2011: 14) concludes, "The current status of the law in Canada is such that children are less protected from physical violence than are adults."

The Public Health Agency of Canada warns on its website, "Never spank! It simply doesn't work—for the child or the parent." This warning is based on statistics from the National Longitudinal Survey of Children and Youth (NLSCY) that indicate that parents who spank are more likely to have children with low self-esteem and emotional damage. Such children tend to be aggressive, particularly against children smaller than themselves, and they exhibit anti-social behaviour such as gang fighting, hitting parents and teachers, and sexual assault. These are the bullies who have been bullied. They have learned to retaliate; when their friends do not give up their games or phones, they hit their friends to make them co-operate. Their emotional damage is long-term, and there are clear connections between having been spanked as a child and anxiety disorder, spousal abuse, and substance abuse in later life (Gershoff, 2013). Judge Bitensky (2006: 301) comments, "Section 43 impairs the equal right of children, already a vulnerable group, to bodily integrity and security . . . There is no feature of section 43 that redeems the devastation it wreaks."

My experience with the students I teach demonstrates that children who were regularly spanked become adults with high emotional needs. This conviction is based on students' reactions to the debate around Section 43. Students who were spanked occasionally (two or three times a year) usually comprise 30 per cent of the group. These students tend to remember the behaviours for which they were spanked, and tend to be ambivalent about the effects of the spanking on their behaviour; sometimes it helped, and sometimes not. Then there are the 10 per cent who admit to being spanked regularly. This group tends to defend spanking vociferously, citing its beneficial effects on their behaviour and morality. After much class discussion and reading, this 10 per cent typically waver and some even change their position and become highly emotional and reactive, often disclosing horrendous histories of their own childhood abuse. The following is an excerpt from a letter sent to me several years ago from a student who was regularly spanked as a child:

> Last night's class actually brought up quite a few emotions for me and I left feeling sad and quite victimized. I guess I never realized how much I have been abused in my life. As you know I have a disability and this is severe anxiety problems. The class sheds some light for me on my childhood years. I was "accidentally" slapped hard at two years old that sent me flying down a stair-

Note from the Field 10.2

Spanking Advice

A single dad with two preschoolers came to ask me about their tantrums. He described his children as "way out of control." When I asked him what he did when they screamed and had tantrums he admitted to spanking them. He said he didn't really want to, but his friends had told him that spanking would stop the tantrums. Spanking hadn't stopped the tantrums, though. In fact, his children's behaviour had only become worse. I asked him if his friends were also parents. He said they weren't. I asked him if he valued their advice, and we talked about his relationship with them, most of which centred on playing darts. We also talked about following advice and when that helps. Then he talked about what he really valued, which was his one night out a week with his friends. He asked about the tantrums and what they meant, and together we worked on understanding the behaviours of his two young children. We made a map of times and places, and he began to see a pattern develop. He saw the triggers (antecedents) and together we developed a plan to change these triggers and restore the love and fun of his family without the fear of spanking.

case. I broke my right leg femur in half and it was protruding through the skin. I do not remember this incident at all, but remember being in hospital for what seemed a long time.

This boy was returned home after the "accident," only to be spanked again and again and again. This contributed to his addiction problems in adolescence and a subsequently troubled adult life. As Alice Miller (2005) and Joyce Dugard (2011) remind us, recovery from childhood assault is long and hard, and not always successful.

Spanking has an immediate effect. The violence of spanking captures children's attention as they tense with fear, anger, and sadness when they are spanked (Gershoff, 2013: 135). Spanking can bring about short-term behavioural change. Restraints and social isolation, such as a "time-out" sitting on a chair or 20 minutes alone in the bedroom, have a similar impact. Restraints are a means of holding or containing the child, and social isolation holds the child in a place away from other persons. Through restraints and/or social isolation, the child stops the behaviour, at least for a short period of time.

Restraints can keep a child safe. A parent restrains a child who is about to run in front of a speeding car. A teacher restrains a student who is about to turn on a propane burner without taking safety precautions. When behaviour escalates and the child is at risk of hurting self or others, restraints contain the child and keep the child safe. The child's arms may be restrained so that the child cannot hit another child. The child's whole body may be restrained so that the child cannot hurl herself off a ledge and into danger.

Caregivers of children in state care, educational assistants in classrooms, and workers in residential settings are taught physical restraint methods such as Therapeutic Crisis Intervention and Non-Violent Crisis Intervention so that they can safely administer restraints when children or youth are at risk of hurting themselves or others. Safe arm and leg restraints; correct methods of pulling out of a bite, hair pull, or choke hold; de-escalation techniques to prevent the spiral of behavioural aggression; and **life space interviews** to debrief and learn from the behavioural crisis: these techniques and understandings are taught in certified restraint programs. This training is both reactive and proactive: it prepares workers to react to behavioural outbursts and to proactively de-escalate behaviours. Workers who are trained and certified in these methods rarely use physical restraint holds because their training provides them with an array of de-escalation techniques.

Untrained workers, on the other hand, use physical restraints on children more often, sometimes causing injuries and even deaths. Physical restraint can be deadly when the person performing the restraint is untrained and unaware of other less physically intrusive de-escalation techniques. Lists of fatalities are incomplete, although some children's advocacy websites do try to keep the national numbers that government cannot or will not record.[1] Nine-year-old Gabriel Poirier's teachers at Hautes-Rivières School in Saint-Jérôme-sur-Richelieu restrained him in a blanket until he died.

Sixteen-year-old Kyle Young's guards handcuffed him to an elevator door and shackled his legs. When the elevator opened he fell to his death at the Edmonton Courthouse. Then there are the children who are tasered by officers while they are held in restraints. The RCMP alone used these electronic control devices or conductive energy weapons (tasers) on children aged 16 and younger 90 times from 2004 to 2010, sometimes for behaviours as innocuous as peeling paint off the wall (Canadian Coalition for the Rights of Children, 2011: 8).

Children and youth are also chemically restrained with psychotropic medications that range in type from over-the-counter tranquillizing medication to prescription drugs such as anti-depressants, stimulants, antipsychotics (neuroleptic medications), benzodiazepines, and other anxiolytics. **Chemical restraints** offer a quick fix for behavioural outbursts and non-compliance. They are increasingly popular because of their immediate, short-term effect on behaviour. As more children are medicated, more diagnoses of behavioural disorders are made. Merrill Singer (2008: 163) remarks, "Overprescription of drugs by physicians . . . has been traced to advertising efforts of the pharmaceuticals. Increasingly the advertising campaigns of the pharmaceutical industry are targeted via the mass media directly to consumers, creating a demand for pharmaceutical psychotropics and other drugs by the parents and teachers who are looking for chemical controls of these children."

This cause-and-effect cycle of chemical restraint merits further discussion. Do the disorders and illness create the medication, or vice versa? The answer is elusive because the history, testing, and marketing of pharmaceuticals are hard to trace globally. However, there is no doubt as to the high financial stakes in their marketing. Two examples—Prozac and Ritalin—suffice.

Prozac (Fluoxetine) is one of many selective serotonin reuptake inhibitors (SSRI) that affect the levels of serotonin present in the brain. Serotonin is a neurotransmitter; it facilitates the conveyance of electrical connections between neurons. Lawrence Diller (2006: 9) explains, "Clinical depression before Prozac's release was a rather infrequent psychiatric diagnosis in America . . . . By the mid-1990s, depression had replaced anxiety as the most frequently diagnosed adult disorder." In 2004, as more and more children, some as young as two years of age, were being prescribed Prozac, clinical-trial results suggested that Prozac increased the risk of children and adolescents having suicidal thoughts (Diller, 2006). Homicidal thoughts were also a side effect, as emerged in a 2011 trial of a Manitoba youth who killed his friend while on Prozac. Called the "Prozac defence," the judge ruled that this SSRI was a major contributor to the murder (Blackwell, 2011).

Another popular drug for children is Ritalin (methylphenidate). Ritalin was released in 1993 for the treatment of dyslexia but it soon became routinely prescribed for attention-deficit hyperactivity disorder (ADHD) too. In the first five years of its release (1993–8) the use of Ritalin by Canadian children increased by 300 per cent (Eberstadt, 1999: 39). The province of Quebec introduced mandatory drug insurance in 1997, and a decade later 44 per cent of Canada's ADHD prescriptions were being written in Quebec (Currie, Stabile, and Jones, 2013). This does not suggest that half of all Canadian children with ADHD live in Quebec. It does suggest that free access to Ritalin has a direct correlation to the chemical restraint of children. Similar in molecular structure to amphetamines, Ritalin can alter a child's mood, slow down the heart rate, and make the child feel more relaxed, pliable, and able to focus—although with reduced mental acuity. Its short-term side effects include drowsiness, lethargy, slurred speech, irritability, psychosis, nervousness, mood changes, high blood pressure, heart palpitations, and diarrhea. The long-term effects are unknown because of the age of the drug, but ample warnings were given by pharmapsychologists such as Richard DeGrandpre in *Ritalin Nation* (1999). The recent shift in neurological thinking regarding the plasticity of the brain (Doidge, 2007) leaves no doubt that the ingestion of this chemical has far-reaching effects on the brain of a child, a brain which in any case is vulnerable because it is still growing and developing. Although Ritalin may cause permanent neurological damage (Tallman, 2010; Sherlock, 2010), it is now so commonly prescribed that it is often referred to as "Vitamin R," which implies that it is a necessary nutrient for all children.

Chemical restraints for children are popular among parents, workers, and teachers who pressure doctors to continue prescribing them, sometimes without even meeting or assessing the child.[2] Chemical restraints are positioned as being necessary, and their use in Canada continues to increase. Very young children are prescribed drugs such as Prozac and Ritalin with alarming, and sometimes fatal, results (Diller, 2006; Lambe, 2006). Between 1997 and 2007, the use of antipsychotic medication by BC children increased tenfold (Beihl, 2011). In a 2009 research study, Yolanda Lambe (2009) revealed that 70 per cent of Canadian youth in foster care had been prescribed psychotropic medication during their time in foster care. This use of chemical restraints may reflect our trust in the biomedical model and our cultural dispositions towards emotional self-control and the painless life. Pushing legal drugs for children is certainly a much bigger business in Canada than pushing illegal drugs.

Although there is little scientific evidence that popular psychotropic

© Itani/Alamy

Photo 10.3 Incarceration may be a lesson, but what is being taught?

medications have a positive long-term effect on the conditions for which they are prescribed, their negative side effects are well-known and include suicidal thinking, disinhibition, agitation, aggression, and depression (Beihl, 2011). Many of these medicated children develop drug dependencies and experience side effects that last much longer than any behavioural change induced by the drugs.

When spanking, physical restraints, and chemical restraints do not work and the child's behaviour leads to illegal activity, the child may become involved with the criminal justice system and face **incarceration**. In Canada, children aged 12 to 17 who are involved with the criminal justice system are re-categorized as young offenders under the Youth Criminal Justice Act (YCJA). This act prioritizes non-punitive correction. Section 42(2) of the Youth Criminal Justice Act outlines non-custodial sentences that range from a reprimand to intensive support and, finally, to deferred custody and supervision. The focus of this intensive support is accountability and healing—"just sanctions that have meaningful consequences for the young person and that promote his or her rehabilitation and reintegration into society" (YCJA, Section 38.1). The Community Restorative Justice Program is one example of this second level. The young offender is required to acknowledge and describe the offence, using the principles of **behavioural contracting**. This second level of support costs one-tenth that of incarceration (Moore, 2007) and has a much lower rate of recidivism.

Those who are incarcerated tend to be marginalized youth, either Aboriginal (one-quarter to one-third of those incarcerated) or former wards of the state (half of those incarcerated) (Munch, 2012).[3] Once their term of incarceration is over, a majority of these young offenders return to custody (Vandergoot, 2006: 175). Recidivism increases with custody, perhaps because of the social learning that happens in youth detention centres. "In fact, more than 80 per cent of youth who are incarcerated will be arrested again within three years of release" (Solomon, 2012: 538).

Motivation to Change

Spanking, physical and chemical restraints, and incarceration can bring about short-term behavioural change. All of these punitive measures focus on the characteristics of the child. A threatened, restrained, or drugged child can be made to be quiet, sit still, and pay attention. A bully can be made to apologize, refrain from a specific action, stay out of the schoolyard, and do chores in the classroom. A young thief can be sent to a residential facility. A young drug dealer can be isolated in a detention centre.

However, long-term behavioural change involves structural change. Rather than locating the cause in the characteristics of the child, and then managing and controlling that child, structural interventions locate the cause in structural determinants that influence the risk behaviour. Structural interventions locate both cause and solution, adapting the structure so that it can support the child as a responsible person with strengths and abilities. The structure provides guidance, modelling, and affirmation for the child during this time of behavioural change and requires the child to take responsibility for change.

Jane Gilgun (2002) describes structural support available in the context of First Nations traditions as a Medicine Wheel in which the major responsibility for the child's change belongs to the adults in the community. She writes, "Questions about what are adults doing or not doing to promote belonging, mastery, independence, and generosity are as important as asking how young people are responding and what blocks their responses to positive interventions" (2002: 69). Gilgun asserts that the responsibility for initial behavioural change belongs with the community and the structure around the child. The adults in the community remind the child of past successes, skills, attributes, and abilities. They believe in the child as a person and a responsible member of the community, and the child or youth who feels their support may begin to consider change. Workers who understand the change process can tune into this pre-contemplative stage (Prochaska and Norcross, 2007) and provide time, space, and support for the child to consider the advantages and disadvantages of change.

Group Exercise   10.1

Match and Mirror

This pairing exercise is an extension of the importance of listening (see Chapter 7); in this exercise, the focus is behaviour. A talker decides in the first minute whether or not to engage with a listener. This unconscious decision is rooted deeply in the nervous system and is triggered by the listener's attentiveness. If the worker's listening response matches and mirrors the talker, the talker automatically engages.

This exercise begins with group members forming pairs. One person in each pair leaves the room while the other person prepares a three-minute story of complaint. The leader then coaches the group outside the room. They are told to listen to their partners' stories without interrupting. In the first minute, they are to match and mirror their partners' body language, breathing, and facial expression. In the next minute, they mismatch their responses, and, in the last minute, they return to matching. The leader cues each change with music, playing soft music for the first minute, slightly louder music for the second, then softer music again for the last minute.

The pairs reunite in the room and, at a signal from the leader, the talker begins to tell a story while the listener attends to the story without interrupting. At the end of the three minutes, the leader stops the exercise and then asks the talkers when they felt less heard. This exercise prompts discussion of the importance of building rapport and trust through matching and mirroring (the empathic response). The leader then asks what this matching reflects and how body language can prompt a response.

Homeostasis is familiar and comforting, and change can be frightening and stressful. Behaviours such as whining, for example, may have been practised for two years, half of a preschooler's lifetime. Imagine learning a behaviour for half of your life and then being asked to change! That change, or unlearning process, requires structural support and takes considerable time, certainly not the few moments that caregivers often demand when they ask a preschooler to "stop whining."

What is the structural determinant that impacts whining? Caregivers who confront the structural determinant of childism and recognize its impact on their caregiving can begin to change their own behaviour and their attitude to the child within the home. Instead of supporting whining, for example, they can support respectful dialogue through listening to the child's request and affirming it. They can respond. This does not mean acceding to every request from the child. It does mean treating the child as a person rather than a nuisance or a helpless, incoherent being.

When the child or youth asks questions about a suggested program or service, this question suggests a readiness to contemplate change. There may be a readiness to engage with a tutor, psychologist, or a new foster home. This behavioural change may mean modifying the behaviour, even eliminating it, but this change impacts every member of the family or resident at the group home. When the behaviour changes, each person responds to the behavioural change. This change process can be difficult for everyone. Sometimes other residents of the home sabotage change, covertly or inadvertently pulling the child or youth back to the familiar old ways, the old roles, even when these old ways and roles are a source of pain and trouble. This is compounded when there is more than one behavioural change happening, or when more than one resident of the home is directly involved in the change process. The unfamiliar behaviour has to be tried out many times in order to fit into the changed home life. Adaptations have to be made by every person in the group home and each person needs encouragement and support to change.

The boy who smokes marijuana every night as a means of coping with problems and falling asleep can modify his behaviour and use half the amount of marijuana when there are structural supports for this change, such as a positive education system, less violence in the neighbourhood, and employment. The boy's reduced intake can be further reduced when he has access to more interesting social alternatives that do not involve the drug. The boy who smokes marijuana may decide to experiment with a different method of winding down (music, yoga, a video) every second night, and then compare the two methods of relaxation. Similarly, the girl who self-harms as a consequence of sexual abuse may decide to write a letter to her abuser, join an advocacy group for youth who have been sexually abused, or lay criminal charges against the abuser. These are healthier, strengths-based and structural ways of making behavioural changes of using less marijuana or of coping with memories of abuse.

Ungar (2007: 121) cautions, "Parents need to seek ways to offer children alternatives to dangerous, delinquent, deviant, and disordered behaviour. Alternatives must, however, offer the same quality of experience that the child achieved through his or her problem behaviour." Attending a social skills group or going to counselling are not substitutes for activities that are risky, exciting, and powerful. Interventions need to be just in time or at the pre-contemplative stage, empathic, and, if possible, communal, especially with youth who have strong peer bonds.

Managing a Behavioural Crisis

A behavioural crisis often seems to erupt from nowhere. The worker misses the preceding events or antecedents, such as bullying, taunts, and sarcasm from other youth in the home. The foster parent misses the classroom incident that the child has thought about for the three hours prior to returning home. The counsellor misses the bus ride in which the youth received terrible news on his phone.

Suddenly, the compliant child is thrashing on the floor and screaming. The youth returns to the home, slams the door, and yells, "I'm done!" The 10-year-old grabs a knife and lashes out at the residential care worker. In all three cases, the worker is meeting this behaviour at its peak. There is no time to analyze structural determinants, motivations, causes within the microsystem and mesosystem, or triggers (antecedents). The worker must respond to ensure the safety of the child and everyone else in the immediate vicinity.

An untrained worker may react, putting the child or youth in even more danger. A worker may lock the thrashing child in her room as a form of punishment. A foster parent may yell back at the youth, "Don't slam the door." A residential care worker may lunge forward and try to grab the knife. In all three cases, the worker's reaction escalates the crisis further and increases the danger to all.

A trained worker responds in a very different way. A trained worker immediately assesses the safety of the situation, focusing on the body language of the young person and simultaneously scanning the room for dangerous objects, presence of onlookers, and exit doors. The worker makes direct eye contact with the young person and stands very still. The worker may then try to reduce the elements of danger by slowly removing the onlookers (other children), dimming the music and light, or simply sitting down on the floor beside the thrashing child. The worker may be silent or speak gently to the child in a soothing voice. The foster parent may affirm the youth's frustration, ignore the slammed door, and engage as an attentive listener: "I'm done too. Let's take a break!" The residential care worker may remove onlookers, speak quietly, and sit on the floor until the child calms. In all three cases, the worker who knows the child or youth best decides how to respond in a way to reduce danger and ensure safety in the moment.

Sometimes the worker needs to make a directive statement clearly communicating that the violence must stop. Sometimes protective interventions are needed and the worker assumes the protective stance, keeping well back from the child or youth and turning slightly so as to reduce the possibility of direct contact. And sometimes it is also necessary to leave the situation and get assistance. The last response is a physical restraint, and only trained and certified workers may apply a physical restraint. Physical restraint controls the acute behaviour of the young person as safely as possible and with the best interests of the young person in mind.

In every situation, the worker responds in an empathic, congruent, and respectful way. The child or youth needs to be reassured that the worker is a safe person who will not react emotionally or violently and that this is a safe place in which no one gets hurt. During this de-escalation stage of the behavioural crisis, the child or youth slowly returns to baseline. The young person needs to regain composure and begin to breathe regularly. This is accomplished through co-regulation as the worker gently holds the child's hand or sits quietly beside the child, giving the child the time and space to recover from the crisis, decompress, and breathe normally again.

The child or youth leads and the worker follows, a pattern that helps to set a pace that does not push back into the triggers or antecedents too quickly. In the following five-minute dialogue, there are periods of silence or rest that are indicated by "pause." These periods may feel awkward and difficult at first, but they provide the time for both the worker (W) and Leah (L) to think through the preceding behavioural crisis in which Leah trashed the common room. The worker is trying to understand what triggers Leah's behaviour. Leah is the teacher, telling the worker bits of her story. The worker calmly keeps Leah on task, steadying her so that she does not spiral back into either aggressive behaviour or avoidance.

W: Does it feel better now?

L : Yeah. (pause) Kind of. (pause) I don't know. (pause) I just don't know how I feel.

W: About?

L : This. (pause) All of this.

W: You mean this room?

L : No. Just being here. Again. (pause) I can't believe I'm in this place again. (pause) It makes me want to scream.

W: And tonight? What made you want to scream?

L : That stupid comment from Reba. So stupid. (pause) She's such a bitch. I hate her.

W: Reba?

L : No, not her. (pause) I just hate her, everything, me, her, the whole thing.

W: And when she said?

L : When she said, "Not you again," I thought, "Yeah, me, here again. Kicked out again. In this place again."

W: And?

L : And I wanted to kill her.

W: Oh?

L : Yeah. (pause) Sort of. I guess I just felt angry. Really mad.

W: So you were feeling really mad, right?

L : Mad at myself kind of. Stupid, eh? (pause) I'm just so stupid.

W: Well, you're teaching me, Leah, so that makes you pretty smart. Help me get this right. You were feeling really mad at Reba and really mad at yourself for being in this group home again, right? And you hate Reba for reminding you or teasing you about that?

L : Well, yeah. (pause) But I guess I don't really hate her. I guess I'm just mad that I'm stuck here again because.

W: Because?

L : (pause) Because I ran away last time. That's why.

W: So you're trying to figure out a way to not run away again so you won't have to move again to another group home. That sounds pretty smart to me.

L : Yeah?

W: Yeah. Sounds like you have a plan in mind.

As upsetting as the crisis can be for the worker, it is also upsetting and scary for the young person who feels out of control and unable to say or do things in a regular way. Emotions take over, and that can feel very frightening. When emotions are highly charged, an event can assume distorted shape. The child or youth needs time to feel safe again, safe enough to reconnect with the worker and reflect on the behavioural crisis in a life space interview. This interview acknowledges and affirms what has just happened, and it is a chance to review the crisis and learn from it. The life space interview also points the way to managing feelings and the behaviours that they prompt.

The first step is to find a calm and quiet place without the distractions of noise, music, or interruptions. This place can be a quiet room inside or a quiet spot outside where nature helps with the healing. The worker begins by asking the child or youth to clarify the event or recall what happened. This affirms who is in control. Because the child or youth now feels some measure of power and control, the child or youth may begin with triggers, albeit in an accusatory tone: "You took my iPod." This accusation is empowering and allows the child to assert control of the situation. The worker is at fault, not the child. The child can identify triggers and take the lead, while the worker stumbles afterwards, making mistakes along the way, taking iPods, guessing incorrectly, and generally doing all the wrong things. Rather than reacting, the worker can respond in a calm and reassuring tone, "Yes, I did."

The child's slow self-regulation and assertion of control stabilizes the situation, restoring some semblance of homeostasis. The child now feels less shaky and unsure and is ready to begin the work of ordering events and clarifying what exactly happened during the crisis. Active listening is an important part of this step so that the young person feels understood and heard. The worker supports the child or youth in reviewing the event in a methodical way until they both agree on what happened. Once this version is clarified the worker echoes back the information to ensure that it is accurate and provides a summary that pinpoints antecedents or triggers. The child may identify a certain person first and then focus on what that person did. This action can be identified as a trigger. Sharing perceptions can also help to strengthen the worker–child relationship as the child identifies alternative ways of acting or coping with triggers.

The next step is making the connection between feelings and behaviours, trying to understand when and how feelings can prompt or trigger behaviours. Anger can prompt aggression, for example. The next step is a search for alternative ways to respond to feelings. Anger prompts aggression, as well as leaving the room, verbalizing the anger, or going out for a walk. These are alternative actions that the young person may want to consider the next time the feeling (anger) arises. It is important for the child or youth to identify some of these alternative actions, choosing those that feel appropriate. These alternative actions can be thought through and acted out in role play. The worker may play the bully, with the child or youth responding in a different way rather than fighting. This planning and practice of behavioural change helps to prepare the young person to deal with upsetting events and aggravations in the future with new ways of behaving that are constructive and positive. The goal of this crucial part of the life space interview is for the young person to feel more confident when confronted with the same situation.

Leah and the worker go for a walk outside and away from the trashed common room. This distance and the ambience of the outdoors add perspective to their recollection of the incident. They reconstruct what happened and put the events in sequence. Leah identifies taunts and shaming as her triggers and connects these to the shaming and taunts of her childhood. The worker expresses confidence in Leah's capabilities and her focus on solutions. Leah suggests positive responses to taunting: leaving the room, affirming the taunt, or turning the taunt into a positive. Each of these responses is acted out so that Leah feels more comfortable with them. Leah and the worker slide into a humorous story, and then they are ready to re-enter the home and begin cleaning up the common room together.

Summary

This chapter presented the child's perspective on behaviour as a way to learn, to communicate, and to feel power. Risky behaviours were seen to be growth experiences rather than simply "bad behaviour." Seen in this way, the child's behaviour takes on a new meaning as we better understand what role the behaviour plays in the child's life and the life of the child's family, too. Traditional interventions such as spanking, physical and chemical restraints, and incarceration have only short-term effects; sometimes they actually exacerbate the negative effects of the behaviour and have very damaging long-term effects on the child. Such interventions rarely prompt the child to make positive and substantive behavioural changes. When the child is the manager of behavioural change, deciding when and where to make these changes, the effects last longer. But what happens when a child is at immediate risk and there is no time to wait for the child to want to change? In these high-risk situations, the worker brings a different understanding to the intervention. The next chapter challenges you to go beyond risk assessment and to find a new meaning for the risky behaviours and the risky situations in which children sometimes live.

Review Questions

1. Describe how the social construction of behaviour is both cultural and co-relational.
2. State one behaviour that can be seen as both negative and positive, and explain how social location affects this evaluation of behaviour.
3. What is the difference between an antecedent and a structural determinant? Give one example that illustrates this difference.
4. What was Vygotsky's behavioural theory? Do you agree with his theory? Why or why not?
5. How is cause and effect learned differently by an infant, toddler, and an older child?
6. When toddlers scream, what might they be communicating? When adults do not respond to the scream, how might toddlers perceive this?
7. What does Section 43 of the Criminal Code of Canada allow? What is the rationale for this law?
8. Why has the use of medication by children in Canada increased? Can this increase be described as both positive and negative? Explain.
9. What effect does incarceration have on the behaviour of children?
10. Why is the life space interview such an essential part of managing a behavioural crisis?

Discussion Questions

1. Suggest a child's behaviour that can be seen only as a negative behaviour. What makes this behaviour negative?
2. Reflect on your learning during childhood. Which behaviours helped you to learn? Were there any behaviours that prevented your learning? How might the adults around you have helped?
3. A child's behavioural change can happen quickly or slowly and can be controlled by the adult or the child. Explain this statement, giving examples of behavioural changes you have made in your life and how these changes have happened.

11 High-Risk Interventions

"Would you tell me, please, which way I ought to go from here?"
"That depends a good deal on where you want to get to," said the Cat.
"I don't much care where—" said Alice.
"Then it doesn't matter which way you go," said the Cat.
"—so long as I get somewhere," Alice added as an explanation.
"Oh, you're sure to do that," said the Cat, "if you only walk long enough."

—Lewis Carroll, *Alice's Adventures in Wonderland*

Reports are not written and interventions are not attempted with children and families who are content. It is discontent that brings in the worker. A behavioural crisis erupts and the worker is called. The worker meets the child and the family when the crisis is peaking. The worker has known neither the child nor the family beforehand, so has no baseline for understanding the situation. The meaning of the crisis is different for the worker and for each member of the family who is affected by it. The parents may engage in self-blame or blame their partners. They may try to avoid the crisis by staying away from the family or by using drugs and alcohol to dull the pain of the behavioural crisis. The parents usually want the worker either to stop or to change the child's behaviour. The worker also wants a quick solution and a file closure; in fact, the worker's performance is often measured by the number of these file closures. Neither the adults nor the child are ready for the Cat's suggestion of the long walk to get somewhere.

These are high-risk situations in which children do need the intervention of workers, and workers need to be prepared to take the long walk to protect the child. Infants have urgent basic needs and they cannot leave the home to get the help that they need. Toddlers who try to find help by themselves are sometimes found frozen or dehydrated miles from their bedroom walls. Immediate worker intervention can be crucial in saving a young child's life.

High-risk interventions typically happen quickly with little time to prepare. A home support worker arrives for a scheduled visit with the family in the evening, assesses an immediate risk to the child, and calls for assistance in removing the child from the home. The counsellor at the drop-in centre observes the child at play and recognizes that the child's play indicates abuse. The teacher sees injuries on the child's legs or arms. In each situation, the worker, counsellor, or teacher intervenes because the child has been injured or is at high risk of being injured. Then other workers become involved: police officers, hospital staff, foster care providers, child protection workers, and more.

In situations deemed to be high-risk, child welfare interventions have swung between family support and keeping the child with the family at home, to child support and apprehending whenever risk is detected. Child protection work today has changed to **risk assessment** and has moved to a mid-point between support and policing. This mid-point has been termed differential response, alternative response, or family assessment response. This response, like risk assessment, does not focus on either structural determinants of risk or advocacy for structural change. The response does not account for or explain the resiliency of the child or the family, except as a notation under "protective factors." Because of these gaps, high-risk interventions sometimes are as wayward and unfocused as Alice's wanderings in Wonderland.

Objectives

By the end of this chapter, you will:

- Understand how to evaluate and manage a high-risk situation, considering both risk factors and protective factors.
- Identify how resiliency impacts children who are trafficked and children who self-harm.
- Demonstrate how to handle a disclosure of abuse or neglect.

The Meaning of Risk

Any action can be considered risky. A newborn who roots for milk is taking a risk. The milk may or may not be there, and the newborn risks dehydration in the search. Infants take a risk when they learn to roll, sit, crawl, and then toddle. Learning to walk is risky: there are stairs to negotiate, uneven surfaces to manage, and toys that get in the way. The child learns and develops skills through meeting and overcoming these risks, and the child who has a risk-free life is unlikely to develop a sense of personal competency and independence.

Risk-taking behaviour is cheered on a sports team or in a sports competition, but punished in the schoolyard. Michael Ungar (2005: xxi) cautions, "To categorically say that risk-taking socially deviant behaviours are all bad, or all good, overlooks the variability in children's pathways to health." Baking cookies is risky: the stove may be too hot, the ingredients wrong, or the recipe faulty. Whitewater rafting, hockey, and skiing all are risky sports that have resulted in injury and even death. Ungar (2005) demonstrates the value of taking age-appropriate risks in his resiliency research project in which children and youth overcome the risks of war, discrimination, displacement, and hard labour, and feel both successful and self-reliant. Ungar (2005: xxiv) warns against the risk-free life: "Improving children's well-being is never as simple as removing risk from their lives."

Is it risky to pierce a newborn's ears? Some adults would call this a risky practice, considering the possibility of infection and irritation and considering the pain inflicted on a child who cannot choose or defend her/himself. Is it risky for a child to sell lemonade on the street? Some adults would say that it is an open invitation to stranger danger. Is it risky for young children to travel on aircraft alone? These three questions can be answered reasonably in many different ways, depending on the social setting, the adult's culture, and personal definition of risk.

Adults assess risk according to their personal culture. Celia Haig-Brown and Carl James (2004: 217) remind us that the terminology of risk is imbued with personal bias and personal experience with risk: "When we use the term 'at risk' youth, we mean that a young person is at risk for not being middle-class, not being white, not holding down a job or going to university." Adults who assess behaviour as bad or risky may themselves be averse to risk. A father might intervene, while a community worker advises the father to let the child manage the risky experience alone. On the other hand, the community worker might intervene while family members refuse to do so, feeling the child needs to experience loss or failure and learn from it. Adults intervene to protect or remove children from what they assess to be high-risk situations, such as rock climbing, playing hockey, or skateboarding, or try to minimize the risks by their close supervision. This supervision lessens as children join social groups and take part in activities in school and recreational groups. At that point, adults try to minimize the risks by imposing curfews, setting limits, and curtailing the use of technology, vehicles, and credit cards.

A risk factor is a predictor of an undesired outcome; a risk factor signals that this undesired outcome has higher than average potential for happening. Risk factors for parenting in Canada include low family income, low maternal education, single parenthood, and early (youth) parenthood. Parents struggling with poverty, for example, may minimize the risks of high fat content in foods simply because so many of these foods are cheap and readily available at food banks. Parents with little education themselves may minimize the risks of truancy, just as young parents may minimize the risks around household hazards. Risk factors of poverty, minimal education, or youth do not preclude warm and nurturing parenting; they simply make parenting more challenging and potentially more risky.

Risk factors can be described as **proximal** or **distal** and can be quantified as low, medium, or high. Proximal risk factors are immediate triggers or precipitants, such as a loaded weapon on the kitchen counter or an inebriated parent supervising a very young child. Distal risk factors are potentiating influences, such as isolation, lack of support, or illness. A distal risk factor can change to a proximal one, increasing the volume or degree of risk. A parent's illness, for example, can change from a distal risk factor to a proximal one when the parent suddenly requires hospitalization and there is no one in the family to care for the child and no money to pay for a childcare provider. Suddenly, the child is at high risk and an out-of-home placement may have to be arranged.

Risk factors can be identified at every system level (micro, meso, and macro). The microsystem risks involve only the child and caregiver and include low birth weight, premature birth, low **Apgar score** at birth, physical or cognitive delay, loss of hearing or sight, unhealthy attachment, emotional or behavioural disorders, mental health issues, and difficult temperament. These immediate microsystem risk factors put the child at some potential risk for difficulty.

The mesosystem risk factors involve the child's interaction with the immediate environment of family and community. Mesosystem risk factors include the family's mental health issues, history of abuse and violence, family structure, family communication skills, and personal boundaries. Mesosystem risk factors also include the health and positive attributes of the child's peer group, teachers, and neighbours.

The macrosystem or structural risk factors include those biases that erode the child's self-esteem and deny the child equal access to supports and services; childism, poverty, homophobia, racism, classism, and gender inequality, for example, are

© Somos Images/Alamy

Photo 11.1 A zoom lens and a trained eye would help to identify whether this restraint is a risk or protective factor.

macrosystem or structural risk factors. The level of friction, acrimony, violence, and disorganization in society also are potential risk factors that affect the child's personal wellness and potential. The greatest structural or macrosystem risk factor for any child in Canada, however, is poverty (see Chapter 1).

The identification of risk factors at these three ecological levels (micro, meso, macro), two location levels (proximal, distal), and three severity levels (low, medium, high) is a precursor to risk assessment. These factors can be combined and assessed in almost unlimited configurations in an effort to begin to understand and identify the level of risk for the child. The constellation or grouping of risk factors in a family, for example, is often identified and assessed as a high-risk situation for the child. Because of this identification, a worker can try to manage the risk through supportive interventions, which are often limited, if available at all.

Group Exercise 11.1

Assessing Risk

This risk assessment exercise demonstrates that personal bias and personal experience with risk affect the identification and assessment of risk (Haig-Brown and James, 2004). Group members bring their own bias and experience to this risk assessment, making this a powerful group exercise.

This exercise begins with the large group being divided into five small groups of three to five members. Each small group is then given a card on which five activities are written that correspond to a particular age of a child. (The activities on the card can be modified to include local street names, restaurants, and sports.)

1. Ten-month-old child crawling on a rug at home; being pulled in a baby carrier behind a bicycle; sitting alone on a deerskin ottoman; being cared for by two grandparents who are over 70 years old; being cared for by a lone mother addicted to alcohol.
2. Four-year-old child being pushed in a stroller; using a mobile phone; eating a hamburger and fries in a fast food outlet; living with a lone father addicted to cocaine; playing street hockey.
3. Eight-year-old child skating without a helmet; walking two kilometres to school; selling lemonade on a street corner with a friend; canoeing on the river with a friend; staying overnight with a school friend.
4. Twelve-year-old child babysitting a six-year-old brother after school; snow-mobiling alone; shopping for clothes at a mall with friends; going on a weekend camping trip with an older brother; living with a lone mother (27 years of age) and her new boyfriend.

continued

5. Fifteen-year-old child staying in Pakistan for a month with a family friend; travelling to Las Vegas with a school trip; working on Sundays at a local restaurant; volunteering at a drop-in centre three nights a week; babysitting a newborn on Saturday mornings.

The leader gives one card to each group, asking the group members to put the activities in order from the least risky to the most risky. When all of the small groups have completed this task, each group presents the activities in order from least risky to most risky. The group then accepts and answers questions from the large group. When all of the small groups have presented, the leader asks the participants why this exercise proved to be so difficult and what lessons can be learned from this exercise.

Disclosures of Abuse and Neglect

Children rarely go to an adult with a disclosure of abuse or neglect; in other words, most child abuse and neglect goes unreported and untreated. When a disclosure is made, the words are brief. The child may say simply, "Mommy hurt me" or "My pee-pee is sore." These verbal disclosures are rarely listened to and understood as disclosures of abuse and neglect; in fact, they tend to be ignored. Only one-quarter of these disclosures are listened to, and only 8 per cent of these disclosures result in a criminal investigation (Bottoms, Rudnicki, and Epstein, 2007: 181). When the abuse and neglect continues, children sometimes increase the volume of their verbal disclosures, disclose through their play, or add another layer to their secret and keep it tightly inside them.

Children learn from an early age that it is safer to disclose through their play. They articulate their abuse and neglect through their play and then hope that an empathic adult will watch attentively and respond. If the wrong adult sees their disclosure, they can always deny it by saying, "I was just playing!" These disclosures of abuse and neglect may take many forms. The following are some examples.

- Crystal may show her art teacher a painting—a black square with a red dot. When the teacher asks her about the red dot, she may say that the red dot is blood on her dolly that her daddy put all over her.
- Tyler may run to his daycare provider, crying and saying that Angie keeps putting her tongue into his mouth.
- Mohammed may appear listless and hungry and does not bring a lunch to day camp all week.
- Baby Noah may arrive at his home daycare wearing the same soiled diaper from the previous day and he may have a severe diaper rash.
- Reilly may stay after pottery class to help clean up and then refuse to go home, saying she is afraid.

- Omar may "forget" his winter boots and his snow pants every day even though there has been snow for over a month now.
- Katya may wear an oversized woollen sweater on a hot day. When her teacher suggests she remove her sweater, she may refuse even though she is sweating. Later the teacher notices Katya pushing up her sleeves and the teacher sees untended burn marks on Katya's forearms.
- Kyle may hit the other children whenever he can, even though the teacher responds with time-outs. His aggression increases during the day and he responds angrily to his teacher's attempts to control his behaviour.

Some disclosures happen during regular play in the neighbourhood. A parent at a wading pool notices alarming injuries on a young bather's upper thighs. A shopper in a parking lot sees a young child left unattended in a public place or in a locked car. A grandmother sees the next-door neighbour's school-aged child engaged in dangerous and unsupervised play. In any of these situations, the child may be at risk or not. The injuries on the child's body may be from skipping rope in the playground or the bruises may be a result of medical treatments. The seemingly unattended young child may, in fact, be with a family member the shopper does not recognize. The dangerous play of the school-aged child may be skateboarding, a sport seen as risky by some adults and as healthy by others.

The abuse and neglect of children is upsetting and disturbing, and so tends to be ignored. Adults try to mind their own business and not interfere with other people's children, especially in Canada with its family-based culture. As Jaycee Dugard (2011: x) writes in her memoir, "We live in a world where we rarely speak out and when someone does, nobody is there to listen. . . . I know I am not the only child to be hurt by a crazy adult. I am sure there are still the families that look great on the outside, but if someone were to delve deeper they would discover horrors beyond belief." When a pregnant girl refuses to disclose the father's name to a clinic nurse, that nurse may not provide the empathy the girl needs to feel safe enough to talk about her home situation. The nurse may assume the girl has a boyfriend rather than an incestuous relationship with an abusive brother, uncle, or father.

Even when adults clearly hear a disclosure through play or behaviour, they may fear upsetting the family by calling the authorities. Adults do not want to confront parents or tell children not to play in a dangerous area. When children or youth do use their words to disclose abuse and neglect to adults, these disclosures are often met with reactions of disgust, disbelief, and anger. An angry guardian who hears the pregnant girl's disclosure may say, "That's awful. I'm going to kill your brother!" The shocked teacher may say, "What? That's horrible!" The dismissive camp counsellor may minimize physical abuse and say, "That's nothing! My dad used to spank me, too, and I learned from it." Adult reactions range from willful blindness to disgust, all of which further humiliate, frighten, and silence the child. Jaycee Dugard was sexually abused by her kidnapper for 18 years while neighbours visited, police called, and parole officers inspected the home. When two police officers finally questioned her situation, Jaycee lapsed into fearful silence. She reacted as do many abused children who often retract their disclosures.

However, the law is clear in Canada: adults must report any suspicion of abuse and neglect of a child even when they have promised the child and family that their information is confidential (Bala, Zopf, and Vogl, 2004: 29). Mandatory reporting law affirms the rights of children and the wrongs of abuse and neglect. The only exception to this is solicitor–client privilege, but even then the solicitor (or lawyer) is enjoined to report child abuse on ethical grounds, particularly in cases in which the abuse is likely to continue. Non-verbal and often unintentional disclosures of abuse and neglect could be revealing a very serious situation; when an adult observes or overhears such disclosures, the response needs to be immediate. The adult's responsibility is not to interrogate the child or to ask the child for details but to inform the local child protection agency of any suspicion of abuse or neglect.

The penalties for not reporting suspected child abuse and/or neglect vary across Canada, but they usually include fines or imprisonment or both. Professionals and paraprofessionals, staff and volunteers—all adults in the community who work with children—are obligated to report suspected child abuse and neglect. In addition, professionals such as doctors, teachers, early childhood educators, and social workers may face disciplinary sanctions from their licensing bodies for failing to report suspected child abuse or neglect. If the suspected abuse is not reported and the abuse continues, there could be a civil suit for damages against the professional who fails to report.

 Note from the Field   11.1

Handling Infant Disclosures

Rania welcomes you warmly on your first home visit as her family support worker. She shows you her apartment, brews you wonderful coffee, and serves you delicious baklava. She tells you that her baby is sleeping and she asks you appropriate questions about immunizations, feeding, and what toys to buy. She also tells you how exhausted she is, especially as her husband works long hours driving a taxi. At the end of your visit, you insist on seeing her baby and you notice that the baby appears listless and pale. You ask Rania to show you how she changes her baby's diaper and, when she complies, you notice bruises on the front of her baby's legs. Rania says that the baby had a fall, but the bruises are inconsistent with her explanation. You telephone your supervisor who advises you that the local child protection agency will be informed. Your supervisor also tells you not to leave the home but to stay with Rania until the child protection worker arrives. You wait with Rania for two hours. What do you say to her?

When the adult response to a verbal disclosure is appropriate, the child feels a moment of safety and relief. Finally, there is a safe and dependable adult who listens without judgement or pity. When the adult continues to actively listen, the child may add details to the initial disclosure. The child may conclude with the plea, "Don't tell anyone," or "Promise me you'll keep my secret." At this point, the listening adult reflects Rogerian respect, congruence, and empathy, and responds with four key messages. These can be reworded so that they are developmentally and culturally appropriate for the individual child:

- Acknowledgement: "That [disclosure] must have been difficult for you to say."
- Respect: "I believe what you are telling me."
- Contextualization: "Sometimes children are hurt or injured. You are not alone."
- Promising action: "I am going to call a worker who will talk to you about this."

All four messages are equally important. The first is an acknowledgement of the child's courage in revealing the secret and making the disclosure. The second is a statement of respect, a statement that the child's words are believed. This does not mean that the abuse has happened or that all of the details of the abuse or neglect are accurately recalled by the child. This *does* mean that the listener believes the child's statement and contextual message. The third key message counters that of the abuser and reassures the child that this has happened to other children too. Finally, the adult promises action and solution seeking.

The adult's next step is to call the local child protection agency to report the disclosure. This is the point at which the child typically becomes very angry with the adult. Usually, the child has held the secret for a long time and is fearful of letting go of the secret. The child may have been told repeatedly that the abuse or neglect is deserved because the child is bad or that the abuse is protecting another member of the family from being harmed or even killed. The child may believe that telling the secret will result in a family member leaving or the child being sent away to a foster home. Fearing abandonment, loss of family, or further harm, the child wants to know that this secret will be kept: "You told me you wouldn't tell anyone." The child may also deny the initial disclosure or minimize parts of the disclosure. The child may scream, cry, or yell at the adult, "I hate you!"

Considering the abuse or neglect that the child has already experienced alone and without support, this is a rational and logical response. Disclosures are very frightening and risky for the child. The silence and secrecy imposed by the abuser is now broken. The child's relief from making a verbal disclosure fades quickly when outside workers are called and a child protection investigation begins. The child now faces an interview by a stranger, a third party whom the child neither knows nor trusts. The courage needed to make the initial disclosure is now going to be retested through the involvement of this stranger who may bring trouble, punishment, or even more abuse. This stranger may not listen to the child's disclosure and leave the child alone to cope with the anger of a parent who is interviewed by the worker and then excused. The child may remain in the home to be further and more cruelly revictimized because of the disclosure. The child feels even more at risk because of the disclosure and is likely to be angry, retract the disclosure, or withdraw in silence.

Children Who Are Trafficked

The internationally accepted definition of **child trafficking** comes from Article 3(c) of the United Nations' *Protocol to Prevent, Suppress and Punish Trafficking in Persons, Especially Women and Children* (2000) which defines child trafficking as "the recruitment, transportation, transfer, harbouring or receipt of a child for the purpose of exploitation." Children are trafficked to Canada for purposes of sexual exploitation, domestic servitude, forced labour, and adoption, and some are trafficked to Canada as a gateway to the United States. Typically, younger children are trafficked to be adopted, while older children are trafficked to be used for other purposes. Some are put to work in the sex or drug trade, and others work as unpaid nannies. Older children may even come willingly on the pretext of a better life here with their boyfriend or in a legitimate job, only to realize later that they have been duped by the traffickers.

The number of children who are trafficked to Canada is unknown as there is no national data collection on these children. Globally, it is estimated that 1.2 million children are trafficked per year (Singh and Fairholm, 2012), about half of all globally trafficked persons (Hartjen and Priyadarsini, 2012: 152). Most of these trafficked children never come into contact with social services and are well hidden by the adults who traffic them. They are a valuable commodity. Clayton Hartjen and S. Priyadarsini (2012: 138) argue, "Children, like consumer goods, have become cargo. As a voiceless segment of societies across the globe, lacking resources and power, children become extremely vulnerable to this kind of victimization." Trafficked children exist in every urban area in Canada, but most Canadians are unaware that these children have been forcibly removed from their parents and their homelands before being brought to Canada.

There are commonalities among these children, however, which indicate that they have been trafficked. These children tend to live with strangers who may be called uncle, aunt, or grandfather. These children usually have a well-rehearsed story about these strangers but, when questioned, they become fearful and anxious and demonstrate no in-depth knowledge about these people. These children typically do not have legitimate birth certificates, health cards, or records of citizenship status. Their birth certificates may be falsified, especially in cases of intercountry or international adoption. School-aged children who have been trafficked may lack educational history and records. They may claim to have attended schools elsewhere but they cannot describe the school or any school friends. When asked the name of their last school they may reply, "I don't remember." They may not even be aware of the name of the city, province, or territory in which they live. This lack of knowledge about Canada or recent schooling can be understood with recent immigrants and refugees, but a total lack of knowledge may also indicate child trafficking.

Children who are trafficked tend to be suspicious of all adults, particularly those in uniform, and they are likely to be hypervigilant and reticent to answer questions. As with most children who have been abused or neglected, they have been warned to keep their condition secret. These children may have been told that their families will be killed, or they will be killed, if they disclose their condition. They may also believe that their lives depend upon the strangers with whom they live. If concerned adults do approach them or offer to help them, they usually tell their handlers who immediately relocate them to another home, city, or province. Even when child welfare becomes involved and the children are moved to a safe foster home, their handlers usually find them, establish contact, and convince them to run away. These children are then shipped to other parts of Canada or even to other countries. They simply vanish.

In June 2012, the Human Trafficking Taskforce replaced the interdepartmental federal working group that was set up in 2004 to develop procedures for handling trafficked children. This task force developed procedures but did not include any federal support specific to child victims of trafficking, aside from the possible issuance of a 180-day temporary resident permit to these victims.[1] In March 2013, the British Columbia Ministry of Justice published an *Action Plan to Combat Trafficking in Persons* that specified immediate and long-term actions to increase the number of school-based awareness-raising sessions on human trafficking in BC.[2] However, most of the victims live under the radar in Canada, and, when child welfare is alerted to potential cases of trafficking, the mechanisms are so slow that these children usually vanish before they can be apprehended.

Children Who Self-Harm

Self-harm or self-injurious behaviour is behaviour that involves the deliberate destruction of body tissue without suicidal intent. This behaviour includes activities such as skin burning, pinching, scratching, cutting, and hair pulling. Self-injurious behaviour also includes self-embedding, or planting paper clips, wood slivers, staples, needles, pencil lead, stones, and other objects underneath the skin. When workers describe self-harm or self-injurious behaviour they do so in terms of severity and regularity. Severity refers to how harmful the behaviour is to the child, with the most harmful being the amputation of a body part and the least harmful being the faint pinching of skin. Regularity refers to how often the behaviour occurs, from daily to occasionally.

Self-injurious behaviour is categorized in the biomedical model as a symptom of the child's deficits: mental illness, depression, anxiety, poor communication skills, inability to cope, lack of social skills, or low self-esteem. The child who is depressed and has low self-esteem may become self-injurious, turning psychic distress inward. The child with mental health issues may begin to self-mutilate. The child with poor social skills and limited communication skills may become suicidal. The underlying assumption is that self-harm is a risk factor and a gateway or precursor to suicide, with suicide being the extreme form of self-injurious behaviour.

This biomedical categorization of self-injurious behaviour as a symptom of the child's deficits, with the underlying assumption that this behaviour is a risk factor, suggests interventions that focus on the child's deficits or weaknesses. The child is positioned as a sick, helpless person who is unable to cope with difficulties. The interventions for the child's behaviour might include foster care, support groups, crisis hotlines, intensive therapy, group work, or chemical restraints.

The structural and strengths-based approach changes this categorization of self-harm from a risk factor to a **protective factor**. The child is seen as a resilient person who copes with structural determinants (poverty, childism, racism, sexism, and homophobia) through self-injurious behaviour. This covert and maladaptive behaviour is seen as a protective factor that keeps the child from engaging in even riskier activities. The child is

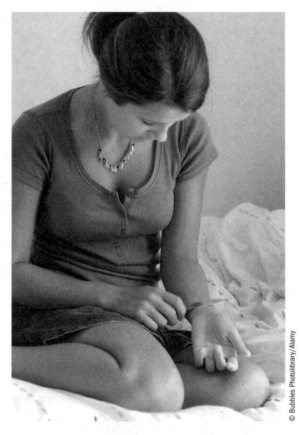

Photo 11.2 Scarification may be a risk factor and self-injurious behaviour, or a protective factor and coping mechanism.

strong and manages personal pain without resorting to medication: cutting and burning can produce fast-acting endorphins that numb or anaesthetize emotional distress. The child not only manages personal pain without medication but also covers up the scars and wounds in order to carry on with daily life. The rock band One Republic summarizes this use of self-harm in their song, "Counting Stars": "Everything that kills me makes me feel alive."

Is this a positive behaviour, one that leads to success in the child's life? No, this leads to neither joy nor success; nor does it build the child's self-esteem. However, it does allow the child to manage pain over which the child feels no control. The girl who self-mutilates as a way to escape the hurt of homophobia and the boy who seeks relief from memories of childhood sexual abuse both gain temporary relief through cutting, burning, or starving. Self-injurious behaviour becomes a way to regain control and power over their bodies, a coping mechanism or stress-reliever rather than simply pathology. When this dangerous behaviour becomes addictive and a necessary part of everyday life, however, the child loses control. The addiction takes control away from the child and the self-injurious behaviour is no longer a coping mechanism or stress reliever; instead, it becomes another risk factor in an already painful life.

Instead of assessing the child as the problem, the worker assesses the structure as the problem. The worker identifies structural risk factors and the structural changes that are needed to lessen, or even extinguish, self-injurious behaviour. The worker asks the child open-ended questions that affirm the child as a problem solver, a controller and director of self-injurious behaviour rather than a sick and helpless person:

- Where did you learn how to cut/burn yourself?
- If you could put a voice to your cutting/burning, what would it sound like?
- When you decide not to cut/burn yourself, what do you tell yourself that works?
- When you feel like cutting/burning yourself, which one of your friends do you turn to first?
- What advice has he/she offered you in the past that was helpful?
- Is there anyone, other than your parents, that you typically turn to for support when the going gets rough?

The worker listens to each answer carefully, affirming the child's ability to cope in a problematic world that sends messages encouraging self-harm and suicide. The worker and the child together create a re-authored narrative through recalling times when the behaviour was needed less or not at all. At the same time, each structural determinant for self-injurious behaviour is deconstructed. The child joins with the worker as an advocate for structural change, an active change agent rather than a passive recipient of care or a sick person.

Suicide is the most extreme form of self-injurious behaviour, and Canadian statistics for child and youth suicide are alarming. According to Stanley Kutcher and Magdalena Szumilas (2008), suicide is the leading cause of non-accidental death for children aged 15 to 19 years, with the suicide rate in this population being 1.02 per 10,000. On average, 762 youth in Canada die by suicide each year, and these numbers continue to rise. Suicide rates of Canadian children surpass those in many developed countries, including the United States, Australia, and the United Kingdom (Kirby, 2013). Child suicide is even more common among children and youth who are First Nations, Inuit, and GLBTQ. The suicide rates among identified First Nations children and youth are currently five to six times higher than the rate in the mainstream population, and the rates for Inuit children and youth are ten times higher than the mainstream population (Kirmayer, 2012). These statistics are alarming because both self-injurious behaviour and suicide are greatly under-reported. Family shame, religious prohibitions, and financial considerations surrounding insurance have shrouded suicide in secrecy, leaving the real numbers of Canadian children who die through suicide unknown and unreported.

Risk Assessment

"Risk" is a term borrowed from the world of business and finance, and risk discourse is a product of institutions and agencies. Risk assessment is the systematic classification or measurement of risk, a measurement used by insurance agents, health inspectors, and human resources staff in an attempt to assess or evaluate factors (lifespan, danger, ability to work) that are not easily quantified. It is an *inexact* science that attempts to predict the future, and it is often described as an attempt to measure the immeasurable. A risk assessment is an estimate or prediction that a particular negative event will occur in the future.

All child welfare jurisdictions in Canada require the use of risk assessment tools to predict the child's potential risk of harm, injury, illness, or failure. These tools contain checklists of factors, primarily from the child's microsystem, which are believed to determine the level of risk to the child. The constellation of risk or cumulative risk factors is quantified. The family's domestic violence (mesosystem) coupled with the child's developmental level (microsystem) and the isolation of the family (macrosystem) are quantified and assessed against protective factors such as an acceptable level of income, a peaceful neighbourhood, and a well-organized community structure. When cumulative risk factors outweigh protective factors, the child may be assessed as at risk of getting caught up in the domestic violence of the home.

Workers bring their own culture, race, gender, ethnicity, and socio-economic status—or monocultural bias—to their understanding of the meaning of risk. Workers rarely concur on the level of risk in the same situation, despite the scales and checklists that they use, their "universal wisdom," and their long years of service within their particular agencies. They may exaggerate, minimize, or even dismiss risk. If the worker is white, Eurocentric, and middle-class, the risk may be assessed very differently from the risk assessed by a worker who is black, Jamaican, and working class. The white worker may see an eight-year-old child helping in his parents' store as being **parentified** and at risk of missing important schooling, whereas the black worker may see this as a competency-enhancing activity. These are **stereotypes**, of course. The opposite may also be true.

Risks are balanced by protective factors and the child's resiliency; in a sense, risk gives meaning to both protective factors and resiliency. Parents, for example, can be described in many different ways: those who nurture, neglect, abuse, and use. However, if the child is at risk of injury and parents move in to protect the child, these same parents become a protective factor. Protective factors act as a buffer to cushion the effects of risk; they may interrupt a negative series of risks, and they may also prevent the initial occurrence of a risk factor.

Protective factors can also be described as **promotive factors** or developmental assets because they promote the healthy development of the child. Traditional descriptions follow Urie Bronfenbrenner's ecological framework (1979) or the developmental assets framework developed by Arturo Sesma, Marc Mannes, and Peter Scales (2005).

Both frameworks are complementary and interactive, and both describe the details of protective factors. Sesma, Mannes, and Scales' developmental assets are observed in the child's high Apgar score, healthy birth weight, high self-esteem, motivation, engagement with learning, enjoyment of reading, sense of honesty and responsibility, as well as, on Bronfenbrenner's microsystem level, a consistent and responsive caregiver, adequate nourishment, safe living conditions, and resiliency. Sesma, Mannes, and Scales (2005) also developed a framework of external factors that very much parallels Bronfenbrenner's mesosystem and macrosystem. Their framework of developmental assets is a set of 40 actions; for example, "youth spends three or more hours per week in lessons or practice in music, theatre, or other art" (283). Each action depends on protective factors, such as categories of support, empowerment, boundaries, and constructive use of time.

In addition to the factors identified by Sesma, Mannes, Scales, and Bronfenbrenner, some Canadians describe the most important protective factor to be a sense of community and spirituality. Aboriginal Canadians, for example, value community as a protective factor and the child's co-parent. The child is connected with the earth and with those who have gone before the child. The child may take in the spirit of a recently deceased relative in the community. Madeleine Dion Stout and Gregory Kipling (2003: 25) note, "They are thus named after the dead family member who, in turn, gives the child certain physical characteristics, skills or personality traits." This naming tangibly connects the newborn to the past and to the community. The child is a gift or a loan from the Creator to the community and is connected forever with that community and with the circle of life. Actions such as preserving the child's umbilical cord in amulets, or telling traditional sayings and holding traditional ceremonies engender the child's feelings of being wanted, loved, and valued as a person in the community. Most active faith communities also prioritize the child, include naming ceremonies and other birth ceremonies, and honour the memory of community members who have died. Naming a child after a close relative or an honoured friend is seen as a spiritual tie to that person, a protective factor.

Sometimes all of the child's actions suggest that the child is at risk. The cumulative risk factors indicate a serious threat that is not counterbalanced by adequate protective factors. However, the child continues to succeed and to meet developmental milestones and maintain emotional stability. The reason for this success is said to be the child's resiliency, that characteristic of positive adaptation despite severe adversity.

Resilient children take risks and engage with the environment to get what they need; they have problem-solving skills and a sense of purpose and future; they rebound in situations of risk and adversity; they meet challenges and endure in situations when other children withdraw or fail to thrive. They tend to be firstborns: active, healthy, and good-natured infants who recover more quickly from childhood illness than other children do. They develop into independent and generally optimistic children who seek out new experiences and take an active approach to problem solving. These resilient children are not always the class presidents or team captains. Such apparently successful children may or may not be resilient, depending on what risks they over-come to achieve their success or popularity.

Risk assessment is a quick, cheap, and seemingly efficient way to categorize a child's situation. Checklists that balance risk and protective factors offer a quantifiable prediction of the risk potential in the child's life and lead to decisions regarding **risk management**. Risk assessment at the same time commodifies children and positions them as vulnerable and unable to manage risk. Children who are assessed as being at-risk fall outside the broad category of children and are seen to be in need of protection. This label may persist well beyond any of the risk factors in the child's life.

Risk Management through Placement

Risk management is an attempt to manage the assessed and recorded risk factors and protective factors, or to quantify the child's situation with a number or grade that the agency and the worker can understand. This process purports to benefit children in that it may lead to decisions to add in-home family support services or apprehend the children from their family and potentially dangerous situations. Risk management led to the apprehension of 40 children from a Mennonite community in Manitoba in February and June of 2013. As a result of a community phone call to the RCMP in 2011, an investigation was launched and a risk assessment was made. In 2013, despite the lack of tangible evidence of abuse, the local child protection agency applied risk management. All of the children in the community were apprehended and placed in state care to mitigate any potential for physical abuse ("discipline") from certain parents in that community (Puxley, 2014).

In situations of high risk when the child cannot be protected from an alleged perpetrator at home, the child is sometimes apprehended and brought to an emergency foster home, residential facility, or group home. Apprehension can also happen when the parent is unable to care for the child because the parent is ill or incapacitated or when family support services are not available to keep the home safe enough for the child. Marginalized parents who cannot navigate the system typically fall into this category. They do not have extended family to help them or they may live in poverty, and they expose their problems to the authorities. Darcie Bennett and Lobat Sadre-hashemi (2008: 5) observe, "Apprehensions are generally the result of a parent's struggle with poverty, addiction, mental health issues or family violence." Child protection workers need to manage risk, and they do not distinguish between parents who abuse and neglect their children and those who cannot provide for their children because of poverty. Sometimes the safest option for the worker is apprehension and placement. Kim Strom-Gottfried (2008: 14) notes that apprehensions target "those who are already powerless and most in need of the social worker's help. Risk-driven decisions, by definition, put the professional's needs before the client's."

In the initial days after their children are placed in foster care, the family is given deadlines, schedules, and service agreements in an attempt to make their home safer and to minimize the risk. The family court judge then decides whether the children will remain in care and whether or not the parents will have access visits with their children. Six of the 40 Mennonite children were returned to their community in November 2013 with the rest remaining in culturally dissonant foster homes in which no one spoke their language (High German) or practiced their faith. Their Mennonite parents were assessed as high risk factors despite their co-operation, signing of agreements, and attendance at parenting classes (Cole, 2013). Risk management is an inexact tool that is litigation-based. It can also be a tool for punishment.

That is certainly how it feels for children, even when they have been abused and neglected at home. The home may mean danger, pain, and injury, but it also means friends in the neighbourhood, brothers and sisters, a family pet, a familiar bedroom, and a classroom with a favourite teacher. Apprehension means moving to a new home, new friends, new school, and a new foster family. Yolanda Lambe (2009: 11) explains, "They typically feel that they are being punished for the abuse they have suffered. After all, it is not the parents who are removed from everything that is secure and known; it is the young person who must shoulder the burden of loss and family separation." Faced with sudden separation from everything and everyone who is familiar, children and youth may deny earlier disclosures, even if these disclosures were made only hours earlier. They may express shock and denial, refusing to go to the placement, or going under the assumption that tomorrow everything will be back to normal. They may scream, hit others, or throw things at the worker, the new foster parent, or the new foster sister or brother.

Later, they may bargain with the worker or the foster parent, promising good behaviour on condition of being allowed to return home. They may call home, asking their parents or siblings to pick them up at the foster home. They may beg over the

Photo 11.3 His bedroom may be clean and bright but right now it feels like loneliness.

telephone, "Come and get me. This place sucks." When bargaining does not produce results, depression follows. Some children accept being in care but many others remain in a state of depression for years, unable to accept the loss of their own home and family. Apprehension and placement can cause long-term physical, cognitive, and emotional damage to children as well as attachment injuries evidenced in social withdrawal, depression, maladaptive development, cardiovascular, and neurohormonal problems, and increased predisposition to disease (DiCiacco, 2008: 28–30).

Most foster parents have good intentions but, as noted in Chapter 4, these good intentions can fade in the face of daily child care. Foster care is not always a place of safety: children have been beaten, starved, sexually abused, and killed in placements in Canada. Jeffrey Baldwin was beaten, tortured, and starved before he died in foster care at age five. He weighed 21 pounds, the same weight as he did when he was apprehended from his parents three years earlier. At the inquest into his death, it was revealed that his foster parents (also his grandparents) were convicted child abusers, having tortured and abused their own children. Journalist Christie Blatchford (2013) observed, "The agency decision that the grandparents were superb caregivers was unsupported, untested, and made with only negligible information."

The sexual abuse of children in foster care is well-documented, beginning with the care formerly provided in residential schools and church-run orphanages. Placement in care may be the beginning of a life characterized by trauma, rejection, sexual and physical violence, self-blame, and self-destructive behaviour. One of the respondents in a recent British Columbia study of foster care commented, "I was sexually abused in the foster home and I reported it to the social worker. The social worker didn't do nothing about it. The foster parents told me that my mom would call me a liar, so I never mentioned it to my mother. The social worker knew about it" (Bennett and Sadrehashemi, 2008: 25).

Risk management is filtered through the cultural expectations of the worker, the agency, and society at large and often results in decisions that are inappropriate, even dangerous, for the child. Risk management resulted in Inuit children being placed with southern families, First Nations children being placed with white adoptive families, children who were blind being institutionalized, and poor children in England being transported to Canada. Risk management does not have a proud history in child welfare.

No-Home Placement

The term "no-home placement" is intended to provoke a response from those who accept children living on our streets. "No-home" means no birth home, no adoptive home, no foster home, and no treatment home. Some Canadian children and youth are placed on the streets without a home by a social structure that fails to recognize and honour the Convention rights of these children.

Homeless children usually do not choose their social location. Nor are they placed on the streets by workers concerned for their welfare. Foster placement graduates comprise 42.7 per cent of the street youth in Canada (Goldstein et al., 2011: 21). Either their foster parents find them difficult or their group home staff feel that their behaviours are non-compliant and frightening. Apprehended from their own family and rejected by child protection, these youth in care soon find that they have nowhere to go but the streets (Gaetz et al., 2013).

Canadian adults do not think of themselves as having placed children on the streets. The current popular fiction is that these children are runaways who choose to live on the street because of their lifestyle choices, which include drugs and sex, that motivate them to leave home. This fiction may be comforting for adults eating dinner in a warm home on a frosty January night. However, it fails to explain the throwaways and the castaways who, like the runaways, are adrift and alone and unsupported in their no-home placements.

Children are excluded from homes, even group homes, and from birth, adoptive, and foster families for a variety of reasons. They may have special needs, behavioural issues, mental health issues, or addictions; they may seem to pose a risk to the other family members because of their violent behaviour; or they may simply be disliked and disowned by the adults living in the home. Some adults throw out their children (even infants), and others drop them off at the local child protection agency. Sometimes the police remove children from their home because of behaviour. Sometimes parents change the locks on their doors when their child is away for a weekend. A large percentage (25 to 40 per cent) of homeless youth are GLBTQ, which suggests that their family may not accept their sexual orientation and either throw out their children or make their life at home intolerable (Gaetz et al., 2013: 77).

In most provinces and territories, children can leave their foster home (by signing themselves out of care) when they turn 16 years old. Children might do this to escape their foster home, and then turn back to child protection for services. However, the door is now shut. If the child is 16 years old or older, the child welfare agencies in most jurisdictions will not provide protective services. The throwing away of these older children is less overt but the result is the same: children trying to survive alone on the streets of Canadian cities and towns.

Children also run away from their birth, adoptive, and foster families for a variety of reasons, including abuse, neglect, anger, or simply the lure of living on their own or with friends. Children may couch surf for a few nights; they may stay at shelters for periods of time; they may even live with family or friends on the streets. Street-involved children are a diverse group that Statistics Canada has yet to count, partly because of the transient nature of their lives and partly because they live under the radar. They are described as throwaways, runaways, street youth, homeless youth, and at-risk youth. They have varying cultures and backgrounds, dreams and talents. What they have in common is that they all have to quickly learn to live and survive on the streets without any of the fundamental rights guaranteed in the Charter and the Convention, rights that most Canadians take for granted. Fay Martin (2003: 268) describes these no-home children: "Most of my research participants had never had a childhood and never

Photo 11.4 A no-home placement means no food, no warmth, no hope, and nobody to care.

would; they had always had to take care of themselves, in natal families, in foster families, group settings, and living on their own. Some had a perpetual childhood; they had never taken care of themselves and never would." Some no-home children survive on the streets for many years without support, whereas others seek the parenting and care they have not yet experienced, often by becoming victims to predatory adults.

No-home children share similar wellness issues. They tend to suffer from respiratory illnesses, skin problems, lice, foot problems, and depression. This suffering has been described as "street sickness, which is a constant feeling of malaise related to exposure to the elements, sleep deprivation, and the inability to maintain personal hygiene" (Kelly and Caputo, 2007: 732). Some become addicted to drugs and/or alcohol. Whether the drugs and alcohol numb the pain or cause the pain, whether they are risk factors or protective factors, is open to debate. No-home children are more likely to be involved in crime, generally theft for survival or theft to cope with life on the streets. As Stephen Baron (2013: 357) explains, "Homelessness exposes youth to an alternative culture that values many forms of offending including property offending, drug dealing, and violence. . . . Together, youth on the street develop new standards and expectations for behaviour."

There are emergency youth shelters in some cities. However, most of these shelters depend on annual municipal and provincial funding. The shelters have limited numbers of beds and even more limited supports. Child welfare provides housing for children who are under 16 years of age, if they attend school and follow the rules of the home.

Social assistance may provide limited income for children over that age, provided they have a social insurance number and a home address. Street children often have neither; many do not even have a birth certificate. Sonja Grover (2007: 336) remarks, "In a real sense, neither home nor street belong to the homeless child in Canada. Street-involved children are not welcome in public spaces, yet they have no decent place of their own to inhabit. They are forced to be constantly on the move within the community and between communities as their integration at even the most marginal level is blocked in a myriad of ways."

Child Protection Work

The child protection system is constructed to be deficit-based, non-voluntary, and childist. Child protection workers still follow the biomedical model of sickness. They go to targeted families to assess their deficiency and dysfunction and compel these families to fit into the risk management system. Neither children nor their families voluntarily turn to this system for protection and support: only 2 per cent of abuse and neglect disclosures come directly from the child (Public Health Agency of Canada, 2010). Children and youth are positioned as helpless and vulnerable, in need of direction and supervision from child protection experts.

This system is an oppressive structural determinant. The child protection worker is the assessor and the expert, while the family is under the microscope (LaLiberte and Crudo, 2012). Families who refuse to co-operate risk losing their children. While some workers enjoy this power and this policing role, others bury themselves in paperwork and quietly smoulder or burn out. Marty, an experienced child protection worker, explains this in recounting a typical work day. Marty might want to "do good" but, at the end of the day, Marty seems to have only temporarily managed risk and litigation demands.

> I got to work early (8:15 a.m.) so that I could check my emails before the school meeting at 9:00 a.m. This meeting had taken months to organize because of the many people involved—foster mom, foster care worker, principal, teacher, educational assistant, and myself—so I did not want to miss it. Sam had been sent home from school three times last week under the zero tolerance policy, and the foster mom is threatening to have him moved. She works part-time and just cannot care for Sam during the day. When I got to my desk, there was a message from the emergency-after-hours worker about a call regarding the neglect of an infant (report from a neighbour). There was also an urgent call from Amanda, one of the mothers on my caseload. Her 12-year-old daughter had stayed out until midnight last night, and Amanda was feeling at the end of her rope. She was asking that her daughter be put into a group home. My co-worker was on sick leave, so I was covering her files. She had a court date tomorrow, and the affidavit was not ready yet.

I developed a quick plan and left a message for my supervisor, asking her to assist with the affidavit. I also left her the address for the infant and for Amanda. I would need to attend to both of these files as soon as possible. As I was driving to the school meeting, my supervisor called me. I pulled over and we had a quick consult. My supervisor offered to have the affidavit finalized for tomorrow's court date and was sending a worker to the infant's home immediately. Thank goodness for teamwork!

The school meeting started late, but there were several new ideas presented. The educational assistant suggested that Sam's speech and language be assessed. I was able to tell her that this had not been done (according to the case file), so could be scheduled right away. The foster mother agreed to call her doctor for a referral. The foster mother explained Sam's home situation and how difficult it was for her to leave work when he was sent home. The teacher listened, and together they developed a strategy that would include a behaviour chart that could go home every day for the foster mother's input. Sam was new at the school, and the principal was unaware that he was in foster care and would most likely only be at the school for another month. With a greater understanding of the disruptions in this child's life, everyone agreed to work together to keep Sam in school as much as possible for the month.

We left the meeting at 10:15 a.m. with a solid plan for Sam. I wrote out the notes in my car, intending to finish them for the file later, and then drove right away to Amanda's home, as promised. She was just getting started with her day and hadn't yet listened to her messages so was unaware that I would be visiting her. She was still angry with her daughter (who was asleep) but also somewhat embarrassed by the state of the house and her late start. Amanda said that Chelsea usually got herself off to school every day, made her own lunch, and often missed dinner. When I asked how Chelsea was doing in school, the answers were vague. It seemed as though Amanda had already decided to put Chelsea into a group home. Noises from the bedroom let me know that someone else was in the apartment, and Amanda mumbled something about her boyfriend spending the night.

I asked Amanda to come to my office for a meeting at 4:00 p.m. I emphasized how important it was to work on a mother-daughter relationship so that Chelsea could feel more secure and settled at home. While I was talking to her there were several urgent calls on my phone, so I left her with a reminder about the importance of our meeting today. The first urgent call told me to arrange to meet the intake worker at the agency right away as the infant had been brought into care. The second urgent call was from the lawyer, again requesting the affidavit as soon as possible. I let the lawyer know that my supervisor was sending the affidavit that afternoon, and then I called a trusted infant foster mother. Her home was full, but she made several suggestions, which I followed up on, finally finding a home in the east end that could take the baby as an emergency placement. Then I drove to the agency.

The intake worker arrived a few minutes after I did and filled me in briefly on the home situation. She handed me her case notes and the initial safety assessment. The priority would be feeding and bathing baby Destiny. She was sleeping at the moment after being in the warm car for half an hour, but I knew that when she awoke the strange environment of an agency would be unsettling and scary. I carried Destiny into my office, gathering supplies on the way. While she slept I had a quick lunch and watched her. At the same time, I went over the notes from the intake worker. It seems that Destiny had screamed herself to sleep the night before (according to a neighbour). Mom was sleeping soundly when the worker went to her unheated trailer this morning. There was evidence of drug use and there was no food in the refrigerator. One crusty jar of uneaten baby food was on the kitchen counter, and there were several dirty baby bottles on the couch. The worker had completed the first phase of the safety assessment, and I would complete the risk assessment tomorrow. Then I would have to prepare an interim care and custody order to present to the court.

Destiny awoke and I held her, rocking her gently, and soothing her with some warm milk. Then I bathed her and did a rudimentary top to toe examination. Her skin was chafed and she had severe diaper rash. Destiny would have to be examined by a physician prior to going to the foster home. While I was dressing her my supervisor popped in and I updated her. She held Destiny while I completed the body chart notes. My supervisor confirmed the time for Destiny's medical check and then handed her back to me.

After a short feeding, Destiny and I went to the physician. While we were waiting in the reception area, Amanda left a message to say she had to reschedule. I left myself a note to call her tomorrow. The physician gave me a prescription for baby ointment and noted that Destiny was in the lowest percentile for weight. That would have to be monitored closely. Destiny had fallen asleep again, so I bundled her into the baby seat and drove to the foster home.

The foster mother gathered up Destiny, and I gave her a quick summary of her needs. I also left supplies (formula and diapers) and asked her to be especially attentive for the first 24 hours. I knew this foster mother would be ideal for Destiny. She asked me to stay for dinner too so that I could meet the other foster children in the home. I thanked her, but told her I needed to get back to my own family.

On the way home, I dictated my case note regarding Destiny's doctor's visit and placement. Then I made a note to complete my case note of the morning meeting. Court was tomorrow at 11:00 a.m., and if my co-worker was still ill, I would be speaking to the affidavit. I would also need to prepare an interim care and custody order for Destiny. Tomorrow would be another full day!

Marty is well on her way to burnout as she regularly works 10-hour days, sometimes doing notes at home after she puts her own children to bed. The secondary trauma of doing child protection work is well documented (Barford and Whelton, 2010) and has been described as burnout, vicarious traumatization, secondary traumatic stress, post-traumatic stress disorder, compassion fatigue and, quite simply, the emotional costs of caring. Child protection workers express feelings of inadequacy, emotional exhaustion, trauma, burnout, and depression. Heavy caseloads, increasing bureaucracy, paperwork requirements, and public scrutiny add to the general stress on child protection workers.

Structural Interventions

High-risk interventions tend to be reactive and crisis-driven; there are foster care crises, abuse crises, children in critical condition, and so on. Adults react quickly to situations that are identified as high-risk and temporary. Children are housed on a short-term basis in emergency foster care placements, emergency shelters, or crisis units. Because these situations are considered to be temporary, long-term supports and solutions, if available, are usually not deployed. These placements are not seen as learning opportunities; nor are the voices of children part of the solutions. James Anglin (2003: 127), in his study of residential care in Canada, observes, "This type of care was derisively labelled by the youth as 'babysitting' or 'putting in time.'" In a follow-up review of care facilities in British Columbia almost a decade later (British Columbia Ministry of Children and Family Development, 2012), the average duration of stay had increased from five years to seven years, and the percentage of Aboriginal children in care had increased from 38 to 56 per cent. There was no mention of Anglin's earlier report or the pain-based behaviours he observed; nor were youth in care consulted. Adults take charge of these situations and often continue to dictate the rules once the crisis is over.

The reactions to high-risk situations are often the same interventions of a century ago under new names. "Orphanages" are now "permanency planning," and "work-houses" are "preparation for independence" programs. The focus on "family support" changes to a focus on "the best interests of the child," then back again. "Clinical work" changes to "risk management," then back to "differential response," a combination of both. The child who suffers abuse and neglect is removed, moved, returned, and then removed again in a downward spiral of very expensive and reactive casework, spurred on by bureaucratic risk management tools from the biomedical model. Ken Barter (2005: 317) calls this a "reactive response to cope with symptoms."

Targeted programs for at-risk children, such as Headstart, infant stimulation programs, and social skills groups, are typical of this reactive, biomedical model with its deficit approach to children. The focus is on fixing the child's deficits rather than changing the structural determinants for the child. The child is positioned as the problem, categorized as at-risk, and becomes unlikely to move beyond that category. Strengths are not identified, except as they correspond to or counter risks.

These quick-fix interventions for at-risk children may be highly effective for the enrolled children while they are in the programs. However, there is little or no evidence that these short-term programs have long-term benefits, even for the children who participate. These targeted programs have little impact on community rates of childhood difficulties or on siblings in the family who do not attend the program. As with the system of foster care, the child who is removed from the home and given a dose of middle-class medicine and returned to the same set of home conditions is unlikely to change.

The structural and strengths-based approach begins with the assumption that the child and family are competent and are partners in change. Children are positioned as persons with rights and persons who have promise, rather than persons with needs and persons at risk. This strengths-based positioning is fundamental to the structural approach. Begin with health and wellness, and the abuse and neglect of the child become structural issues that can be addressed. Social change is the methodology, rather than social control of children and families through service plans, time limits, apprehensions, and litigation.

Structural determinants can foster and support resiliency in children, while still responding to the safety of these children and preventing their abuse and neglect. Community capacity-building projects in Canada (see Chapter 5) have done just that. Reported cases of child abuse and neglect lessen, and parental participation increases in well-baby clinics, in the child's classroom, and in family recreation programs. Children in these communities feel a sense of belonging. They feel communal support rather than individual compensation for perceived or real injuries. They demonstrate civic pride and participate more actively in school, sport, and volunteer work. They are valued participants within their communities. They have a placement and it is permanent.

Jane Gilgun (2002) describes this approach in her study of resilience in First Nations children in care. She applies the Medicine Wheel framework to identify which structural factors actually support resiliency in children as they journey through the foster care system. She indicates that a key structural factor is spirituality as it is offered through the guidance, modelling, and affirmations of the Elders in the Native community. Her framework assumes that there is trust, mutuality, and reciprocity in the relationship, and that children are willing and able to listen and to learn. A summary of her structural supports for resiliency is depicted in Figure 11.1.

The risk and protective factors that affect children are embedded within multiple levels of the child's world. Unless fundamental changes happen at all of these levels, any high-risk intervention will be inadequate for the child. Structural and strengths-based interventions can meet the challenges of high risk while valuing families and keeping children within their own families and communities.

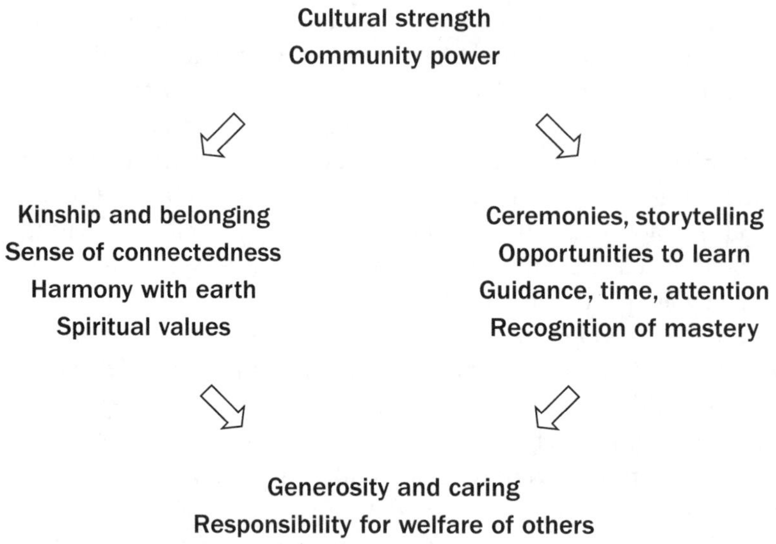

Cultural strength
Community power

Kinship and belonging
Sense of connectedness
Harmony with earth
Spiritual values

Ceremonies, storytelling
Opportunities to learn
Guidance, time, attention
Recognition of mastery

Generosity and caring
Responsibility for welfare of others

Figure 11.1 Structural Supports for Resiliency

Summary

This chapter outlined how risk and protective factors can be assessed and managed, how resiliency can be supported, and what steps can be taken to address structural determinants in high-risk situations. Protective factors are balanced against risk factors, with the child's resiliency being one of those protective factors. This system appears logical, yet the human factors involved in high-risk situations defy such quantitative measures. Resiliency, for example, may be genetic and may be a reaction to structural factors; certainly, it does not fit neatly into a risk assessment checklist.

High-risk situations demand a worker who is culturally competent and knowledgeable. Children who are trafficked, who are self-injurious, or who live on the streets expect and deserve respect and empathy rather than help and sympathy. In high-risk situations, a child is often removed from the community and placed in another home and another community. This can feel like punishment, especially when one move is compounded by many more and then a final move into poverty on the streets. Children and youth often get more support and attentive listening from their peers, and they turn to these social contacts when they join a group or gang. In this next chapter, we will consider whether groups or gangs can be helpful in high-risk situations. Risk assessment and risk management will be useful when considering the dynamics, leadership, and membership of both groups and gangs.

Review Questions

1. Describe a high-risk situation. Differentiate between the protective and risk factors in the situation. Describe the risk factors as either proximal or distal. Now identify the bias in your description.
2. When a child discloses abuse, what four key messages should be given to the child?
3. Why are most disclosures never reported? What do children and youth do when their disclosures are not heard?
4. Explain what is meant by "trafficked children." How would you identify such children, and what makes this identification so difficult?
5. How can self-injurious behaviour be described as both a risk and a protective factor?
6. How does risk management lead to placement, and what kinds of placements are available for children and youth?
7. How does a child perceive risk management and placement? Why?
8. How can foster placement be both a protective factor and a risk factor for a child?
9. What is meant by "no-home placement"? How many children in Canada are in this situation?
10. Which structural and strengths-based determinants mitigate risk for children?

Discussion Questions

1. How do you apply risk management in your own life? Has your risk management ever proved to be faulty? Why has this happened?
2. Has a child ever made a disclosure of abuse or neglect to you? If so, what steps did you follow in supporting the child's disclosure? If not, how do you think you might react to such a disclosure?
3. After reading about Marty's day as a child protection worker, did you feel she was uncaring, inattentive, or simply overwhelmed? Have you ever considered doing this kind of work? Would you have handled her day differently? Explain.

12 Groups and Gangs

You are never really alone in the city at night. There are always taxi drivers, coffee shop people, the 7-Eleven guy, people in their homes watching talk shows. It just feels lonely.

—Mariko Tamaki, *Skim*

Human beings are social and have an innate need to belong. In evolutionary terms, humans who separated from the group were at risk, and those who stayed with the group tended to survive. The novel's namesake, Skim, is a Goth heroine who describes the loneliness of exclusion, particularly in the city at night. She samples many different groups and attaches herself briefly to the English teacher, the preppy boys, her best friend Lisa Soor, and random Wicca friends in her search for inclusion. When one of her classmates feels excluded from the group because of his sexual orientation and commits suicide, Skim begins to understand and absorb the price of exclusion. On the outside looking in, she can only conclude, "Being sixteen is officially the worst thing I've ever been" (103).

The family is the first natural group that a young child experiences. This group can be supportive or threatening, comforting or abusive, or anywhere within this range. This group may also be larger, more extended through the generations, or constantly evolving. Skim's family is dual: herself and her mom in one home, and herself and her dad in another. Canadian writer Mariko Tamaki describes the group skills that Skim learns from each family group model. Even a very young child who joins a group or a gang has experienced group leadership and group dynamics and has learned group skills that are shaped and sharpened by this family group experience.

The child may have already developed quite a different construct of turn-taking. For the child, it may not be the regularity of **maypole** communication—the leader prompting each member to make a contribution in turn. Turn-taking in the family may mean pushing very hard to have your voice heard. It may mean shouting, screaming, or edging out other family members. Because the child has learned these turn-taking skills over many years in the family, these skills are entrenched and may take an equally long time to change.

The worker recognizes and builds on the diversity of group skills that children bring to groups and tries to pull these skills together to form a cohesive, strengths-based group. The worker relies on the contributions of all the members, for they are the glue that holds the group together. The influence that they exert on one another and their interactions with one another are powerful agents for change. Members and leaders construct a power dynamic that can have a tremendous influence on the child within the group and on the group as a whole.

The same skills are used by gang leaders who engage children in activities that can be described both as deviant and empowering. Power and control are used by leaders to engage members; when the power is shared, members benefit. In this chapter, we will examine the social construction of gangs, as well as the structural interventions that can change gang membership into group membership.

We will start by defining a "group" and then will discuss several models of gangs and groups, each with a specific goal and dynamic. We will review techniques for leadership, which include facilitation, mediation, and reinforcement. The worker can use this information in matching the child to the group so that **group work** can be a positive and helpful intervention. The worker can also use this information in understanding gang formation and dynamics and in working with gang members.

Objectives

By the end of this chapter, you will:

- Differentiate between groups and gangs, in their development, leadership, and membership.
- Identify a leadership skill set that matches your own skill set.
- Demonstrate your understanding of how to initiate and facilitate a group for children or youth that attracts their voluntary participation and meets their evolving needs.

Gang Models

When two or more children gather together with one focus, this gathering is sometimes called a group and sometimes called a gang. These labels are value-charged. "Group" tends to be a neutral, benign, or positive label. "Gang" has become a pejorative label that connotes drugs, violence, illegal activities, and possible incarceration.

This difference in labelling reflects the changing social construction of children and their relative (to adults) powerlessness in society. When several senior citizens walk through the neighbourhood at night, they are called a group of walkers, women, or friends. When several children walk through the same neighbourhood on the same night, they may be called a gang. The person making these assessments may be the same adult; the location (neighbourhood) is the same; and the activity (walking) is the same. Only the age of the members differs. Therein lies the power differential and the reason for the label of "gang" being applied to the children's group.

Gangs that are labelled today are quite different from *Our Gang* or *The Little Rascals*, groups of small-town neighbourhood children who played pranks and had dangerous and comedic adventures in the 1930s Hal Roach comedies. The Little Rascals were a "play-tough" gang with wild schemes. Neighbours scolded them, shouted at them, and threatened them; and the police occasionally chased them. But the Little Rascals always outwitted the police and escaped to enjoy another day of freedom. These comedies reflected the prevailing social construction of the child as mischievous and vulnerable. Childhood was seen as a time of innocence and waywardness, and children were seen to be susceptible to moral corruption (see Chapter 2).

The social construction of children today as social capital has put a quite different spin on the word "gang." The susceptibility to moral corruption is still there, but youth gangs are now seen as a source of this moral corruption: anti-social and unproductive at best, criminal at worst. Much of the research on youth gangs is American, and much of what we think about gangs tends to be influenced by the American law-and-order urban context or "get tough on crime" approach (Wortley and Tanner, 2004). Canadian statistics on gangs are compiled by Public Safety Canada, the RCMP, and provincial, territorial, and municipal police forces. Gangs are studied by criminologists rather than by sociologists, and many view the first solution to youth gangs to be the arrest and incarceration of the members.

Adults have been taught to fear the congregating of both children and youth when adult leadership is absent. Media reports about youth gangs and gun violence fuel this fear and change the meaning of the word "gang." The Little Rascals are now the fourth-graders of the animated show *South Park* who get together to trick their teachers, their parents, and other adults who seem to be uninformed and rather silly. The children, on the other hand, are smart and provide provocative social commentary. They talk tough and strong in this mountain town. Kenny, a main character on the show, is eaten by rats; a boy toasts marshmallows over a burning Vietnam vet; and another boy calls his school bus driver a "fat ugly bitch." These little rascals—the *South Park* gang—prompt fear in the world of adults.

Youth gangs are associated with criminal activity rather than waywardness, and all youth who informally congregate are seen as suspect. In fact, a youth's member-ship in a gang can be cause for detention (Chatterjee, 2006; Wortley and Tanner 2007; Mourani, 2009). A youth participant in Scot Wortley and Julian Tanner's (2007: 98) study on youth gang activity in Toronto remarked, "Like the brothas in our crew always get hassled by the cops. They like get stopped all the time. Police always searching them and shit." Even when the focus of a youth group is legal, such as attending a rock concert, walking at night, skateboarding, or playing music, the members are suspected of violence and involvement with weapons and criminal activity. They may also be subjected to random police checks and unprovoked searches.

Definitions of youth gangs reflect the biomedical model and the deficit approach to children and youth. The Montreal Police Service defines a youth gang as "an organized group of adolescents and/or young adults who rely on group intimidation and violence, and commit criminal acts in order to gain power and recognition and/or control certain areas of unlawful activity" (Public Safety Canada, 2008). Similarly, the International Centre for the Prevention of Crime (2011: 3) defines a gang as "a group of young people who self-identify as a group, are generally perceived by others as a distinct group involved in a significant number of delinquent incidents that produce consistent negative responses from the community." One of the few non-police studies of Canadian gangs (Mellor et al., 2005) takes a strengths-based approach and describes five gang models: Group of Friends, Spontaneous Criminal Activity Gang, Purposive Gang, Youth Street Gang, and Structured Criminal Organization. Each model has a specific focus and goal-directed activity, and all five models fit into the three classic group types identified by social psychologists John R.P. French and Bertram Raven (1959): task, growth, and treatment. Understanding each gang model is essential to understanding the member's role within the gang.

The first gang model is the Group of Friends. This gang tends to be interest-based and usually does not involve criminal activity even though the gang may be subject to police scrutiny. A girl may describe her friends as "my gang" because they share a common social interest, such as shopping, going to movies or clubs, skateboarding. A boy may hang out with his "gang" because they all live in the same neighbourhood; in fact, most youth gangs are neighbourhood-based and multi-ethnic (Wortley and Tanner, 2004; Mourani, 2009). The Group of Friends gang model can also be described as a "growth" group or a "mutual aid" group, using classic group typologies, because the members derive support from their friends in the gang and develop peer skills through their interactions with other gang members. Their membership in their respective gangs persists as long as they share the same social interests or neighbourhoods as other gang members.

The second model is the Spontaneous Criminal Activity Gang. This gang is social in nature and usually located in the neighbourhood. Membership is transitory and tied to the fun or spontaneous activity that the gang offers at that moment. In many ways, the Spontaneous Criminal Activity Gang is like a task group, and membership is similarly short-lived. The tasks of this gang include activities such as socializing while roaming streets and attending concerts; gratuitous violence and bullying are spontaneous and occasional acts rather than regular events. Criminal activity, when it occurs, is situational, impromptu, and peripheral to the main task of having fun.

The third model is the Purposive Gang, which comes together for a specific purpose such as stealing cars, engaging in vigilante-type violence, or mob activity. This model can be described as both a task and a growth group. The task is specific and typically illegal. Accomplishing this task develops or grows the members' feelings of competence, power, and self-esteem. These gang members tend to be disenfranchised children and youth who use their gang membership and the risky gang tasks as a way to ameliorate their feelings of depression, alienation, and low self-esteem. These members gradually build their social skills and feelings of competence (and their cash flow too!) through carrying out a specific plan or activity. Once this plan or activity is accomplished the purposive gang disbands.

The fourth model is the Youth Street Gang. These highly visible and cohesive hard-core gangs come together primarily for illegal activities. Like the Spontaneous Criminal Activity Gang, the members tend to live in the same neighbourhood. They usually have a gang name, a uniform (tattoos, brand-name clothing), and meeting place or turf. Their illegal activity is profit-driven and continuous, unlike that of the Purposive Gang. The Youth Street Gang can also be described as a task group because membership cohesion revolves around the task, or it can be described as a mutual aid group because of the peer support offered within this gang.

The fifth model is the Structured Criminal Organization in which children and youth play only peripheral roles, such as drug mules or runners. The gang leader uses these young members only for specific jobs because the Youth Criminal Justice Act protects these young members from adult prison. They take the risks but tend to have low or no status within the gang. This type of task group may function as a treatment group for the children and youth on its margins who seek an escape from their own marginalized lives and an entry to the social life of adults.

Each gang model is a discrete category. There is no current research evidence that children move from one gang model to another. Some children may find that they enjoy the risky behaviour, and their engagement increases as the risks increase; they may move from stealing a bicycle to stealing a car, for example. Other children may belong to the gang as long as they live in the neighbourhood; when their family moves, their membership in the gang ceases. Many adults tend to assume that children in gangs all belong to the fifth model, the highly structured criminal network. Whether or not the majority of youth gang members engage in criminal activity is unknown. Much depends on who is doing the survey, how "children" and "youth" are defined, and what is said by the key informants.

Group Models

Group work preceded individual worker–client work. It was the first kind of recorded social work in Canada and was often political or religious in nature (Jennissen and Lundy, 2011). Groups of people gathered in settlement houses to discuss labour and citizenship issues, went to progressive education centres to learn, and participated in recreational groups and church groups. This early group work was intrinsically strengths-based; the underlying principle of the group was that people have much to share both intellectually and materially and much to learn from one another. There was always a struggle for internal cohesiveness and integration as members argued, exchanged ideas, joined and left the group.

Structural determinants were the original focal issues of these political and labour groups, and these same determinants impact the recreational, educational, and social skills groups that children and youth are encouraged to join today. These

Photo 12.1 Task groups come together to accomplish a specific goal within a time frame.

groups are categorized according to their group work as task, treatment, and growth groups. Sometimes a group is a combination of two types—"treatment and growth," for example. The group work may be focused on treatment for a particular difficulty, and through this work the child grows both cognitively, in terms of understanding, and socio-emotionally, in terms of a change in attitude and feeling towards that difficulty. Sometimes a group begins as a task group and the task is forgotten or put aside as the group evolves into a growth group.

Task groups have a specific goal to accomplish, such as building a garden, writing a report, making a video. The focus is the task, and there are time frames within which to achieve the task. When the task is complete, the group disperses. A task group may also be organized according to knowledge needs; children learn about specific topics such as eating disorders, anger management, prenatal health, or healthy sexuality each time the group meets. The group has a leader and often a manual or a colouring book to guide the group sessions. The group considers a particular topic each week, considers pre-set discussion questions, and perhaps has a video to watch. Sometimes the structured, time-limited, and educational group is run in tandem with another related group. For example, a group for the parents might run at the same location and the same time as the group for the parents' children. In this way, both groups follow the same curriculum. The parents learn about healthy meal preparation, for instance, while the children learn about healthy eating.

Task groups can also be growth groups for some members who benefit from the interpersonal dynamics of the group. They feel empowered by the group dynamics and the accomplishment of the group task, and they develop new skills through completing a set task with other group members.

Treatment groups include both psychodynamic treatment and growth, self-help, or mutual aid groups. The psychodynamic treatment group is a structured and time-limited group organized to address behavioural or mental health needs. Members of this group may have been diagnosed as aggressive, addictive, violent, anorexic, or anti-social, and typically have been directed or ordered to attend this group. Others—victims of bullies, children of alcoholics, or victims of abuse, for example—attend a group voluntarily, with some initial encouragement from significant adults in their lives. The leader pre-selects and pre-screens members for the group and usually follows a set program and booklet, adapting the materials to meet the specific behavioural needs of the members.

! Point to Consider   **12.1**

What Kind of Group Do You Want?
Some workers attribute stereotypical motivations to children who join groups. They assume children want to have fun, eat pizza, learn more, watch movies, or just hang around together. Other workers ask children to state anonymously what they want from the group. High school students forced to participate in a lunch-hour social skills group anonymously submitted their requests:

> I want to be a member, not a kid with a problem.
> I want to be me, not holding back, not pretending.
> I want you to be real, too, and I want to know who you are.
> I want the group to be real, not some phoney, "turn to page 3" thing.
> I want to be the leader sometimes but not every time.
> I want to talk about my stuff and my life, not some stuff from a book.
> I want to feel connected, not just with the group, but with the whole school too.
> I want to feel like my ideas are valued and needed by the group.
> I want to have fun and laugh, and do fun stuff, not just talk all the time.

The growth group, also called the self-help or mutual aid group, is more open-ended and flexible. A child may choose to attend for a month, a year, or longer, and membership is determined by felt social and emotional needs. The focus of the group is personal growth in each or all of the domains as children learn from the experiences of other children in similar situations. The theory is that children enjoy being with their peers and that children learn best by actively engaging and participating with others. The most common technique is role play. Children reflect on and act out situations and emotions, sometimes alone and sometimes with other members of the group. In family support growth groups, family members sometimes change roles and engage in dialogue in an attempt to gain insight into the roles of other family members.

Leadership

Leaders in groups and gangs have much in common. The leader of a group may wear a suit and carry a briefcase, but that leader needs to recruit, motivate, and retain members just as much as a gang leader wearing tags and tats. Recognizing the similarities and the differences in leadership is important, especially when children gravitate to gang leaders and reject groups.

Workers are often asked to lead a group, form a group, talk to a group, or engage a child or parent in a group. Groups are more cost-effective than individual client work. Workers can deal with 10 or 15 children in an hour rather than spending time with each child during the week. When the worker looks for more information about the group, the answer is often thematic. The group is described according to its content or theme as a "self-esteem group," or "for kids on drugs." There is little information about the factors that influence a successful match between the child and the group, factors such as

- purpose of the group;
- current leadership style;
- composition of the group;
- applicability of the group model to the temperament and the perceived needs of the child;
- length of the meetings;
- timing of the meetings (day of the week, time of day); and
- accessibility of the group (cost, space, location, transportation issues).

The right match between the child and the group is essential for the group to function and for the child to function in the group. Because the child is often placed in a group by an adult who does not understand the factors that determine a successful match, it is up to the leader in the group to gently place the child out of the group before the child is in any way damaged by the group experience. This is the worker's first task as leader of the group: to recruit and retain members who can benefit from the group experience. A weak leader may choose to recruit only followers, while a strong leader recruits those challenging members who might benefit from the group experience by taking on an indigenous leadership role themselves. Sharing the leadership role with members is the mark of effective leadership.

Leadership of both groups and gangs involves power and power sharing, and leaders exert their power in complex and often covert ways. A leader may claim to be democratic and invite members to both participate and develop gang or group rules and activities. As each member contributes, however, the leader may mock, undermine, or dismiss the contribution and the contributor. This solidifies the leader's power and undermines the member. The member's weakness bolsters the leader. French and Raven's (1959) original typology of leadership power is useful in understanding this dynamic. They identify five sources of leadership power: rewards, coercion, legitimacy, reference, and expertise. These sources of power are used both openly and covertly to solidify the leader's power, influence members, and build membership in the five leadership roles of organizer, seller, teller, tester, joiner, and consultant. Table 12.1, an adaptation of the French and Raven typology, delineates how this is accomplished by leaders of gangs and groups.

Organizing is the leader's primary role. As described earlier, the leader decides on membership, recruiting, and pre-selecting members. The leader finds a space to accommodate all of the members. The group leader provides refreshments and materials for the first meeting, and the gang leader may add cash, drugs, or alcohol to the mix. The leader designs and controls the first meeting, deciding who speaks, when, and on what subject. This organizing role continues and evolves as new situations arise, such as the need for new members, a change of dates or activity, a new location, a need for resources, and so on. With each new situation, the leader may gradually share this organizing role with members or tighten this role further so that all power remains vested in the leader.

The next role is that of selling or trying to convince members to continue to participate and attend. When members do not accept or enjoy the activity or structure, or when they are passive and unmotivated, the leader tries to sell them on the activity or the structure. The leader sells a focus group by convincing children or youth that their participation and written comments make a difference. The leader sells a fight by convincing members that their honour is at stake. Selling keeps the members motivated and task-oriented.

Stagnant, controlling, and power-hungry leaders take the more coercive role of telling. These leaders are the gatekeepers and decision makers who control membership and activities on the assumption that members need constant direction and supervision. Group leaders may say, "If you want to stay with us, you'll have to behave."

Table 12.1 Gang Leaders and Group Leaders

Gang Leader	Group Leader
Rewards such as money, cars, drugs, status in neighbourhood	Rewards such as praise, certificates, badges, marks, field trips
Coercion such as threats, violence, shaming	Coercion such as threats to notify parents, shame, marks
Legitimacy through intelligence, knowledge, experience, age, personal status, physical characteristics, family, money	Legitimacy through intelligence, organizational status, knowledge, experience, age, personal status, physical characteristics
Reference through personal attractiveness, ethnicity	Reference through power attribution from others
Expertise such as experience, social skills, street smarts, physical skills, and information	Expertise such as experience, social skills, knowledge and information

Gang leaders may add threats of violence or exclusion to this dictum, doubling up on the testing role, "If you want to stay, you'll have to do this job." When members lose interest, argue, defy the leader, or fail to accomplish their tasks, the leader may assign them an additional task to prove their loyalty to the gang or avoid exclusion from the gang. When the member does the task, this member's loyalty is broadcast to the others and universalized: what one member can do, all members can do. Similarly, the leader of a group may test involvement by asking for input, coaxing and urging the members to participate and act, or setting a written or physical test. Group leaders may ask individual members to make a presentation or tell their story to the entire group.

The fourth role is joining, and at this point indigenous leadership is strong within the gang or group. The leader steps back and observes members talk with one another and exchange ideas. The leader does not control the conversation but participates as a member or waits to be asked for a decision. Three or four members may decide to rob a local store and bring the proceeds back to the gang. The affirmation of the leader is still important but members feel empowered to take on actions and responsibility without being overtly ordered or enjoined to do so. Similarly, three or four group members may organize and run a fundraising activity that benefits the entire group.

The fifth role is consulting. When the group or gang is cohesive and there is capable indigenous leadership, the leader who is able to share power begins to divest control and openly consult members. Those who are consulted feel special and important, and the other members take on more tasks in hopes of being consulted. The leader is able to step aside and let the members evolve into a stronger unit and develop their direction from within rather than without. In both gangs and groups, empowerment is engendered when members are encouraged to take on leadership roles such as organizing, selling, or telling. When every member is seen to have some leadership potential and is given the chance to take a leadership role in evolving leadership, then the interpersonal dynamic is democratized and the power dynamic is equalized.

Membership

Adults usually encourage children and youth to form and join groups and discourage them from forming or joining gangs. In addition, adults subsidize and support groups, and offer social rewards to those children and youth who join groups. The rewards are generous: adult approval, social legitimacy, and points/certificates/badges/prizes. Despite these tangible and generous rewards, children and youth sometimes choose to join gangs over groups. Who are these children and youth, and why do they make this choice?

Gang members are depicted as low-functioning misfits, marginalized youth who lack social skills, impulse control, and cognitive ability, or dropouts without school or work in their lives. Yet youth gang members often meet in schools: "positive school attendance was actually sometimes linked to gang involvement, where gang members attended school to associate with each other" (Public Safety Canada, 2012: 5). They recruit members, organize their activities, and make elaborate plans without adult support or direction. It seems that these members are self-motivated and street smart. Jane Wood and Emma Alleyne (2010) characterize gang membership by four qualities: durability, street orientation, youthfulness, and identity.

Durability refers to the brevity of membership: most children and youth belong to a gang for one year or less (Chatterjee, 2006: 5). The excitement of gang membership does not appear to endure, and membership is often as short-lived as task group membership. While some children stay in the Girl Guides or a choir for their entire childhood, most sample a task group for a year or less and then leave to join another task group. Childhood is a period of rapid change and evolution of ideas. Children and youth have a wide spectrum of interests and social contacts, and interest in one group or gang, one activity or sport, tends to be short-lived and transitory. Gang membership is typically brief.

The quality of street orientation differentiates gang members from group members. Gang members tend to congregate anywhere but the home, school, or place of worship. They might meet up at school, but they quickly move out onto the street where there is less adult control and direction. Gang members do not appear to be comfortable in adult-sanctioned spaces; in addition, they do not have access to these spaces. They often live in neighbourhoods characterized by disorganization, violence, family instability, inadequate schooling, and little or no real recreational facilities (Wortley and Tanner, 2006; Wood and Alleyne, 2010). Group members, on the other hand, are encouraged to meet in community spaces, schools, and homes and are usually supported and rewarded for doing so.

Youthfulness is the third quality of gang membership, but not all youth gang members are between the ages of 12 and 17. Maria Mourani's (2009) study of street gangs in Quebec notes that street gang members are usually males between the ages of 16 and 23. Mourani refers to these males as "youth." The Wortley and Tanner (2007) study of Toronto youth gangs refers to "youth" as persons aged 16 to 24, thus drawing adults into a range that legally includes children. Police reports on gangs never refer to "children"; their term of choice is "youth" even when gang members are 14 and 15 years old. In this way, "youth" becomes a pejorative term associated with violence and crime.

The fourth gang membership quality—identity—refers to the counterculture identity that is specific to gangs. Members tend to question or reject adult authority rather than acquiesce and follow. Members may have turned to adults for help in their lives (see Chapter 11) or relied on their caregivers only to be disappointed and rejected over and over again. They may also have been ridiculed and punished by adults in authority. The following comments from two Toronto youth gang members describe the identity and the protection that they experience through their gang membership:

> "In my area, man, if you ain't with a crew, you gonna get punked and jumped all the time. If ya can't beat em join em. The gang got your back and people don't mess with you cause they know you got backup."

"It got so you would like not even bring like a gold chain or anything to school cause it would be taken from you by lunch. So we needed to join up to fight them back. Meet force with force, you know what I'm sayin? We needed to . . . show those guys to show respect." (Wortley and Tanner, 2007: 105)

These comments describe the very unsafe world of school and neighbourhood that gang members inhabit. Children and youth congregate for protection in this unsafe world in which they experience violence, ridicule, and disrespect. Protection against larger children and bullies is often cited as a rationale for joining or forming gangs. Pejorative terms such as "punk," "loser," and "nobody" are ascribed to children living in poverty in neighbourhoods that lack resources and in situations in which school success and even part-time employment is limited. Gang members, on the other hand, have status and a sense of safety and support. As Kiaras Gharabaghi (2012: 16) explains, "The brotherhoods and sisterhoods of edgy youth are about reassurance, confirmation and rationalization. They reassure each brother or sister that they are not alone and that their path to the edge is a path well traveled; in other words, they are not weird."

When youth have the protection of their gang, the stress of being marginalized and living in neighbourhoods that are fraught with violence is lessened. Michael Ungar (2008: 27) observes, "Gang behaviour is not always emblematic of a desire to be bad, but is more often a response to threats from others." On the fringes already because of their family lives and relative poverty, children and youth join with neighbourhood friends who accept them. When all of the other doors are shut tight, the path to gang membership and social connectedness looks promising, and members find safety, reassurance, respect, and self-worth through interacting with one another.

Group members also describe feeling empowered by their group membership and the common purpose of a task group. The shared values or the shared triumph

Point to Consider   12.2

Child Soldiers

Child soldiers have always been a part of war. A 2009 working paper from the Refugee Studies Centre at Oxford University estimated that 300,000 children from 41 countries are child soldiers, and the majority are involved in civil wars (Lee, 2009). They are recruited and kidnapped to become soldiers because they are plentiful and expendable, particularly in countries such as Ethiopia and Burundi, where half of the population is under 18. They tend to obey adults without question, do not ask for pay, and follow out of fear. An increasing percentage of child soldiers are girls. They are less likely to run away than boys and more amenable to doing a variety of jobs, including serving as sexual partners for commanders. *continued*

Most child soldiers are abducted or kidnapped from their villages, but some are recruited by persuasive leaders or other child soldiers. The children of Soweto, for example, fought for an end to apartheid, and the children of Palestine strap bombs to their bodies to fight for their cause. Religious, community, and political causes prompt some children to fight.

Child soldiers have been studied, pitied, and condemned. They fit the age category of children but do not fit its social construction. Most of those who survive are resilient and strong, having seen and participated in atrocities that Western adults cannot even imagine. Their life span is short unless they are rescued. Even when rescued, only those who are relocated outside of their country seem to survive. Others return to their army or to soldiering as a way of life and their only means of survival. The power of gang membership pulls them back even to this precarious and deadly task.

Researchers identify lack of family, poverty, and group identity as commonalities among child soldiers. They may be the only surviving member of their family, and may in fact have helped to massacre their own family to prove their loyalty to the cause. They may have no skills, education, or any other means of survival. They may also identify with their fellow child soldiers, the leader, or the cause of their army.

Child soldiers tend to be resilient and mature, much as gang members appear to be in Canada. They develop an insensitivity to hardship and violence, and they come to regard their army (gang) as their real family.

of accomplishing a task are empowering. In treatment groups and growth groups, the members feel a similar affiliation and acceptance, necessary components to feeling empowered. As members gain confidence and feelings of competence, they gain self-control or power from within. While absolutely shared or balanced power is unlikely, a sharing of power is empowering for the members.

Culture and Interaction

Internal integration or cohesion of a group or gang involves both cultural issues and interaction patterns. Culture affects interaction and vice versa in an interwoven pattern that may be uniform and cohesive or torn and disjointed. The leader who understands how this dynamic evolves is able to work with members to support the positive internal integration of the group or gang.

Group or gang culture refers to the values, beliefs, customs, and traditions that members hold in common. On the surface, this culture is displayed in symbols and rituals such as special handshakes, opening statements or prayers, tattoos, bandanas, tags, or check-ins. On a deeper level, this culture is shown in the way that members interact with one another. At the deepest level, this culture involves the norms and shared beliefs in such things as religion, anti-racism, money, police corruption, or social action. It is at this deepest level that members integrate into the group or gang and develop their cohesion as a group or gang.

This culture evolves gradually from the first meeting when the members begin to articulate their rules or norms. When an authoritarian leader dictates the rules, members listen and respond either by tacitly agreeing or by questioning, arguing, or withdrawing. The evolving leader solicits member input and supports indigenous leadership. Each member contributes to the rules or norms as the leader tries to achieve initial consensus. This process of identifying norms and beliefs weaves the members together into a cohesive and confident unit. The unit develops confidence through the

---

Group Exercise   12.1

Icebreakers

This large group exercise introduces participants to icebreakers, activities that help the members of a group to develop a sense of comfort with one another and trust in the group. Leaders use icebreakers to support members as well as to identify and assess the cultural undertones at the first meeting. Icebreakers help the leader to understand the members, respond to their group needs, and plan the activities that members might enjoy.

This exercise begins with one of the following icebreakers:

- Form pairs to interview each other about movies, clothes, or sports, and then introduce each other to the group.
- Form pairs to build an object or collage together and then present this object or collage to the group.
- Play the memory game in which the first person states her/his name, the second person repeats this name and then adds her/his own name, and so on until all of the names of the members of the group are known and remembered by all.
- Toss a ball of wool to one member while stating a favourite food/sport/idea. That person then tosses the ball to another member until all members are tied together.

After everyone has had a chance to participate in the icebreaker, the leader initiates a discussion on how and when such icebreakers can be used, keeping in mind ability level and age-appropriateness. The exercise concludes with the group developing a list of effective icebreakers that can be used with groups of children and youth.

members, and the members develop confidence through the unit. Members gradually develop a sense of safety, predictability, acceptance and belonging in the group or gang. This reciprocal relationship creates internal integration or cohesion.

The culture of the leader plays off the culture of each member and the culture of the group or gang as a whole. The leader's culture, for example, may be authoritarian and power-centric. When the members' culture is submissive, the leader is able to take control and become more and more authoritarian. When the members' culture is also authoritarian, the members may quarrel with the leader and with one another over leadership. If the leader does not adjust his or her own authoritarian culture, the task may never be accomplished, and members may gradually drift away from the continuous cycle of arguments and power struggles.

When this happens it is important for the leader to acknowledge the power struggle rather than avoid it. Continuing is pretentious at best, harmful and bullying at worst. A group leader can frame the situation of a disintegrating and fractious group as an opportunity for growth rather than an opportunity for more control and rules: "I guess support group isn't the right name for our group right now. You all seem to agree that you are beginning to feel afraid to speak up, and some feel criticized rather than supported. Am I hearing you right? Okay, this is one thing we all agree on. What else can we agree on?" A gang leader might use a similar tactic, single out the suspected troublemaker, or threaten members with punishment for dissension. Through these leader-member dynamics the cultures of leaders and members begin to change to match the culture of the gang or group. This shift does not happen at the first meeting

Photo 12.2 Body language and clothing convey gang culture.

but evolves over time as the membership becomes stronger through consistent attendance and active participation.

Interaction happens through established communication patterns. Interaction may follow the maypole pattern of communication, with the leader asking or prompting each member to speak in turn. This prompt may be phrased as a challenge: "What're you doin' here?" It may be phrased as a question: "What are your hopes for this group?" Alternatively, this prompt may be a look or a nudge. Either verbally or with body language, the leader asks each member for input, and the member replies. The leader then asks the next member the same question, and so on. The regularity of the maypole pattern is comforting and safe in an initial meeting in which the members do not know one another and do not trust the leader or the process. The maypole pattern also establishes the leader as the pivot around which the group or gang revolves.

Sometimes members take turns talking in a **round robin** pattern, and the leader steps back from the questioner role. The leader actively observes as each member makes a statement or introduction and each speaks in turn. Sometimes a visual cue such as a talking stone or feather is passed around to signal each member's opportunity to talk while other members listen. This has a comforting regularity for members and adds to the feeling of safety and security. The round robin pattern can be used to end meetings, also. In traditional treatment groups, the members may sit or stand in a circle, holding a length of ribbon or rope as each member states a positive thought about the group meeting. When the meetings end, the ribbon is cut, and a piece is given to each member.

Sometimes interaction stalls or breaks down when one member is more animated or defensive or aggressive than others. This member may block any action suggested by the leader, asking endless questions or telling unrelated personal stories that stop the action. This member may joke about the task or action or about other members, scoffing and making snide remarks that stop the gang or group from developing cohesion. The leader may engage this member in one-to-one dialogue called the **hot-seat** pattern of communication. Other members observe the tone and mood of this intensive interchange and may learn to keep quiet and withhold their own opinions or to challenge one another. Soon the members start to hot-seat one another.

Beyond maypole, round robin, and hot-seat modes of group interaction is a democratic communication pattern called **floating** communication in which members are free to contribute at any time. They learn to take turns, listen empathically, advise their peers, share their stories and opinions, and deal with other members' anger, lateness, silence, or sadness. This interaction encourages members to take responsibility for one another and for the whole unit; for example, a member might challenge another member who interrupts, teases, intimidates, or laughs at others.

The culture of the whole group or gang affects each member's contribution and the entire pattern of interaction. In the dynamic of communication, the child or youth tests certain words and certain ideas; in a sense, this is a skill-practising session. This is a chance to rephrase, to explain, maybe to back off, and to express other thoughts. The member develops these social skills and communication skills within the safety of the gang or group until the skills are razor-sharp and ready for the street.

Note from the Field   12.1

Fitting in with the Group

Chantal, a 12-year-old girl, is referred by the court to your social skills group after her second charge of shoplifting. She arrives late for the pre-group meeting and appears to be very unwilling to talk. Her denim jacket smells strongly of smoke. In the ensuing half hour, you create a genogram together and she describes her position as the eldest daughter in a blended family. Her father's partner has three younger children, aged 6, 4, and 18 months, whom Chantal occasionally babysits in the evening. Although she is not paid to babysit, she says she enjoys her younger stepsisters and thinks they are "cute." She especially loves the baby and expresses the wish to have a baby of her own some day. Chantal denies the shoplifting charge and says that the clerks were hassling her and that she only wanted to show the clothes to her friends. It appears that Chantal has very few friends because most of her evenings and weekends are spent either babysitting or helping out at home. She says that her stepmom sometimes gets on her case about chores and that her parents are "really mad" about the shoplifting. Chantal says she doesn't really have time to go to the group but will join "if she really has to." How would you assess this group's suitability for Chantal?

The Importance of Social Networks

Groups and gangs offer children and youth the opportunity to play and work with a common focus, problem solve, collect ideas from others, discuss, and argue. The learning opportunities are immense and multi-faceted. Sugata Mitra noted this when he began his hole-in-the-wall experiments in New Delhi in 1999. His research team embedded a computer in a wall in front of a public lot that was used as a toilet by local street children. The team also installed a camera to record the interaction between computer and passersby. Over a six-month period, the camera captured peer learning and social interaction as the children learned computer skills, taught one another English, argued about software programs, and acquired functional numeracy and literacy skills through play. Over 300 children interacted with the computer, and typically this interaction was in groups of 3 to 20 children aged 6 to 12 years old.

The researchers evaluated the effectiveness of this group learning and replicated the hole-in-the-wall experiment in other Indian cities. Their evaluation results prompted more hole-in-the-wall experiments in Asia and in South America. It was found that street children and youth learned more skills in groups than would ever be possible in the far more expensive traditional school setting. Mitra (2009) explains,

"They were driven purely by their own interests. Conventional pedagogy, on the other hand, focuses on the teacher's ability to disseminate information in a classroom setting." It seems that the absence of adult teachers and the resulting reliance on peers is a key ingredient in the effectiveness of these groups. Sometimes the six-year-olds give directions and sometimes an older child does. The leader (director) is the one with skills, not necessarily the eldest. In the hole-in-the-wall experiments, none of the children spoke English at the outset, and most spoke some rudimentary English words by the end of the six months. The children learned a new language and skill set and developed problem-solving and group skills out of necessity; they had to work together in order to play on the computer (Mitra, 2013).

Members of groups and gangs share experiences, advice, and stories of survival. This is empowering for the member who feels isolated and alone in a personal narrative. Other members have solutions, each one different and each one unique to that person. Each member can provide an example of resiliency, as well as potential stability and social support for other members. A child or youth who hears another member talk about a treatment centre or a foster home as being a positive place, for example, is more likely to be open to going there. Victims of sexual abuse, victims of war, children of divorced parents, children whose parents are incarcerated, youth who live in poverty, and youth with addictions—these children and youth know the value of support from their peers.

From middle childhood onwards peer-based social networks are more influential than family members (Bastiampillai, Allison, and Chan, 2012), and this influence is often dubbed **social contagion**. This term suggests a diseased spread of negativity. Obesity, smoking, depression, drug use, and feelings of anger, competence, worthlessness, helplessness, and happiness spread through social networks as one person influences another and as tasks change to suit the evolving mood and behaviour of the membership. Social contagion

Photo 12.3 Social contagion leads children to take risks and develop new skills.

© vario images GmbH & Co.KG/Alamy

is a powerful force that can also be called social learning, a positive influence in encouraging the development and testing of skills.

Despite this evidence of the power of social contagion, most groups for children and youth are still controlled by adults. Children may be assigned to do small group work without an adult, but their small group reports are written or spoken in front of the large group and screened, chosen, and assessed by the adult leader. Similarly, provincial, territorial, and national youth groups bring their reports and their discussion papers forward to adults who then decide on continued funding and support for these groups. This is to be expected in our socio-political structure. Children do have much to learn from adults, and adult leadership is helpful when children are learning a skill (e.g., skiing, karate, woodworking), developing socio-emotionally (social skills groups, co-operative playgroups), or recovering from traumatic life events (bereavement groups).

Children are *placed* in groups but they *choose* gangs, although sometimes this choice is coerced or influenced by peers. This element of choice changes the child's participation to "voluntary" and makes the length and the quality of membership the child's prerogative until, of course, adult or peer sanctions may end or change membership. It is this element of choice that differentiates gang membership from group membership. This choice may be based on factors such as the child's situation or the gang activities. Both may preclude the child's participation in groups and may actually prompt the child's participation in gangs.

Point to Consider   12.3

Forum Theatre

As both a co-leader and observer of treatment groups for over a decade, I have often witnessed children's unease, discomfort, and misery at being asked to act out their emotions. Regardless of the skill and enthusiasm of the group leader, not all children feel comfortable in a performance role and not all children benefit from public performance. The additional stress of role-playing in front of peers can compound a child's problems and cause the child to withdraw further or become hostile and aggressive. In the gang situation, role-play also is demanded, albeit in a less structured and more spontaneous way. The shy child may try to engage and act out situations but the role-play may prove too stressful and the shy child may find recourse in sidelining, encouraging other members to take the lead parts.

An exception to the discomfort of role-play is forum theatre, developed by Augusto Boal and used with children in many countries. Forum theatre involves both players and audience in finding solutions to local structural oppression. There are three set roles in forum theatre: oppressor, oppressed, and joker. The first two children act out the local problem—one child playing the oppressor and the other child playing the oppressed. The third child, the joker, describes what is happening. The joker asks the audience for ideas, new dialogue, or new actions. Everyone (audience and players) is part of the play and everyone is responsible for finding a solution to the oppression. Boal shows how effective this is in positioning problems within the structure and in collectivizing both problems and solutions. Workers who take the structural approach use forum theatre to build the group dynamic and to help children and youth to identify structural determinants relevant to them (Hawkins, 2012).

Some children and youth choose neither groups nor gangs. They may be anxious, depressed, withdrawn, or shy and may not want to join a group of children in which there is social interaction, role play, and close contact with other children. They may be developmentally delayed and may fear the ridicule of other members of the group or gang. They may have a syndrome or disorder (Asperger's syndrome or autistic spectrum disorder, for example) that makes communication with other children and following directions problematic. They may have behaviours that frighten or threaten other children. They may have different norms and values and may find the group or gang threatens their personal norms and values. Alternatively, they may not have the transportation and time to get to the group and may not have the financial resources to buy the equipment to join the group.

In any of the above situations, forced or coerced group membership may prove to be a negative experience; in Steve de Shazer's (1984) terminology, these children are visitors. They do not want to be there (in the group or gang). They may struggle to function as members and may repeatedly fail, an experience that compounds their difficulties and makes them feel more inadequate and socially inept. As Sarah Dufour and Claire Chamberland (2003: 7) explain, "Groups are contraindicated for people whose behaviour is so alien to others that it results in negative rather than positive interactions or when it leads to the failure of others to continue with the group."

From Gangs to Groups

Consider membership in both groups and gangs. The dominant Canadian culture overtly encourages membership in groups. Adults subsidize and sanction membership in adult-led groups such as Girl Guides, choirs, sports groups, and social skills groups. The dominant culture overtly discourages children from gang membership, imposing sanctions on gang members. At the same time, structural determinants such as poverty, violence, and inadequate educational and child welfare systems encourage children and youth to form and join gangs (Wortley and Tanner, 2006; Wood and Alleyne, 2010). They get together in gangs for comfort and safety in an unsafe world. The gang provides them with a secure base from which to operate. "Gang violence is a visible, public culmination of violence that begins in the private sphere and that shapes children's lives" (Singh and Fairholm, 2012: 352).

Jharna Chatterjee (2006: 4) describes the effects of structural determinants such as poverty in encouraging youth gang membership. His study also pinpoints mesosystem factors such as family-related difficulties, lack of school success and low attachment to school, and community violence and disorganization. Chatterjee describes how these factors interact when marginalized youth without educational, employment, and recreational opportunities look around their neighbourhood for an outlet and find only weapons, alcohol, and drugs. When they do this, the only safe place they find is their neighbourhood gang.

A lack of community resources in poor neighbourhoods does not in any way justify the violence in these gangs, but it does provide a context for understanding why youth turn to gangs and violence and suggests what sort of structural interventions could be developed to counter the violence, or at least convert gangs to groups. When structural issues change—alternate educational facilities open, community houses develop, or part-time employment becomes available—gang membership tends to decrease or at least evolve into something more positive. Interventions such as Chicago's Little Village Program and Boston's Operation Ceasefire, for example, have been highly successful in decreasing gang membership. Both are structural approaches that do not focus on the elimination of gangs. Instead, both interventions follow the Comprehensive Gang Model, developed by the late Irving Spergel, a leading authority on gangs. Rather than criminalizing gangs, Spergel (2007) urged adults to implement structural interventions such as community mobilization and the provision of academic, economic, and social opportunities for youth who are drawn to gangs. Gang structure is not dismantled but is used to transmit messages about viable and safe opportunities for gang members. Gangs become a source for safe and secure employment and housing opportunities, reducing the members' need to carry handguns for self-protection. In this way, the structural changes obviate the felt need for protection and security through violence.

Programme de suivi intensif de Montréal also follows the Comprehensive Gang Model. Prevention, intervention, and suppression are the three prongs of the program that offers street gang members education, employment, and real power in the program. Similarly, the Remix Project in Toronto offers cultural opportunities for 40 to 50 street gang members each year. Choices Youth Program (Winnipeg) and InReach (Kitchener, Ontario) are adult-led programs that focus on gang members and at-risk youth, with the Winnipeg program specifically targeting children in Grades 6 through 8. The support offered in these Canadian programs is structural and involves the prime determinant identified in Chapter 1: poverty. When children and youth have access to employment and educational opportunities in safe spaces in which their voice is respected and valued, gang membership loses its luster.

Vancouver media regularly report on Indo-Canadian youth gangs. Filipino-Canadian Albert Lopez describes his own membership in one such gang. Albert fed and cared for his siblings while his parents worked. He juggled school, caregiving, and learning English with little or no support from either school or community. In fact, his high school classmates called him "Flip" and laughed at his attempts to learn English. When he reacted angrily school authorities expelled him, along with 20 other Filipino-Canadian students.

This drove him to join a gang that engaged in criminal activity while also giving him a sense of security and a chance to earn money. Albert's experience replicates that of other high school boys as described by Sandra Smidt (2013: 87): "Adolescent boys often feel that they receive no respect at school but can earn respect on the streets through their adoption of the culture of the streets." Fortunately, a less violent political group called Filipino-Canadian Youth Alliance offered him the opportunity to speak out about racism in his high school and to take anti-racist political action (Makilan, 2007). At the same time, the school system opened up to him and accepted him as a student again. Albert's experience, described by Aubrey Makilan (2007) in his report on youth gangs in Vancouver, demonstrates the power of timely and appropriate intervention that can draw children and youth away from gangs and into groups.

Summary

In this chapter, we explored the similarities between groups and gangs—how they are formed, their styles of leadership, communication, and group dynamics. We also saw the differences and the dangers offered by the third gang model: the Purposive Gang. This understanding will help you to design and develop groups that are play-based and exciting, groups that appeal to children and youth while supporting their strengths and encouraging indigenous leadership. Recognizing strengths has been an ongoing theme, and both gangs and groups offer their members an opportunity to support the strengths of other members and to have their own strengths validated, too.

Review Questions

1. What is the first natural group to which a child belongs? Explain why this is a "group" rather than a "gang."
2. List the five gang models, correlating each model with a type of group.
3. Compare and contrast treatment groups, task groups, and mutual aid groups.
4. Compare group leaders and gang leaders according to their rewards, coercion, legitimacy, reference, and expertise.
5. What factors make gang membership empowering? Can these same factors be applied to group membership? Why or why not?
6. How does the leader's culture affect the members, and what happens when these cultures clash?
7. State the four styles of communication in a group or gang, and explain how each one evolves as members begin to feel empowered.

8. What do children and youth learn by being members in groups and gangs?
9. What factors could influence a gang member to join a group instead?
10. Name four Canadian projects designed to join with youth to tackle structural determinants that support gang membership. How do you think they will succeed?

Discussion Questions

1. Have you ever belonged to a gang or known someone who has belonged to a gang? If so, how does this experience compare with the information presented in this chapter? What information about gangs do you feel is missing?
2. Imagine that your task is to facilitate a group for 10-year-old boys who have been excluded from the classroom because of their aggressive behaviour. What kind of group would you choose? How would you design this group, and how would you encourage the boys to become customers rather than visitors in this group?
3. One of the groups described in this chapter is forum theatre. Why do you think this kind of group works so well with children? Suggest other kinds of groups that you have found children voluntarily join and enjoy.

Afterword

Setting Structural and Strengths-Based Targets

I shot an arrow into the air,
It fell to earth, I knew not where.

—Henry Wadsworth Longfellow

Interventions with children are often random shots in the air, and where they land is anyone's guess. We try one intervention and, when it does not work, we try another. We review a child's file with its history of failed interventions and sadly note that the original behavioural difficulty is much worse now and that the child is even more troubled and unhappy.

Interventions often are ineffective, although the case file or the agency mythology may suggest the opposite. The child goes back to class; the letter of apology is written; the child promises not to drink. Two weeks later, the behaviour recurs. Another intervention is tried, sometimes at the same agency and sometimes at another one. The first intervention is reapplied over and over again with a continuing lack of success. The worker is now invested in the intervention and believes it to be right; the child is simply being "uncooperative." The child may be described as being "damaged" or having a "mental health issue," umbrella phrases that hold off the rain.

When we look at a child's case file, why do we see these years of repeated interventions and a spiral of escalating behaviours? The answer to this question lies in a systemic lack of ongoing qualitative and quantitative evaluation of intervention effectiveness—in other words, evidence-based practice. Science is replaced by ideology. Interventions are used because we believe in them, whether or not they have been proven to be effective. This lack of intervention evaluation in Canadian child welfare agencies is described by Marie Hoskins and Jennifer White (2010). They cite many examples of the lack of discernment in interventions that continue to be applied because they are "what the agency does" or because "everyone knows they work." The agency may specialize in specific interventions such as residential treatment for addictions. A child being served by that agency is sent to residential treatment, whether or not this intervention is appropriate or what the child would choose. Without the child's commitment to the treatment, this intervention is likely to fail.

Furthermore, the intervention offered by the agency may no longer be relevant to the child. It is offered simply because that funding silo, that executive director, or that board of directors believes in its efficacy. There is no evidence-based practice. Instead, the outcome measurements are based on anecdotes from random children who praise the staff and claim to be "saved." These children are the success stories who are routinely selected as guest speakers at award dinners and annual general meetings. They are the bursary winners, the college graduates, the ones who made it. The edgy youth who are critical of the agency or of their workers; those who are homeless and addicted; and those who are "uncooperative" and are not "saved" by the interventions are never the keynote speakers and they never get the rose bouquets. They are the "failures" or "kids with issues."

But whose failure? Is the child a failure, or are we the failures for using the same tired interventions that fail to meet the needs of today's children? Learning about interventions is learning about self. The questions we ask and the questions we are asked begin to balance out. In each child, we meet our own limitations of service and of self. In each one of our child-specific interventions, we learn about the effectiveness of that intervention for that child at that time, and we learn to question the intervention itself. The next time we use that intervention with a different child, we learn more. Carl Rogers (1980: 66), who never ascribed to the universal wisdom claimed by many workers, remarked, "I have confidence in the young, from whom I have continuously learned."

Lifelong learning includes training and experience. Training is valuable and we need it to work effectively. Yet, to identify only with know-how is to turn the child–worker relationship into one of control. We say—and the child does. We teach—and the child is taught. We order—and the family complies. This power imbalance is contingent on a social construction in which the child is a dependent and helpless person, unable to change without adult intervention. Training sometimes leads us to see children and youth in categories, as subjects for intervention, as labelled case files: "deadbeat dads"; "abuse victims"; and "exceptional children." Analysis of behaviour is important, but it is equally important to see and develop a relationship with the whole person.

The structural and strengths-based approach challenges this traditional biomedical and deficit approach by providing defined structural targets and clear concepts of what achievement means in altering systems for the child: those concentric micro, meso, and macrosystems. In 2014, the federal government took this approach and launched Digital Canada 150. This program involved children in a national hackathon to create CODE (Canadian Open Data Experience) and a public awareness campaign on cyber-bullying. Structural change such as this will undoubtedly impact interventions, and we need to incorporate this impact and adjust. Such a shift may feel new and strange. However, it is clear that the traditional methods of assessing and intervening do not meet the current needs of Canadian children.

Children teach us to pause and observe play, watching each episode closely to uncover hidden meanings within the play. They teach us to listen affirmatively in the here and now and to unravel the subtexts of behaviour. In solitary play, digital play, or in play within groups or gangs children reveal their strengths and their understandings of their personhood. By refocusing on the child as a capable person, and by taking the structural and strengths-based approach, we can change that weary and ultimately costly habit of shooting arrows into the sky. We can hear the lessons children teach us, shoot straight, and finally find the target.

Glossary

Aboriginal According to the 1982 Constitution Act of Canada this collective name for the first peoples of Canada includes Indians, Inuit, and Métis.

abuse Physical, emotional, and/or sexual maltreatment of children.

advocacy Writing or speaking in order to support (advocate for) a person or cause.

affect Demeanour or facial expression.

affidavit Legal and sworn document attesting to facts of relevance in a court case.

affirmation Validation of the importance and worth of feelings, condition, or personhood.

age of majority The threshold of adulthood as legally determined. At the age of majority, a person can be held responsible for personal debts accrued, for example.

AHA! Method Listening method that requires the listener to affirm, stay in the present (here and now), and always be authentic.

antecedent Preceding event, prompt, or trigger that leads to a particular behaviour.

Apgar score Score from 1 to 10 that indicates the appearance, pulse, grimace, activity, and respiration level of an infant in the first one to five minutes of life.

app Application or piece of software that can run on a computer, a mobile phone, or another electronic device.

apprehension Removal of a child from the family because of a perceived risk of physical, sexual, and/or emotional abuse or neglect.

at risk Situation in which the cumulative risk factors in the child's life outweigh the protective factors.

attachment Strong, lifelong commitment that develops, usually from infancy, between a person and that person's significant caregiver or community of caregivers.

attachment injuries Emotional wounds caused by the sudden and inexplicable loss of the attachment figure or by abuse or neglect being perpetrated by this same attachment figure.

attunement Internal working model of a positive relationship between two persons in which each responds to the other's inner emotional messages. When applied to the caregiver–baby dyad, this is described as the caregiver following the baby's cues.

authoritarian Parenting or caregiving style that uses punitive, forceful methods to ensure children obey commands and comply.

authoritative Parenting or caregiving style that provides nurturance and structure for children while still respecting their input.

autobiographical reasoning Lifelong reflective process in which a person tries to make sense of both past and current events as they fit into that person's dominant narrative.

avatar Icon that represents a person, idea, or emotion in a digital game or simulation.

behavioural contracting Verbal or written agreement on the rewards contingent to behaving in certain ways.

best interests of the child Approach that prioritizes the interests and needs of the child over those of the adults (family).

best practice Benchmark agreed to be the ideal way of performing a certain task.

bisexual Person whose sexual orientation is towards both men and women.

blamestorming Reciprocal and self-sustaining process of assigning blame that continues without resolution.

bonding Process in which a socio-emotional or affective bond develops between the infant and the primary caregiver.

boundaries Closeness or proximity between two persons.

bullying Aggressive behaviour intended to cause harm or distress to another.

case note Simple, honest, accurate, and objective recording of an event.

categorization of persons Division of persons into discrete categories or subsets in order to manage or control these persons effectively.

cephalocaudal Neurological development that proceeds downward from the head.

characterization Attribution of particular character traits to certain persons.

chemical restraints Psychotropic medication that is administered in order to restrain, modify, or curb behaviour.

child carers Children who provide care and support to another family member and assume care responsibilities that would usually fall to an adult.

childism Systematic devaluing of children in which children are stereotyped as inferior and incapable, underdeveloped, or still developing as persons.

child protection Legislated state protection of children and youth from abuse and neglect. Child protection services may also include abuse prevention, support to children over the age of eighteen, and support to families.

child support Privately arranged or court-ordered financial support for the child that is paid by the non-custodial parent.

child trafficking Recruitment, transfer, harbouring, or receiving of children by fraudulent means for the purpose of exploitation.

child welfare This is a broader term than child protection and includes the public provision of support to children and their families when they are in need of these supports.

classical conditioning Behavioural learning that associates a neutral stimulus with a significant stimulus for behaviour; for example, keys may be associated with the fun of a drive so that when a child hears keys rattle, the child may smile in anticipation.

client de Shazer's term to describe a person who shows some interest in receiving services but does not necessarily ask for these services.

coercive power Control over others that influences them to do things against their preferences or better judgement.

cognitive-behavioural theory   Theory that behaviour is prompted or motivated by cognition or thinking.

cognitive development   Gradual change or evolution of the organizing and thinking systems of the brain.

collaborative practice   Respectful sharing of viewpoints or power rather than a struggle to control and dominate.

collateral   Person who has some interest in or influence over another.

commodification   Conversion of a person into a consumer good so that the person can be bought, sold, displayed, or transferred to another person.

community capacity building   Process of building on individual and community assets that begins inside the community and continues due to the will of the community.

competence   Ability to perform or function.

conduct disorder   Behaviour labelled as a syndrome and characterized by persistent, repetitive anti-social activities that violate the rights of others. Symptoms of this disorder include physical or verbal aggression directed towards others, repeated violation of age-appropriate social rules and norms, stealing, and lying.

congruence   Being direct and honest in sharing information, provided this information does not harm the person.

conscientization   Internal, exploratory process of reflection during which people develop an understanding of collective oppression and the structural impacts on their lives.

contact comfort   Socio-emotional reassurance provided by close physical contact with a trusted person.

contextualizing   Process of placing an individual's narrative within the ecological environment that impacts the narrative.

co-regulation   Balanced and soothing interaction or acting in response to a person moment by moment in order to calm that person.

co-relational   Interconnected or allied in an equal relationship in which one entity affects the other.

countertransference   Interactive process in which the child's narrative stimulates the worker's unconscious thoughts, emotions, and memories, and the worker responds by projecting these thoughts, emotions, and memories onto the child's narrative.

critical learning periods   Specific times in the life cycle at which a person most readily absorbs crucial information or skills needed to develop. Before or after the critical learning period, this same learning or skill acquisition is more difficult and sometimes impossible.

crowdfunding   Online solicitation of funding for particular projects from an anonymous crowd of online donors.

crowdsourcing   Open call to the online (digital) community for contributions such as services, ideas, or content.

cultural competency   Understanding of personal culture and its inherent bias in relating to the culture of others.

customary adoption   Traditional practice in which a relative or member of the community adopts another woman's child while promising to retain that child's birth name and identity. This practice usually happens within Aboriginal communities.

customer   de Shazer's term for a person who comes voluntarily and willingly to participate in counselling.

cyberbullying   Digital attempt to deliberately and repeatedly harm or harass others. This includes impersonation, fraud, identity theft, spreading rumours or flame throwing, sexual harassment, trolling, and spam.

deculturation   Systematic devaluing and stripping away of the cultural identity of others.

dependency   Degree to which we rely on others to meet our physical, social, spiritual, and emotional needs.

determinants of health   Structural and personal factors that have a major impact on health or wellness.

development   Sequential change or unfolding that is brought about by increasing age and accumulating life experiences. Development can be stopped or slowed down in response to both genetic and environmental factors.

developmentalists   Those who advocate that development occurs in a linear progression through prescribed stages.

developmentally appropriate practice   Provision of structural supports that meet both the individual and developmental needs of the child. This practice is based on close observation of a child or youth's interests, social location, culture, and overall development.

developmental perspective   Theory that children evolve or develop in a linear progression through set stages and that particular milestones must be reached before the child can move on to the next stage.

digital media   Media that can be created, stored, changed, enhanced, and downloaded via a digital device such as a computer or mobile phone.

digital natives   Those who were born into the world of digital technology as contrasted to digital immigrants who were born prior to the advent of digital technology.

distal   Potentiating influence or risk factor rather than an immediate and close risk.

domains   Interrelated areas of human development: physical, cognitive, spiritual, and socio-emotional.

dominant narrative   Family narrative that permeates and overshadows the individual narratives of each member of the family.

e-counselling   Online (digital) counselling.

emotionally focused therapy (EFT)   Therapeutic approach rooted in attachment theory that focuses on intrapsychic and interpersonal processes.

empathy   Ability to understand the feelings and thoughts of another person and to communicate this understanding to that person.

empowerment   Process or experience in which a person gains self-assurance through successfully overcoming obstacles or solving problems.

encrypted   Digitally altered using a code that renders written material unintelligible to unauthorized users.

e-tribe   Online group or community of users with similar interests.

Eurocentrism   Western-centred or European-centred cultural bias that reflects a perspective of privilege and dominance.

evidence-based practice   Practice based on what empirical research demonstrates to be effective.

exception questions   Questions that elicit descriptions of times when identified problems were less severe or absent.

express consent   Oral or written expression of consent that is valid when the person has the mental capacity to understand consent, is fully informed, and freely gives such consent.

externalizing   Placing a problem outside of or external to the person by identifying its role in the person's life and its antecedents.

family systems theory   Theory premised on a concept of the family as a mutually supportive unit rather than as a mere collection of individual members. The members act to keep the unit intact and healthy rather than solely to pursue individual goals.

flaming   Rude, hostile, offensive, and insulting online behaviour that can involve flame trolling in order to throw out flame bait. Flaming can escalate into flame wars.

flash mob   Group that assembles solely to perform one brief action (dance, song, or theatrical event) and then quickly dissolves.

floating   Pattern of communication in which group or gang members dialogue with one another rather than through or to the leader.

fontanel   Space between the bones in the skull of a newborn that allows the newborn's head to be compressed during its passage through the birth canal without this compression causing injury to the brain.

foster care   Temporary, short-term alternative (to the home) placement for a child or youth whose safety in the home is at risk.

foster care drift   Placement practice of moving the child or youth among different foster home, group home, and residential care placements over several years without considering permanency planning.

gang   Three or more people who interact with one another, share similar interests, and have a collective identity.

gender construction   Building of role scripts, cultural norms, expectations, and behaviours related to a specific sex.

gender roles   Culturally and historically specific social and behavioural norms that are arbitrarily assigned to individuals of a specific sex. Gender roles today cross these historic norms but are still dependent on their cultural context.

gender stereotype   Biased and oversimplified generalizations about which gender attributes and roles should apply to which sex.

generationing   Classification of persons according to socially constructed age-restricted generations; for example, teenagers and tweens.

genogram   Pictorial case note of family relationships that is simple to read and that evolves as the family relationships change.

GLBTQ   Acronym that stands for gay, lesbian, bisexual, transsexual, and queer or questioning.

group   Three or more people who interact with one another, share similar interests, and have a collective identity.

group work   Goal-directed activity by individual members in a group and by the group as a whole.

growth-faltering   Non-organic failure of an infant to thrive or grow.

heterosexual   Person attracted to and sexually preferring members of the opposite sex.

homeostasis   State of stability or equilibrium.

homophobia   Irrational fear, hatred, and intolerance of GLBTQ persons.

homosexual   Person attracted to and sexually preferring members of her/his own sex.

hot-seat   Pattern of communication in which a leader engages only one member in dialogue.

implied consent   Unwritten and unspoken (tacit) consent or agreement demonstrated by coming to the worker with a problem or by staying with the worker until help arrives.

imprinting   Pattern of spontaneous attachment to a figure who supplies nutritional needs.

incarceration   Imprisonment or forced detention in an institution such as prison.

infanticide   Murder of a person who is less than one year old.

in loco parentis   Latin phrase meaning "in the place of the parent," which refers to an acceptance of the legal and functional responsibility of a parent.

intersex   Socially constructed category that reflects the wide spectrum of sexual anatomy.

intervention   Action taken to lessen or alleviate an individual's challenges or problems.

intimacy   Contact comfort or feelings of closeness and connection with another person.

joining   Finding that first point of connection or commonality in a working relationship.

kidfluence   Child's coercive influence over family or parent purchases.

learned helplessness   Belief that personal effort does not yield results, a belief that results from multiple experiences of being positioned as vulnerable, incapable, and needy.

lifeline   Drawn line that begins at birth and maps significant events in a person's life.

life space interview   An interview between worker and child that acknowledges, affirms, and reviews a preceding behavioural crisis in order to understand antecedents and triggers.

LIM   Acronym for low income measure after tax, an internationally accepted measure of poverty.

lone mothers   Single mothers who live with their never-married children.

macrosystem   Overarching socio-political and cultural context that affects every aspect of life.

marginalized   Excluded from mainstream society because of bias and discrimination.

maternal deprivation   Theory that a healthy relationship with the mother is crucial to a child's healthy development.

mature minor   Child who is chronologically below the age of majority but who demonstrates the competence and maturity of that age.

maypole   Pattern of communication in which a leader acts as a pivot or maypole around and through which members communicate.

meme   Single humorous unit (melody, image, word, or symbol) that is copied, often with minor changes, and sent out to other Internet users.

mesosystem   Interrelationships among community systems, such as school, daycare, and sports teams, that affect a person living within that community.

metaphor   Word, object, or symbol that is used to represent a problem or difficulty.

microsystem   Immediate and proximal daily environment of a person.

milestone   Marker of a critical learning achievement in a person's development.

mindfulness   Fully attending to the present moment with an open and accepting attitude.

miracle question   Question that prompts visualization of the potential for a better future.

monocultural bias   Ethnocentrism or the tendency to judge or value all cultures from the perspective of one's own culture which is tacitly assumed to be superior.

neglect   Child maltreatment that includes abandonment, inadequate supervision, and failure to provide adequate food, clothing, shelter, and daily care.

neonaticide   Murder of a person in the first 24 hours of life; also called post-natal abortion.

netiquette   Manners or etiquette for communicating online.

netnography   Research that involves participation in an online forum, e-tribe, or other open source social media to observe and record the discussion for analysis.

object relations   Relationships with the important people in our lives and the continuing impact of these relationships on our lives.

open-ended questions   Questions with no definitive answer that allow the respondent to give detailed answers. Open-ended questions can begin with such words as "why," "how," "explain," and "describe."

oppression   Injustice resulting from the domination of one group or person over another group or person; policy and practice that entitles or favours certain persons or groups over others.

paraphrasing   Rewording the speaker's words so that both the speaker and the listener share the same understanding of the meaning of those words.

paraprofessional   Person with specialized knowledge but no professional accreditation.

parentified   Descriptor of young persons who take on the role and responsibility of parenting.

persistent poverty   Chronic poverty that is severe and long-lasting, usually persisting through several generations.

play   Activity that is usually pleasant and voluntary.

play episodes   Specific, time-limited units of play that have a beginning and an end.

play therapy   Approach to working with children through their play towards their self-realization.

post-traumatic growth   (PTG) Personal growth or positive change that results from the survival of trauma.

post-traumatic stress disorder (PTSD)   Debilitating condition that results from experiencing trauma. This condition is characterized by hyperarousal, flashbacks, memory blocks or lapses.

praxis Informed action based on reflection, education, training, and sound practice principles.

presenting problem Expressed problem, rarely the primary one, that is the focus for the child or the family.

promotive factors Developmental assets that promote the healthy development of the child.

protective factors Positive influences that are obvious only when measured against risk factors or factors that have the potential to harm a person.

proximal Immediate or precipitating.

proximodistal Physical growth and development that proceeds outwards from the midline.

psychoanalytic theory Theory based on the premise that intrapsychic processes—repressed memories, dreams, and the unconscious—determine the behaviour of the individual.

re-authoring Development of an alternative, more hopeful personal narrative based on a new understanding of past events.

reframing Paradigm shift that changes the context of an event or incident.

relational aggression Covert aggression such as gossiping, rumour mongering, and exclusion that harms another person's social relationships.

resiliency Positive adaptation to adverse circumstances or the ability to rebound when faced with severe hardships or obstacles.

resistance Lack of co-operation or movement in the opposite direction.

respect Complete acceptance or unconditional positive regard for the person.

restraint Application of physical force to reduce, restrict, or immobilize the ability of an individual to fully move.

risk assessment Systematic classification or measurement of risk in order to predict outcomes.

risk factor Element considered to be a predictor or signal of an undesired outcome.

risk management Attempt to manage and minimize risk by balancing or weighing risk factors against protective factors.

Rogerian model Client-centred social work practice based on mutual respect and shared power and control.

role model Person whose behaviour is patterned by another person.

round robin Pattern of communication in which each group or gang member speaks in turn when prompted by the leader.

routine Regularity and rhythm in activities and tasks.

self-concept Conscious sense of being separate and distinct because of one's intrinsic qualities, relationships, and culture.

self-control Power from within, or a feeling of self-confidence and competence that is evidenced in outward emotional control.

self-injurious behaviour Deliberate destruction of body tissue without suicidal intent.

sexual identity Identification with a sex or sexes associated with or antithetical to personal genitalia.

sexual orientation   Interest in developing a sexual relationship with members of one's own or the opposite sex or both.

silo approach   Person-centred or agency-centred approach to solving social problems that does not include collective problem solving through sharing information, opinions, and expertise.

social capital   Valuable collective investment shared between family and state.

social construction   Socio-political act that attributes social meaning to information, persons, or events through culturally shared assumptions; a view that may be expressed as "context is everything."

social contagion   Spread of emotion through groups of intimates in social networks.

social history   Summary of key life events that is prepared prior to a child being placed for adoption.

social learning   Observational learning that takes place in a social context.

social location   Person's position of relative power that includes that person's race, ethnicity, class, socioeconomic status, gender, and sexual orientation.

social referencing   Looking first to the caregiver to read social clues regarding a new event or a new person in the room.

social structure   Macrosystem that includes the political, legal, economic, health, social, and educational systems as well as the culture, mores, and traditions of the larger society.

sociogram   Visual depiction or mapping of a person's social networks or community.

stereotype   Association of a word or image with an activity, emotion, group, or class of persons. This association is an oversimplification because no one word or image can capture individual differences.

strategy   Action that is deliberately designed and executed to achieve desired objectives.

strengths-based approach   Approach to working with people that focuses on their assets and strengths rather than their deficits.

structural approach   Approach to working with people that focuses on how societal structures and their aligned systems influence and determine people's lives.

structural determinant   Specific macrosystem or structural factor that impacts the individual; for example, sexism or racism.

subpoena   Legal document requiring a person to attend before a court or tribunal as a witness to a legal proceeding.

synapses   Multiple connections between individual nerve cells in the human brain.

synchrony   Natural and ongoing attunement that develops over time between two persons, enabling one person to instantaneously sense the unspoken needs of the other. Synchrony is marked by the split-second timing of responsiveness between the two persons.

tableau   Story that is told through carefully posed figurines or miniatures.

transitory poverty   Income instability that is not expected to last.

trauma   Enduring adverse response to an event such as abuse, death, illness, war, or torture.

trial and error   Unsystematic method of solving problems through repeated attempts until one attempt is successful.

triangulation   Relationship between two persons in which communication or messages are exchanged through a third person.

trolls   Persons who spread inflammatory arguments or off-topic messages online so as to derail a forum or blog.

two-spirited   First Nations descriptor of individuals who are considered to have extra power because they are gay, lesbian, intersex, transsexual, questioning, or queer.

unfriending   Online process on a social media site whereby a person's name is dropped or excluded from the site.

visitor   de Shazer's term for a person who does not participate in services voluntarily but is brought to these services by a control agent or person in authority.

Notes

Chapter 1

1. *The Well-Being of Canada's Young Children* (2011) is the federal government's fifth report about young Canadian children (up to the age of six). It uses data from the 2006 Aboriginal Children's Survey, the 2006 Census, and the *National Longitudinal Survey of Children and Youth (NLSCY)*, Cycles 3, 4, 5, 6, and 7. Because the *NLSCY* does not include children living in the territories, and the Census data does not include children living in Quebec, the report is not inclusive of all Canadian children.

2. Campaign 2000 is a non-partisan, cross-Canada coalition of over 120 national, provincial, and community organizations that advocate for the eradication of child and family poverty in Canada. The complete list of partner organizations is on the Campaign 2000 website at www.campaign2000.ca.

3. Heather O'Neill's novel *Lullabies for Little Criminals* (2006) portrays the daily life of Baby, a child living in a poor Montreal neighbourhood rife with homelessness, hunger, addictions, and criminality. Baby's father is a single dad struggling with poverty and addictions, and Baby is seen by her neighbours and her teachers as a little "criminal-in-waiting." O'Neill's descriptor aptly captures the seemingly hopeless situation of children who struggle with persistent poverty.

4. The minimum age for employment varies according to the province and territory. See The Workers' Mandate section for more detail.

5. This statistic was released by Statistics Canada in May 2013 and shocked Aboriginal leaders. The full article, "Nearly half of children in foster care Aboriginal, Statistics Canada," can be read at APTN National News, May 8, 2013, http://aptn.ca/pages/news/2013/05/08/nearly-half-of-children-in-foster-care-aboriginal-statistics-canada/.

6. The story of Jordan's Principle can be read on the "Jordon's Principle" webpage on the First Nations Child and Family Caring Society of Canada website at http://www.fncaringsociety.com/jordans-principle.

Chapter 2

1. The Famous Five are five Canadian women (all from Alberta) who advocated in support of the Persons case of 1927: Emily Murphy, Irene Marryat Parlby, Nellie Mooney McClung, Louise Crummy McKinney, and Henrietta Muir Edwards. The Supreme Court of Canada upheld the ruling, supported by the British North America Act, that women were not persons and, therefore, could not sit in the Canadian Senate. With the help of Canadian Prime Minister Mackenzie King, the Famous Five appealed the Supreme Court of Canada's decision to the Judicial Committee of the Privy Council in England, at the time the highest court of appeal for Canada. They won in 1929, and, in 1930, the first Canadian female senator took her place in the Canadian Senate.

2. This legislation regarding sexual activity is further explained on the Government of Canada's Department of Justice webpage, "Age of Consent to Sexual Activity"; see http://www.justice.gc.ca/eng/rp-pr/other-autre/clp/faq.html.

3. David Bjorklund (2007: 172–6) describes systems such as BabyPlus and the Classwomb that aim to educate the fetus, as well as instruments such as the "pregaphone" that purport to enable a mother to talk to her fetus. Even without such devices, the fetus can hear from about the fourth prenatal month and, as a result, distinguishes the sound of the mother's voice from others at birth.

4. The multimedia stories of youth on the verge of losing their child welfare funding can be heard on the Youth in Care Canada website at http://www.youthincare.ca/.

Chapter 3

1. *NLSCY* provides data for researchers only, and it is listed on the Statistics Canada website as "inactive," which implies that it has been discontinued. The latest cycle (8) was released in 2010. It tracks over 56,000 children and

youth and can be viewed at http://www23. statcan.gc.ca/imdb/p2SV.pl?Function=getIns tanceList&SDDS=4450&InstaId=16044&Sur vId=25609.

2. The American Psychological Association (APA) provides a summary of this research at http://www.apa.org/helpcenter/sexual-orien-tation.aspx.

3. The 10 per cent estimate is from the 2010 CHEO pamphlet, "What You Need to Know about ... Sexual Orientation and Supporting Children and Youth Who Are Gay, Lesbian, Bisexual, Two-spirit, Queer, & Questioning," which can be downloaded at http://www.cheo. on.ca/uploads/Gay,%20Lesbian%20and%20 Bisexual%20Youth/LGBT%20youth.pdf.

Chapter 4

1. In this chapter the caregiver is assumed to be female, although many caregivers, guardians, and parents of children are male. This sex-specific attribution is made because the references are largely to infants and, in infancy, caregivers are predominantly female.

2. This estimate of seven moves per foster child was made by Andrée Cazabon, director of the National Film Board of Canada film *Wards of the Crown* (2005). A former foster child herself, Cazabon lives in Ontario today and is an award-winning filmmaker and national advocate for children in care in Canada.

3. In addition to David Kirschner, many other psychologists have studied the effects and the pathology of Adopted Child Syndrome. These psychologists include Joyce Maguire Pavao, Katarina Wegar, David M. Brodzinsky, and Marshall D. Schecter.

4. According to the 2011 Census, roughly 15 per cent or 213,400 of the 1,400,685 persons of Aboriginal descent in Canada speak an Aboriginal language. See Statistics Canada, 2011, "Linguistic Characteristics of Canadians," http://www12.statcan.gc.ca/census-recensement/2011/as-sa/98-314-x/98-314-x2011001-eng.cfm.

Chapter 5

1. "Minor" and "major" are terms that relate to the legal age of majority or of adult responsibility. The age of majority is 18 in the provinces of Ontario, Quebec, Manitoba, Saskatchewan, Alberta, and Prince Edward Island. In all other provinces and in the territories, the age of majority is 19.

2. This happens when one parent has custody of one child and the other parent has custody of a sibling. The parents may live in the same city but deal with different child welfare agencies in that city. These agencies are bound by confidentiality not to disclose client information without express consent.

3. The RCMP has a national sex offender registry that is inaccessible to the public. This may change with the passage of Bill C-26 which had second reading in the House on June 2, 2014.

4. This process is called community mapping. Peter Benson (2006) presents a 156-item survey that can be modified to suit individual communities. Implementing this survey is one way to map community assets or strengths.

Chapter 6

1. Katharine Kelly and Mark Totten (2002) describe the singularity of the child's culture within the family in *When Children Kill: A Social-Psychological Study of Youth Homicide*. Within one family only one child commits murder while the others appear to be reticent and non-aggressive. Similarly, the parents may be violent and homicidal, but their only child may be the opposite.

Chapter 7

1. Parenting books advise listening to children but this listening is often just a foil for interjecting parental wisdom, judgement, or direction. The following popular parenting books feature this strategy of offering guidance rather than listening: Adele Faber and Elaine Mazlish, *How to Talk So Kids Will Listen and Listen So Kids Will Talk* (2002); Kevin Leman, *Parenting Your Powerful Child: How to Bring an End to the Everyday Battles* (2013); and Nancy Rose, Dorothy Carico Smith, Dianne O'Connell, *Raise the Child You've Got—Not the One You Want: Why Everyone Thrives When Parents Lead with Acceptance* (2013).

Chapter 8

1. These poems and songs can be found on Ingrid Johnson's website, *In the Closet Productions*, http://www.intheclosetproductions.com.

Chapter 9

1. In 2013, the *Canadian Internet Registration Authority Factbook* reported that Canadians are the heaviest Internet users in the world,

despite the high cost of broadband speed in Canada. The world average for Internet use is 24.4 hours per month per person, and the Canadian average is 45.6 hours per month per person. For more information, including reasons for this frequent Internet use, see *Huffington Post*, "World's Heaviest Internet Users: Canada Tops List Despite Uncompetitive Prices, Speed" (2013, January 22) http://www.huffingtonpost.ca/2013/01/22/canada-worlds-heaviest-internet-users_n_2527319.html.

2. Faye Mishna and co-authors (2012: 63) give the statistic of 98 per cent but qualify this with references from 2010.

3. See *Huffington Post*, "Zora Ball, First Grader, Becomes Youngest Person to Develop Mobile Game App," (2013, April 2), http://www.huffingtonpost.com/2013/02/04/zora-ball_n_2586140.html4.

4. See Hopeworks 'N Camden's website, www.hopeworks.org/, for more information about the organization.

5. Haydn Shaughnessy's March 11, 2013 article in *Forbes.com*, "Kony 2012: Successes and Failings in the Stop Kony Campaign" summarizes the quick reaction from youth (largely 13- to 17-year-olds) to the Stop Kony Campaign. See http://www.forbes.com/sites/haydnshaughnessy/2012/03/11/kony-2012-successes-and-failings-in-the-stop-kony-campaign/.

6. More information on continuous partial attention and the Attention Project can be found on Linda Stone's website, http://lindastone.net/qa/continuous-partial-attention.

7. The story of Brandon Crisp was told in the CBC *Fifth Estate* documentary, *Top Gun*. This documentary identified Brandon's problem to be the violent games he was seeing. Later reviews of both the videogames and Brandon's gaming showed that the violence of the games did not factor into his accidental death.

8. These materials can be downloaded for free from the website of the Office of the Privacy Commissioner of Canada at http://www.priv.gc.ca/youth-jeunes/index_e.asp.

Chapter 10

1. The deaths of children killed by staff who restrain them are usually investigated only by the chief coroner. This investigation is recorded in a report and sometimes this investigation leads to an inquiry. Injuries of children through restraint may be investigated by child protection agencies in individual municipalities. There are no national statistics on these deaths and injuries because child welfare is a provincial or territorial concern. Advocacy groups for these injured and killed children are volunteer-driven and donor-funded, so tend to be short-lived. One such advocacy group is People Assisting Parents Association (http://www.pa-pa.ca/impact.html).

2. I have attended many child protection case reviews in which the attending psychiatrist prescribed medications for children he or she had never met. These prescriptions were made at the request of the social worker. Children did not attend these case reviews and were often not seen by the psychiatrist until several months later.

3. Munch (2012) shows that, in 2010/2011, 34 per cent of incarcerated female youth were Aboriginal and 24 per cent of incarcerated male youth were Aboriginal. Munch's statistics on former children in care are taken from the National Crime Prevention Centre's *A Statistical Snapshot of Youth at Risk and Youth Offending in Canada* (2012: 3), which also indicates that 48 per cent of incarcerated youth are former youth in care.

Chapter 11

1. The child would have to apply for this permit. The permit allows the child to get health benefits and remain in Canada for a maximum of 180 days. Details are explained on a Government of Canada webpage, "Protection and Assistance for Victims of Human Trafficking" at http://www.cic.gc.ca/english/information/applications/trp.asp.

2. BC's *Action Plan to Combat Trafficking in Persons* is a living document with continual updates and may be viewed online at http://www.pssg.gov.bc.ca/octip/about.htm.

Afterword

1. Further information on Digital Canada 150 can be viewed at www.ic.gc.ca/eic/site/028.nsf/eng/home.

References

Abramovich, Alexa. 2013. "No fixed address: Young, queer, and restless," in *Youth Homelessness in Canada: Implications for Policy and Practice*, edited by Stephen Gaetz, Bill O'Grady, Kristy Bucchieri, Jeff Karabanow, and Allyson Marsolais, 387–405. Toronto: Canadian Homelessness Research Network Press.

Acier, Didier, and Laurence Kern. 2011. "Problematic internet use: Perceptions of addictions counsellors," *Computers and Education* 56, 4: 983–9.

Action Canada. 2013. "Who cares about young carers? Raising awareness for an invisible population," February 6, *Scribd*, www.scribd.com/doc/124089317/Who-Cares-About-Young-Carers-Raising-Awareness-for-an-Invisible-Population.

Ainsworth, Mary D. Salter, Mary C. Blehar, Everett Waters, and Sally Wall. 1978. *Patterns of Attachment: A Psychological Study of the Strange Situation*. Hillsdale, NJ: Erlbaum.

Akhtar, Monisha C. 2011. "Remembering, replaying, and working through: The transformation of trauma in children's play," in *Play and Playfulness: Developmental, Cultural, and Clinical Aspects*, edited by Monisha C. Akhtar, 85–104. Lanham, MD: Jason Aronson.

Ambert, Anne-Marie. 2007. *The Rise in the Number of Children and Adolescents Who Exhibit Problematic Behaviours: Multiple Causes*. Ottawa: Vanier Institute of the Family.

Ames, E. 1997. *The Development of Romanian Orphanage Children Adopted to Canada*. Final Report to National Welfare Grants Program, Human Resources Development Canada. Burnaby, BC: Simon Fraser University.

Anglin, James. 2003. *Pain, Normality, and the Struggle for Congruence: Reinterpreting Residential Care for Children and Youth*. London: Haworth Press.

Aphek, Edna. 2000. "A study in reciprocity: Minimizing the digital divide and the intergeneration gap: Children tutor seniors at computer and internet skills and get a lesson in history." *21Learn.org*, accessed November 2, 2014, www.21learn.org/archive/a-study-in-reciprocity-minimizing-the-digital-divide-and-the-intergeneration-gap-children-tutor-seniors-at-computer-and-internet-skills-and-get-a-lesson-in-history/.

Armstrong, Jeanette C. 2005. "Blue against white," in *An Anthology of Native Literature*, edited by Daniel David Moses and Terry Goldie, 240–2. Toronto: Oxford University Press.

Arsenault, Michael. 2008. "Child's play," *The Walrus* (Oct.–Nov.): 26–8.

Ávila, JuliAnna, and Jessica Zacher Pandya, eds. 2013. *Critical Digital Literacies as Social Praxis: Intersections and Challenges*. New York: Peter Lang.

Axline, Virginia M. 1964. *Dibs: In Search of Self*. Boston: Houghton Mifflin.

———. 1969. *Play Therapy*. Boston: Houghton Mifflin.

Baker, Maureen. 2005. *Families: Changing Trends in Canada*. Toronto: McGraw-Hill Ryerson.

———. 2007. *Choices and Constraints in Family Life*. Toronto: Oxford University Press.

Bala, Nicholas, Michael K. Zopf, and Robin Vogl, eds. 2004. *Canadian Child Welfare Law: Children, Families and the State*. Toronto: Thompson Educational.

Bandura, Albert. 1997. *Self-Efficacy: The Exercise of Control*. New York: W.H. Freeman.

Barbara, Angela M., and Farzana Doctor. 2007. *Asking the Right Questions 2: Talking with Clients about Sexual Orientation and Gender Identity in Mental Health, Counselling and Addiction Settings*. Toronto: Centre for Addiction and Mental Health.

Barcons, Natalia, Neus Abrines, Carme Brun, Claudio Sartini, Victoria Fumado, and Diana Marre. 2014. "Attachment and adaptive skills in children of international adoption," *Child & Family Social Work* 19, 1: 89–98.

Barford, S.W., and W.J. Whelton. 2010. "Understanding burnout in child and youth care workers," *Child and Youth Care Forum* 39, 4: 271–87.

Baril, R., P. Lefebvre, and P. Merrigan. 2000. "Quebec family policy: Impact and options," *Choices* 6, 1: 1–52.

Barnett, Laura. 2008. *The "Spanking" Law: Section 43 of Criminal Code*. Library of Parliament, Parliamentary Information and Research Service, PRB 05-10E, revised June 20, http://www.parl.gc.ca/content/lop/researchpublications/prb0510-e.htm.

Barnett, Lisa M., Trina Hinkley, Anthony D. Okely, Kyle Hesketh, and Jo Salmon. 2012. "Use of electronic games by young children and fundamental movement skills?" *Perceptual and Motor Skills* 114: 1023–34.

Baron, Stephen. 2013. "Why street youth become involved in crime," in *Youth Homelessness in Canada: Implications for Policy and Practice*, edited by Stephen Gaetz, Bill O'Grady, Kristy Bucchieri, Jeff Karabanow, and Allyson Marsolais, 353–68. Toronto: Canadian Homelessness Research Network Press.

Barron, Christie L. 2000. *Giving Youth a Voice: A Basis for Rethinking Adolescent Violence*. Halifax, NS: Fernwood.

Barter, Ken. 2005. "Alternative approaches to promoting the health and well-being of children: Accessing community resources to support resilience," in *Handbook for Working with Children and Youth: Pathways to Resilience across Cultures and Contexts*, edited by Michael Ungar, 343–55. Thousand Oaks, CA: Sage.

———. 2009. "Community capacity building: A re-conceptualization of services for the protection of children," in *Canadian Social Welfare*, edited by Joanne C. Turner and J. Francis Turner, 270–88. Toronto: Pearson.

Bastiampillai, Tarun, Stephen Allison, and Sherry Chan. 2012. "Is depression contagious? The importance of social networks and the implications of contagion theory," *Australia & New Zealand Journal of Psychiatry* 47, 4: 299–301.

Bauerlein, Mark, ed. 2011. *The Digital Divide*. London, UK: Penguin.

Beauvais, Caroline, and Jane Jenson. 2001. *Two Policy Paradigms: Family Responsibility and Investing in Children*. Ottawa: Canadian Policy Research Networks.

Beihl, Hans. 2011. "Treating psychological problems with drugs: Some thoughts," *BC Psychologist*: 12–14.

Bennett, Darcie, and Lobat Sadrehashemi. 2008. *Broken Promises: Parents Speak about B.C.'s Child Welfare System*. Vancouver: PIVOT.

Benson, Peter L. 2006. *All Kids Are Our Kids: What Communities Must Do to Raise Caring and Responsible Children and Adolescents*. San Francisco: Jossey-Bass.

Béres, Laura. 2009. "Mindfulness and reflexivity: The no-self as reflexive practitioner," in *Mindfulness and Social Work*, edited by Steven F. Hick, 57–75. Chicago: Lyceum.

Bettelheim, Bruno. 1987. "The importance of play," *Atlantic Monthly* 3 (March 1): 35–46, accessed April 1, 2014, www.theatlantic.com/magazine/archive/1987/03/the-importance-of-play/305129/.

Bitensky, Susan H. 2006. *Corporal Punishment of Children: A Human Rights Violation*. Ardsley, NY: Transnational.

Bjorklund, David F. 2007. *Why Youth Is Not Wasted on the Young: Immaturity in Human Development*. Maiden, MA: Blackwell.

Blackstock, Cindy, and Nico Trocmé. 2005. "Community-based child welfare for Aboriginal children," in *Handbook for Working with Children and Youth: Pathways to Resilience across Cultures and Contexts*, edited by Michael Ungar, 105–20. Thousand Oaks, CA: Sage.

Blackstock, Cindy, Terry Cross, John George, Ivan Brown, and Jocelyn Formsma. 2006. *Reconciliation in Child Welfare: Touchstones of Hope for Indigenous Children, Youth, and Families*. Ottawa: First Nations Child and Family Caring Society of Canada.

Blackwell, Tom. 2011. "'Prozac defence' stands in Manitoba teen's murder case." *National Post*, December 7, http://news.nationalpost.com/2011/12/07/prozac-defence-stands-in-manitoba-teens-murder-case/.

Blatchford, Christie. 2013. "Catholic Children's Aid Society testimony in Jeffrey Baldwin case not off to an auspicious start," *National Post*, October 15, http://fullcomment.nationalpost.com/2013/10/15/christie-blatchford-catholic-childrens-aid-society-testimony-in-jeffrey-baldwin-case-not-off-to-an-auspicious-start/.

Bottoms, Bette L., Aaron G. Rudnicki, and Michelle A. Epstein. 2007. "A retrospective study of factors affecting the disclosure of childhood sexual and physical abuse," in *Child Sexual Abuse: Disclosure, Delay, and Denial*, edited by Margaret-Ellen Pipe, Michael E. Lamb, Yael Orbach, and Ann-Christin Cederborg, 175–94. Mahwah, NJ: Lawrence Erlbaum Associates.

Bowlby, John. 1969. *Attachment and Loss*. Vol. 1, *Attachment*. London: Hogarth Press.

———. 1988. *A Secure Base: Parent–Child Attachment and Healthy Human Development*. London: Routledge.

Brant, Beth. 2005. "A long story," in *An Anthology of Native Literature*, edited by Daniel David Moses and Terry Goldie, 145–50. Toronto: Oxford University Press.

Brazier, David. 2013. "Mindfulness reconsidered," *European Journal of Psychotherapy & Counselling* 15, 2: 116–26.

Brendtro, Larry K. 2004. "From coercive to strength-based intervention: Responding to the needs of children in pain," accessed November 2, 2014, http://graingered.pbworks.com/f/Coercive%20to%20Strength-based.pdf.

British Columbia Ministry of Children and Family Development. 2012. *Residential Review Project Final Report*, www.fcssbc.ca/CoreBC/projects/residential-review.

British Columbia Ministry of Justice. 2011. "Human Trafficking: Canada is Not Immune. Online Training Program," www.pssg.gov.bc.ca/octip/training.htm.

Brockman, John, ed. 2011. *Is the Internet Changing the Way You Think?* New York: Harper Perennial.

Brodzinsky, David M., Daniel W. Smith, and Anne B. Brodzinsky. 1998. *Children's Adjustment to Adoption: Developmental and Clinical Issues*. Thousand Oaks, CA: Sage.

Bronfenbrenner, Urie. 1979. *The Ecology of Human Development: Experiments by Nature and Design*. Cambridge, MA: Harvard University Press.

Buckingham, David, and Rebekah Willett, eds. 2006. *Digital Generations: Children, Young People, and New Media*. Mahwah, NJ: Lawrence Erlbaum Associates.

Butler, Ian, and Caroline Hickman. 2011. *Social Work with Children and Families: Getting into Practice*. London: Jessica Kingsley Publishers.

Campaign 2000. 2013. *Canada's Real Economic Action Plan Begins with Poverty Eradication: 2013 Report Card on Child and Family Poverty in Canada*. Toronto: Family Service, www.campaign2000.ca/news.html.

Canadian Association of Social Workers (CASW). 2005. *Code of Ethics for the Canadian Association of Social Workers*, http://www.casw-acts.ca/sites/default/files/attachements/CASW_Code%20of%20Ethics.pdf.

Canadian Coalition for the Rights of Children. 2011. *Children's Rights in Canada 2011 Working Document: Violence Against Children, Research Report*, http://rightsofchildren.ca/wp-content/uploads/Working-Document-Violence-Against-Children-Research-Report-update-Sept-2011.pdf.

———. 2012. *Right in Principle. Right in Practice: Implementation of the Convention on the Rights of the Child in Canada*, http://rightsofchildren.ca/monitoring.

Canadian Council on Social Development. 2013. *Alternative Federal Budget 2013: Doing Better Together*. Ottawa: Canadian Centre for Policy Alternatives.

Canadian Institute for a Healthy Society. 2013. *Upstream Thinking*. Video posted October 24, http://healthcaretransformation.ca/video-upstream-thinking.

Canadian Marketing Association. 2011. *Marketing Facts: Statistics and Trends for Marketing in Canada*. Don Mills, ON: Canadian Marketing Association.

Cantwell, Nigel. 2014. *The Best Interests of the Child in Intercountry Adoption*. Florence, Italy: UNICEF.

Cappon, Paul. 2011. *Exploring the 'Boy Crisis' in Education*. Canadian Council on Learning, January 27–9, www.ccl-cca.ca/pdfs/Other-Reports/Gendereport20110113.pdf.

Carr, Nicholas. 2011. 'Is Google making us stupid?' in *The Digital Divide*, edited by Mark Bauerlein, 63–76. London: Penguin.

Carrière, Jeanine, ed. 2010. *Aski Awasis/Children of the Earth: First Peoples Speaking on Adoption*. Halifax, NS: Fernwood Publishing.

Cartwright, D., ed. 1959. *Studies in Social Power*. Ann Arbor: University of Michigan Press.

CBC News. 2013. "Unlicensed daycares operate free from oversight," February 21, *http://www.cbc.ca/news/canada/unlicensed-daycares-operate-free-from-oversight-1.1319698*.

Cech, Maureen. 1991. *Globalchild: Multicultural Resources for Young Children*. Menlo Park, CA: Addison-Wesley.

———. 1995. *Globalsense: A Leader's Guide to Games for Change*. Menlo Park, CA: Addison-Wesley.

———. 2000. *Adoption: An Annotated Bibliography*. Ottawa: PFNCR.

Cederborg, Ann-Christin. 1997. "Young children's participation in family therapy talk," *American Journal of Family Therapy* 25, 1: 23–38.

Chamberlain, David B. 1995. "What babies are teaching us about violence," *Pre- and Perinatal Psychology Journal* 10, 2: 57–74.

Chamberlain, Mark, and Liz Weaver. 2008. "Feds must join child poverty fight," *Hamilton Spectator*, December 12.

Chansonneuve, Deborah. 2005. *Reclaiming Connections: Understanding Residential School Trauma among Aboriginal People*. Ottawa: Aboriginal Healing Foundation.

Charles, Grant, Tim Stainton, and Sheila Marshall. 2012. *Young Carers in Canada: The Hidden Costs and Benefits of Young Caregiving*. Ottawa: Vanier Institute of the Family.

Chatterjee, Jharna. 2006. *Gang Prevention and Intervention Strategies*. Ottawa: Royal Canadian Mounted Police.

Cheung, Connie, Kristen Lwin, and Jennifer M. Jenkins. 2012. "Helping youth in care succeed: Influence of caregiver involvement on academic achievement," *Children and Youth Services Review* 34, 6: 1092–1100.

Child Welfare League of Canada (CWLC). 2013. "Lexicon of Child Welfare." Unpublished document.

Chunn, Dorothy E. 2003. "Boys will be men, girls will be mothers: The legal regulation of childhood in Toronto and Vancouver," in *Histories of Canadian Children and Youth*, edited by Nancy Janovicek and Joy Parr, 188–207. Toronto: Oxford University Press.

Cicchetti, D., F.A. Rogosch, and S.L. Toth. 2006. "Fostering secure attachment in infants in maltreating families through preventive interventions," *Development and Psychopathology* 18: 623–49.

Cole, Alana. 2013. "Mennonite community regrets harshly disciplining children," *CBC News*, October 17, www.cbc.ca/news/canada/manitoba/mennonite-community-regrets-harshly-disciplining-children-1.2075497.

Cottrell, Barbara. 2003. *Parent Abuse: The Abuse of Parents by Their Teenage Children*. Ottawa: National Clearinghouse on Family Violence.

Couture, Ernest. 1940. *The Canadian Mother and Child*. Ottawa: Ministry of Pensions and National Health

Covell, Katherine, and R. Brian Howe. 2001. *The Challenge of Children's Rights for Canada*. Waterloo, ON: Wilfrid Laurier University Press.

Criminal Code of Canada, Section 43. RSC, 1985, c C-46, s 43, http://laws-lois.justice.gc.ca/eng/acts/C-46/section-43.html.

Criminal Code of Canada, Section 279. RSC, 1985, c C-46, s 279, http://laws-lois.justice.gc.ca/eng/acts/C-46/section-279.html.

Currie, Janet, Mark Stabile, and Lauren E. Jones. 2013. "Do stimulant medications improve educational and behavioral outcomes for children with ADHD?" Working paper 19105, National Bureau of Economic Research, Cambridge, MA.

Darwin, Charles. 1877. "A biographical sketch of an infant," *Mind* 2: 285–94. *Classics in the History of Psychology*, http://psychclassics.yorku.ca/Darwin/infant.htm.

Dass, Ram, and Paul Gorman. 1997. *How Can I Help? Stories and Reflections on Service*. New York: Knopf.

Davey, Ian E. 2003. "The rhythm of work and the rhythm of school," in *Histories of Canadian Children and Youth*, edited by Nancy Janovicek and Joy Parr, 108–22. Toronto: Oxford University Press).

Davis, Wade. 2009. *The Wayfinders: Why Ancient Wisdom Matters in the Modern World*. Toronto: House of Anansi Press.

DeGrandpre, Richard. 1999. *Ritalin Nation*. New York: Norton.

deMontigny, Gerald A.J. 1995. *Social Working: An Ethnography of Front-line Practice*. Toronto: University of Toronto Press.

Deresiewicz, William. 2011. "The end of solitude," in *The Digital Divide*, edited by Mark Bauerlein, 307–18. London: Penguin.

de Shazer, S. 1984. "The death of resistance," *Family Process* 23: 79–93.

Deslandes, Rollande. 2006. "Designing and implementing school, family, and community collaboration programs in Quebec, Canada," *The School Community Journal* 16, 1: 81–105.

DiCiacco, Janis A. 2008. *The Colors of Grief: Understanding a Child's Journey through Loss from Birth to Adulthood*. London: Jessica Kingsley.

Diller, Lawrence H. 2006. *The Last Normal Child: Essays on the Intersection of Kids, Culture, and Psychiatric Drugs*. Westport, CT: Praeger.

Dirix, Chantal E.H., Jan G. Nijhuis, Henk W. Jangsma, and Gerard Hornstra. 2009. "Aspects of fetal learning and memory," *Child Development* 80, 4: 1251–8.

Doidge, Norman. 2007. *The Brain that Changes Itself: Stories of Personal Triumph from the Frontiers of Brain Science*. New York: Viking Penguin.

Dufour, Sarah, and Claire Chamberland. 2003. *The Effectiveness of Child Welfare Interventions: A Systematic Review*. Montreal: Centre of Excellence for Child Welfare.

Dugard, Jaycee. 2011. *A Stolen Life: A Memoir*. New York: Simon & Schuster.

Duong, Kevin. 2012. "2012 Canada Digital Future in Focus." White paper, *ComScore.com*, http://www.comscore.com/Insights/Presentations_and_Whitepapers/2012/2012_Canada_Digital_Future_in_Focus.

Dwyer, Sonya Corbin, and Lynn Gidluck. 2010. "Pre- and Post-Adoption Support Services in Canada: Implications for Policy Makers." Working paper 31, Atlantic Metropolis Centre, www.community.smu.ca/atlantic/documents/WP31CorbinDwyer.pdf.

Dyck, D. Ryan. 2012. *Guide for the Development of an LGBTQ Youth Suicide Prevention Strategy*. *Egale.ca*, December 12, http://egale.ca/all/guide-for-the-development-of-an-lgbtq-youth-suicide-prevention-strategy/.

Eberstadt, Mary. 1999. "Why Ritalin rules," *Policy Review* 94 (April): 24–46.

El and Jae. 2012. "Top 10 cool kid bloggers," *Eljae* (blog), July 8, http://eljae.com/2012/07/08/top-10-cool-kid-bloggers/.

Elkind, David. 1981. *The Hurried Child: Growing Up Too Fast Too Soon*. Reading, MA: Addison-Wesley Publishing.

Erikson, Erik. 2000. *The Erik Erikson Reader*. New York: Norton.

Esbensen, Steen. 1985. *Good Day Care Makes a Difference: A Review of the Research Findings on the Effects of Day Care on Children, Families and Communities*. Report submitted to the Task Force on Child Care. Ottawa: Status of Women.

Fahlberg, Vera. 1988. *Fitting the Pieces Together*. London: BAAF.

Fechter-Leggett, M.O., and K. O'Brien. 2010. "The effects of kinship care on adult mental health outcomes of alumni foster care," *Children and Youth Services Review* 32, 2: 206–13.

Feeney, Judith A. 2005. "Attachment and perceived rejection: Findings from studies of hurt feelings and the adoption experience," *E-Journal of Applied Psychology* 1, 1: 41–9.

Fewster, Gerry. 2002. "The hardest advice: Listen to your kids," *Journal of Child and Youth Care* 15, 4: 17–19.

Field, Tiffany. 2007. *The Amazing Infant*. Maiden, MA: Blackwell.

Fifth Estate. 2009. "Top Gun," CBC-TV, March 6, http://www.cbc.ca/player/Shows/Shows/the+fifth+estate/ID/1368429043/.

Fivush, Robyn. 2011. "The development of autobiographical memory," *Annual Review of Psychology* 62: 559–82.

Fletcher, Fay, Daniel McKennitt, and Lola Baydala. 2008. "Community capacity building: An Aboriginal exploratory case study," *Pimatisiwin* 5, 2: 9–32.

Flynn, Robert J., Peter M. Dudding, and James G. Barber, eds. 2006. *Promoting Resilience in Child Welfare*. Ottawa: University of Ottawa Press.

Foucault, Michel. 1977. *Discipline and Punish*. London: Allen Lane.

Fox, Bonnie J. 2001. *Family Patterns, Gender Relations*. Toronto: Oxford University Press.

Freire, Paulo. 2000. *Pedagogy of the Oppressed*. New York: Continuum.

French, J.R.P., Jr, and B. Raven. 1959. "The bases of social power," in *Studies in Social Power*, edited by D. Cartwright, 259–68. Ann Arbor: University of Michigan.

Freud, Anna. 1935. *Psycho-analysis for Teachers and Parents: Introductory Lectures*. New York: Emerson Books.

Fusco, Dana. 2012. "The use of self in the context of youth work," *Child & Youth Services* 33: 33–45.

Gaetz, Stephen, Bill O'Grady, Kristy Buccieri, Jeff Karabanow, and Allyson Marsolais, eds. 2013. *Youth Homelessness in Canada: Implications for Policy and Practice*. Toronto: Canadian Homelessness Research Network Press.

Garcia, Antero. 2013. "Utilizing mobile media and games to develop critical inner-city agents of social change," in *Critical Digital Literacies as Social Praxis*, edited by JuliAnna Ávila and Jessica Zacher Pandya, 107–25. New York: Peter Lang.

Garrett, Paul Michael. 2003. *Remaking Social Work with Children and Families: A Critical Discussion on the Modernisation of Social Care*. London: Routledge.

Gershoff, Elizabeth T. 2013. "Spanking and child development: We know enough now to stop hitting our children," *Child Development Perspectives* 7, 3: 133–7.

Gharabaghi, Kiaras. 2012. *Being with Edgy Youth*. New York: Nova Science Publishers.

Gibbs, John C. 2014. *Moral Development and Reality: Beyond the Theories of Kohlberg, Hoffman, and Haidt.* New York: Oxford University Press.

Gil, Eliana. 2010. "Silent grieving in a world without words: A child witnesses his brother's murder," in *Working with Children to Heal Interpersonal Trauma: The Power of Play,* edited by Eliana Gil, 67–91. New York: Guilford Press.

Gilgun, Jane. 2002. "Completing the circle: American Indian medicine wheels and the promotion of resilience of children and youth in care," *Journal of Human Behavior in the Social Environment* 6, 2: 65–84.

Gilligan, Robbie. 2006. "Promoting resilience and permanence in child welfare," in *Promoting Resilience in Child Welfare,* edited by Robert J. Flynn, Peter M. Dudding, and James G. Barber, 18–34. Ottawa: University of Ottawa Press.

Girls Action Foundation, Juniper Glass, and Lee Tunstall. 2013. *Beyond Appearances: Brief on the Main Issues Facing Girls in Canada.* Montreal: Girls Action Foundation.

Glad, Kristin Alve, Tine K. Jensen, Tonje Holt, and Silje Mørup Ormhaug. 2013. "Exploring self-perceived growth in a clinical sample of severely traumatized youth," *Child Abuse & Neglect* 37, 5: 331–42.

Gokiert, Rebecca J., Winnie Chow, Betsabeh Parsa, Nasreen Rajani, Jeffrey Bisanz, Christine Vandenberghe, and Yvonne Chui. 2010. *Early Childhood Screening in Immigrant and Refugee Populations.* Edmonton, AB: Canadian Council on Learning.

Goldstein, Abby L., Touraj Amiri, Natalie Vilhena, Christine Wekerle, Tiffany Thornton, and Lil Tonmyr. 2011. *Youth on the Street and Youth Involved with Child Welfare: Maltreatment, Mental Health and Substance Use.* Toronto: University of Toronto.

Goldstein, Sam, and Robert B. Brooks. 2005. *Handbook of Resilience in Children.* New York: Kluwer Academic/Plenum.

Gordon, Andrea. 2013. "Growing up with same-sex parents," *The Star (Toronto),* August 16, www.thestar.com/life/2013/08/16/growing_up_with_samesex_parents.html.

Gosse, Douglas, and Steven Arnocky. 2012. "The state of Canadian boyhood—Beyond literacy to a holistic approach." *In Education* 18, 2: 67–97.

Gottman, John. 1997. *Raising an Emotionally Intelligent Child.* New York: Simon and Schuster.

Government of Canada, Early Childhood Development. 2011. *The Well-Being of Canada's Young Children: Government of Canada Report 2011,* www.dpe-agje-ecd-elcc.ca/eng/ecd/well-being/page00.shtml.

Greenberg, Gary. 2013. *The Book of Woe: The DSM and the Unmaking of Psychiatry.* New York: Blue Rider Press.

Greene, Sheila, and Diane Hogan, eds. 2005. *Researching Children's Experience: Methods and Approaches.* Thousand Oaks, CA: Sage.

Griffin, Sandra. 2007. *Why the Investment in Children? Costs and Benefits of Investing in Children.* Ottawa: Centre of Excellence for Early Childhood Development.

Grover, Sonja. 2007. "Homeless children and street-involved children in Canada", in *A Question of Commitment: Children's Rights in Canada,* edited by Brian R. Howe and Katherine Covell, 343–73. Waterloo, ON: Wilfrid Laurier University Press.

Habermas, T., and S. Bluck. 2000. "Getting a life: The emergence of the life story in adolescence," *Psychological Bulletin* 126: 748–69.

Haig-Brown, Celia, with Carl James. 2004. "Supporting respectful relations: Community-school interface and youth 'at risk,'" in *From Enforcement and Prevention to Civic Engagement: Research on Community Safety,* edited by Bruce Kidd and Jim Phillips, 216–35. Toronto: Centre of Criminology, University of Toronto.

Hamilton, Claire E. 2000. "Continuity and discontinuity of attachment from infancy through adolescence," *Child Development* 71, 3: 690–4.

Haner, Dilys. 2010. "Adolescent experiences of confidential Internet counselling at Kids Help Phone." MA thesis, York University, Toronto.

Harlow, H., and M. Harlow. 1962. "Social deprivation in monkeys," *Scientific American* 207: 136–46.

Harlow, H., and S. Suomi. 1972. "Social rehabilitation of isolate-reared monkeys," *Developmental Psychology* 6: 487–96.

Harris, Barbara. 2006. "What can we learn from traditional Aboriginal education? Transforming social work education delivered in First Nations communities," *Canadian Journal of Native Education* 29, 1: 117–46.

Hartjen, Clayton A., and S. Priyadarsini. 2012. *The Global Victimization of Children*. New York: Springer.

Hawkins, Stephen. 2012. *Dramatic Problem-Solving: Drama-Based Group Exercise for Conflict Transformation*. London: Jessica Kingsley.

Heckman, James J., and Dimitry V. Masterov. 2007. "The productivity argument for investing in young children." Working paper 13016, National Bureau of Economic Research, Cambridge, MA.

Hick, Steven F., ed. 2009. *Mindfulness and Social Work*. Chicago: Lyceum.

Hill, Heather D., Pamela Morris, Lisa A. Gennetian, Sharon Wolf, and Carly Tubbs. 2013. "The consequences of income instability for children's well-being." *Child Development Perspectives* 7, 2: 85–90.

Hillis, W. Daniel. 2011. "Introduction: The dawn of entanglement," in *Is the Internet Changing the Way You Think?* edited by John Brockman, xxv–xxix. New York: Harper Perennial.

Hollander, J.A. 2002. "Resisting vulnerability: The social reconstruction of gender in interaction," *Social Problems* 49, 4: 474–96.

hooks, bell. 1994. *Teaching to Transgress: Education as the Practice of Freedom*. New York: Routledge.

Hoskins, Marie L., and Jennifer White. 2010. "Processes of discernment when considering issues of neglect in child protection practice," *Child & Youth Care Forum* 39, 1: 27–45.

Howe, R. Brian, and Katherine Covell. 2005. *Empowering Children: Children's Rights Education as a Pathway to Citizenship*. Toronto: University of Toronto Press.

Howe, R. Brian, and Katherine Covell, eds. 2007. *A Question of Commitment: Children's Rights in Canada*. Waterloo, ON: Wilfrid Laurier University Press.

Human Resources and Skills Development Canada (HRSDC). 2004, April. *A Canada Fit for Children*, www.canadiancrc.com/PDFs/Canadas_Plan_Action_April2004-EN.pdf.

International Centre for the Prevention of Crime. 2011, March. *Comparative Report on Types of Intervention Used for Youth at Risk of Joining a Street Gang: Practices from Belgium, Canada and France*, www.crime-prevention-intl.org/en/publications/report/report/article/comparative-report-on-types-of-intervention-used-for-youth-at-risk-of-joining-a-street-gang-2.html.

Jackson, Linda A., Edward A. Witt, Alexander Ivan Gomes, Hiram E. Fitzgerald, Alexander von Eye, and Yong Zhao. 2012. "Information technology use and creativity: Findings from the Children and Technology Project," *Computers in Human Behavior* 28, 2: 370–6.

James, Allison, and Chris Jenks. 1996. "Public perceptions of childhood criminality," *British Journal of Sociology* 47, 2: 315–30.

Janovicek, Nancy, and Joy Parr, eds. 2003. *Histories of Canadian Children and Youth*. Toronto: Oxford University Press.

Jenkins, Mary Ann. 2008, July. *What Makes It Ours: Lessons Learned from the Our Place—Learning in Motion Initiative*, www.betterbeginnings.ca/What_Makes_It_Ours.html.

Jenks, Chris. 2005. *Childhood*. New York: Routledge.

Jennissen, Therese, and Colleen Lundy. 2011. *One Hundred Years of Social Work: A History of the Profession in English Canada, 1900–2000*. Waterloo, ON: Wilfrid Laurier University Press.

Jent, Jason F., Larissa N. Niec, and Sarah E. Baker. 2011. "Play and interpersonal processes," in *Play in Clinical Practice*, edited by Sandra Russ and Larissa N. Niec, 23–47. New York: Guilford Press.

Johnson, Steven. 2011. "The Internet," in *The Digital Divide*, edited by Mark Bauerlein, 26–34. London: Penguin.

Johnson, Sue. 2004. *The Practice of Emotionally Focused Marital Therapy: Creating Connection*. New York: Bruner/Routledge.

———. 2008. *Hold Me Tight: Seven Conversations for a Lifetime of Love*. New York: Little, Brown and Company.

Jones, Laura, and Edward Krak. 2005. "Life in government care: The connection of youth and family," *Child and Youth Care Forum* 34, 6: 405–21.

Jordan, Judith V. 2005. "Relational resilience in girls," in *Handbook of Resilience in Children*, edited by Sam Goldstein and Robert B. Brooks, 79–91. New York: Kluwer Academic/Plenum.

Jud, Andreas, and Nico Trocmé. 2013. "Physical Abuse and Physical Punishment in Canada." CWRP information sheet 122E, Centre for Research on Children and Families, McGill University, Montreal, QC, *Canadian Child Welfare Research Portal*, http://cwrp.ca/sites/default/files/publications/en/122E.pdf.

Jukes, Ian, Ted McCain, and Lee Crockett. 2010. *Understanding the Digital Generation*. Vancouver: Corwin.

Kail, Robert V., and Theresa Zolner. 2005. *Children*. Toronto: Pearson.

Keen, Andrew. 2012. *Digital Vertigo: How Today's Online Social Revolution is Dividing, Diminishing, and Disorienting Us*. New York: St Martin's Press.

Kelly, Katharine, and Tullio Caputo. 2007. "Health and street/homeless youth," *Journal of Health Psychology* 12, 5: 726–36.

Kelly, Katharine, and Mark Totten. 2002. *When Children Kill: A Social-Psychological Study of Youth Homicide*. Peterborough, ON: Broadview Press.

Kidd, Bruce, and Jim Phillips, eds. 2004. *From Enforcement and Prevention to Civic Engagement: Research on Community Safety*. Toronto: Centre of Criminology, University of Toronto.

Kids and Media. 2012. "Quotes from children," March 13, http://www.kidsandmedia.co.uk/quotes-from-children/.

Kimelman, E.C. 1985. *No Quiet Place: Review Committee on Indian and Metis Adoptions and Placements*. Winnipeg: Manitoba Department of Community Services.

Kingsley, Jason, and Levitz, Mitchell. 2007. *Count Us In: Growing up with Down Syndrome*. New York: Harcourt & Brace.

Kirby, Michael. 2013. "We are failing young Canadians on mental health" *The Star (Toronto)*, October 7, www.thestar.com/opinion/commentary/2013/10/07/we_are_failing_young_canadians_on_mental_health.html.

Kirmayer, Laurence J. 2012. "Changing patterns in suicide among young people," *Canadian Medical Association Journal* 184, 9: 1015–16.

Kirschner, David. 2007. *Adoption: Uncharted Waters*. Woodbury, NY: Juneau Press.

Klapper, Stacy A., Nancy S. Plummer, and Robert J. Harmon. 2004. "Diagnostic and treatment issues in cases of childhood trauma," in *Young Children and Trauma: Intervention and Treatment*, edited by Joy D. Osofsky, 139–54. New York: Guilford Press.

Klein, Melanie. 1965. *Contributions to Psychoanalysis, 1921–1945*. London: Hogarth Press.

Knapp, Vincent J. 1998. "Major medical explanations for high infant mortality in nineteenth-century Europe," *Canadian Bulletin of Medical History* 15: 317–36.

Kraemer, Gary. 1997. "Psychobiology of early social attachment in rhesus monkeys: Clinical implications," *Annals, New York Academy of Sciences* 807, 1: 401–18.

Kufeldt, Kathleen, and Brad McKenzie, eds. 2003. *Child Welfare: Connecting Research, Policy, and Practice*. Waterloo, ON: Wilfrid Laurier University Press.

Kuhl, P. K. 2011. "Early language learning and literacy: Neuroscience implications for education," *Mind, Brain, and Education* 5: 128–42.

Kummer, Markus. 2012. "Children and the Internet." Briefing paper, *Internet Society*, October 17, www.internetsociety.org/children-and-internet.

Kutcher, Stanley P., and Magdalena Szumilas. 2008. "Youth suicide prevention." *CMAJ* 178, 3 (January 29), www.cmaj.ca/cgi/content/full/178/3/282.

LaLiberte, Traci, and Tracy Crudo, eds. 2012. *Secondary Trauma and the Child Welfare Workforce*, Center for Advanced Studies in Child Welfare, University of Minnesota, www.cehd.umn.edu/ssw/cascw/attributes/PDF/.../CW360_2012.pdf.

Lamb, Charles W., Joseph F. Hair, Carl McDaniel, A.J. Faria, and William J. Wellington. 2012. *Marketing*. 5th Cdn Edn. Toronto: Nelson Education.

Lambe, Yolanda. 2006. *The Chemical Management of Canadian Systems Youth*. Ottawa: National Youth in Care Network.

———. 2009. *Drugs in Our System: An Exploratory Study on the Chemical Management of Canadian Systems Youth*. Ottawa: National Youth in Care Network.

Landreth, Garry L. 2012. *Play Therapy: The Art of the Relationship*. London: Routledge.

Lane, David A., and Andrew Milner, eds. 1992. *Child and Adolescent Therapy: A Handbook*. Buckingham, UK: Open University Press.

Law, Danielle M., Jennifer D. Shapka, José F. Dormene, and Monique H. Gagné. 2012. "Are cyberbullies really bullies? An investigation of reactive and proactive online aggression," *Computers in Human Behavior* 28, 3: 664–72.

Lee, A.J. 2009. "Understanding and Addressing the Phenomenon of 'Child Soldiers': The Gap Between the Global Humanitarian Discourse and the Local Understandings and Experiences of Young People's Military Recruitment." Working paper series no. 52, Refugee Studies Centre, University of Oxford, www.rsc.ox.ac.uk/PDFs/RSCworkingpaper52.pdf.

Lefevre, Michelle. 2010. *Communicating with Children and Young People: Making a Difference*. Bristol, UK: Policy Press.

Levine, H. 2000. "Book review of children's rights education curriculum resource," *International Journal of Children's Rights* 8: 391–4.

Levine, Peter A., and Maggie Kline. 2007. *Trauma through a Child's Eyes: Awakening the Ordinary Miracle of Healing*. Berkeley, CA: North Atlantic Books.

Liebenberg, Linda, and Michael Ungar. 2008. *Resilience in Action: Working with Youth across Cultures and Contexts*. Toronto: University of Toronto Press.

Lifton, Betty Jean. 2009. *Lost and Found: The Adoption Experience*. Ann Arbor, MI: University of Michigan Press.

Livingstone, S., and E.J. Helsper. 2007. "Gradations in digital inclusion: Children, young people and the digital divide," *New Media & Society* 9, 4: 671–96.

Loiselle, Elicia, Sandrina de Finney, Nishad Khanna, and Rebecca Corcoran. 2012. "We need to talk about it!: Doing CYC as political praxis," *Child & Youth Services* 33: 178–205.

Lorenz, Konrad. 1970–1. *Studies in Animal and Human Behaviour*. London: Methuen.

Macdonald, David, and Daniel Wilson. 2013. *Poverty or Prosperity: Indigenous Children in Canada*. Ottawa: Canadian Centre for Policy Alternatives.

Madigan, Sheri, Leslie Atkinson, Kristin Laurin, and Diane Benoit. 2013. "Attachment and internalizing behaviour in early childhood: A meta-analysis," *Developmental Psychology* 49, 4: 672–89.

Madigan, Stephen. 2011. *Narrative Therapy*. Washington: American Psychological Association.

Makilan, Aubrey. 2007. "Filipino youth in Canada driven to gangs, drug tailing," *Philippine Reporter*, February 1, http://philippinereporter.com/2007/02/01/filipino-youth-in-canada-driven-to-gangs-drug-tailing/.

Marin, Andre. 2014. *Careless about Child Care*. Ombudsman Report. Toronto: Queens Printer.

Martel, Yann. 2001. *Life of Pi*. Toronto: Vintage Canada.

Martí, Eduardo, and Cintia Rodríguez, eds. 2012. *After Piaget*. New Brunswick, NJ: Transaction Publishers.

Martin, Barbara. 2011. *Children at Play: Learning Gender in the Early Years*. Stoke-on-Trent: Trentham Books.

Martin, Fay. 2003. "Knowing and naming 'care' in child welfare," in *Child Welfare: Connecting Research, Policy, and Practice*, edited by Kathleen Kufeldt and Brad McKenzie, 261–73. Waterloo, ON: Wilfrid Laurier University Press.

Maslow, Abraham. 1943. "A theory of human motivation," *Psychological Review* 50: 370–96.

Masten, Ann S. 2006. "Promoting resilience in development: A general framework for systems in care," in *Promoting Resilience in Child Welfare*, edited by Robert J. Flynn, Peter M. Dudding, and James G. Barber, 3–18. Ottawa: University of Ottawa Press.

McCain, Margaret N., and J. Fraser Mustard. 1999. *Reversing the Real Brain Drain: Early Years Study Final Report*, accessed December 1, 2013, www.children.gov.on.ca/htdocs/English/.../early_years_study-1999.doc.

McCarthy, Dennis. 2012. *A Manual of Dynamic Play Therapy: Helping Things Fall Apart, the Paradox of Play*. London: Jessica Kingsley.

McElheran, Megan, Allison Briscoe-Smith, Anna Khaylis, Darrah Westrup, Chris Hayward, and Cheryl Gore-Felton. 2012. "A conceptual model of post-traumatic growth among children and adolescents in the aftermath of sexual abuse," *Counselling Psychology Quarterly* 25, 1: 73–82.

Mellor, Brian, Leslie MacRae, Monica Pauls, and Joseph P. Hornick. 2005. *Youth Gangs in Canada: A Preliminary Review of Programs and Services*. Calgary, AB: Canadian Research Institute for Law and the Family.

Merry, Sally N., Karolina Stasiak, Matthew Shepherd, Chris Frampton, Theresa Fleming, and Mathijs F.G. Lucassen. 2012. "The effectiveness of SPARX, a computerized self-help intervention for adolescents seeking help for depression: randomized controlled non-inferiority trial," *British Medical Journal* May 19: 6.

Miller, Alice. 2005. *The Body Never Lies: The Lingering Effects of Cruel Parenting*. New York: Norton.

Mishna, Faye, Mona Khoury-Kassabri, Tahany Gadalla, and Joanne Daciuk. 2012. "Risk factors for involvement in cyber bullying: Victims, bullies and bully-victims," *Children and Youth Services Review* 34, 1: 63–70.

Mitra, Sugata. 2009. "Hole-in-the-wall experiments in India." *Hole-in-the-Wall*. Accessed November 1, 2014. www.hole-in-the-wall.com.

———. 2013. "The internet can harm, but can also be a child's best tool for learning," *Guardian (UK)*, November 3, www.theguardian.com/commentisfree/2013/nov/03/child-safety-internet-web-access#start-of-comments.

Montgomery, Lucy Maud. 1972 [1917]. *Anne's House of Dreams*. Toronto: McClelland & Stewart.

Moore, Shannon. 2007. "Restorative justice: Toward a rights-based approach," in *A Question of Commitment: Children's Rights in Canada*, edited by Brian R. Howe and Katherine Covell, 179–209. Waterloo, ON: Wilfrid Laurier University Press.

Morrisseau, Calvin. 1998. *Into the Daylight: A Wholistic Approach to Healing*. Toronto: University of Toronto Press.

Moses, Daniel David, and Terry Goldie, eds. 2005. *An Anthology of Native Literature*. Toronto: Oxford University Press.

Mourani, Maria. 2009. *Gangs de rue ici: Leurs reseaux au Canada et dans les Amériques*. Montreal: Les Editions de l'Homme.

Munch, Christopher. 2012. "Youth correctional statistics in Canada, 2010/2011." *Juristat*, October 12, Statistics Canada, cat. no. 85-002-X. http://www.statcan.gc.ca/pub/85-002-x/2012001/article/11716-eng.htm.

National Crime Prevention Centre. 2012. *A Statistical Snapshot of Youth at Risk and Youth Offending in Canada*. Public Safety Canada, http://www.publicsafety.gc.ca/cnt/rsrcs/pblctns/ststclsnpsht-yth/ssyr-eng.pdf.

National Film Board of Canada. 2005. *Wards of the Crown*. Directed by Andrée Cazabon.

Nesca, Marc, and J. Thomas Dalby. 2011. "Maternal neonaticide following traumatic childbirth," *International Journal of Offender Therapy and Comparative Criminology* 55, 7: 1166–78.

Newson, Elizabeth. 1992. "The barefoot play therapist: Adapting skills for a time of need," in *Child and Adolescent Therapy: A Handbook*, edited by David A. Lane and Andrew Milner, 89–108. Buckingham, UK: Open University Press.

Nixon, Althea Scott. 2013. "Engaging urban youth in meaningful dialogue on identity through digital storytelling," in *Critical Digital Literacies as Social Praxis: Intersections and Challenges*, edited by JuliAnna Ávila and Jessica Zacher Pandya, 41–62. New York: Peter Lang.

O'Donnell, Susan. 2009. "Learning, not labels, for special-needs students," *Edmonton Journal*, June 9.

O'Neill, Heather. 2006. *Lullabies for Little Criminals*. New York: Harper Perennial.

O'Neill, Tom, and Dawn Zinga, eds. 2008. *Children's Rights: Multidisciplinary Approaches to Participation and Protection*. Toronto: University of Toronto Press.

Ontario Ministry of Community and Social Services. *Risk Assessment Model for Child Protection in Ontario*. 2000. Toronto: Queen's Printer for Ontario.

Osofsky, Joy D., ed. 2004. *Young Children and Trauma: Intervention and Treatment*. New York: Guilford Press.

Owen, Frances, Christini Tardif-Williams, Donato Tarulli, Glenys McQueen-Fuentes, Maurice Feldman, Carol Sales, Karen Stoner, Leanne Gosse, and Dorothy Griffiths. 2008. "Human rights for children and youth with developmental disabilities," in *Children's Rights: Multidisciplinary Approaches to Participation and Protection*, edited by Tom O'Neill and Dawn Zinga, 163–94. Toronto: University of Toronto Press.

Palfrey, John, and Urs Gasser. 2008. *Born Digital: Understanding the First Generation of Digital Natives*. New York: Basic Books.

Parada, Henry Ubaldo. 2002. *The Restructuring of the Child Welfare System in Ontario: A Study in the Social Organization of Knowledge*. Toronto: Ontario Institute for Studies in Education.

Pearson, Landon. 2008. Foreword to *Children's Rights: Multidisciplinary Approaches to Participation and Protection*, edited by Tom O'Neill and Dawn Zinga, vii–ix. Toronto: University of Toronto Press.

Perrin, Benjamin, ed. 2012. *Modern Warfare: Armed Groups, Private Militaries, Humanitarian Organizations, and the Law*. Vancouver: UBC Press.

Perry, B.D., and E.P. Hambrick. 2008. "The neurosequential model of therapeutics," *Reclaiming Children and Youth* 17, 3: 38–43.

Peters, Ray DeV., Bonnie Leadbeater, and Robert J. McMahon, eds. 2005. *Resilience in Children, Families, and Communities: Linking Context to Practice and Policy*. New York: Kluwer Academic/Plenum.

Peters, Ray DeV. 2005. "A community-based approach to promoting resilience in young children, their families, and their neighbourhoods," in *Resilience in Children, Families, and Communities: Linking Context to Practice and Policy*, edited by Ray DeV. Peters, Bonnie Leadbeater, and Robert J. McMahon, 157–77. New York: Kluwer Academic/Plenum.

Peterson, C., and M.E.P. Seligman. 2004. *Character Strengths and Virtues: A Handbook and Classification*. New York: Oxford University Press.

Piaget, Jean. 1929. *The Child's Conception of the World*. New York: Harcourt, Brace.

Pipe, Margaret-Ellen, Michael E. Lamb, Yael Orbach, and Ann-Christin Cederborg. 2007. *Child Sexual Abuse: Disclosure, Delay, and Denial*. Mahwah, NJ: Lawrence Erlbaum Associates.

Point Made Films. 2008. *Adopted*. Directed by Barb Lee.

Pollard, Juliet. 2003. "A most remarkable phenomenon: Growing up Métis: Fur traders' children in the Pacific Northwest," in *Histories of Canadian Children and Youth*, edited by Nancy Janovicek and Joy Parr, 57–71. Toronto: Oxford University Press.

Prensky, Marc. 2010. *Teaching Digital Natives: Partnering for Real Learning*. Thousand Oaks, CA: Corwin/Sage.

Prochaska, James O., and John C. Norcross. 2007. *Systems of Psychotherapy: A Transtheoretical Analysis*. Belmont, CA: Thomson Brooks/Cole.

Public Health Agency of Canada. 2010. *Canadian Incidence Study of Reported Child Abuse and Neglect—2008 Major Findings*, http://www.phac-aspc.gc.ca/cm-vee/csca-ecve/2008/index-eng.php.

———. 2013. "Population Health," www.phac-aspc.gc.ca/ph-sp/.

Public Safety Canada. 2008. *Youth Gangs in Canada: What Do We Know?* www.slideshare.net/vindego/youth-gangs-in-canada.

———. 2012. *The Surrey Wraparound: A Youth Driven Plan for Gang Violence Prevention*, www.publicsafety.gc.ca/cnt/rsrcs/pblctns/srr-wrprnd/index-eng.aspx.

Putnam, Robert D. 2000. *Bowling Alone: The Collapse and Revival of American Community*. New York: Simon & Schuster.

Puxley, Chinta. 2014. "Manitoba Mennonites closer to return of 36 children." *Globe and Mail*, February 17, http://www.theglobeandmail.com/news/national/manitoba-mennonites-closer-to-return-of-36-children/article16928403/.

Regan, Priscilla, and Valerie Steeves. 2010. "Kids R Us: Online social networking and the potential for empowerment," *Surveillance & Society* 8, 2: 151–65.

Richards, John. 2011. *School Dropouts: Who Are They and What Can Be Done?* E-brief, C.D. Howe Institute, January 6, http://www.cdhowe.org/pdf/ebrief_109.pdf.

Richmond, Mary. 1917. *Social Diagnosis*. New York: Russell Sage Foundation.

Rochat, Philippe. 2012. "Baby assault on Piaget," in *After Piaget*, edited by Eduardo Martí and Cintia Rodríguez, 71–82. New Brunswick, NJ: Transaction Publishers.

Roche, J., K. Petrunka, and Ray DeV. Peters. 2008. *Investing in our Future: Highlights of Better Beginnings, Better Futures Research Findings at Grade 9*. Kingston, ON: Better Futures Research Coordination Unit.

Rogers, Carl. 1951. *Client-centered Therapy*. Boston: Houghton Mifflin.

———. 1967. *On Becoming a Person: A Therapist's View of Psychotherapy*. London: Constable.

———. 1980. *A Way of Being*. Boston: Houghton Mifflin.

Rogers, Natalie. 2000. *The Creative Connection: Expressive Arts as Healing*. Ross-on-Wye: PCCS Books.

Rogers, Shelagh, Mike deGagné, and Jonathan Dewar, eds. 2012. *Speaking My Truth: Reflections on Reconciliation and Residential School*. Ottawa: Aboriginal Healing Foundation.

Rosenhan, David. 1973. "On being sane in insane places," *Science* 179: 250–8.

Rozovsky, L. 2003. *The Canadian Law of Consent to Treatment*. Toronto: Butterworths.

Ruane, Janet M., and Karen A. Cerulo. 2004. *Second Thoughts: Seeing Conventional Wisdom through the Sociological Eye*. Thousand Oaks, CA: Pine Forge Press.

Russ, Sandra W. 2004. *Play in Child Development and Psychotherapy: Toward Empirically Supported Practice*. Mahwah, NJ: Erlbaum.

Russ, Sandra W., and Jessica A. Dillon. 2011. "Changes in children's pretend play over two decades," *Creativity Research Journal* 23 (4): 330–8.

Russ, Sandra W., and Larissa N. Niec, eds. 2011. *Play in Clinical Practice: Evidence-Based Approaches*. New York: Guilford Press.

Saleebey, Dennis. 2002. *The Strengths Perspective in Social Work Practice*. Boston: Allyn & Bacon.

Samuels, Gina Miranda. 2009. "Being raised by white people: Navigating racial difference among adopted multiracial adults," *Journal of Marriage and Family* 71: 80–94.

Scales, Peter C., and Nancy Leffert. 2004. *Developmental Assets: A Synthesis of the Scientific Research on Adolescent Development*. Minneapolis, MN: Search Institute.

Scales, Peter C., Arturo Sesma Jr, and Brent Bolstrom. 2004. *Coming into Their Own: How Developmental Assets Promote Positive Growth in Middle Childhood*. Minneapolis, MN: Search Institute.

Schaefer, Charles E., and H.G. Kaduson. 2006. *Contemporary Play Therapy: Theory, Research, and Practice*. New York: Guilford Press.

Schissel, Bernard. 2006. *Still Blaming Children: Youth Conduct and the Politics of Child Hating*. Halifax, NS: Fernwood.

———. 2011. *About Canada: Children & Youth*. Halifax, NS: Fernwood.

Schissel, Bernard, and Terry Wotherspoon. 2003. *The Legacy of School for Aboriginal People: Education, Oppression, and Emancipation*. Toronto: Oxford University Press.

Schmidt, Glen. 2012. *Community Capacity Building in Child Welfare Services*. Victoria, BC: Research in Practice Network.

Seiter, Ellen. 2005. *The Internet Playground: Children's Access, Entertainment, and Mis-Education*. New York: Peter Lang Publishing.

Sesma, Arturo, Marc Mannes, and Peter C. Scales. 2005. "Positive adaptation, resilience, and the developmental asset framework," in *Handbook of Resilience in Children*, edited by Sam Goldstein and Robert B. Brooks, 281–97. New York: Kluwer Academic/Plenum.

Shebib, Bob. 2007. *Choices: Interviewing and Counselling Skills for Canadians*. Toronto: Pearson.

Sherlock, Tracy. 2010. "One in five hyperactive kids possibly misdiagnosed: Study," September 14, *Canada.com*, www.canada.com/health/five+hyperactive+kids+possibly+misdiagnosed+Study/3521890/story.html.

Sinclair, Raven. 2007. "Identity lost and found: Lessons from the Sixties Scoop," *First Peoples Child and Family Review* 3, 1: 65–82.

Sinclair, Raven, Michael Anthony Hart, and Gord Bruyere. 2009. *Wichihitowin: Aboriginal Social Work in Canada*. Halifax, NS: Fernwood.

Singer, Merrill. 2008. *Drugging the Poor: Legal and Illegal Drugs and Social Inequality*. Long Grove, IL: Waveland Press.

Singh, Gurvinder, and Judi Fairholm. 2012. "Violence against children in urban settings: Private hurt, public manifestations," in *Modern Warfare: Armed Groups, Private Militaries, Humanitarian Organizations, and the Law*, edited by Benjamin Perrin, 348–61. Vancouver: UBC Press.

Sinha, Vandna, Nico Trocmé, Barbara Fallon, Bruce MacLaurin, Elizabeth Fast, Shelley Thomas Prokop, Tara Petti, et al. 2011. *Kiskisik Awasisak: Remember the Children. Understanding the Overrepresentation of First Nations Children in the Child Welfare System*. Ottawa: Assembly of First Nations.

Small, Gary, and Gigi Vorgan. 2011. "Your brain is evolving right now," in *The Digital Divide*, edited by Mark Bauerlein, 76–96. London, UK: Penguin.

Smidt, Sandra. 2013. *The Developing Child in the 21st Century: A Global Perspective on Child Development*. New York: Routledge.

Smith, Dorothy E. 1998. *Writing the Social: Critique, Theory and Investigations*. Toronto: University of Toronto Press.

———. 2005. *Institutional Ethnography: A Sociology for People*. Oxford: AltaMira Press.

Smith, Sheila Dorothy. 2012. *Sandtray Play and Storymaking*. London: Jessica Kingsley.

Snow, Rebekah, and Katherine Covell. 2006. "Adoption and the best interests of the child: The dilemma of cultural interpretation," *International Journal of Children's Rights* 14: 109–17.

Sobol, Barbara. 2010. "'I am an artist': A sexually traumatized girl's self-portraits in paint and clay," in *Working with Children to Heal Interpersonal Trauma: The Power of Play*, edited by Eliana Gil, 240–62. New York: Guilford Press.

Solomon, Andrew. 2012. *Far From the Tree: Parents, Children, and the Search for Identity*. New York: Scribner.

Spergel, Irving A. 2007. *Reducing Youth Gang Violence: The Little Village Gang Project in Chicago*. Lanham, MD: AltaMira Press.

SPARX. 2012. *Linked Wellness*, http://linkedwellness.com/play-sparx-the-video-game-for-depression/.

Standing Senate Committee on Human Rights. 2007. *Children: The Silenced Citizens. Effective Implementation of Canada's International Obligations with Respect to the Rights of Children. Final Report of the Standing Senate Committee on Human Rights*, http://www.parl.gc.ca/Content/SEN/Committee/391/huma/rep/rep10apr07-e.pdf.

Stanley, Timothy J. 2003. "White supremacy, Chinese schooling, and school segregation in Victoria: The case of the Chinese students' strike, 1922–1923," in *Histories of Canadian Children and Youth*, edited by Nancy Janovicek and Joy Parr, 126–43. Toronto: Oxford University Press.

Statistics Canada. 2009a. *Canadian Community Health Survey, 2009. The Daily,* June 26, http://www.statcan.gc.ca/daily-quotidien/090625/dq090625b-eng.

———. 2009b. "Population of working age and either gainfully occupied or labour force, in non-agricultural and agricultural pursuits, census years 1881 to 1971," table D1-7, www.statcan.gc.ca/pub/ll-516-x/sectiond/Dl_7-eng.csv.

———. 2010. *National Longitudinal Survey of Children and Youth (NLSCY): Cycle 8, 2008–2009,* November 10, www23.statcan.gc.ca/imdb/p2SV.pl?Function=getSurvey&SDDS=4450&Item_Id=25609&lang=en.

———. 2011. *2011 National Household Survey: Aboriginal Peoples in Canada: First Nations People, Métis and Inuit,* in *The Daily,* May 8, 2013, http://www.statcan.gc.ca/daily-quotidien/130508/dq130508a-eng.pdf.

Stearns, Peter N. 2006. *Childhood in World History.* New York: Routledge.

Steeves, Valerie. 2012. *Young Canadians in a Wired World, Phase III: Talking to Youth and Parents about Life Online.* Ottawa: MediaSmarts.

Steiner-Adair, Catherine. 2013. *The Big Disconnect: Protecting Childhood and Family Relationships in the Digital Age.* New York: Harper Collins.

Stout, Madeleine Dion, and Gregory Kipling. 2003. *Aboriginal People, Resilience and the Residential School Legacy.* Ottawa: Aboriginal Healing Foundation.

Strom-Gottfried, Kim. 2008. *The Ethics of Practice with Minors: High Stakes, Hard Choices.* Chicago: Lyceum Books.

Sutherland, Neil. 2003. "When you listen to the winds of childhood, how much can you believe?" in *Histories of Canadian Children and Youth,* edited by Nancy Janovicek and Joy Parr, 19–34. Toronto: Oxford University Press.

Tallman, Laurna. 2010. *Listening for the Light: A New Perspective on Integration Disorder in Dyslexic Syndrome, Schizophrenia, Bipolarity, Chronic Fatigue Syndrome, and Substance Abuse.* Marmora, ON: Northern Light Books.

Tapscott, Don. 2011. "The eight net gen norms," in *The Digital Divide,* edited by Mark Bauerlein, 130–59. London: Penguin.

Taylor, Catherine, and Tracey Peter. 2011. *Every Class in Every School: Final Report on the First National Climate Survey on Homophobia, Biphobia, and Transphobia in Canadian Schools.* Toronto: Egale Canada Human Rights Trust.

Thompson, Carol C., Jeff Putthoff, and Ed Figueroa. 2006. "Hopeworks: Youth identity, youth organization, and technology," in *Digital Generations: Children, Young People, and New Media,* edited by David Buckingham and Rebekah Willett, 313–29. Mahwah, NJ: Lawrence Erlbaum Associates.

Timimi, Sami, and Begum Maitra, eds. 2006. *Critical Voices in Child and Adolescent Mental Health.* London: Free Association Books.

Todd, Paula. 2014. *Extreme Mean: Trolls, Bullies and Predators Online.* Toronto: Signal.

Tough, Paul. 2012. *How Children Succeed: Grit, Curiosity, and the Hidden Power of Character.* Boston: Houghton Mifflin Harcourt.

Transracial Abductees. 2013, www.archive.today/CUuD6.

Trenka, Jane Jeong, Julia Chinyere Oparah, and Sun Yung Shin, eds. 2006. *Outsiders Within: Writing on Transracial Adoption.* Cambridge, MA: South End Press.

Trocmé, Nico, Marc Tourigny, Bruce MacLaurin, and Barbara Fallon. 2003. "Major findings from the Canadian incidence study of reported child abuse and neglect," *Child Abuse and Neglect* 27, 12: 1427–39.

Turner, Joanne C., and J. Francis Turner, eds. 2009. *Canadian Social Welfare.* Toronto: Pearson.

Ungar, Michael. 2005. *Handbook for Working with Children and Youth: Pathways to Resilience across Cultures and Contexts.* Thousand Oaks, CA: Sage.

———. 2006. *Strengths-based Counseling with At-risk Youth.* Thousand Oaks, CA: Corwin Press.

———. 2007. *Too Safe for Their Own Good: How Risk and Responsibility Help Teens Thrive.* Toronto: McClelland & Stewart.

———. 2008. "Putting resilience theory into action," in *Resilience in Action: Working with Youth across Cultures and Contexts,* edited by Linda Liebenberg and Michael Ungar, 17–39. Toronto: University of Toronto Press.

UNICEF. 1989. *UN Convention on the Rights of the Child,* accessed April 2, 2014, www.unicef.org/crc/.

———. 2013. *Child Well-Being in Rich Countries,* www.unicef-irc.org/Report-Card-11/.

United Nations. 2000. *Protocol to Prevent, Suppress and Punish Trafficking in Persons, Especially Women and Children,* accessed June 7,

2014, http://www.uncjin.org/Documents/Conventions/dcatoc/final_documents_2/convention_%20traff_eng.pdf.

Valkenburg, P.M., and J. Peter. 2009. "The effects of instant messaging on the quality of adolescents' existing friendships: A longitudinal study," *Journal of Communication* 59: 79–97.

Vandergoot, Mary E. 2006. *Justice for Young Offenders: Their Needs, Our Responses*. Saskatoon, SK: Purich.

Vetere, Arlene, and Emilia Dowling, eds. 2005. *Narrative Therapies with Children and Their Families: A Practitioner's Guide in Concepts and Approaches*. New York: Routledge.

Vygotsky, L.S. 1997. *Educational Psychology*. Delray Beach, FL: St Lucie Press.

Webber, Marlene. 1998. *As If Kids Mattered*. Toronto: Key Porter.

Westcott, Helen L., and Karen S. Littleton. 2005. "Exploring meaning in interviews with children," in *Researching Children's Experience: Methods and Approaches*, edited by Sheila Greene and Diane Hogan, 141–58. Thousand Oaks, CA: Sage.

Wharf, Brian, and Brad McKenzie. 2004. *Connecting Policy to Practice in the Human Services*. Toronto: Oxford University Press.

White, Jennifer. 2007. "Knowing, doing and being in context: A praxis-oriented approach to child and youth care," *Child and Youth Care Forum* 36, 5–6: 225–44.

White, Michael. 1989. *Selected Papers*. Adelaide, Australia: Dulwich Center Publications.

———. 2007. *Maps of Narrative Practice*. New York: Norton.

Whitfield, Charles. 2006. "Childhood trauma as a cause of ADHD, aggression, violence and anti-social behaviour," in *Critical Voices in Child and Adolescent Mental Health*, edited by Sami Timimi and Begum Maitra, 89–106. London: Free Association Books.

Willms, J.D., ed. 2002. *Vulnerable Children: Findings from Canada's National Longitudinal Survey of Children and Youth*. Edmonton: University of Alberta Press.

Willoughby, T. 2008. "A short-term longitudinal study of Internet and computer game use by adolescent boys and girls: Prevalence, frequency of use, and psychosocial predictors," *Developmental Psychology* 44: 195–204.

Wilson, Janet. 2011. *Shannen and the Dream for a School*. Toronto: Second Story Press.

Wilson, Jim. 2005. "Engaging children and young people," in *Narrative Therapies with Children and Their Families: A Practitioner's Guide to Concepts and Approaches*, edited by Arlene Vetere and Emilia Dowling, 90–107. New York: Routledge.

Winnicott, D.W. 1953. "Transitional objects and transitional phenomena," *International Journal of Psychoanalysis* 34: 89–97.

Wohlwend, Karen E. 2012. "'Are you guys girls?' Boys, identity texts, and Disney princess play," *Journal of Early Childhood Literacy* 12, 1: 3–23.

Wood, Jane, and Emma Alleyne. 2010. "Street gang theory and research: Where are we now and where do we go from here?" *Aggression and Violent Behavior* 15, 2: 100–11.

Wortley, Scot, and Julian Tanner. 2004. "Social groups or criminal organizations? The extent and nature of youth gang activity in Toronto," in *From Enforcement and Prevention to Civic Engagement: Research on Community Safety*, edited by Bruce Kidd and Jim Phillips, 59–80. Toronto: Centre of Criminology, University of Toronto.

———. 2006. "Immigration, social disadvantage and urban youth gangs: Results of a Toronto-area survey," *Canadian Journal of Urban Research* 15, 2 Supplement: 18–37.

———. 2007. *Criminal Organizations or Social Groups? An Exploration of the Myths and Realities of Youth Gangs in Toronto*, http://canada.metropolis.net/pdfs/WortleyTanner2007.pdf.

Wyness, Michael. 2012. *Childhood and Society*. New York: Palgrave Macmillan.

Yahav, Rivka, and Shlomo A. Sharlin. 2000. "The symptom-carrying child as a preserver of the family unit," *Child and Family Social Work* 5, 4: 353–64.

Youth Criminal Justice Act (YCJA). S.C. 2002, c.1, http://laws-lois.justice.gc.ca/eng/acts/Y-1.5/.

Index